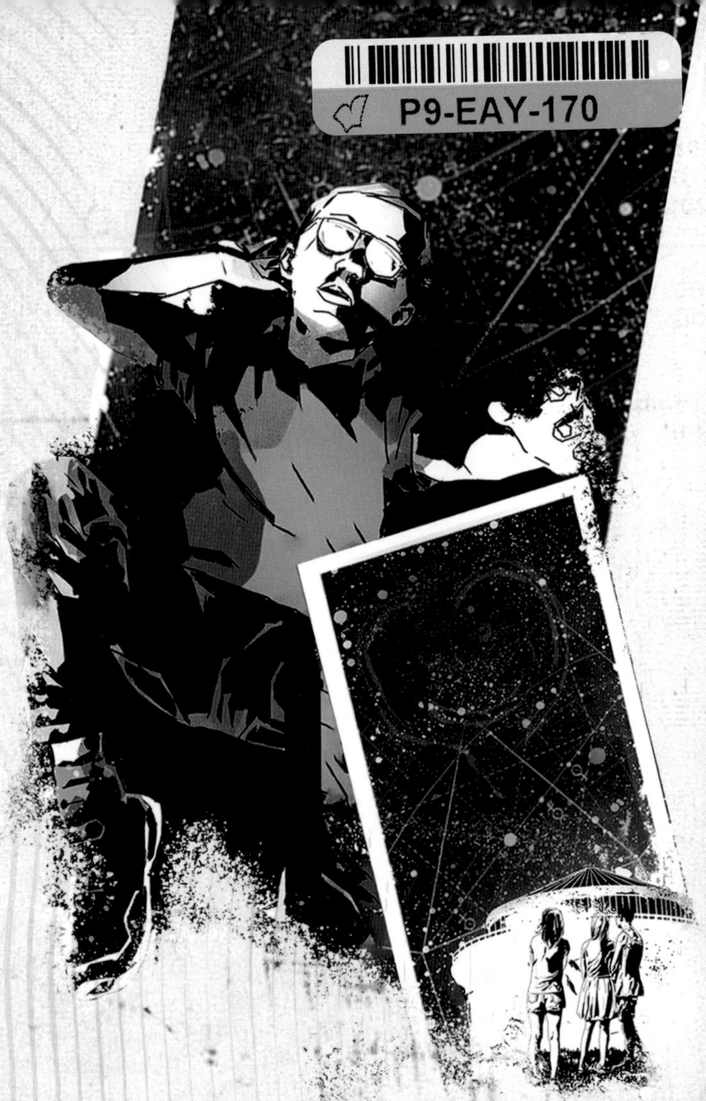

[redacted] **ANTHONY CLEVELAND** WRITER [redacted]

ANTONIO FUSO ARTIST [redacted] **STEFANO SIMEONE** COLORIST

[redacted] **JUSTIN BIRCH** LETTERER [redacted]

CHRIS FERNANDEZ
EDITOR

BRIAN HAWKINS
EDITOR

MIGUEL ÁNGEL ZAPATA
LOGO DESIGNER

DIANA BERMÚDEZ
BOOK DESIGNER

~~TOP SECRET SPECIAL HANDLING NOFORN~~

MAD CAVE

LAURA CHACÓN FOUNDER • **MARK LONDON** CEO AND CHIEF CREATIVE OFFICER
GIOVANNA T. OROZCO VP OF OPERATIONS • **CHRIS SANCHEZ** EDITOR-IN-CHIEF • **CHRIS FERNANDEZ** PUBLISHER • **CECILIA MEDINA** CHIEF FINANCIAL OFFICER
MANUEL CASTELLANOS DIRECTOR OF SALES AND RETAILER RELATIONS MANAGER • **ALLISON POND** MARKETING SPECIALIST • **ASIA HIRSCHENSON** P.R. AND COMMUNICATIONS
MIGUEL ANGEL ZAPATA DESIGN DIRECTOR • **DIANA BERMÚDEZ** GRAPHIC DESIGNER • **DAVID REYES** GRAPHIC DESIGNER • **ADRIANA T. OROZCO** INTERACTIVE MEDIA DESIGNER
NICOLÁS ZEA ARIAS AUDIOVISUAL PRODUCTION • **FRANK SILVA** EXECUTIVE ASSISTANT • **STEPHANIE HIDALGO** EXECUTIVE ASSISTANT

FOR MAD CAVE COMICS, INC.
Stargazer™ Trade Paperback Published by Mad Cave Studios, Inc. 8838 SW 129th St. Miami, FL 33176 © 2021 Mad Cave Studios, Inc. All rights reserved.
Contains materials originally published in single magazine form as Stargazer™ #1-6.

Printed in Canada
ISBN: 978-1-952303-04-3

SECRET

DENY

THE SECRETARY OF STATE

T
H
E

S T A R S

H	N	
A	E	B
V	V	E
E	E	E
	R	N
		C
		L
		O
		S
		E
		R

32 08'59.96"N
110 50'09.03"W

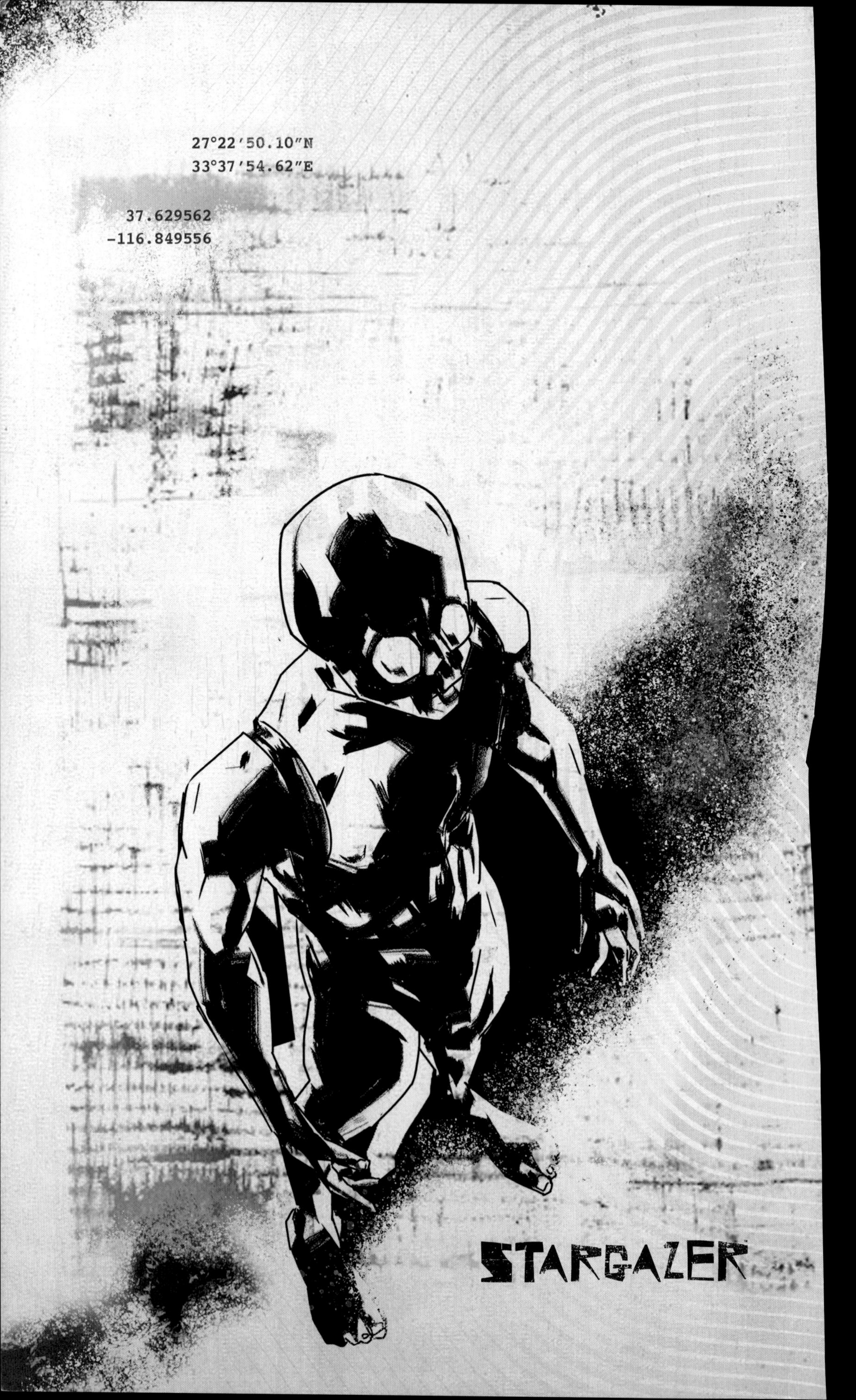
27°22′50.10″N
33°37′54.62″E
37.629562
-116.849556
STARGAZER

SAHARA DESERT.1999.
BIRKSVILLE COLORADO.1999.

32°40'34.19"N
117°9'27.58"W

PART ONE

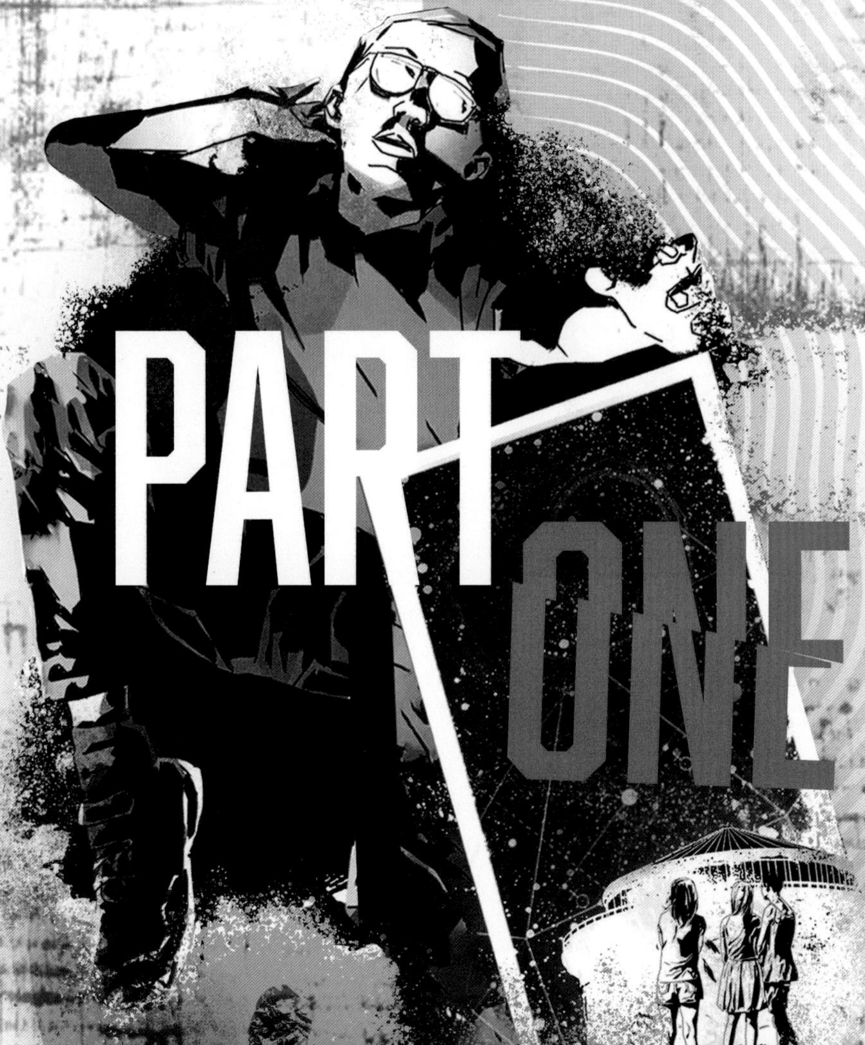

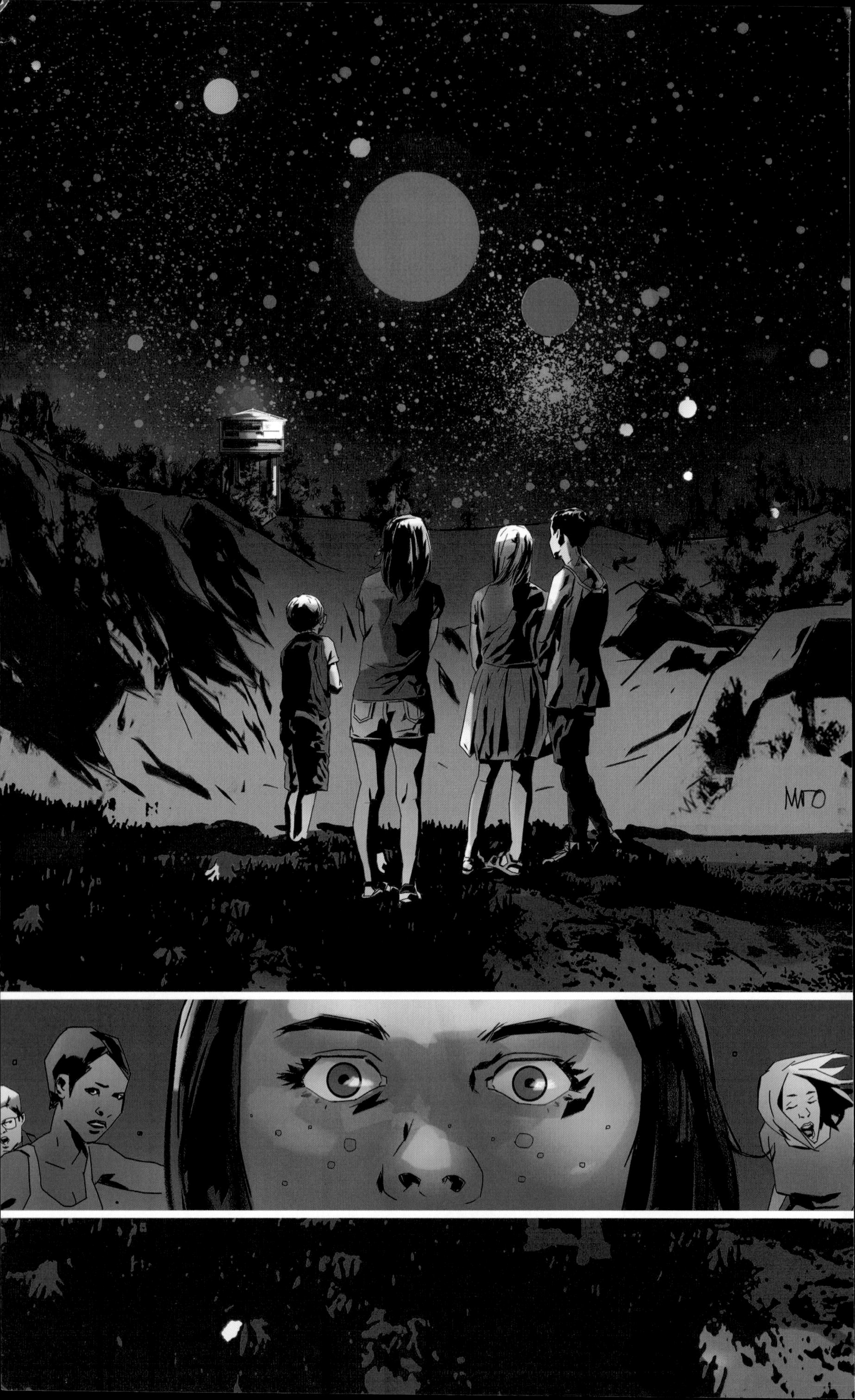
MTO

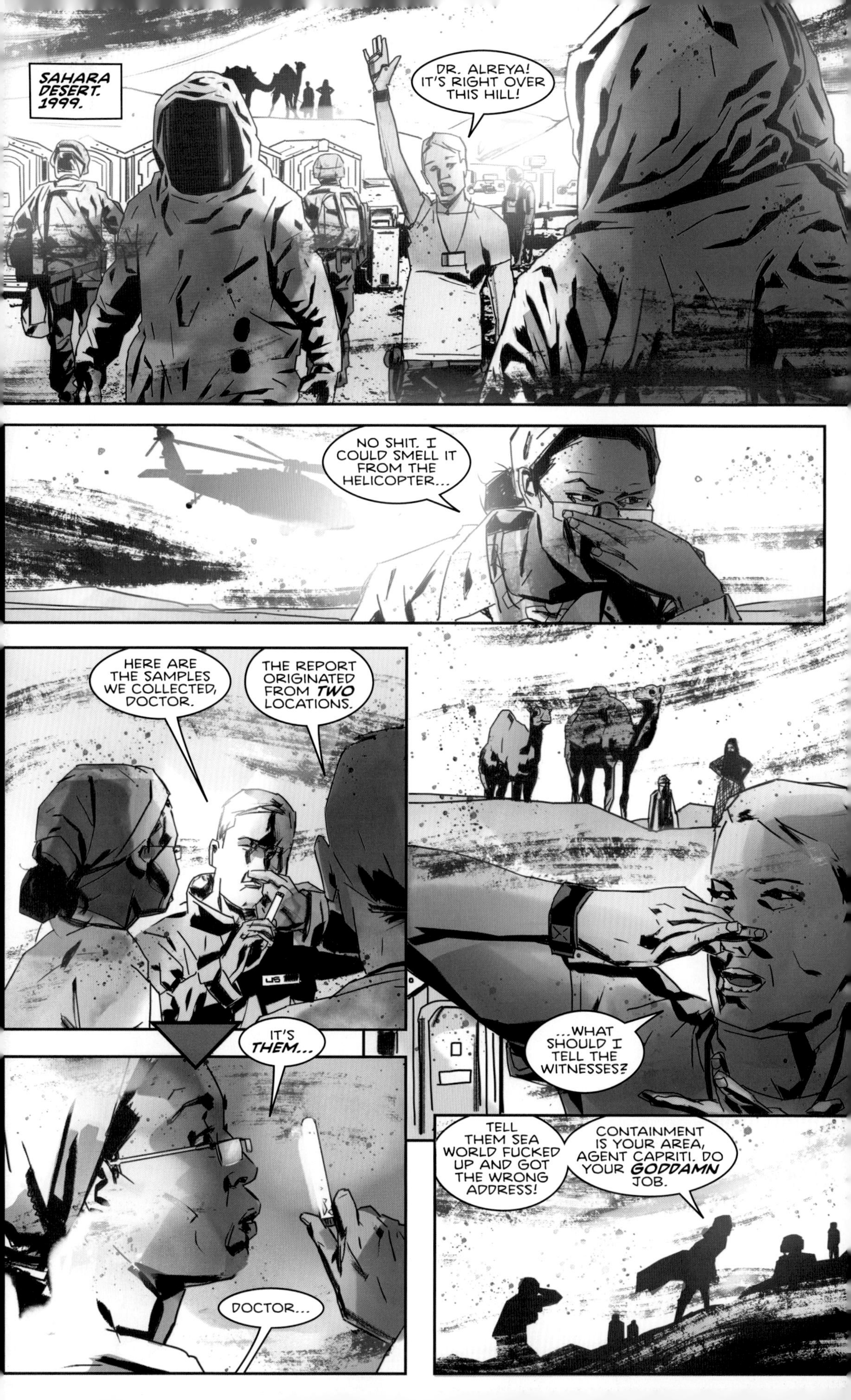
SAHARA DESERT. 1999.
DR. ALREYA! IT'S RIGHT OVER THIS HILL!
NO SHIT. I COULD SMELL IT FROM THE HELICOPTER...
HERE ARE THE SAMPLES WE COLLECTED, DOCTOR.
THE REPORT ORIGINATED FROM *TWO* LOCATIONS.
IT'S *THEM...*
DOCTOR...
...WHAT SHOULD I TELL THE WITNESSES?
TELL THEM SEA WORLD FUCKED UP AND GOT THE WRONG ADDRESS!
CONTAINMENT IS YOUR AREA, AGENT CAPRITI. DO YOUR *GODDAMN* JOB.

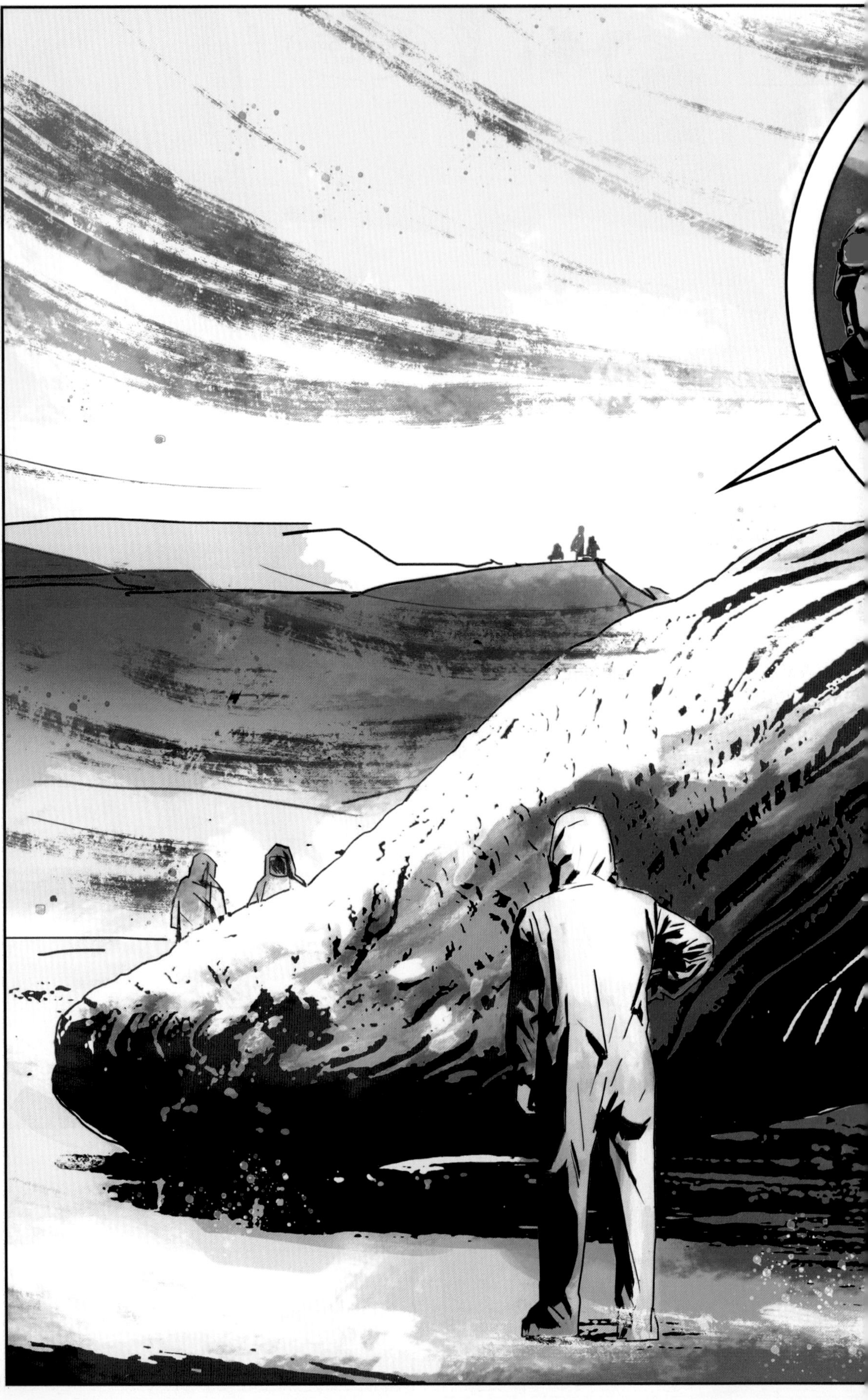

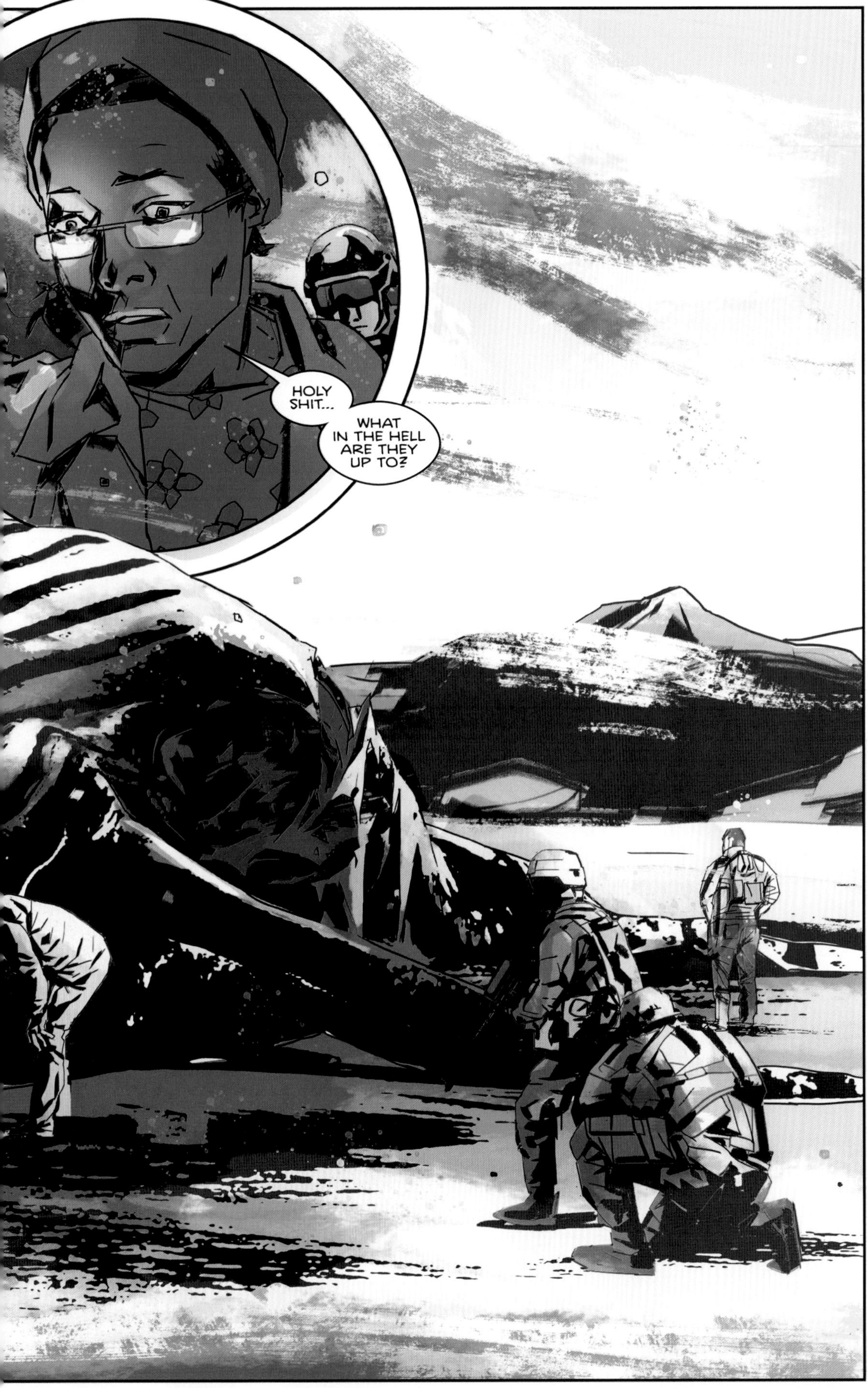
HOLY SHIT...
WHAT IN THE HELL ARE THEY UP TO?

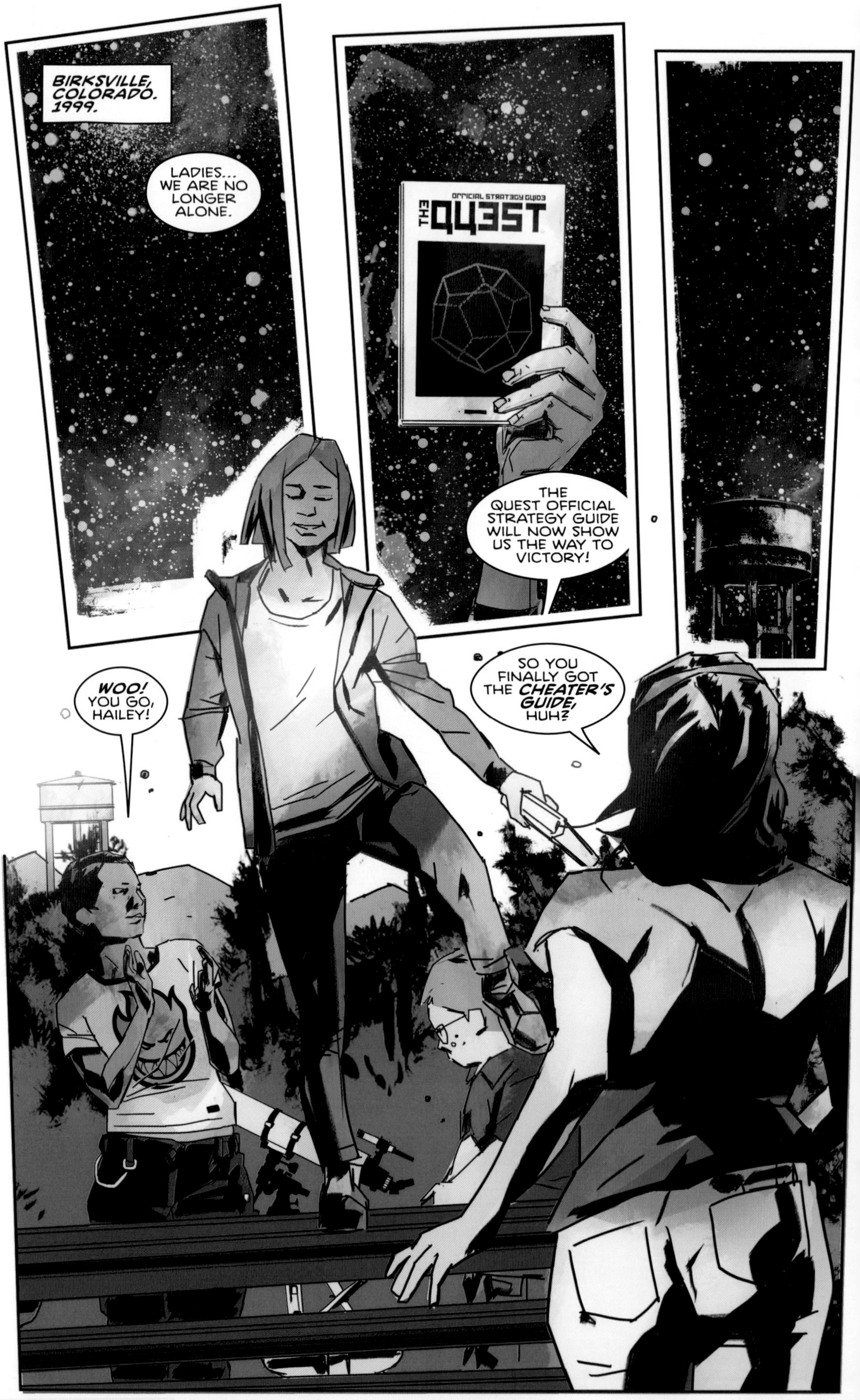
BIRKSVILLE, COLORADO. 1999.
LADIES... WE ARE NO LONGER ALONE.
OFFICIAL STRATEGY GUIDE THE QUEST
THE QUEST OFFICIAL STRATEGY GUIDE WILL NOW SHOW US THE WAY TO VICTORY!
WOO! YOU GO, HAILEY!
SO YOU FINALLY GOT THE CHEATER'S GUIDE, HUH?

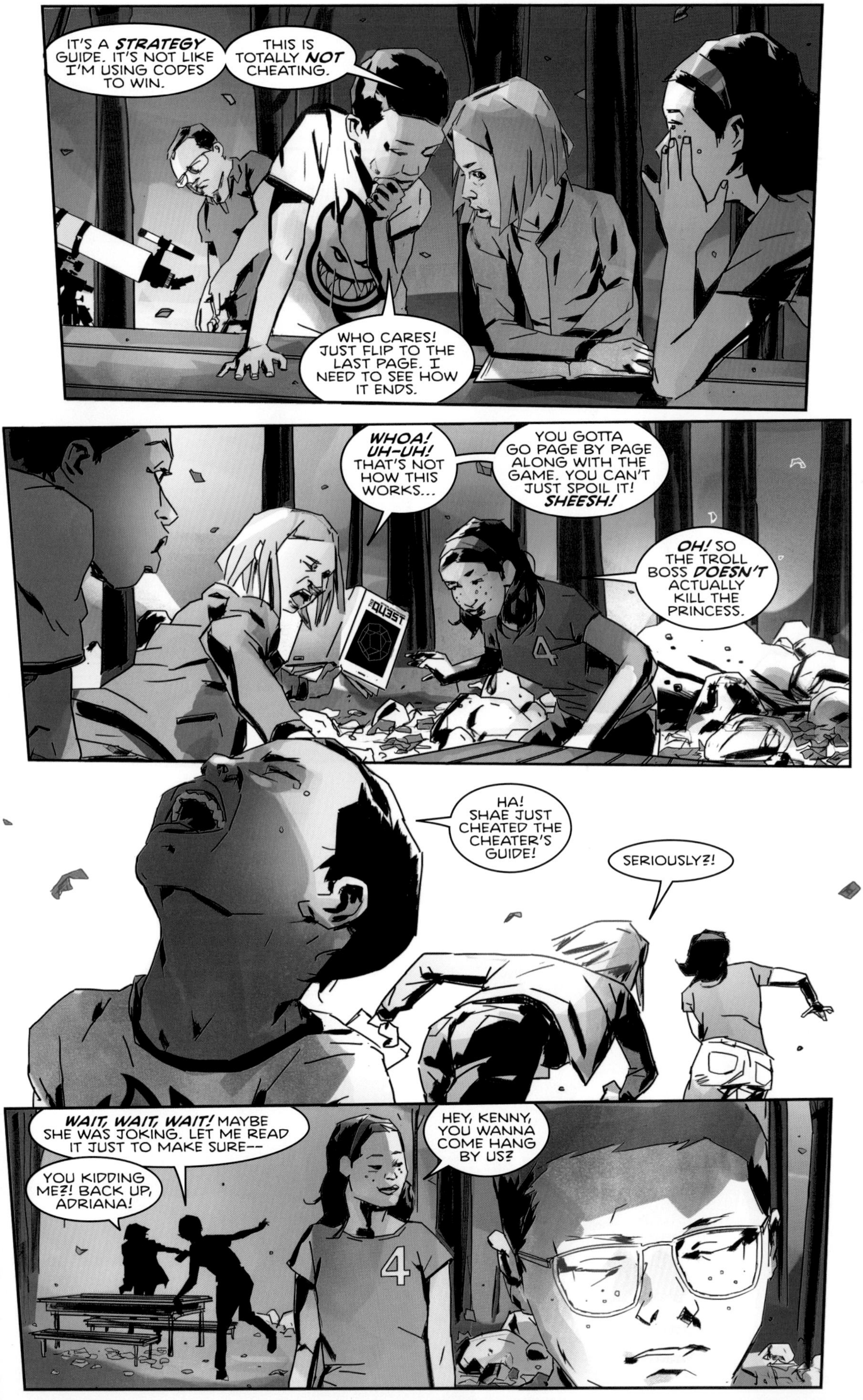
IT'S A **STRATEGY** GUIDE. IT'S NOT LIKE I'M USING CODES TO WIN.
THIS IS TOTALLY **NOT** CHEATING.
WHO CARES! JUST FLIP TO THE LAST PAGE. I NEED TO SEE HOW IT ENDS.
WHOA! UH-UH! THAT'S NOT HOW THIS WORKS...
YOU GOTTA GO PAGE BY PAGE ALONG WITH THE GAME. YOU CAN'T JUST SPOIL IT! **SHEESH!**
THE QUEST
OH! SO THE TROLL BOSS **DOESN'T** ACTUALLY KILL THE PRINCESS.
HA! SHAE JUST CHEATED THE CHEATER'S GUIDE!
SERIOUSLY?!
WAIT, WAIT, WAIT! MAYBE SHE WAS JOKING. LET ME READ IT JUST TO MAKE SURE--
YOU KIDDING ME?! BACK UP, ADRIANA!
HEY, KENNY, YOU WANNA COME HANG BY US?

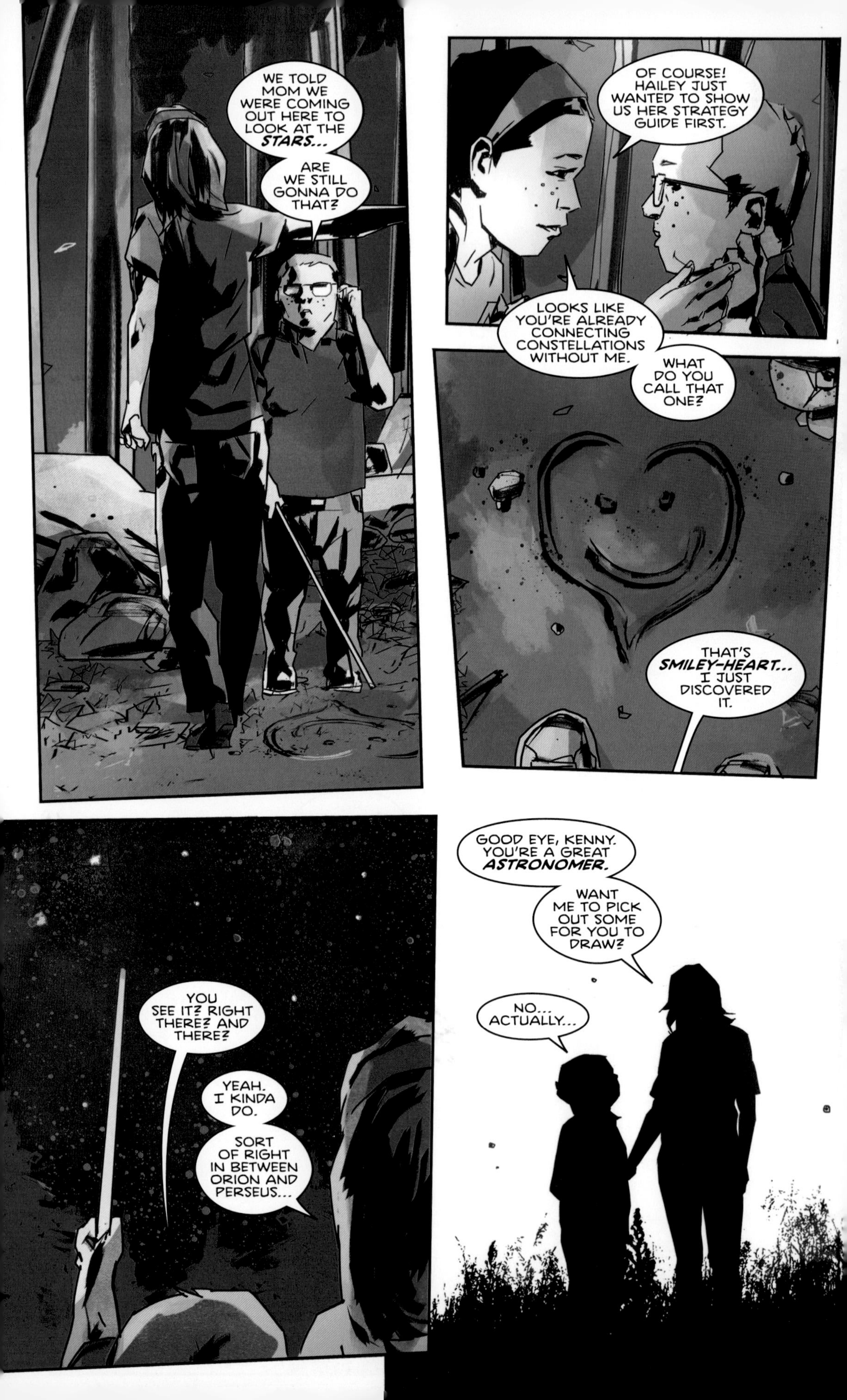
WE TOLD MOM WE WERE COMING OUT HERE TO LOOK AT THE STARS...
ARE WE STILL GONNA DO THAT?
OF COURSE! HAILEY JUST WANTED TO SHOW US HER STRATEGY GUIDE FIRST.
LOOKS LIKE YOU'RE ALREADY CONNECTING CONSTELLATIONS WITHOUT ME.
WHAT DO YOU CALL THAT ONE?
THAT'S SMILEY-HEART... I JUST DISCOVERED IT.
YOU SEE IT? RIGHT THERE? AND THERE?
YEAH. I KINDA DO.
SORT OF RIGHT IN BETWEEN ORION AND PERSEUS...
GOOD EYE, KENNY. YOU'RE A GREAT ASTRONOMER.
WANT ME TO PICK OUT SOME FOR YOU TO DRAW?
NO... ACTUALLY...

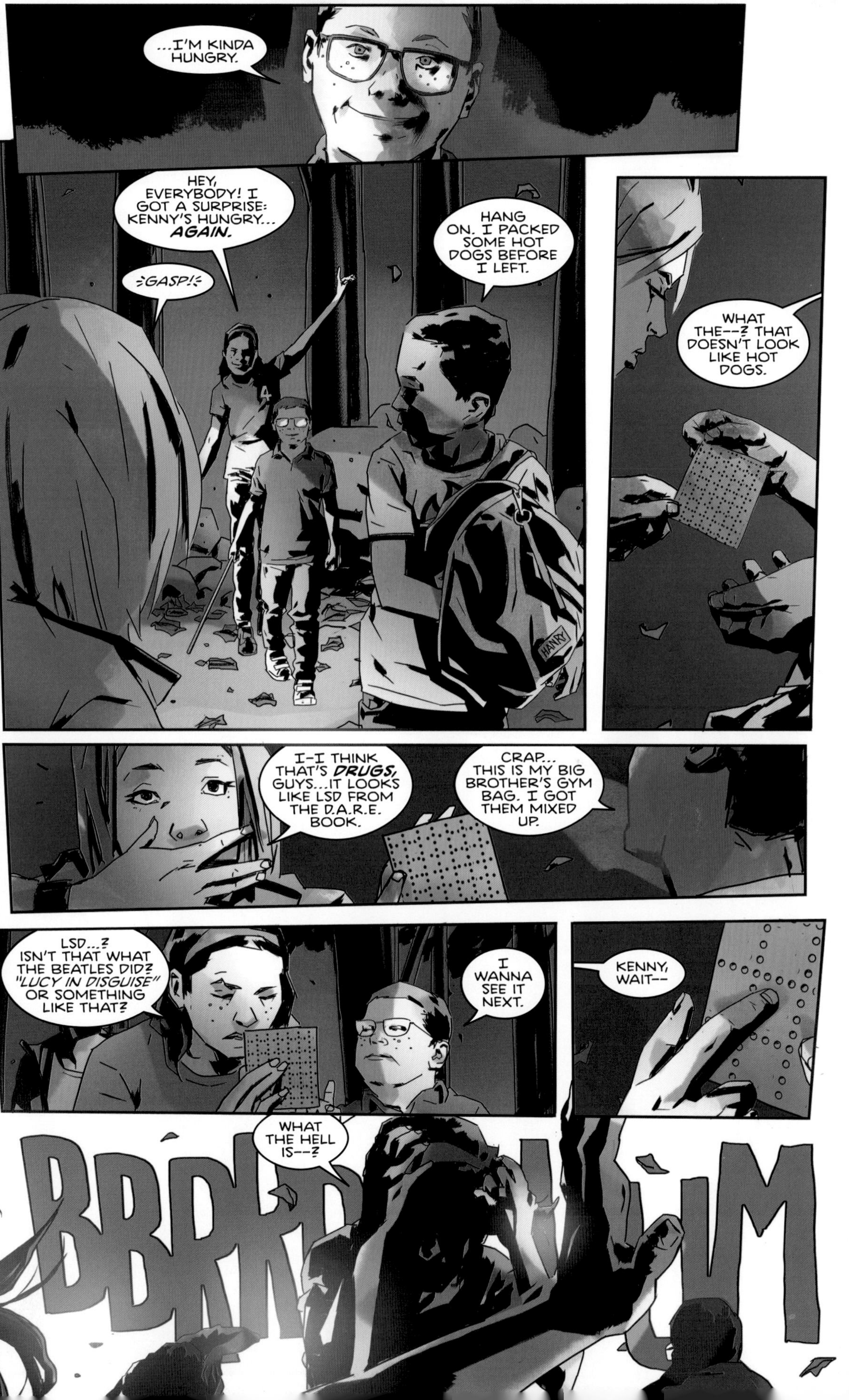

...I'M KINDA HUNGRY.
HEY, EVERYBODY! I GOT A SURPRISE: KENNY'S HUNGRY... AGAIN.
GASP!
HANG ON. I PACKED SOME HOT DOGS BEFORE I LEFT.
HANRY
WHAT THE--? THAT DOESN'T LOOK LIKE HOT DOGS.
I-I THINK THAT'S DRUGS, GUYS...IT LOOKS LIKE LSD FROM THE D.A.R.E. BOOK.
CRAP... THIS IS MY BIG BROTHER'S GYM BAG. I GOT THEM MIXED UP.
LSD...? ISN'T THAT WHAT THE BEATLES DID? "LUCY IN DISGUISE" OR SOMETHING LIKE THAT?
I WANNA SEE IT NEXT.
KENNY, WAIT--
WHAT THE HELL IS--?

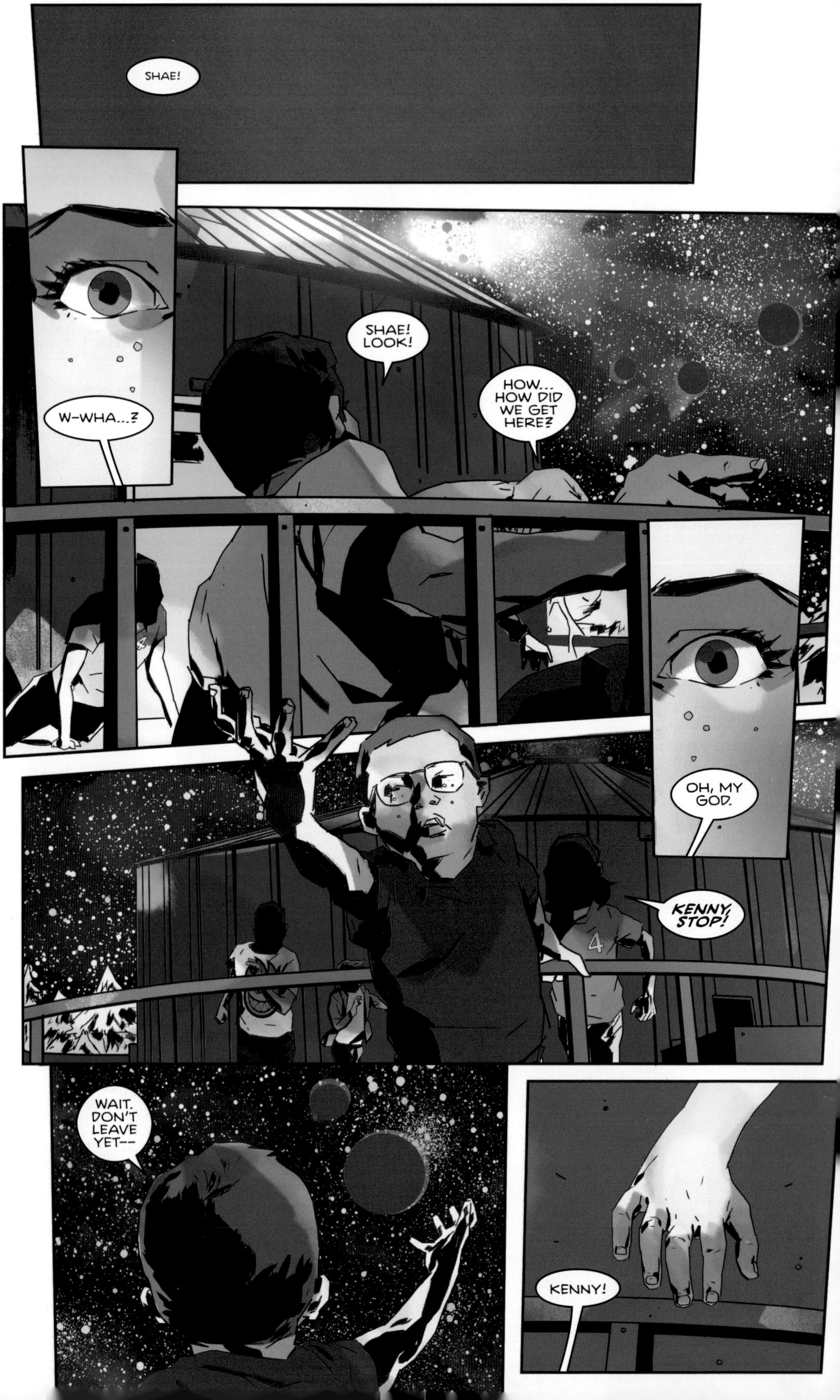
SHAE!
W-WHA...?
SHAE! LOOK!
HOW... HOW DID WE GET HERE?
OH, MY GOD.
KENNY, STOP!
WAIT. DON'T LEAVE YET--
KENNY!

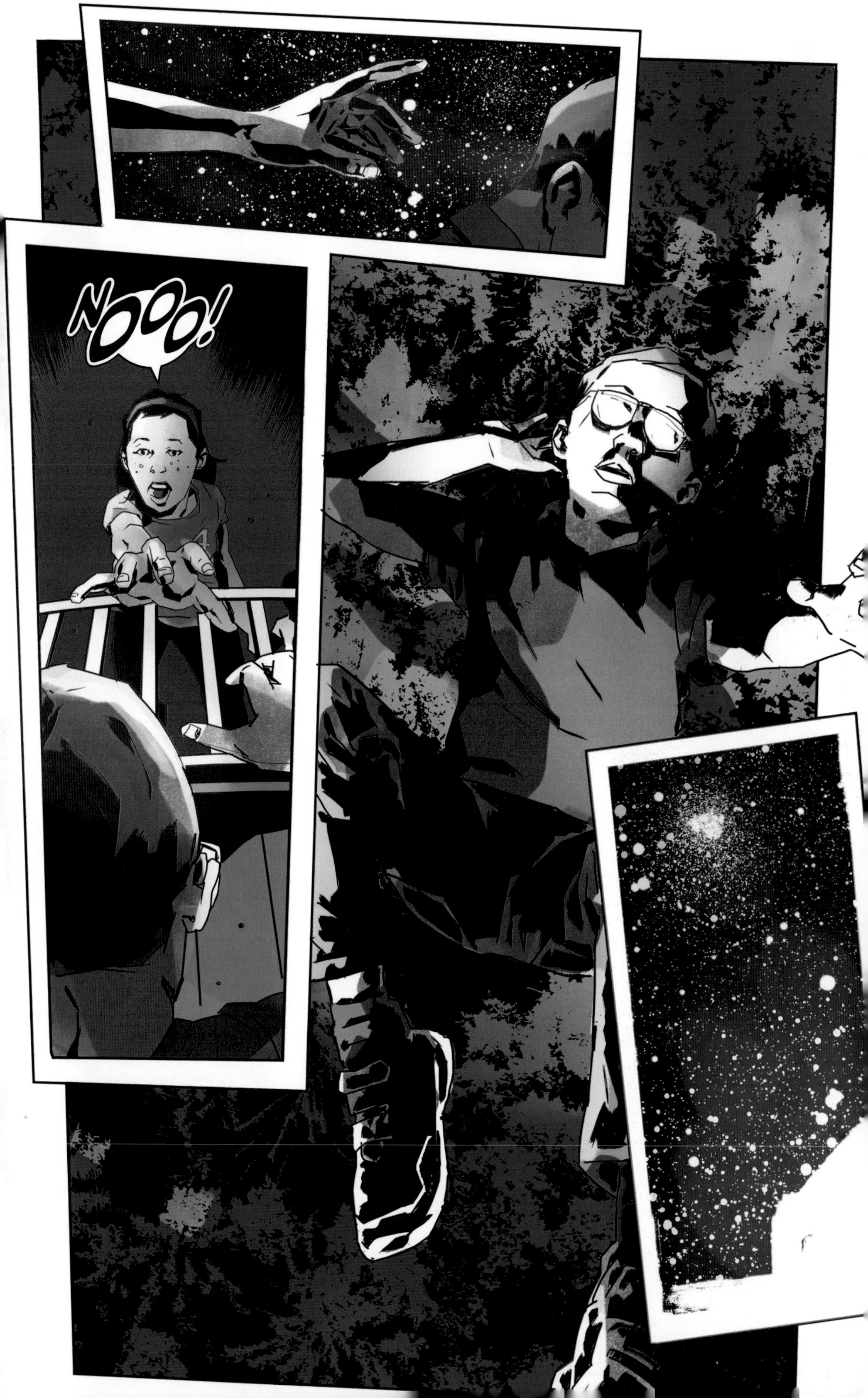
NOOO!

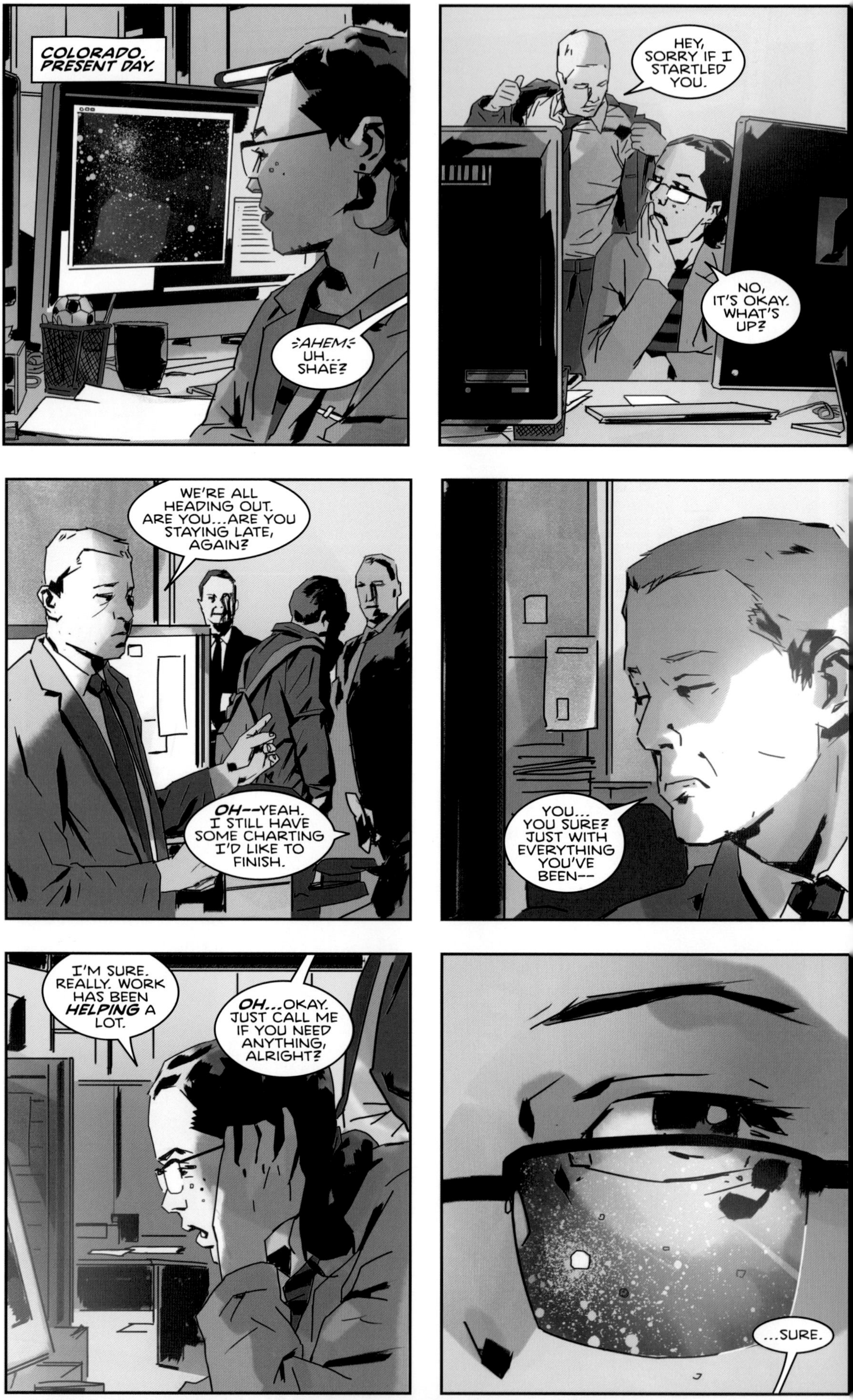
COLORADO. PRESENT DAY.
AHEM UH... SHAE?
HEY, SORRY IF I STARTLED YOU.
NO, IT'S OKAY. WHAT'S UP?
WE'RE ALL HEADING OUT. ARE YOU...ARE YOU STAYING LATE, AGAIN?
OH--YEAH. I STILL HAVE SOME CHARTING I'D LIKE TO FINISH.
YOU... YOU SURE? JUST WITH EVERYTHING YOU'VE BEEN--
I'M SURE. REALLY. WORK HAS BEEN HELPING A LOT.
OH...OKAY. JUST CALL ME IF YOU NEED ANYTHING, ALRIGHT?
...SURE.

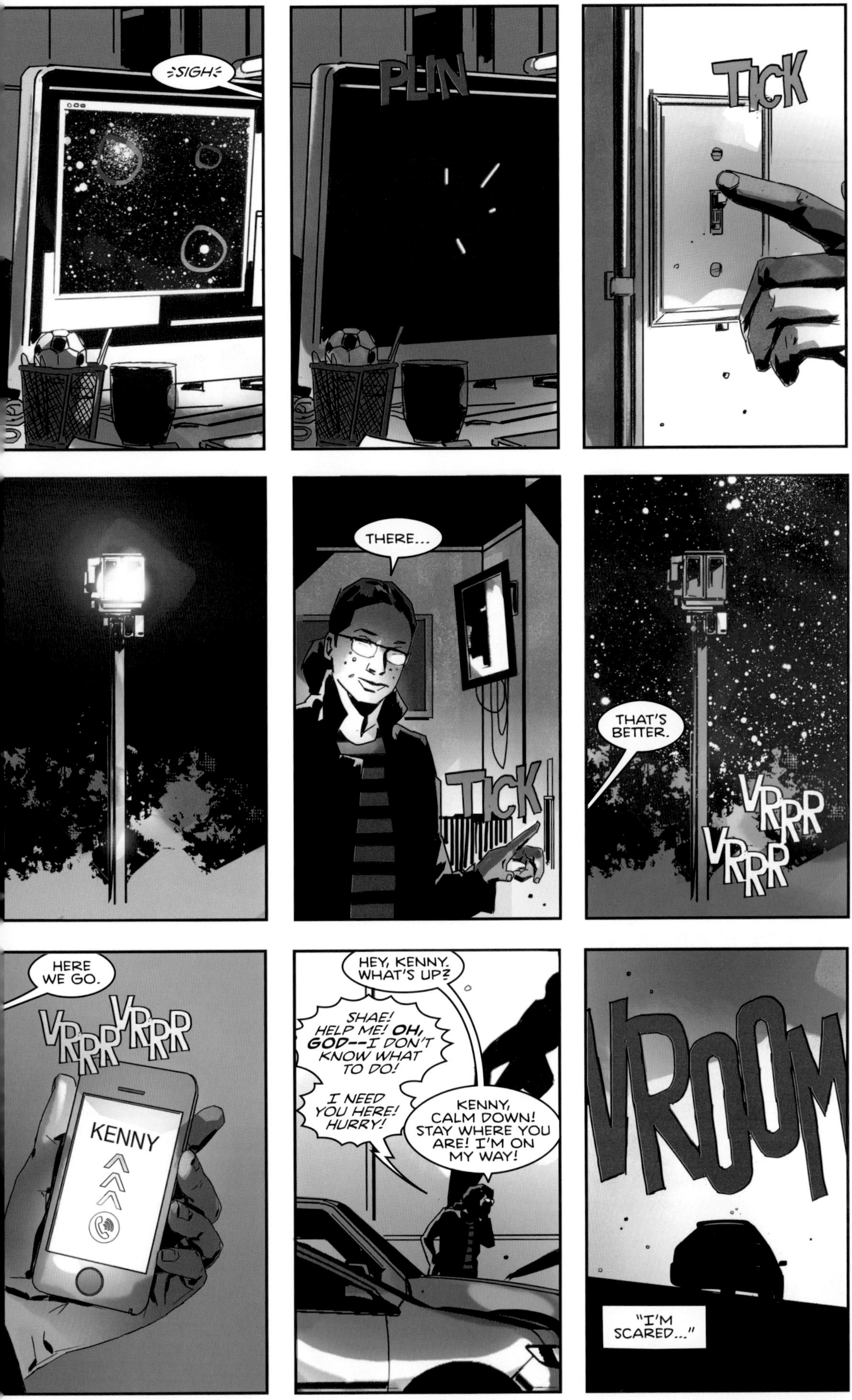
SIGH
PLIN
TICK
THERE...
TICK
THAT'S BETTER.
VRRRR
VRRRR
HERE WE GO.
VRRRR VRRRR
KENNY
HEY, KENNY. WHAT'S UP?
SHAE! HELP ME! OH, GOD--I DON'T KNOW WHAT TO DO!
I NEED YOU HERE! HURRY!
KENNY, CALM DOWN! STAY WHERE YOU ARE! I'M ON MY WAY!
VROOM
"I'M SCARED..."

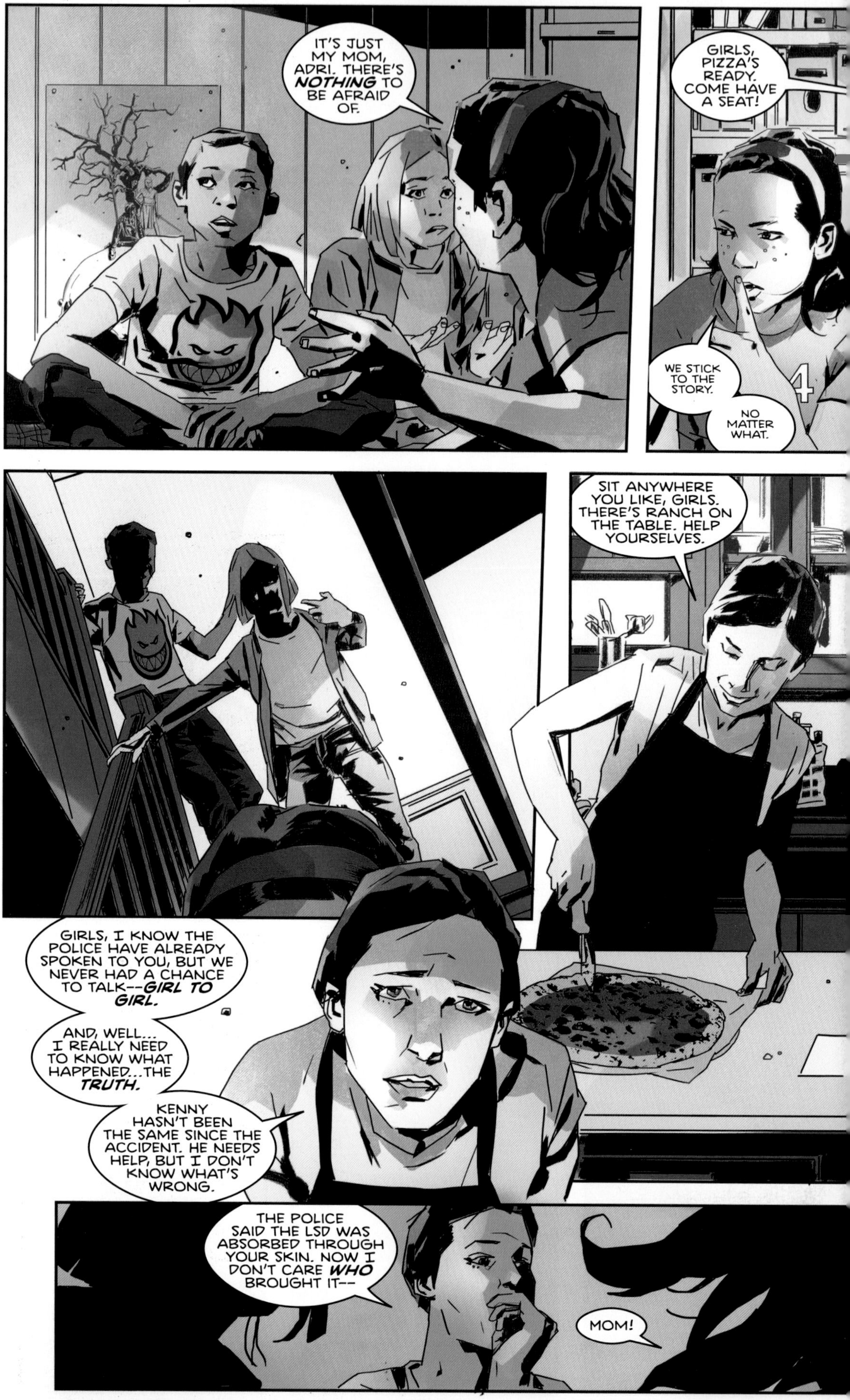
IT'S JUST MY MOM, ADRI. THERE'S NOTHING TO BE AFRAID OF.
GIRLS, PIZZA'S READY. COME HAVE A SEAT!
WE STICK TO THE STORY.
NO MATTER WHAT.
SIT ANYWHERE YOU LIKE, GIRLS. THERE'S RANCH ON THE TABLE. HELP YOURSELVES.
GIRLS, I KNOW THE POLICE HAVE ALREADY SPOKEN TO YOU, BUT WE NEVER HAD A CHANCE TO TALK--GIRL TO GIRL.
AND, WELL... I REALLY NEED TO KNOW WHAT HAPPENED...THE TRUTH.
KENNY HASN'T BEEN THE SAME SINCE THE ACCIDENT. HE NEEDS HELP, BUT I DON'T KNOW WHAT'S WRONG.
THE POLICE SAID THE LSD WAS ABSORBED THROUGH YOUR SKIN. NOW I DON'T CARE WHO BROUGHT IT--
MOM!

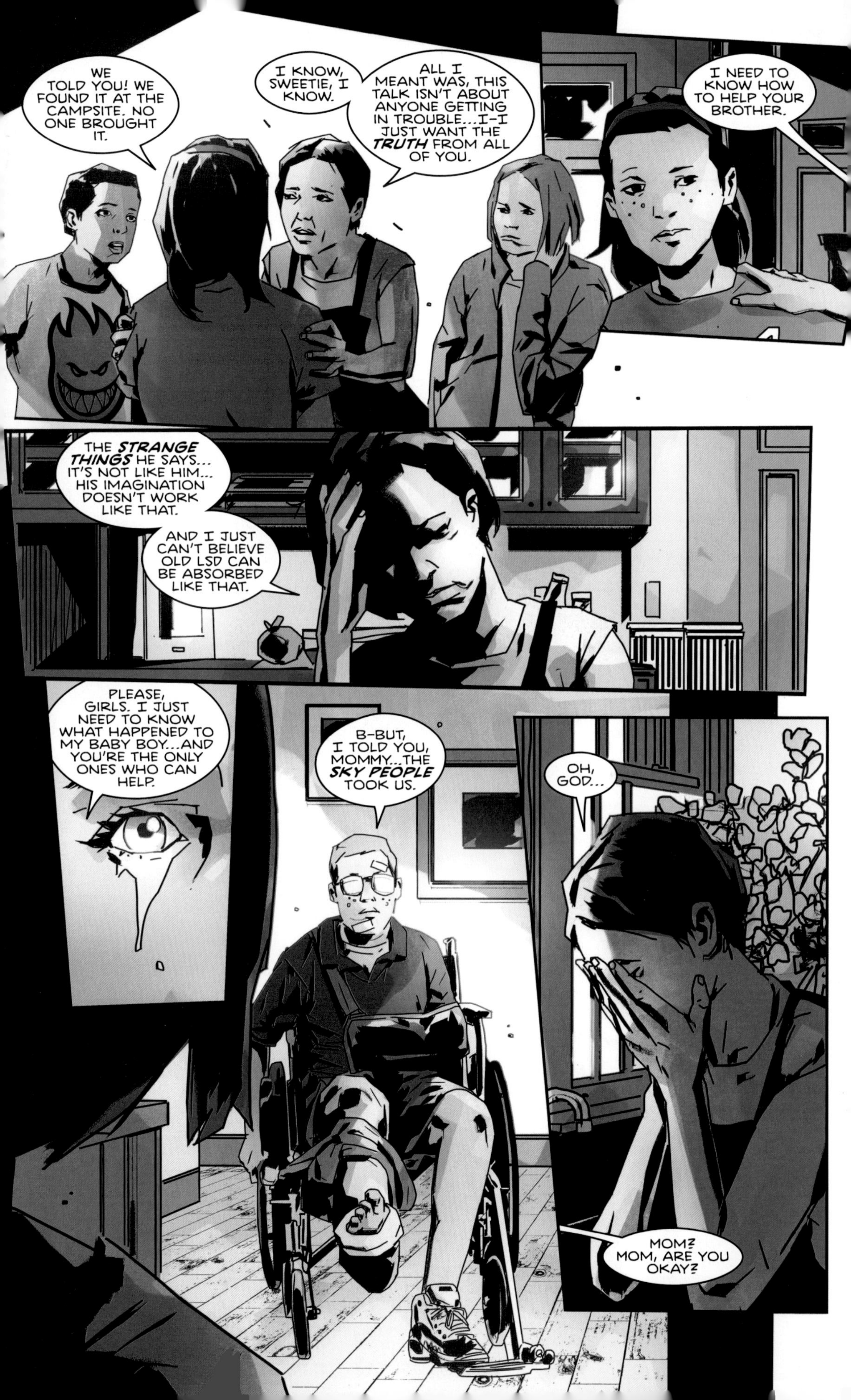
WE TOLD YOU! WE FOUND IT AT THE CAMPSITE. NO ONE BROUGHT IT.
I KNOW, SWEETIE, I KNOW.
ALL I MEANT WAS, THIS TALK ISN'T ABOUT ANYONE GETTING IN TROUBLE...I-I JUST WANT THE TRUTH FROM ALL OF YOU.
I NEED TO KNOW HOW TO HELP YOUR BROTHER.
THE STRANGE THINGS HE SAYS... IT'S NOT LIKE HIM... HIS IMAGINATION DOESN'T WORK LIKE THAT.
AND I JUST CAN'T BELIEVE OLD LSD CAN BE ABSORBED LIKE THAT.
PLEASE, GIRLS. I JUST NEED TO KNOW WHAT HAPPENED TO MY BABY BOY...AND YOU'RE THE ONLY ONES WHO CAN HELP.
B-BUT, I TOLD YOU, MOMMY...THE SKY PEOPLE TOOK US.
OH, GOD...
MOM? MOM, ARE YOU OKAY?

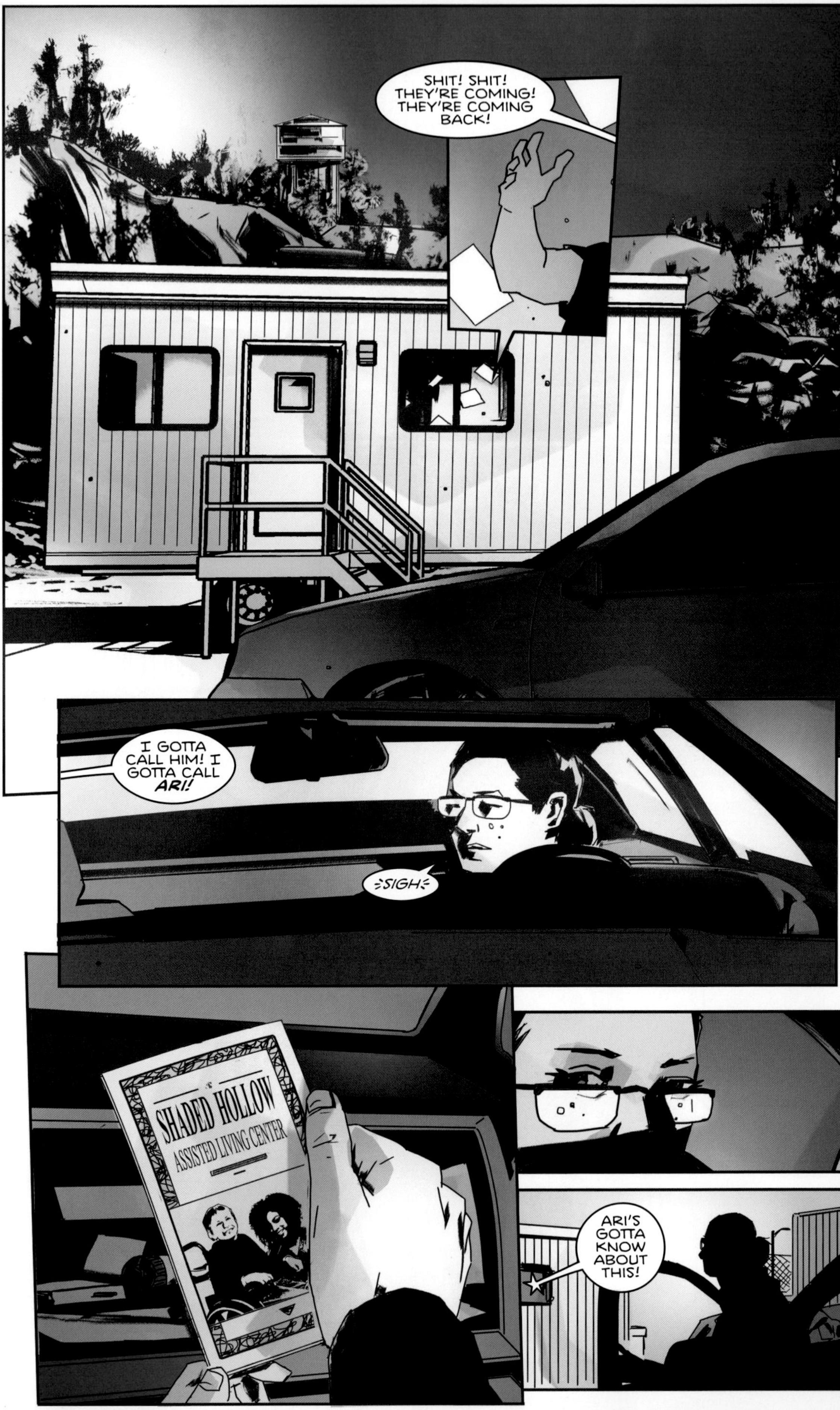
SHIT! SHIT! THEY'RE COMING! THEY'RE COMING BACK!
I GOTTA CALL HIM! I GOTTA CALL ARI!
SIGH
SHADED HOLLOW
ASSISTED LIVING CENTER
ARI'S GOTTA KNOW ABOUT THIS!

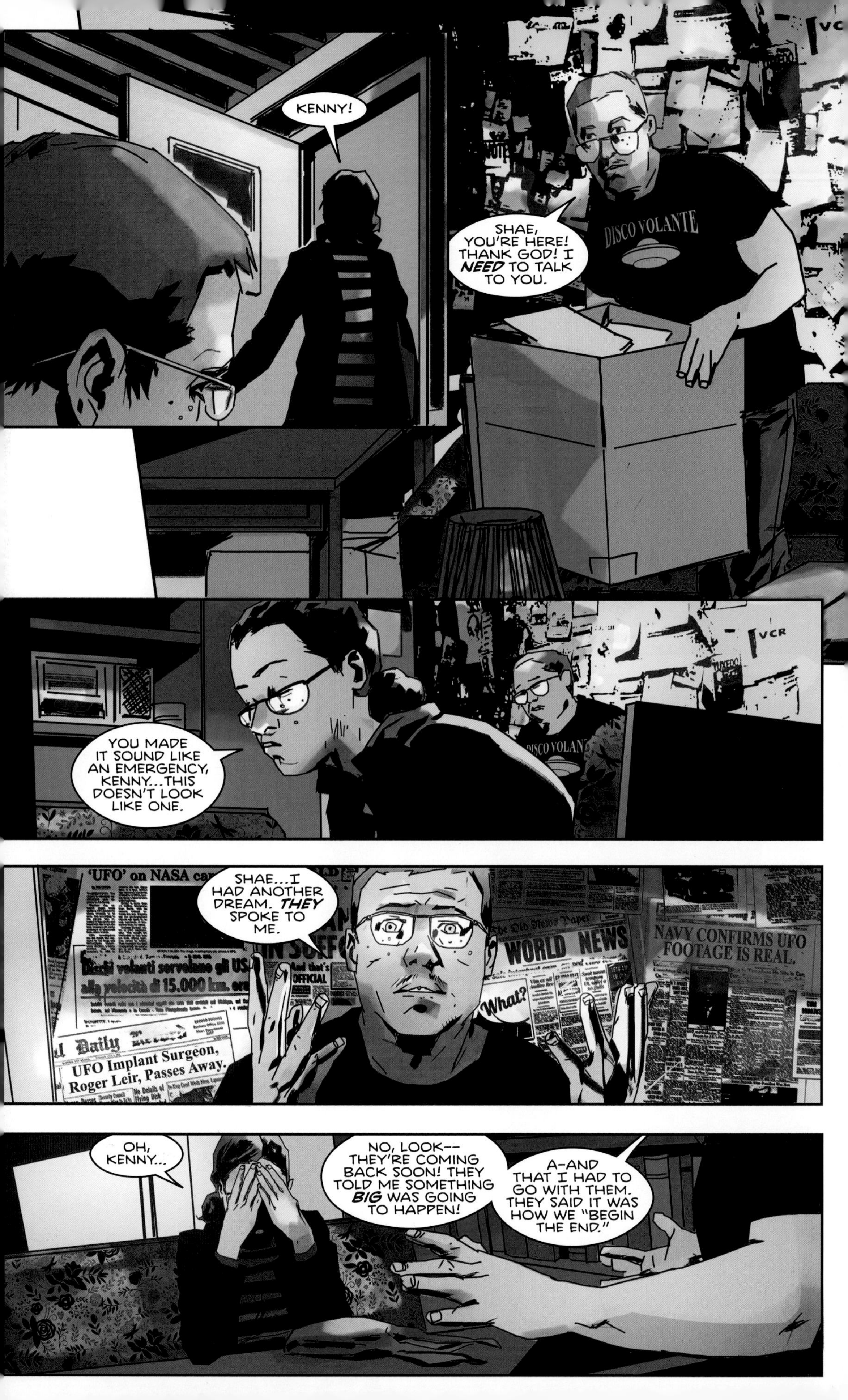
KENNY!
SHAE, YOU'RE HERE! THANK GOD! I *NEED* TO TALK TO YOU.
DISCO VOLANTE
VCR
YOU MADE IT SOUND LIKE AN EMERGENCY, KENNY...THIS DOESN'T LOOK LIKE ONE.
SHAE...I HAD ANOTHER DREAM. *THEY* SPOKE TO ME.
NAVY CONFIRMS UFO FOOTAGE IS REAL.
WORLD NEWS
UFO Implant Surgeon, Roger Leir, Passes Away.
What?
OH, KENNY...
NO, LOOK-- THEY'RE COMING BACK SOON! THEY TOLD ME SOMETHING *BIG* WAS GOING TO HAPPEN!
A-AND THAT I HAD TO GO WITH THEM. THEY SAID IT WAS HOW WE "BEGIN THE END."

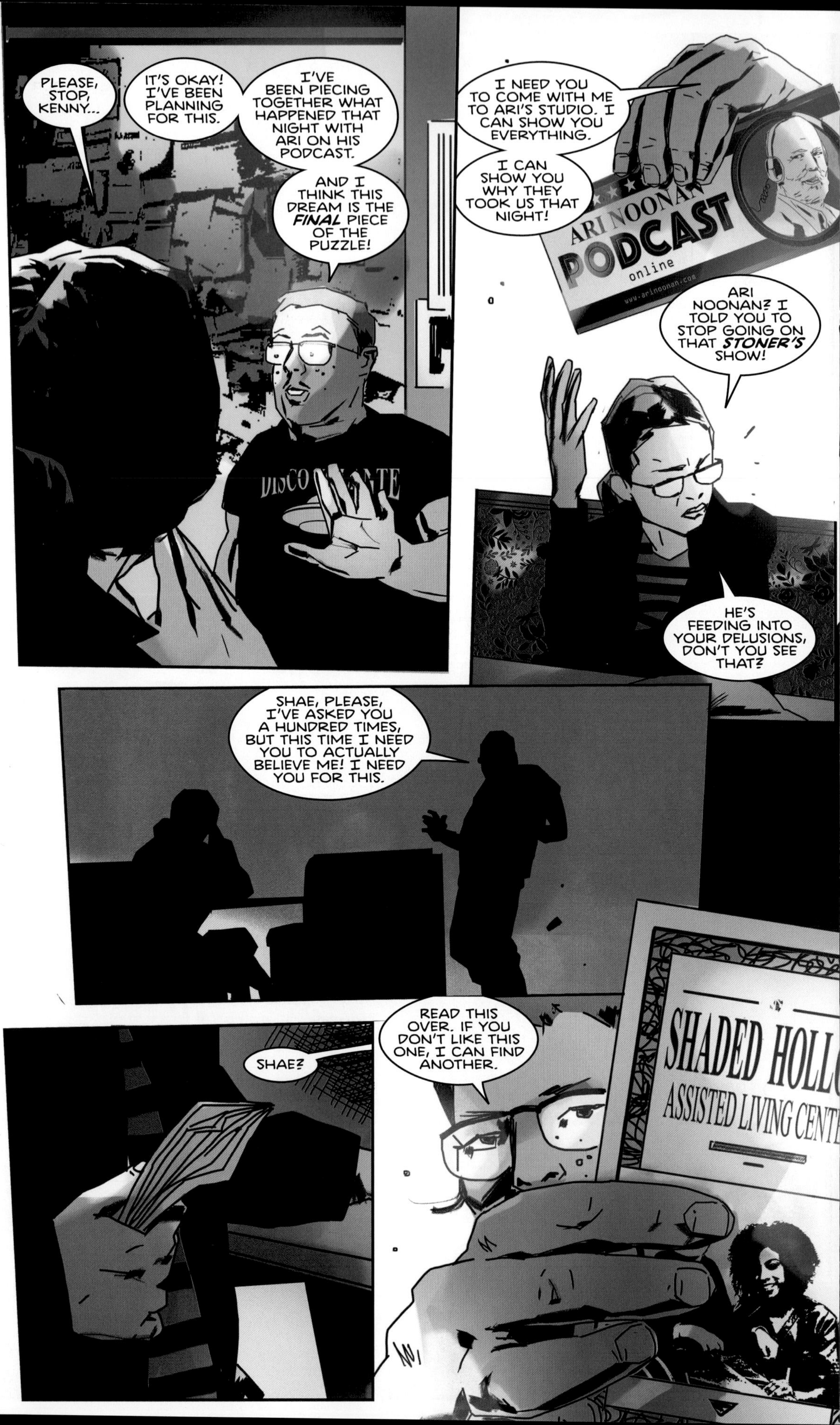
PLEASE, STOP, KENNY...
IT'S OKAY! I'VE BEEN PLANNING FOR THIS.
I'VE BEEN PIECING TOGETHER WHAT HAPPENED THAT NIGHT WITH ARI ON HIS PODCAST.
AND I THINK THIS DREAM IS THE FINAL PIECE OF THE PUZZLE!
DISCO
I NEED YOU TO COME WITH ME TO ARI'S STUDIO. I CAN SHOW YOU EVERYTHING.
I CAN SHOW YOU WHY THEY TOOK US THAT NIGHT!
ARI NOONAN PODCAST
online
www.arinoonan.com
ARI NOONAN? I TOLD YOU TO STOP GOING ON THAT STONER'S SHOW!
HE'S FEEDING INTO YOUR DELUSIONS, DON'T YOU SEE THAT?
SHAE, PLEASE, I'VE ASKED YOU A HUNDRED TIMES, BUT THIS TIME I NEED YOU TO ACTUALLY BELIEVE ME! I NEED YOU FOR THIS.
SHAE?
READ THIS OVER. IF YOU DON'T LIKE THIS ONE, I CAN FIND ANOTHER.
SHADED HOLLO
ASSISTED LIVING CENTE

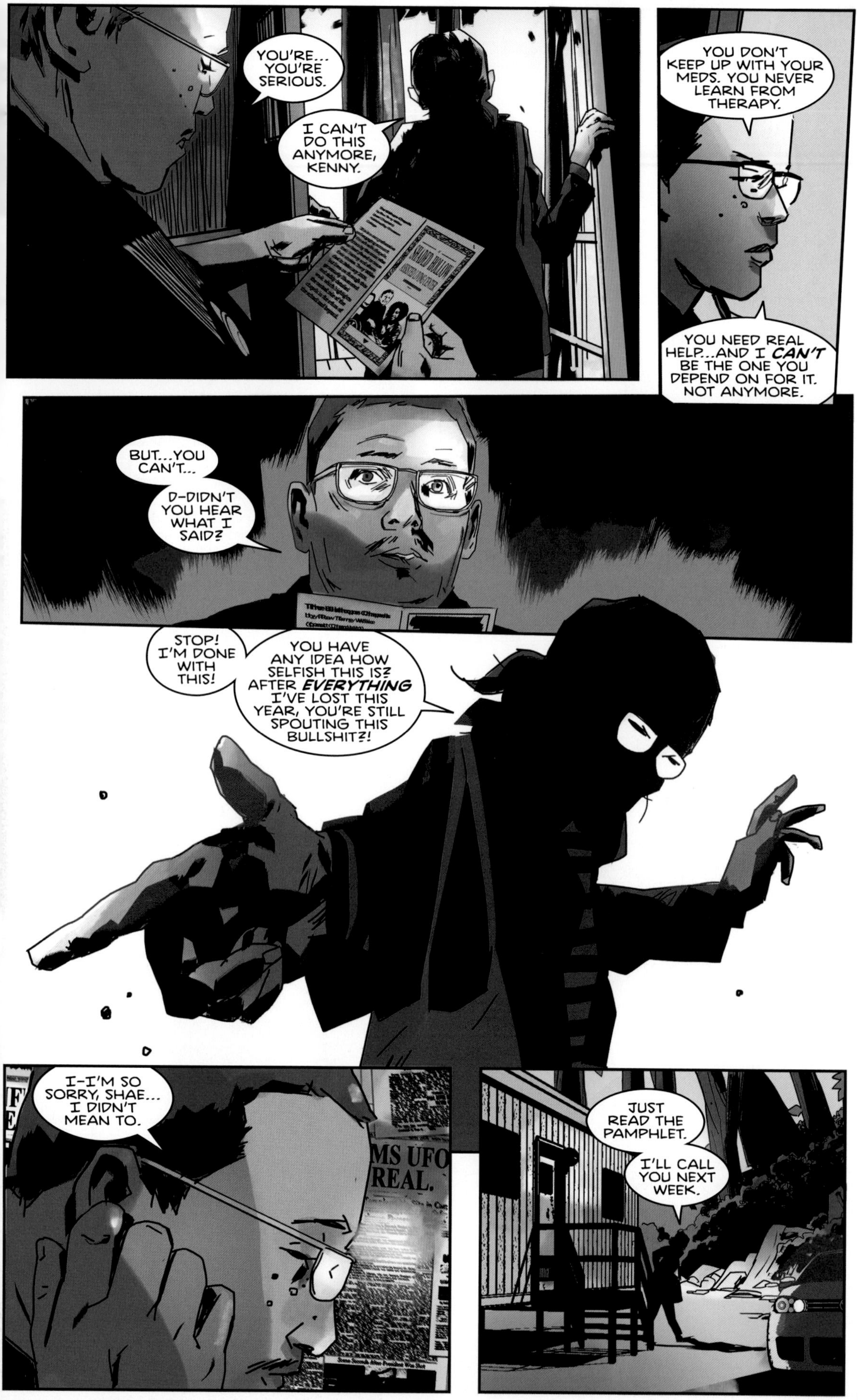
YOU'RE... YOU'RE SERIOUS.
I CAN'T DO THIS ANYMORE, KENNY.
YOU DON'T KEEP UP WITH YOUR MEDS. YOU NEVER LEARN FROM THERAPY.
YOU NEED REAL HELP...AND I *CAN'T* BE THE ONE YOU DEPEND ON FOR IT. NOT ANYMORE.
BUT...YOU CAN'T...
D-DIDN'T YOU HEAR WHAT I SAID?
STOP! I'M DONE WITH THIS!
YOU HAVE ANY IDEA HOW SELFISH THIS IS? AFTER *EVERYTHING* I'VE LOST THIS YEAR, YOU'RE STILL SPOUTING THIS BULLSHIT?!
I-I'M SO SORRY, SHAE... I DIDN'T MEAN TO.
MS UFO REAL.
JUST READ THE PAMPHLET.
I'LL CALL YOU NEXT WEEK.

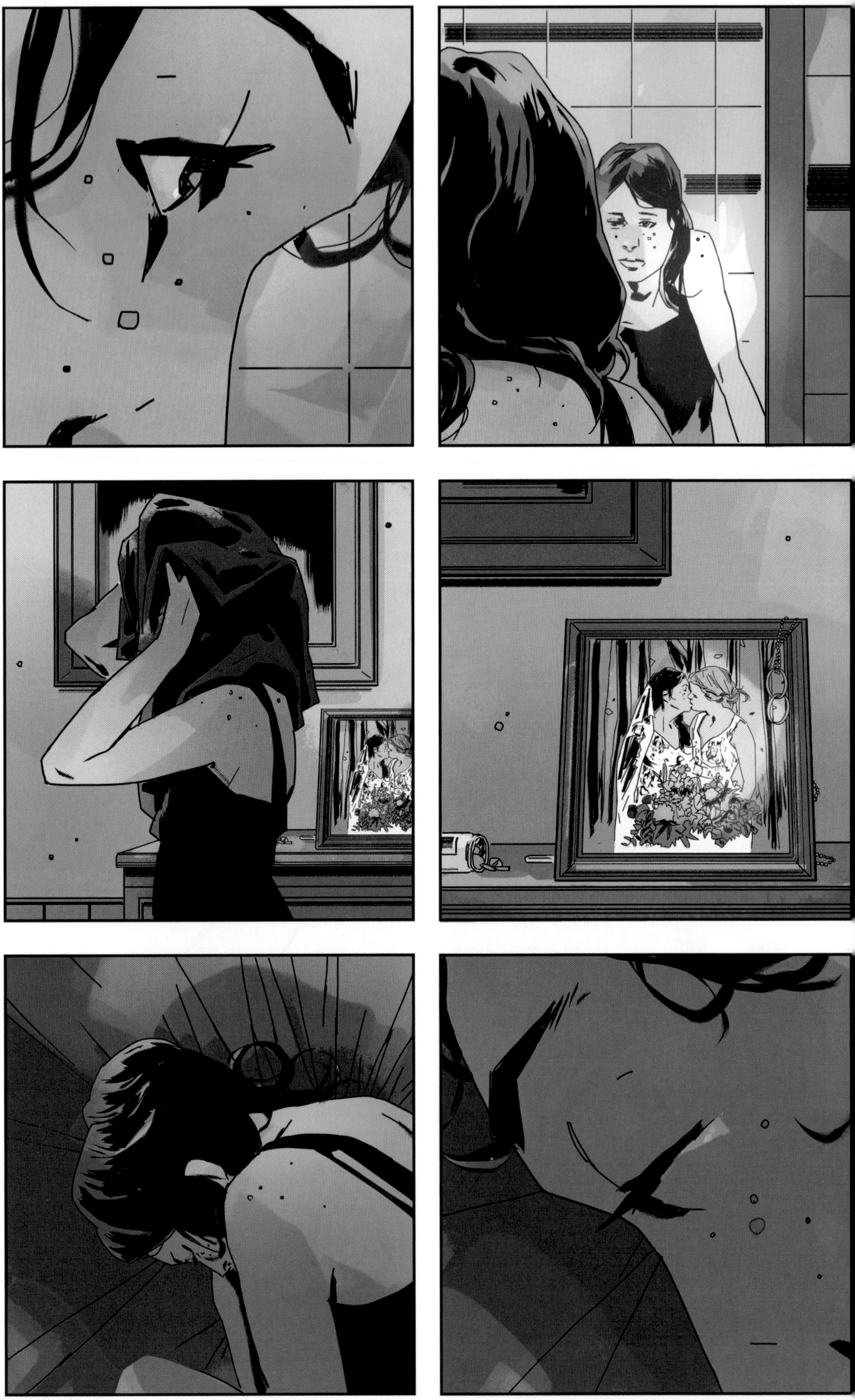

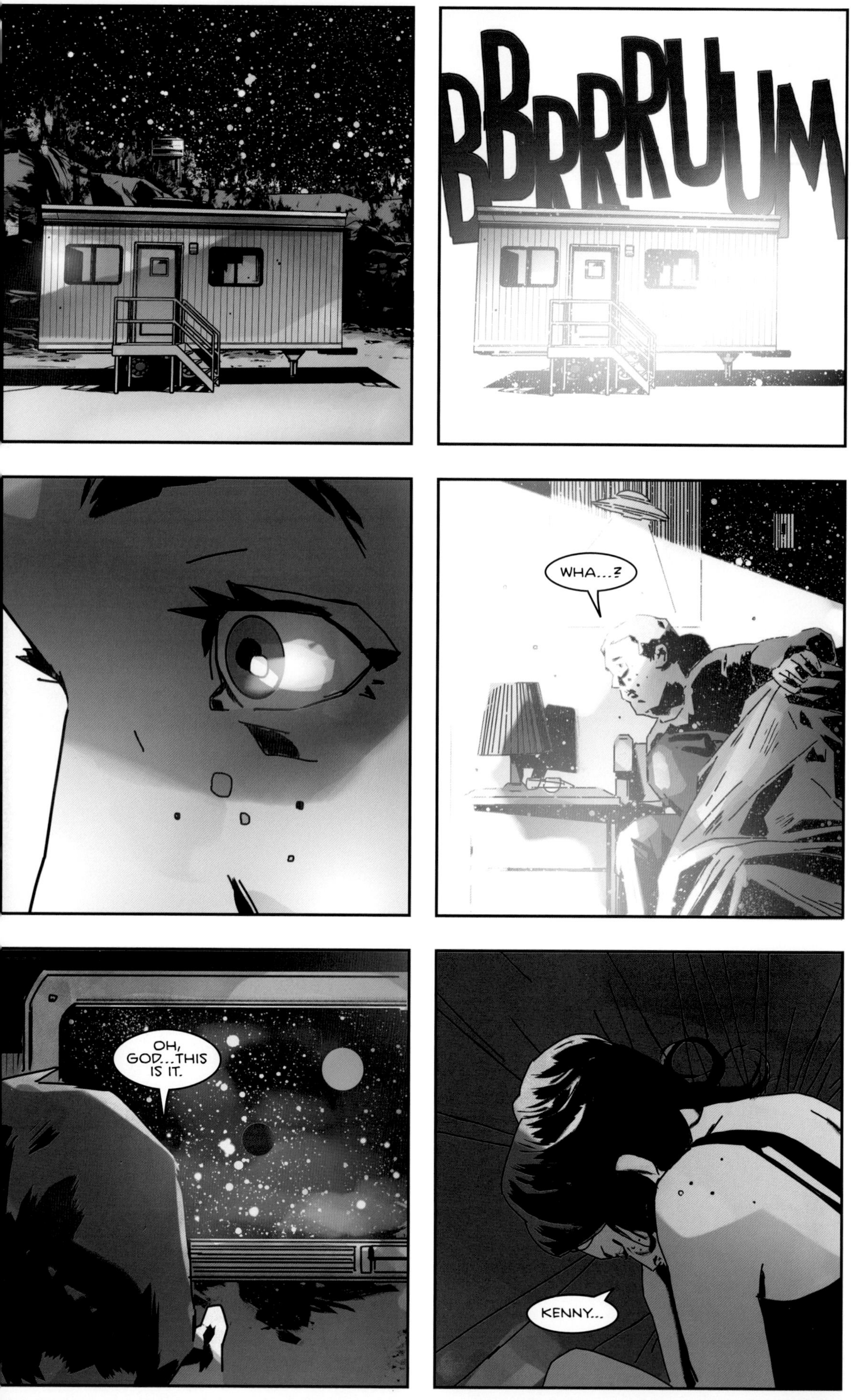
BBRRRUUUM
WHA...?
OH, GOD...THIS IS IT.
KENNY...

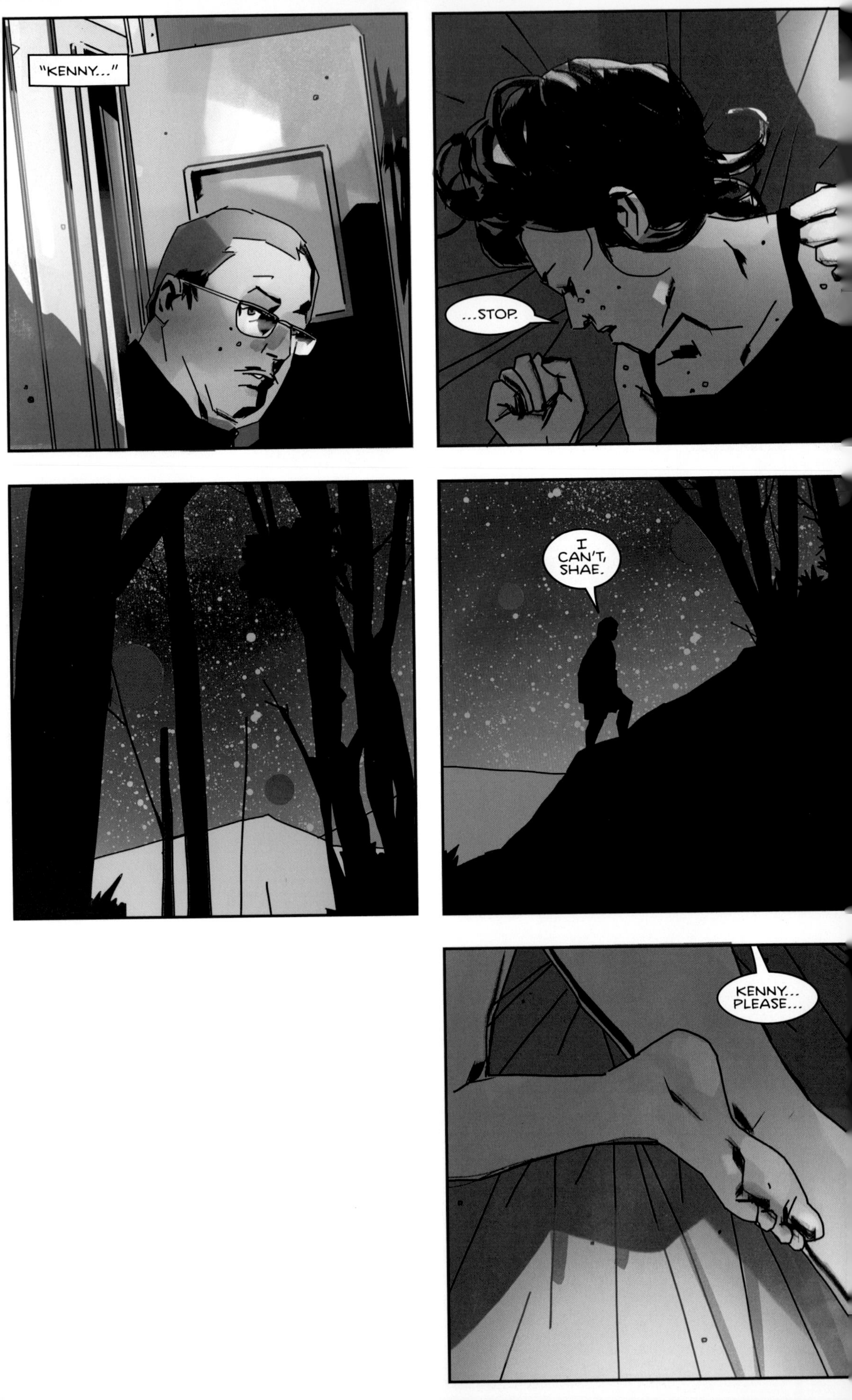
"KENNY..."
...STOP.
I CAN'T, SHAE.
KENNY... PLEASE...

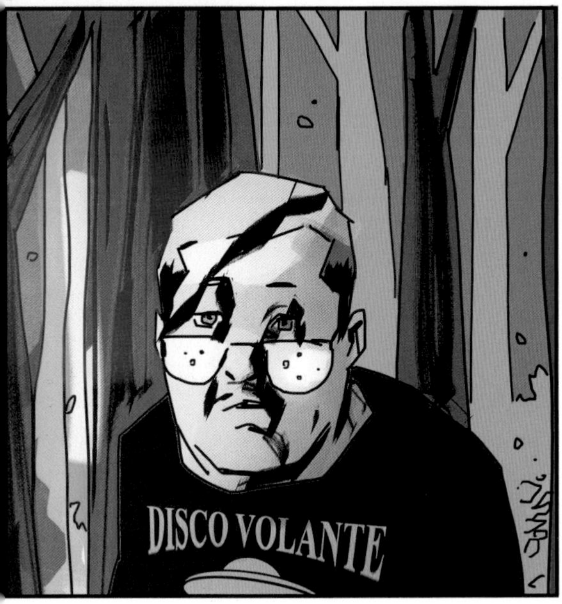
DISCO VOLANTE

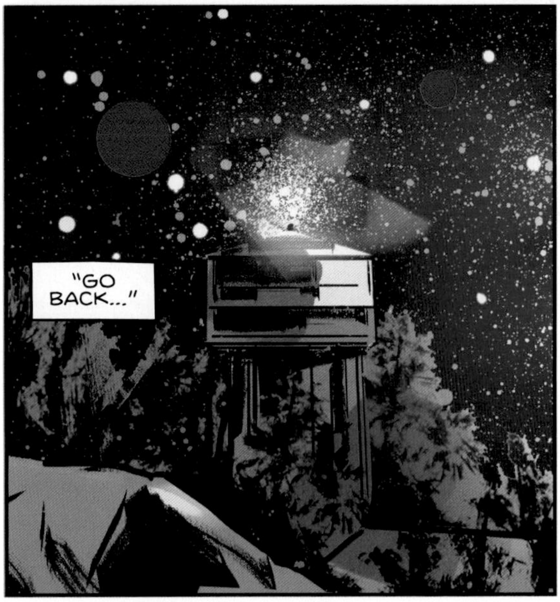
"GO BACK..."

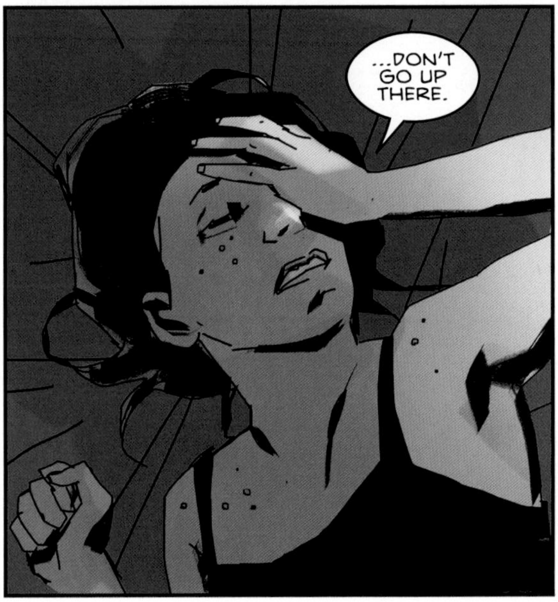
...DON'T GO UP THERE.

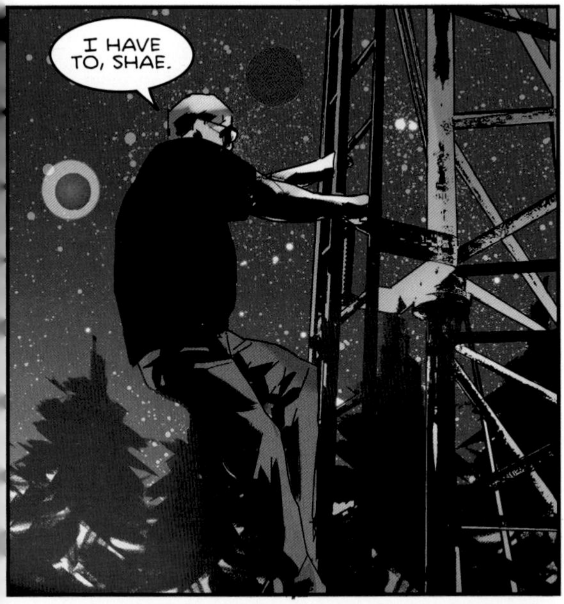
I HAVE TO, SHAE.

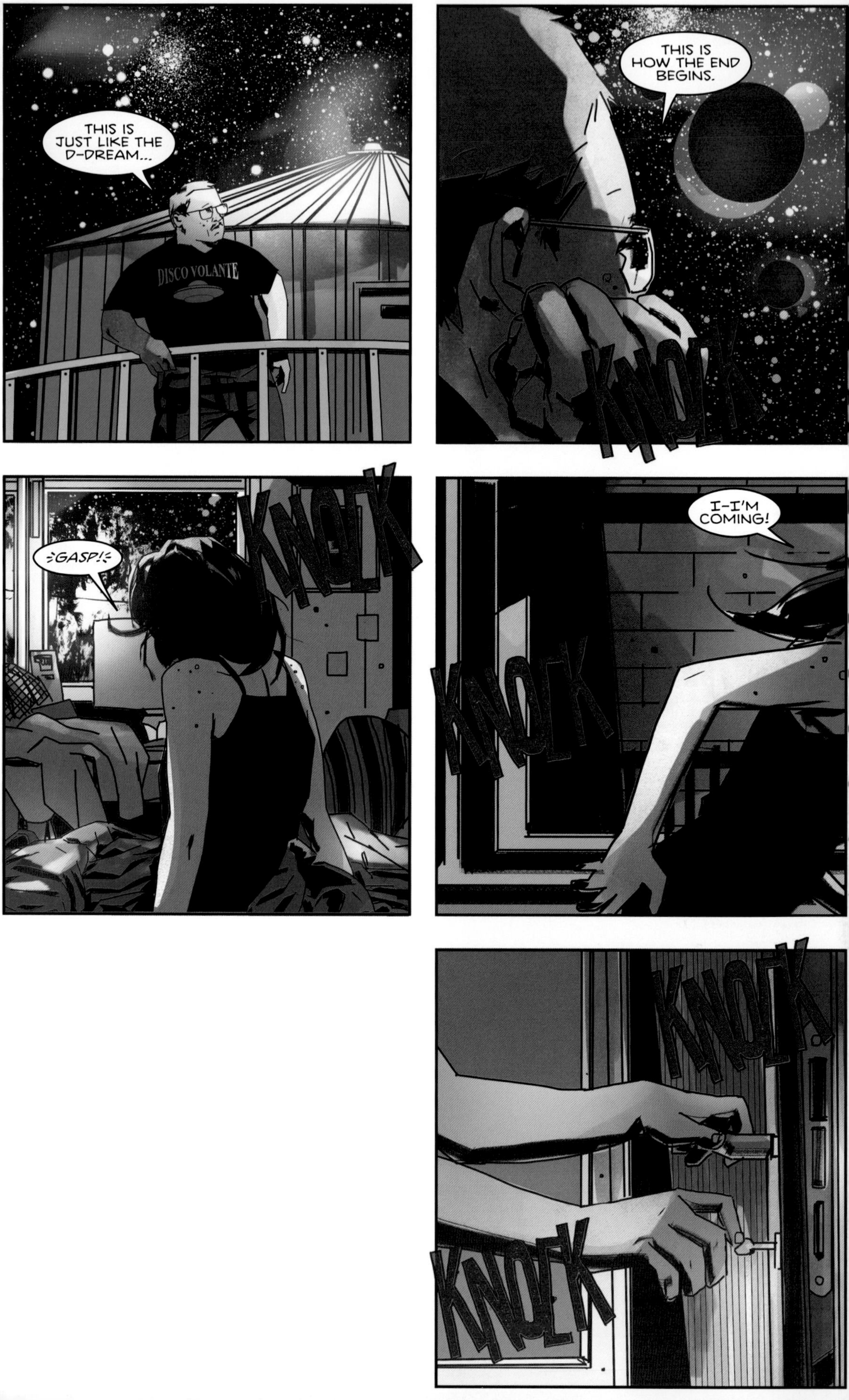
THIS IS JUST LIKE THE D-DREAM...
DISCO VOLANTE
THIS IS HOW THE END BEGINS.
KNOCK
KNOCK
GASP!
I-I'M COMING!
KNOCK
KNOCK
KNOCK

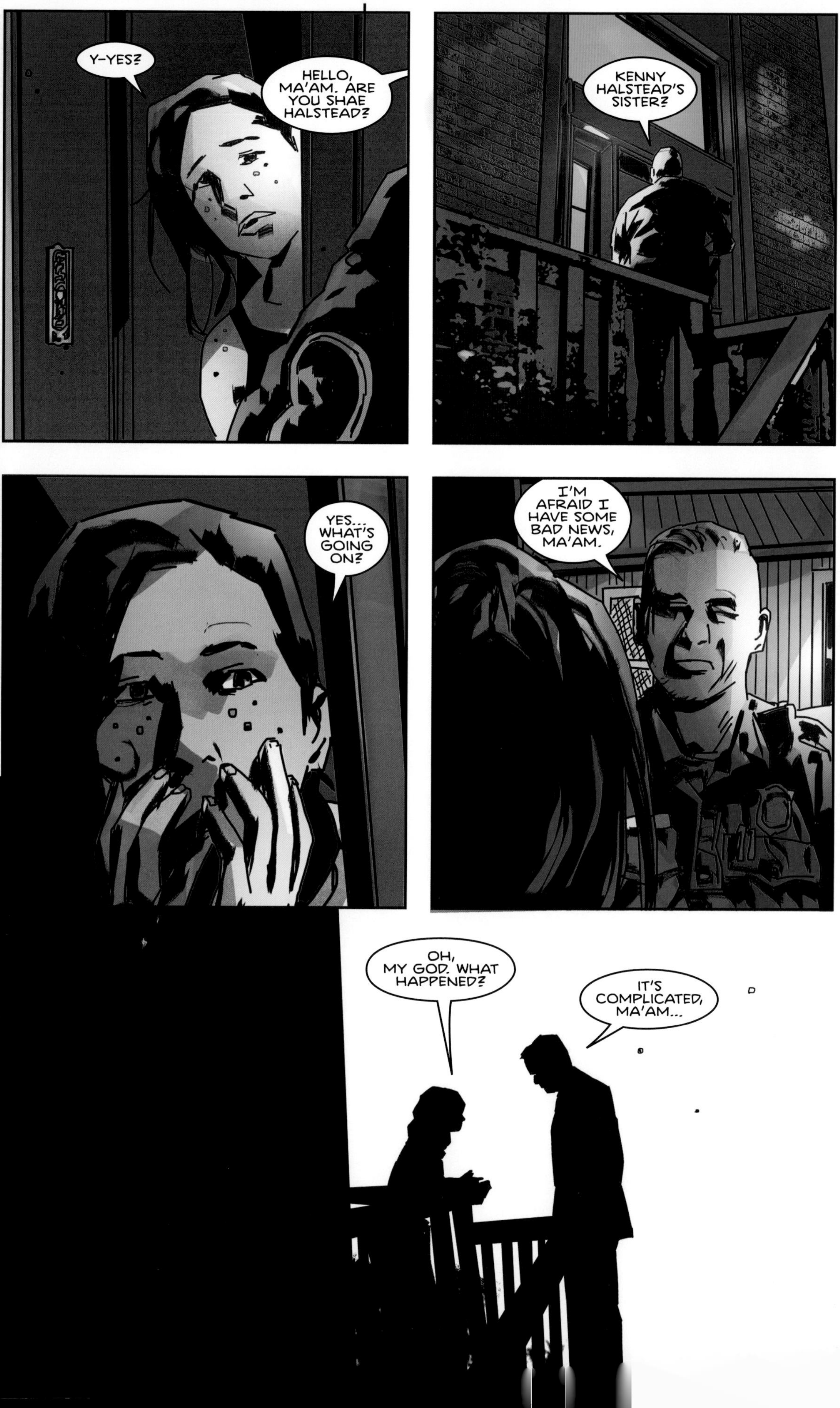
Y-YES?
HELLO, MA'AM. ARE YOU SHAE HALSTEAD?
KENNY HALSTEAD'S SISTER?
YES... WHAT'S GOING ON?
I'M AFRAID I HAVE SOME BAD NEWS, MA'AM.
OH, MY GOD. WHAT HAPPENED?
IT'S COMPLICATED, MA'AM...

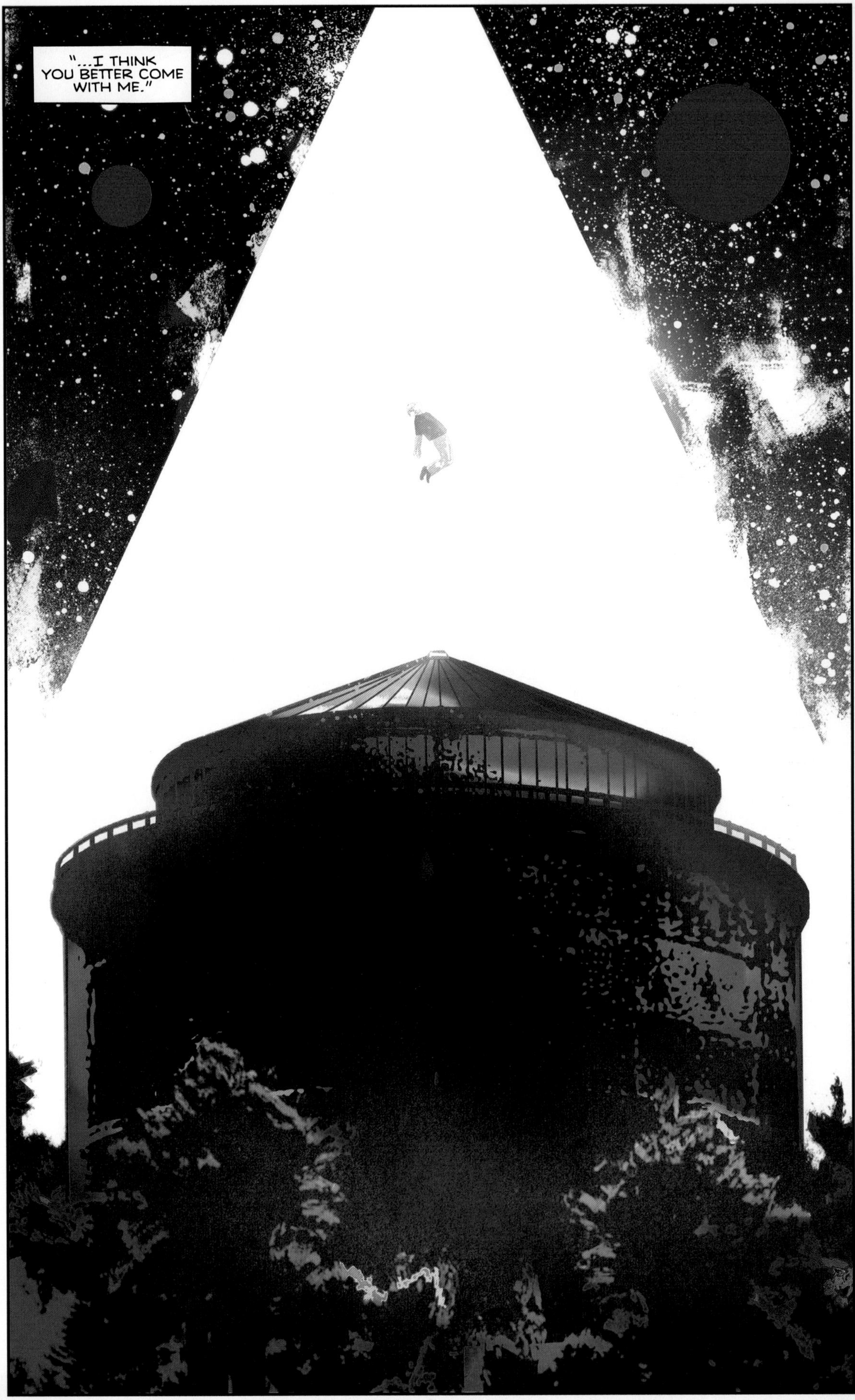
"...I THINK YOU BETTER COME WITH ME."

PART TWO

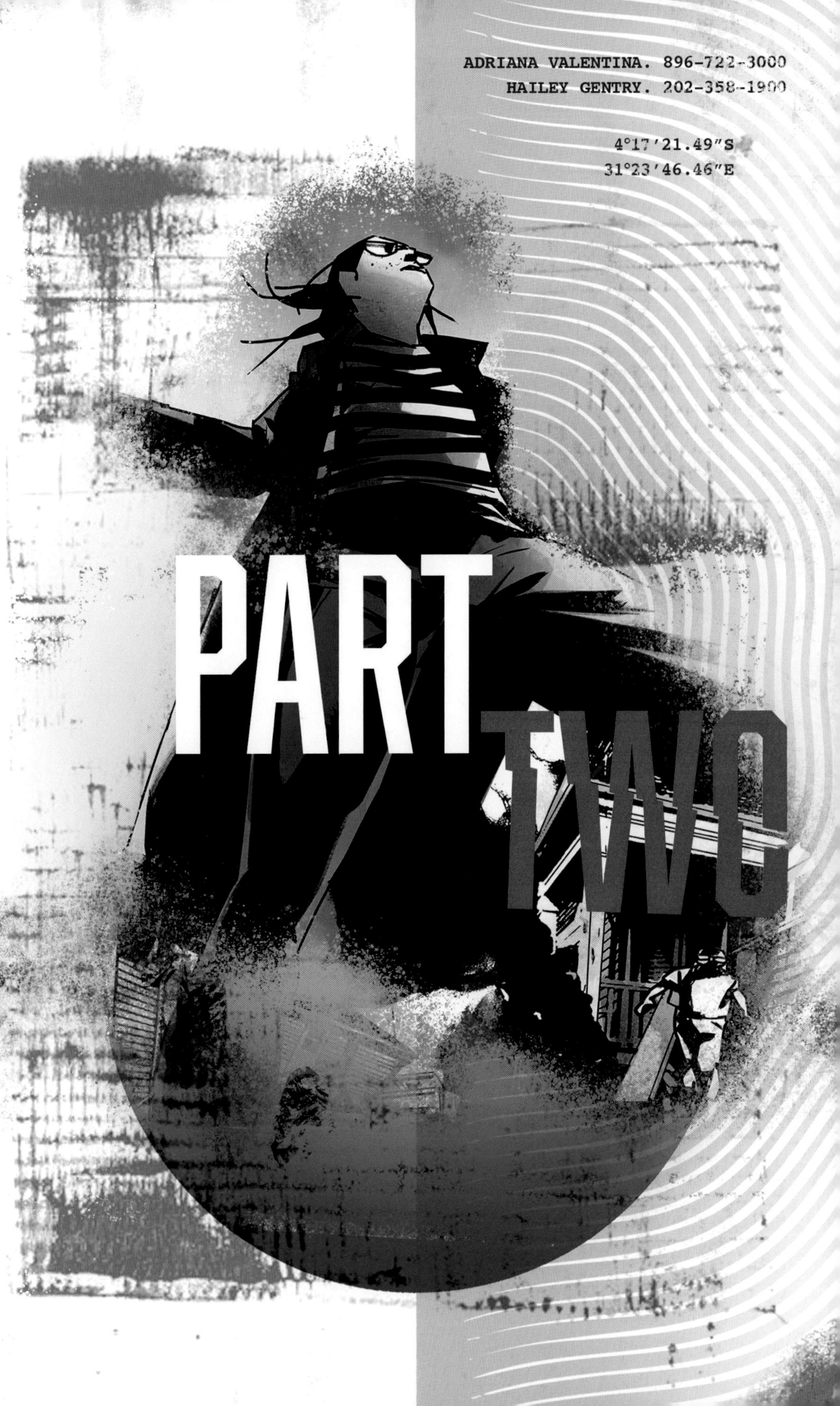

ADRIANA VALENTINA. 896-722-3000
HAILEY GENTRY. 202-358-1900
4°17′21.49″S
31°23′46.46″E

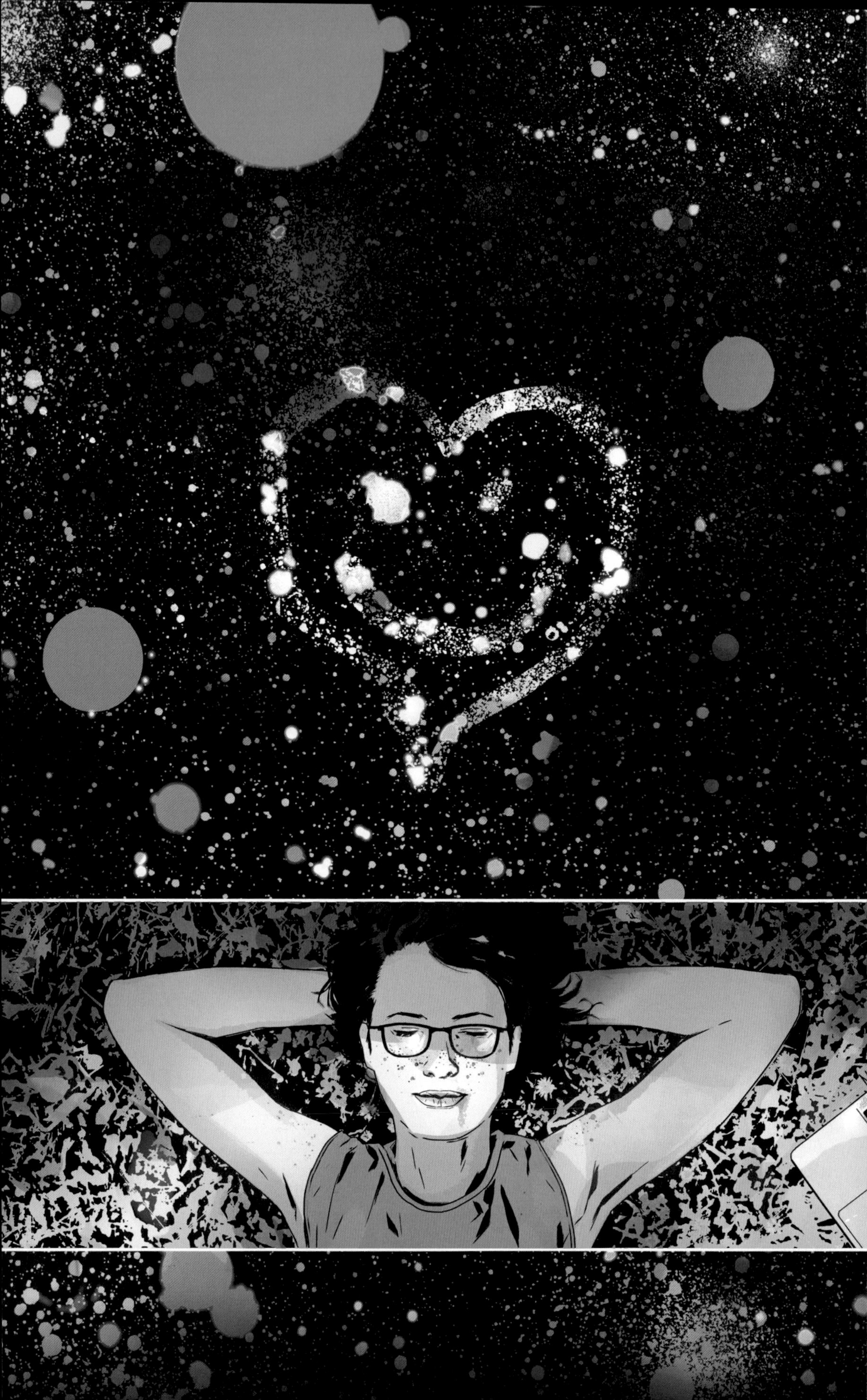

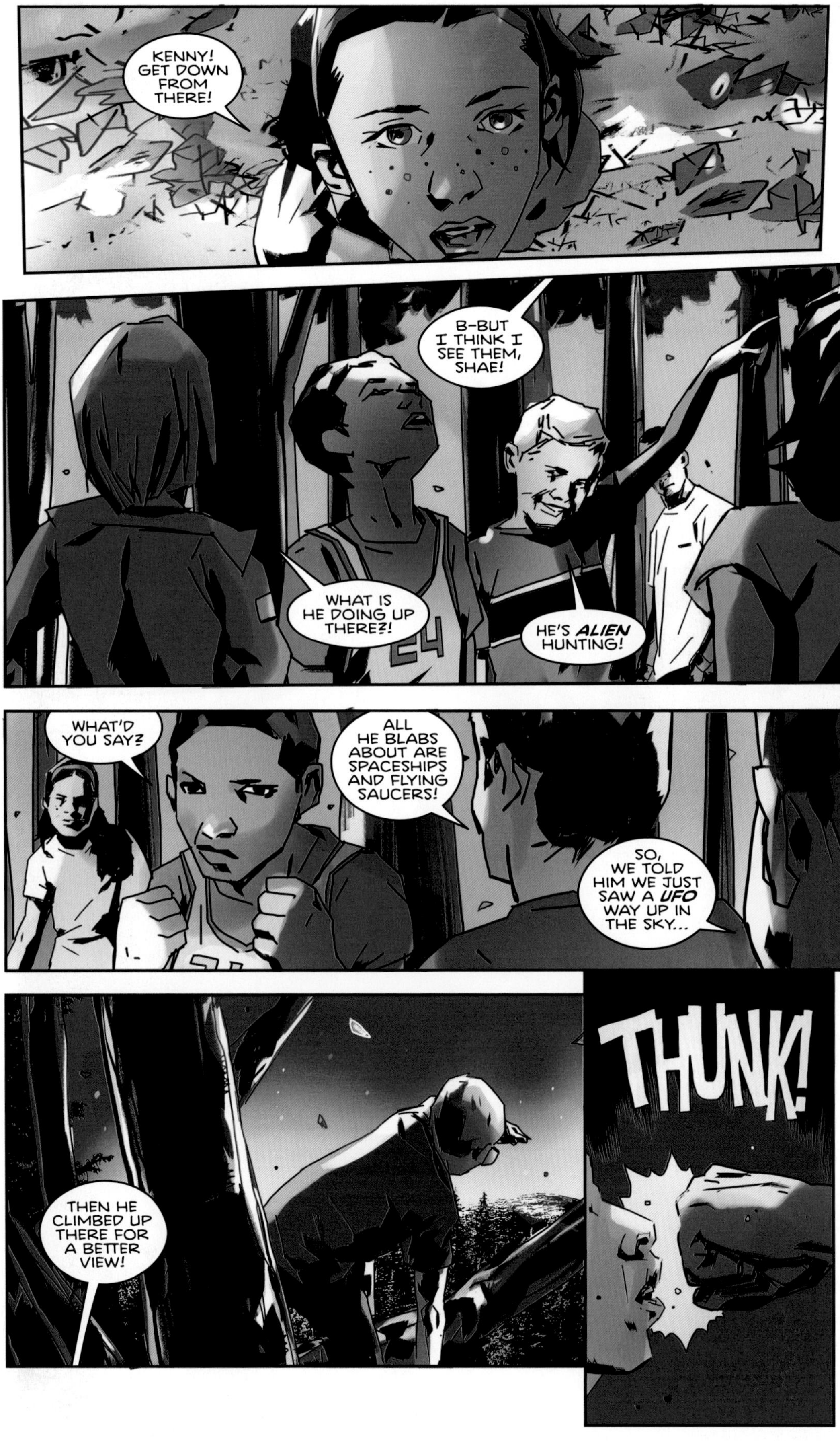
KENNY! GET DOWN FROM THERE!
B-BUT I THINK I SEE THEM, SHAE!
WHAT IS HE DOING UP THERE?!
HE'S ALIEN HUNTING!
WHAT'D YOU SAY?
ALL HE BLABS ABOUT ARE SPACESHIPS AND FLYING SAUCERS!
SO, WE TOLD HIM WE JUST SAW A UFO WAY UP IN THE SKY...
THEN HE CLIMBED UP THERE FOR A BETTER VIEW!
THUNK!

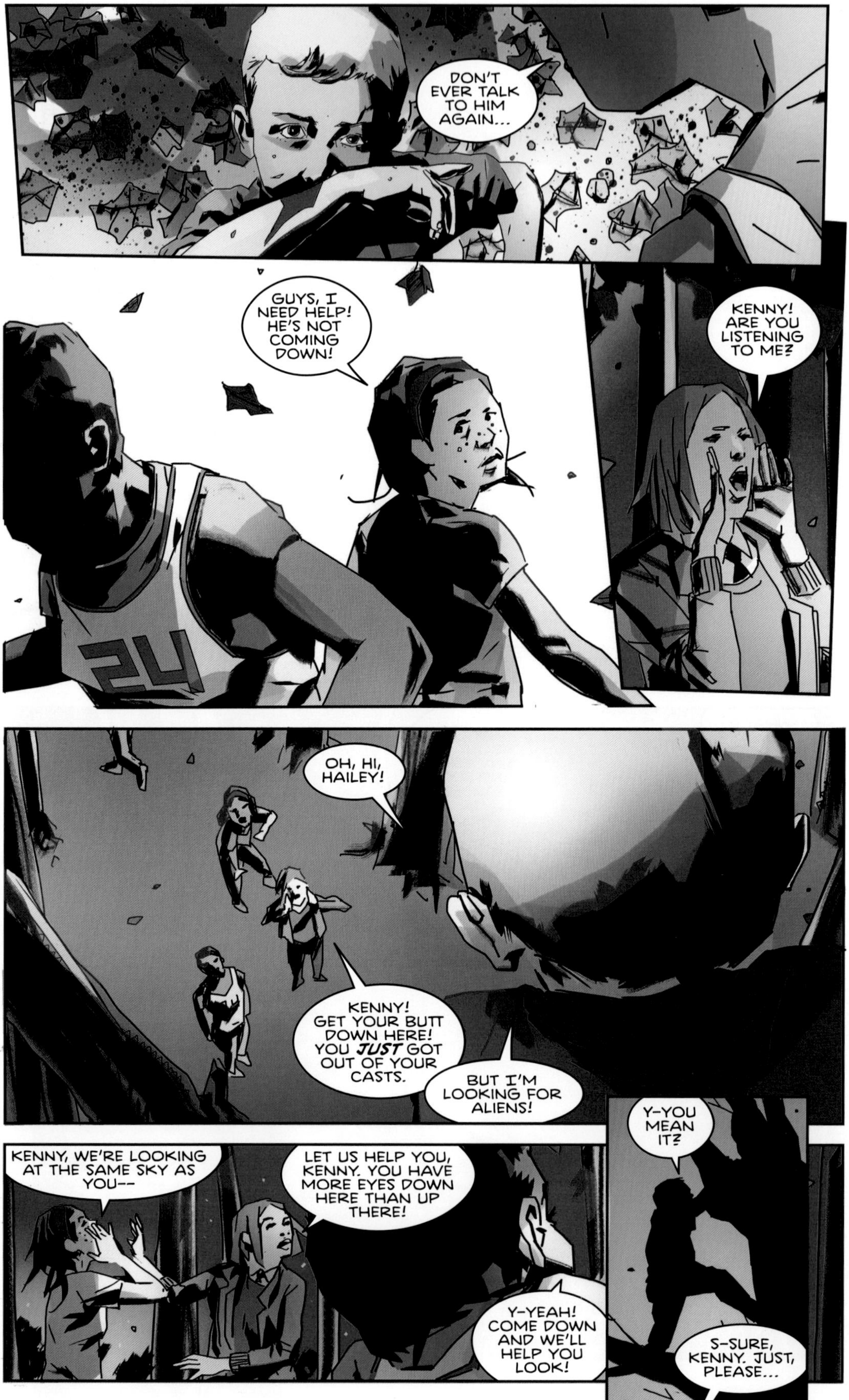
DON'T EVER TALK TO HIM AGAIN...
GUYS, I NEED HELP! HE'S NOT COMING DOWN!
KENNY! ARE YOU LISTENING TO ME?
OH, HI, HAILEY!
KENNY! GET YOUR BUTT DOWN HERE! YOU *JUST* GOT OUT OF YOUR CASTS.
BUT I'M LOOKING FOR ALIENS!
KENNY, WE'RE LOOKING AT THE SAME SKY AS YOU--
LET US HELP YOU, KENNY. YOU HAVE MORE EYES DOWN HERE THAN UP THERE!
Y-YEAH! COME DOWN AND WE'LL HELP YOU LOOK!
Y-YOU MEAN IT?
S-SURE, KENNY. JUST, PLEASE...

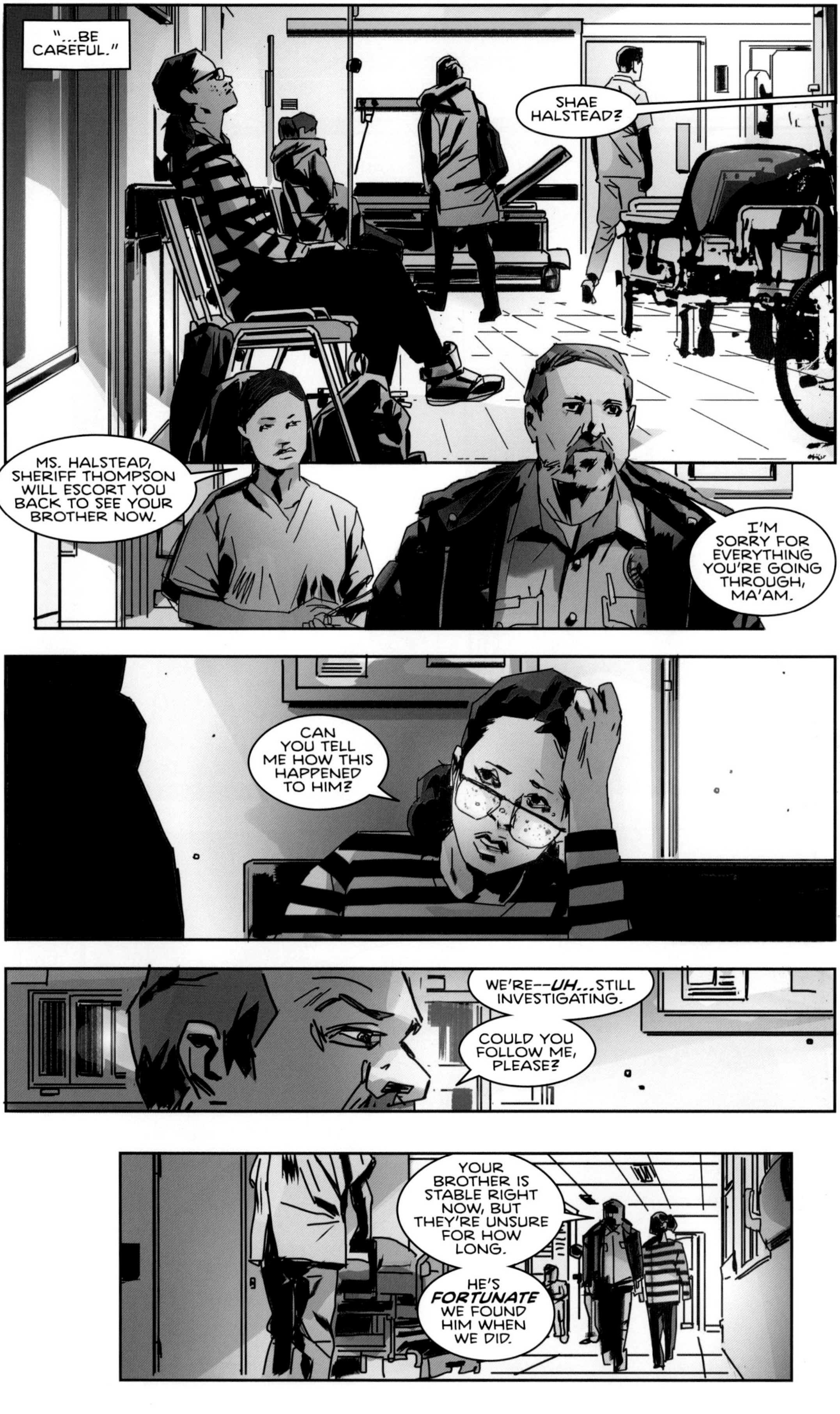
"...BE CAREFUL."
SHAE HALSTEAD?
MS. HALSTEAD, SHERIFF THOMPSON WILL ESCORT YOU BACK TO SEE YOUR BROTHER NOW.
I'M SORRY FOR EVERYTHING YOU'RE GOING THROUGH, MA'AM.
CAN YOU TELL ME HOW THIS HAPPENED TO HIM?
WE'RE--*UH...*STILL INVESTIGATING.
COULD YOU FOLLOW ME, PLEASE?
YOUR BROTHER IS STABLE RIGHT NOW, BUT THEY'RE UNSURE FOR HOW LONG.
HE'S ***FORTUNATE*** WE FOUND HIM WHEN WE DID.

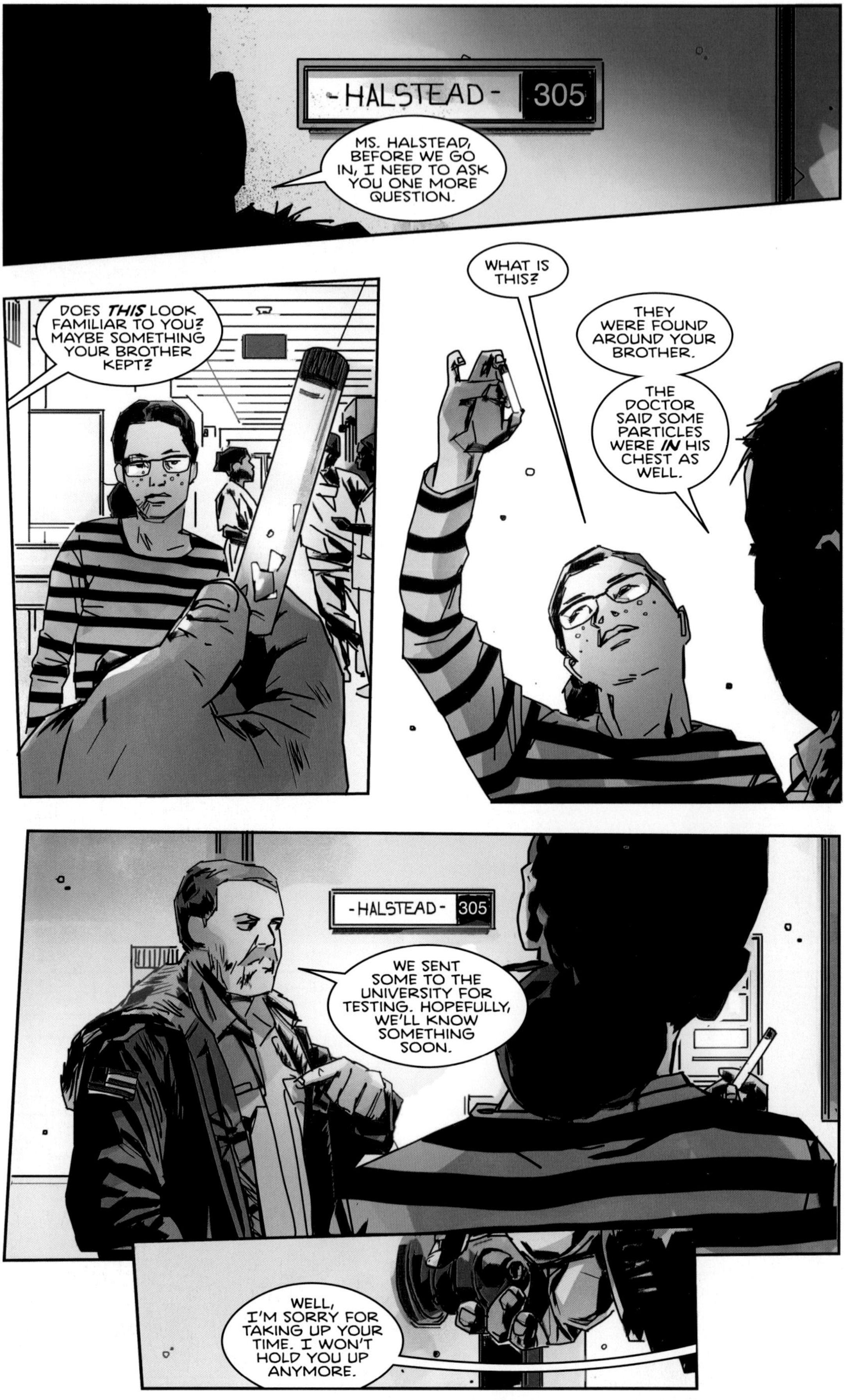

-HALSTEAD- 305
MS. HALSTEAD, BEFORE WE GO IN, I NEED TO ASK YOU ONE MORE QUESTION.
DOES *THIS* LOOK FAMILIAR TO YOU? MAYBE SOMETHING YOUR BROTHER KEPT?
WHAT IS THIS?
THEY WERE FOUND AROUND YOUR BROTHER.
THE DOCTOR SAID SOME PARTICLES WERE *IN* HIS CHEST AS WELL.
-HALSTEAD- 305
WE SENT SOME TO THE UNIVERSITY FOR TESTING. HOPEFULLY, WE'LL KNOW SOMETHING SOON.
WELL, I'M SORRY FOR TAKING UP YOUR TIME. I WON'T HOLD YOU UP ANYMORE.

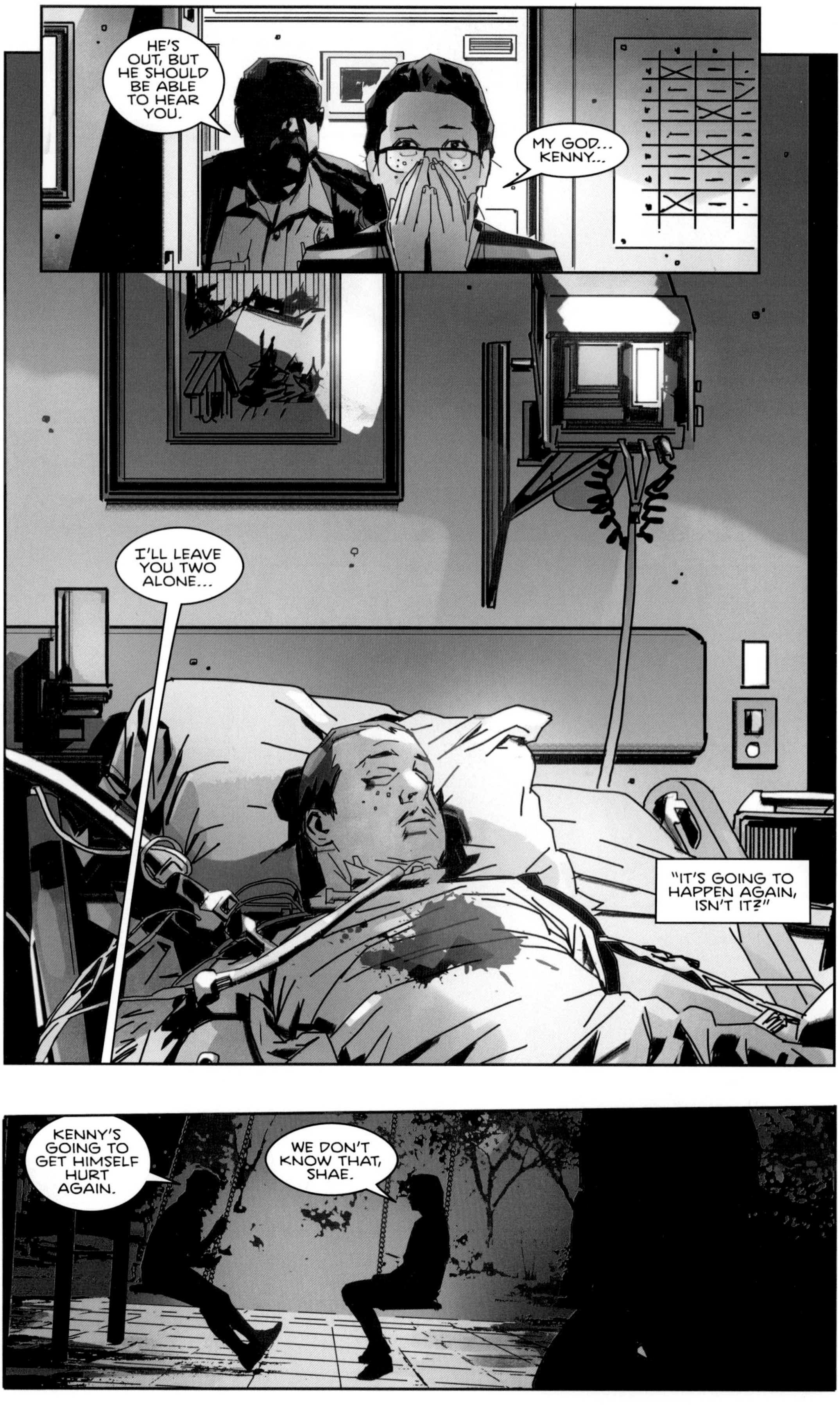
HE'S OUT, BUT HE SHOULD BE ABLE TO HEAR YOU.
MY GOD... KENNY...
I'LL LEAVE YOU TWO ALONE...
"IT'S GOING TO HAPPEN AGAIN, ISN'T IT?"
KENNY'S GOING TO GET HIMSELF HURT AGAIN.
WE DON'T KNOW THAT, SHAE.

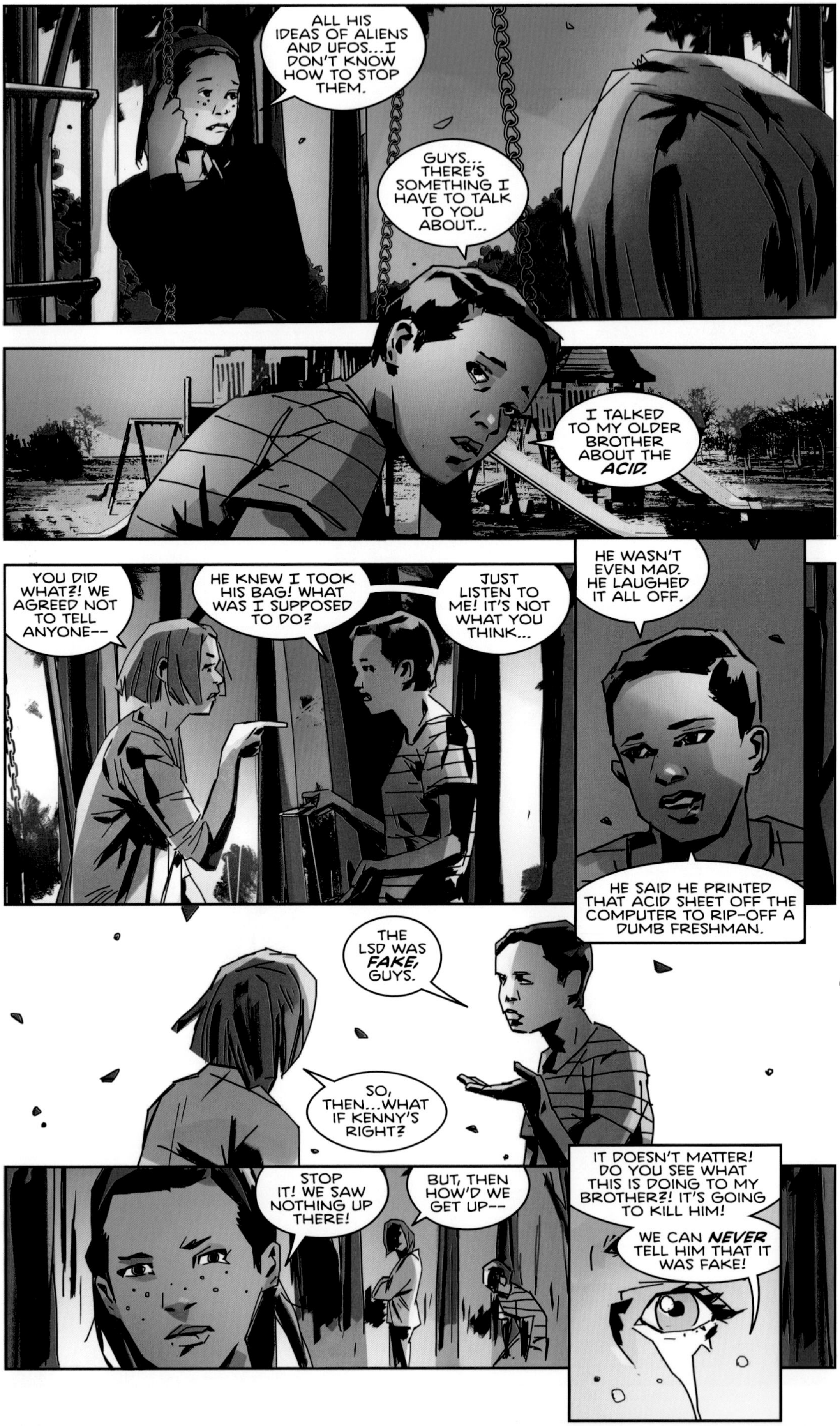
ALL HIS IDEAS OF ALIENS AND UFOS...I DON'T KNOW HOW TO STOP THEM.
GUYS... THERE'S SOMETHING I HAVE TO TALK TO YOU ABOUT...
I TALKED TO MY OLDER BROTHER ABOUT THE ACID.
YOU DID WHAT?! WE AGREED NOT TO TELL ANYONE--
HE KNEW I TOOK HIS BAG! WHAT WAS I SUPPOSED TO DO?
JUST LISTEN TO ME! IT'S NOT WHAT YOU THINK...
HE WASN'T EVEN MAD. HE LAUGHED IT ALL OFF.
HE SAID HE PRINTED THAT ACID SHEET OFF THE COMPUTER TO RIP-OFF A DUMB FRESHMAN.
THE LSD WAS FAKE, GUYS.
SO, THEN...WHAT IF KENNY'S RIGHT?
STOP IT! WE SAW NOTHING UP THERE!
BUT, THEN HOW'D WE GET UP--
IT DOESN'T MATTER! DO YOU SEE WHAT THIS IS DOING TO MY BROTHER?! IT'S GOING TO KILL HIM!
WE CAN NEVER TELL HIM THAT IT WAS FAKE!

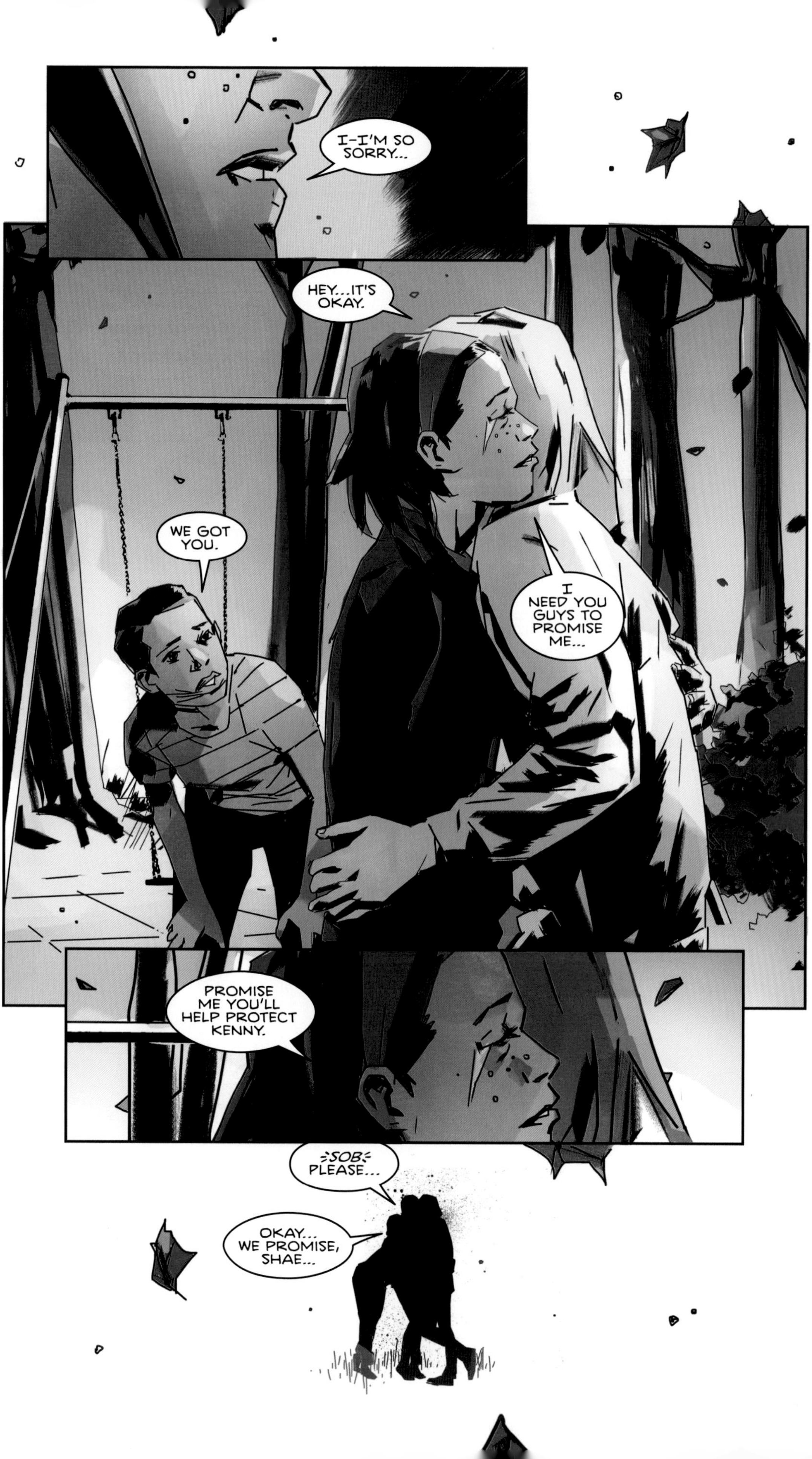
I–I'M SO SORRY...
HEY...IT'S OKAY.
WE GOT YOU.
I NEED YOU GUYS TO PROMISE ME...
PROMISE ME YOU'LL HELP PROTECT KENNY.
SOB PLEASE...
OKAY... WE PROMISE, SHAE...

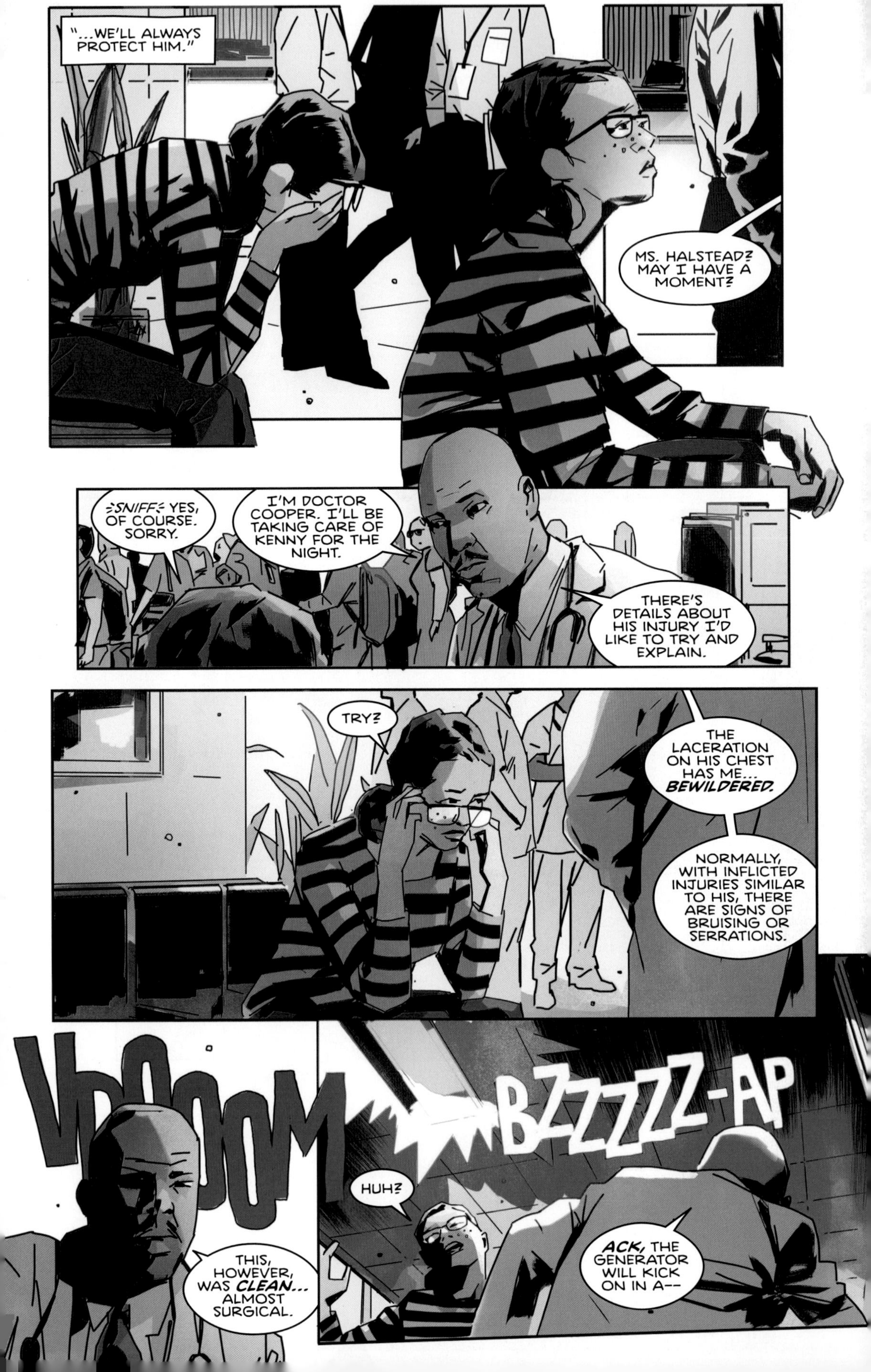
"...WE'LL ALWAYS PROTECT HIM."
MS. HALSTEAD? MAY I HAVE A MOMENT?
SNIFF YES, OF COURSE. SORRY.
I'M DOCTOR COOPER. I'LL BE TAKING CARE OF KENNY FOR THE NIGHT.
THERE'S DETAILS ABOUT HIS INJURY I'D LIKE TO TRY AND EXPLAIN.
TRY?
THE LACERATION ON HIS CHEST HAS ME... ***BEWILDERED.***
NORMALLY, WITH INFLICTED INJURIES SIMILAR TO HIS, THERE ARE SIGNS OF BRUISING OR SERRATIONS.
VRROOOM
THIS, HOWEVER, WAS ***CLEAN...*** ALMOST SURGICAL.
BZZZZZ-AP
HUH?
ACK, THE GENERATOR WILL KICK ON IN A--

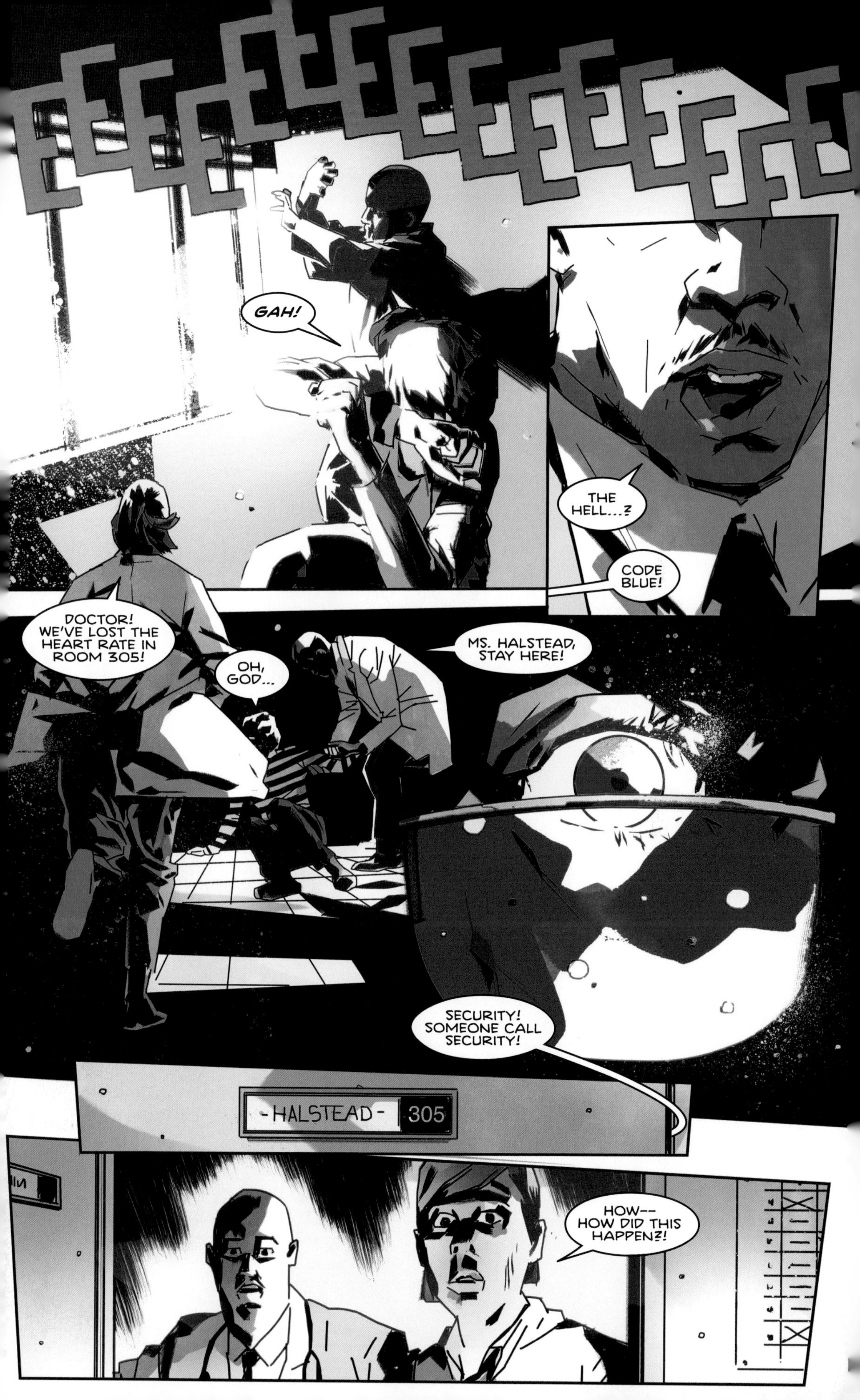
EEEEEEEEEEEEEEEEEEEEE
GAH!
THE HELL...?
CODE BLUE!
DOCTOR! WE'VE LOST THE HEART RATE IN ROOM 305!
OH, GOD...
MS. HALSTEAD, STAY HERE!
SECURITY! SOMEONE CALL SECURITY!
-HALSTEAD- 305
HOW-- HOW DID THIS HAPPEN?!

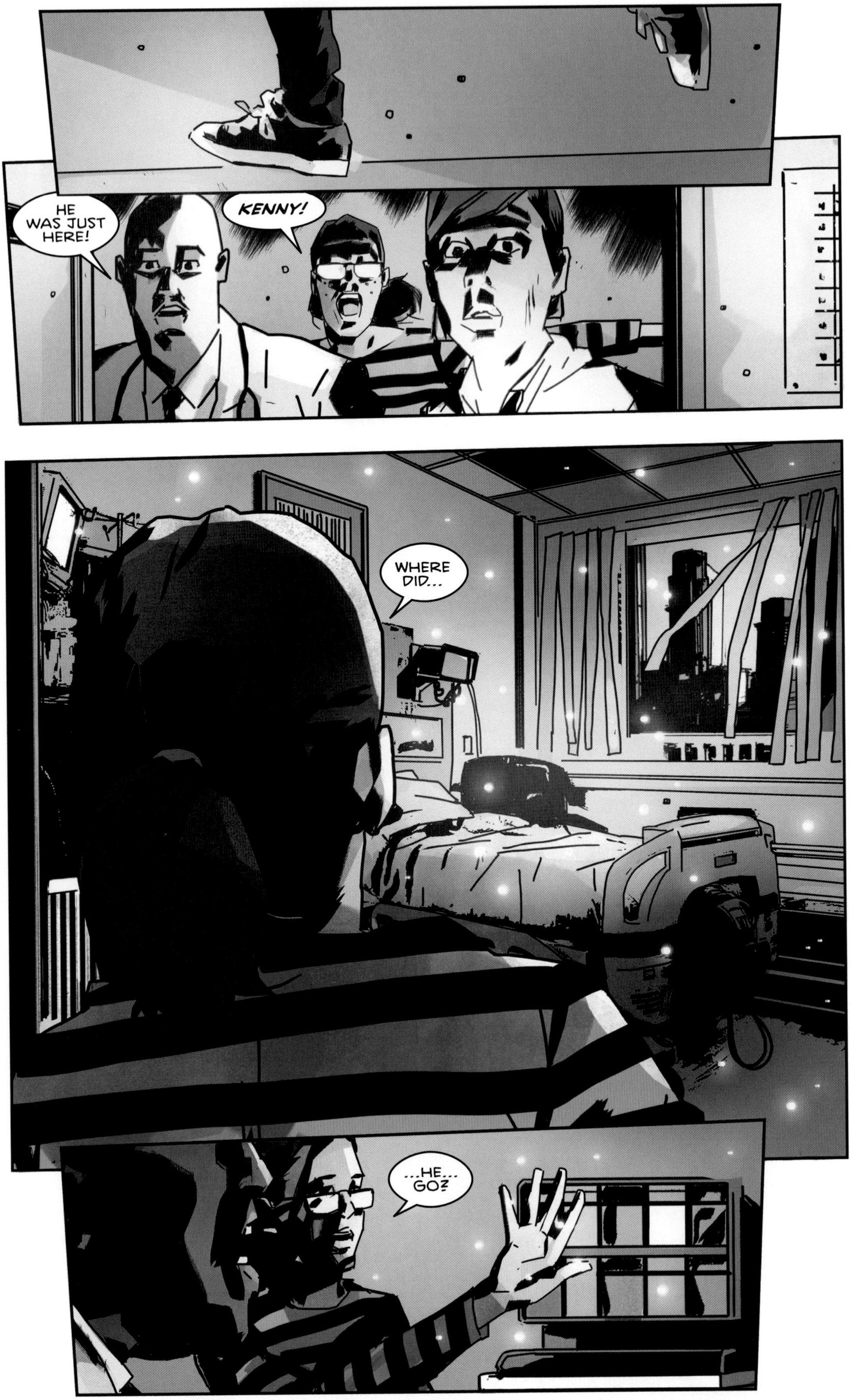
HE WAS JUST HERE!
KENNY!
WHERE DID...
...HE... GO?

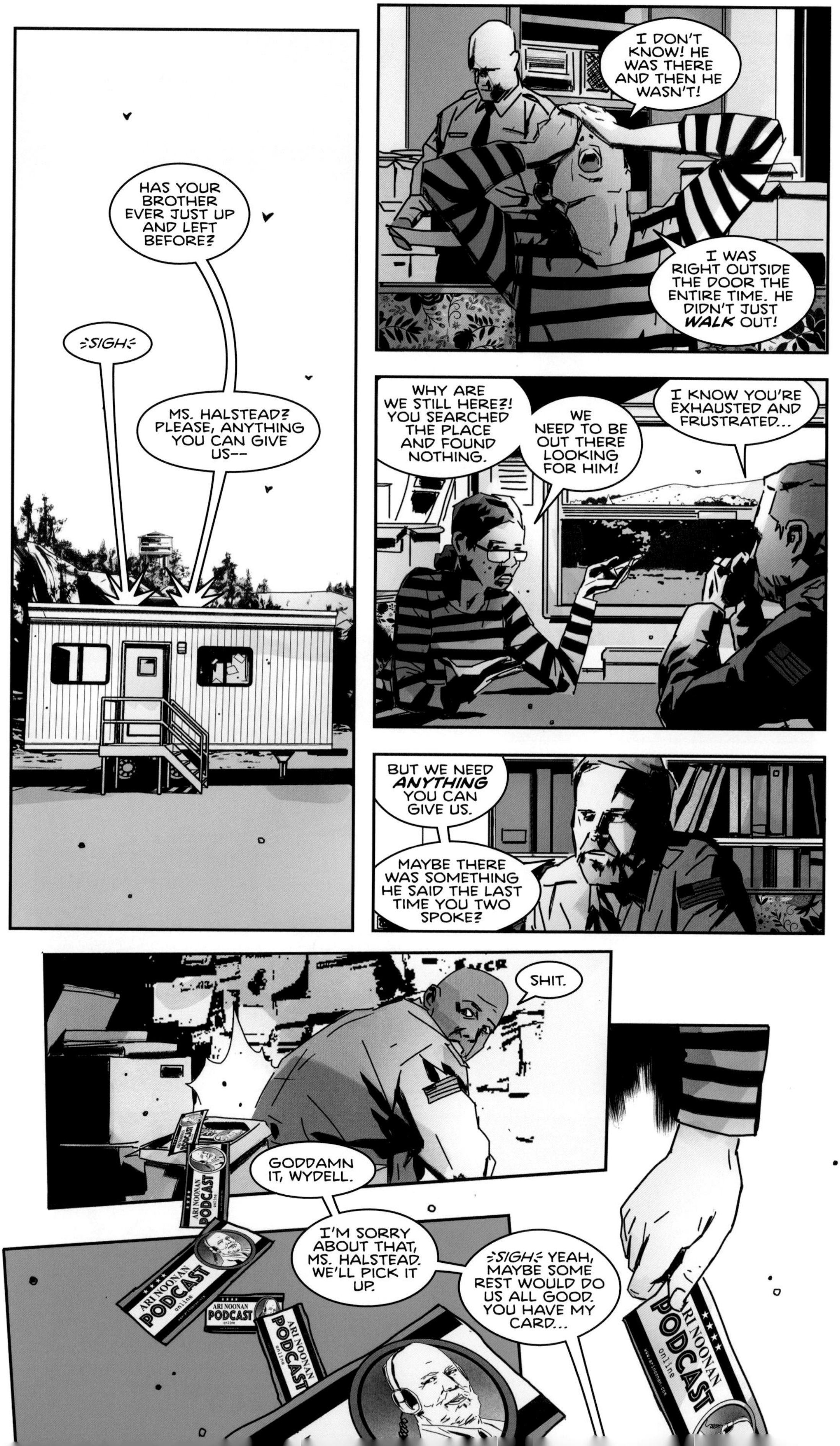
HAS YOUR BROTHER EVER JUST UP AND LEFT BEFORE?
MS. HALSTEAD? PLEASE, ANYTHING YOU CAN GIVE US--
SIGH
I DON'T KNOW! HE WAS THERE AND THEN HE WASN'T!
I WAS RIGHT OUTSIDE THE DOOR THE ENTIRE TIME. HE DIDN'T JUST WALK OUT!
WHY ARE WE STILL HERE?! YOU SEARCHED THE PLACE AND FOUND NOTHING.
WE NEED TO BE OUT THERE LOOKING FOR HIM!
I KNOW YOU'RE EXHAUSTED AND FRUSTRATED...
BUT WE NEED ANYTHING YOU CAN GIVE US.
MAYBE THERE WAS SOMETHING HE SAID THE LAST TIME YOU TWO SPOKE?
SHIT.
GODDAMN IT, WYDELL.
I'M SORRY ABOUT THAT, MS. HALSTEAD. WE'LL PICK IT UP.
SIGH YEAH, MAYBE SOME REST WOULD DO US ALL GOOD. YOU HAVE MY CARD...
ARI NOONAN PODCAST online

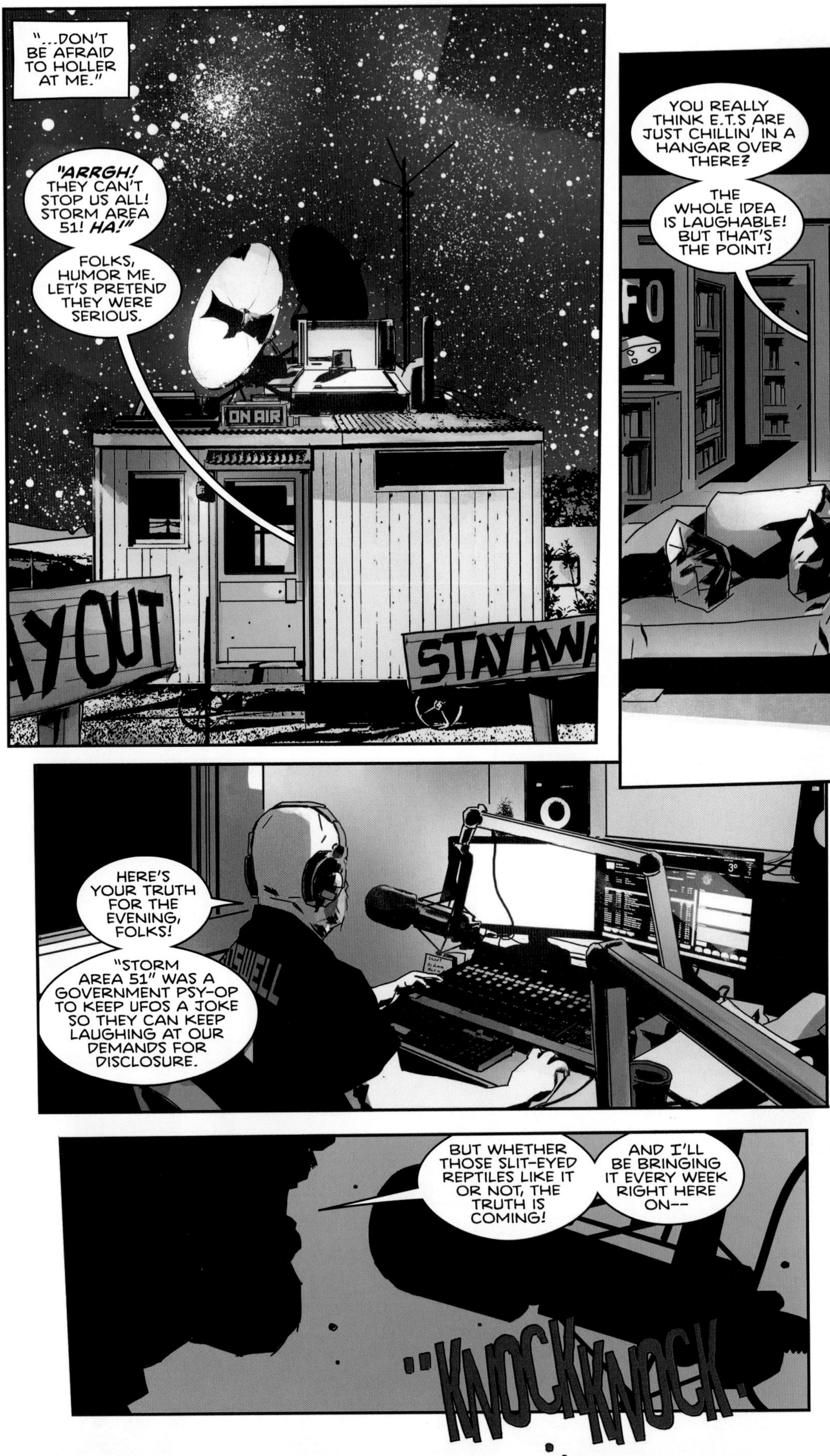
"...DON'T BE AFRAID TO HOLLER AT ME."
"ARRGH! THEY CAN'T STOP US ALL! STORM AREA 51! HA!"
FOLKS, HUMOR ME. LET'S PRETEND THEY WERE SERIOUS.
ON AIR
AY OUT
STAY AWA
YOU REALLY THINK E.T.S ARE JUST CHILLIN' IN A HANGAR OVER THERE?
THE WHOLE IDEA IS LAUGHABLE! BUT THAT'S THE POINT!
FO
HERE'S YOUR TRUTH FOR THE EVENING, FOLKS!
"STORM AREA 51" WAS A GOVERNMENT PSY-OP TO KEEP UFOS A JOKE SO THEY CAN KEEP LAUGHING AT OUR DEMANDS FOR DISCLOSURE.
BUT WHETHER THOSE SLIT-EYED REPTILES LIKE IT OR NOT, THE TRUTH IS COMING!
AND I'LL BE BRINGING IT EVERY WEEK RIGHT HERE ON--
KNOCK KNOCK

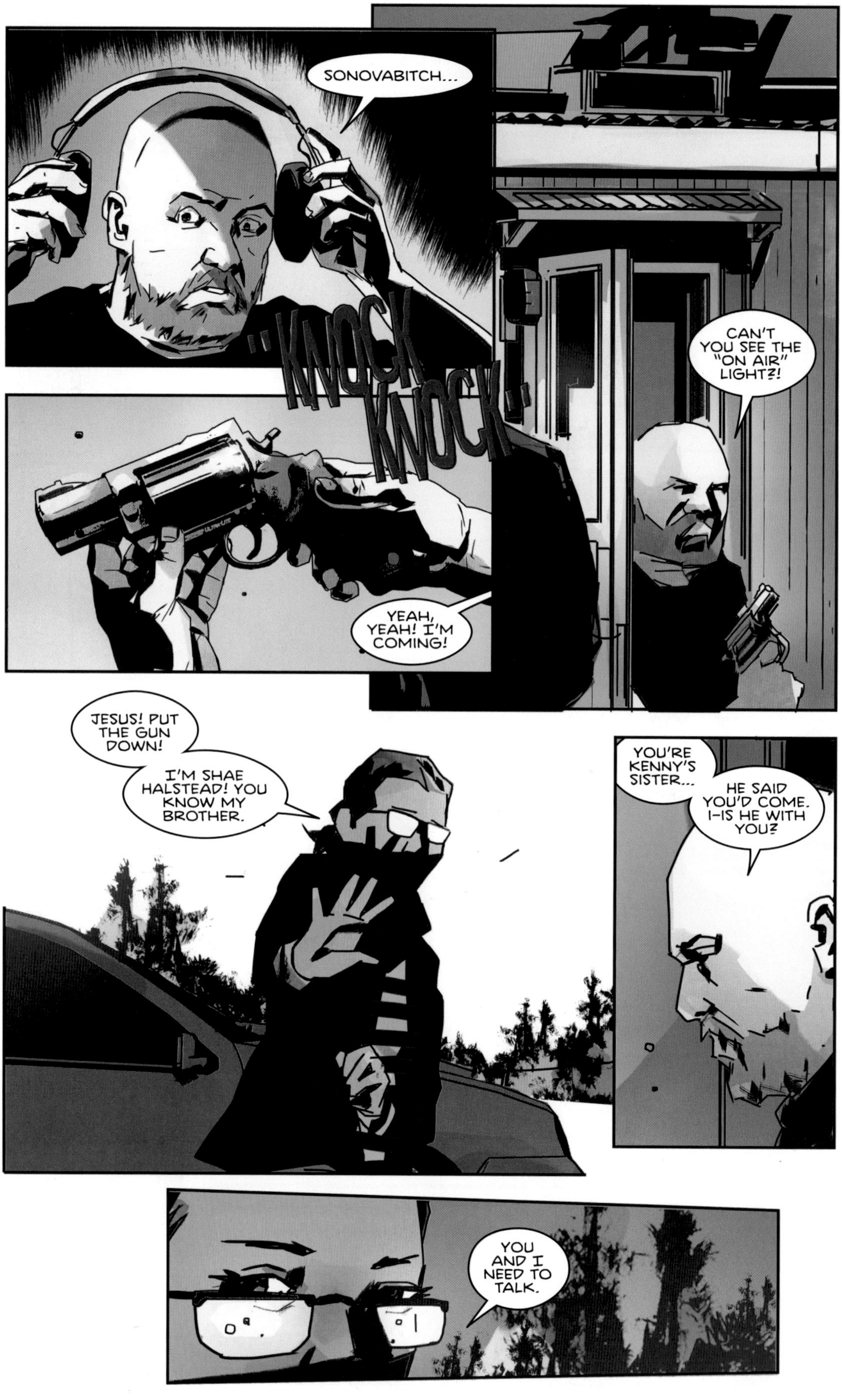
SONOVABITCH...
"KNOCK KNOCK"
CAN'T YOU SEE THE "ON AIR" LIGHT?!
YEAH, YEAH! I'M COMING!
JESUS! PUT THE GUN DOWN!
I'M SHAE HALSTEAD! YOU KNOW MY BROTHER.
YOU'RE KENNY'S SISTER...
HE SAID YOU'D COME. I-IS HE WITH YOU?
YOU AND I NEED TO TALK.

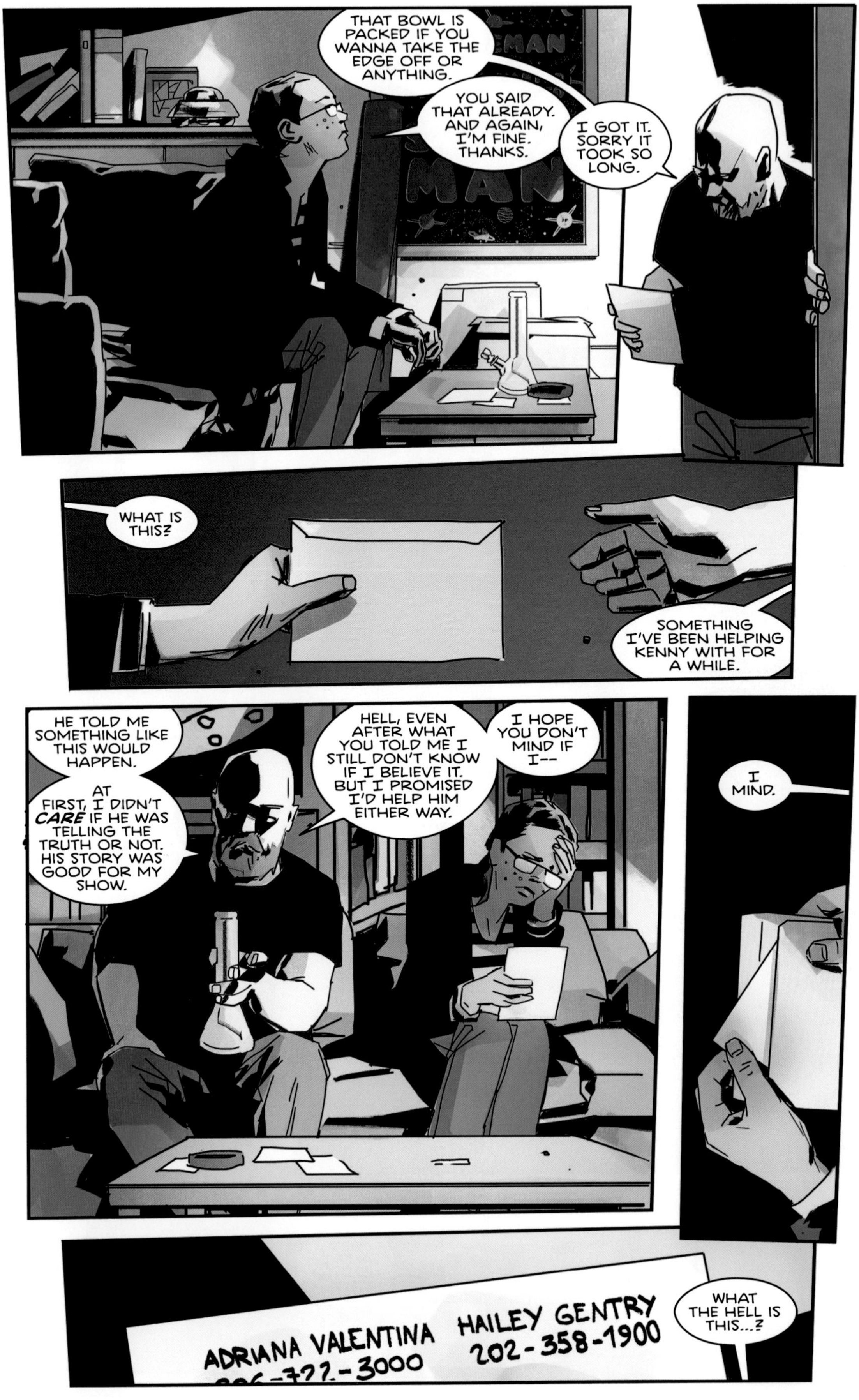
THAT BOWL IS PACKED IF YOU WANNA TAKE THE EDGE OFF OR ANYTHING.
YOU SAID THAT ALREADY. AND AGAIN, I'M FINE. THANKS.
I GOT IT. SORRY IT TOOK SO LONG.
WHAT IS THIS?
SOMETHING I'VE BEEN HELPING KENNY WITH FOR A WHILE.
HE TOLD ME SOMETHING LIKE THIS WOULD HAPPEN.
AT FIRST, I DIDN'T CARE IF HE WAS TELLING THE TRUTH OR NOT. HIS STORY WAS GOOD FOR MY SHOW.
HELL, EVEN AFTER WHAT YOU TOLD ME I STILL DON'T KNOW IF I BELIEVE IT. BUT I PROMISED I'D HELP HIM EITHER WAY.
I HOPE YOU DON'T MIND IF I--
I MIND.
ADRIANA VALENTINA
HAILEY GENTRY
202-358-1900
WHAT THE HELL IS THIS...?

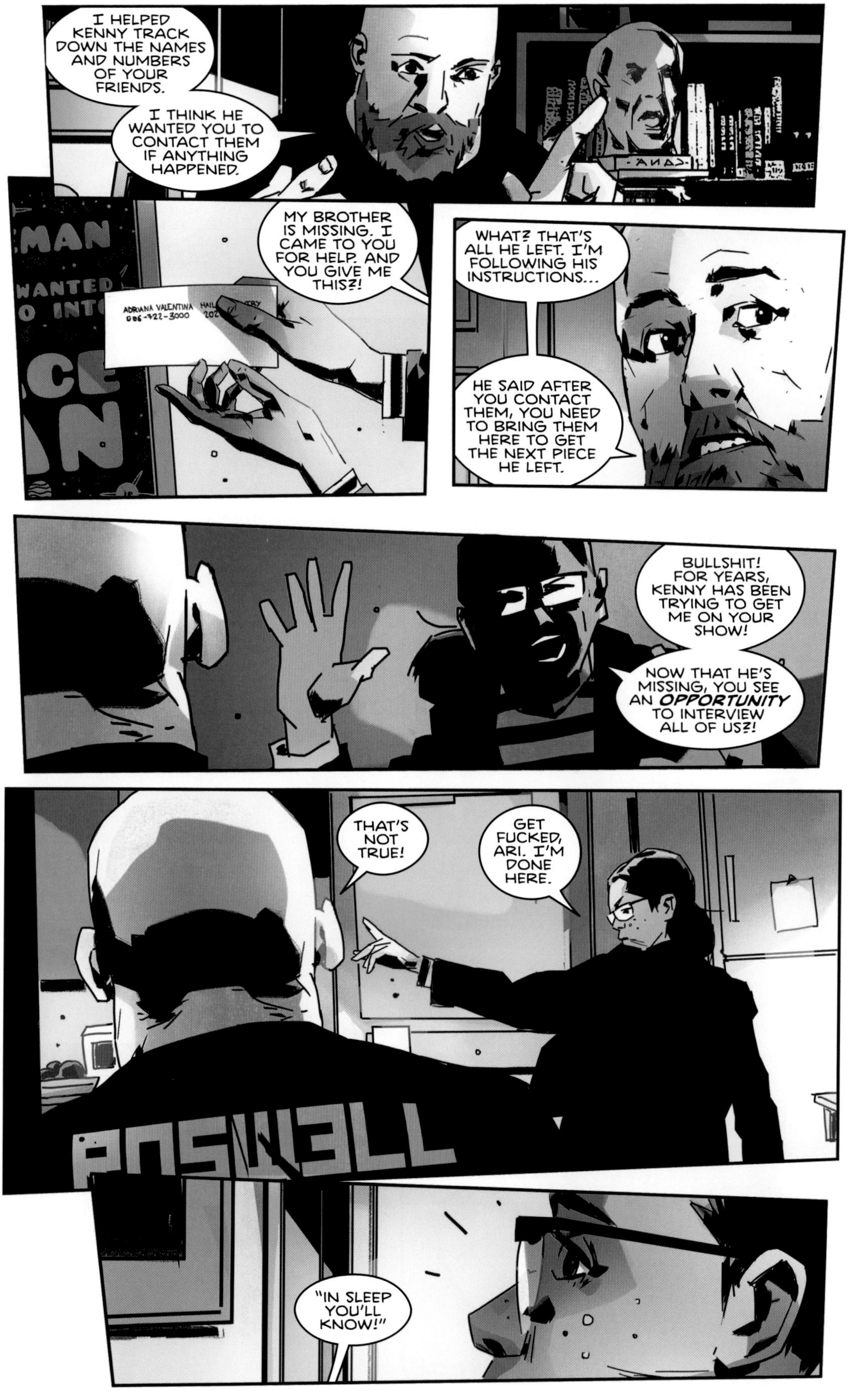
I HELPED KENNY TRACK DOWN THE NAMES AND NUMBERS OF YOUR FRIENDS.
I THINK HE WANTED YOU TO CONTACT THEM IF ANYTHING HAPPENED.
MY BROTHER IS MISSING. I CAME TO YOU FOR HELP. AND YOU GIVE ME THIS?!
ADRIANA VALENTINA
806-722-3000
WHAT? THAT'S ALL HE LEFT. I'M FOLLOWING HIS INSTRUCTIONS...
HE SAID AFTER YOU CONTACT THEM, YOU NEED TO BRING THEM HERE TO GET THE NEXT PIECE HE LEFT.
BULLSHIT! FOR YEARS, KENNY HAS BEEN TRYING TO GET ME ON YOUR SHOW!
NOW THAT HE'S MISSING, YOU SEE AN *OPPORTUNITY* TO INTERVIEW ALL OF US?!
THAT'S NOT TRUE!
GET FUCKED, ARI. I'M DONE HERE.
ROSWELL
"IN SLEEP YOU'LL KNOW!"

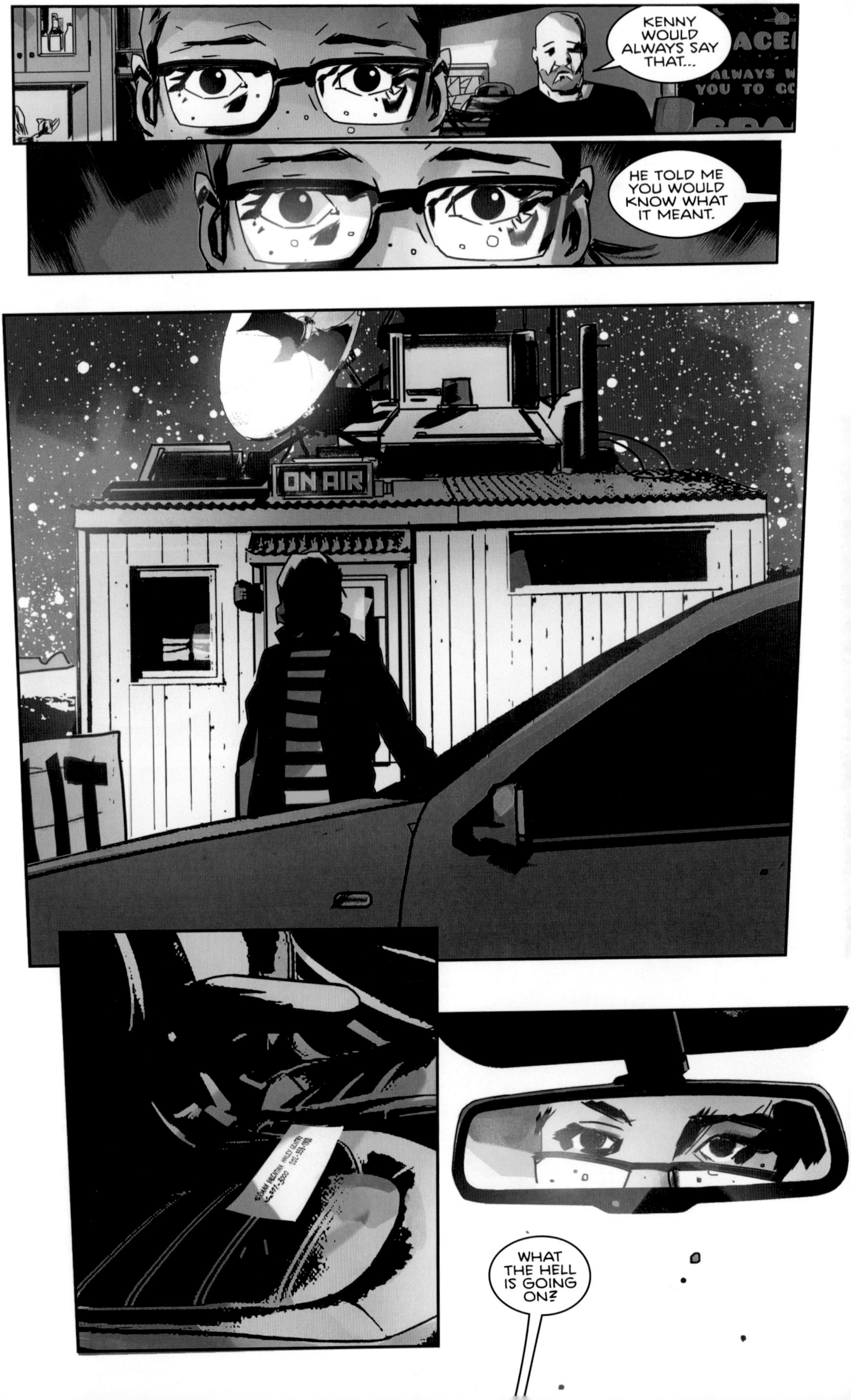
KENNY WOULD ALWAYS SAY THAT...
HE TOLD ME YOU WOULD KNOW WHAT IT MEANT.
ON AIR
WHAT THE HELL IS GOING ON?

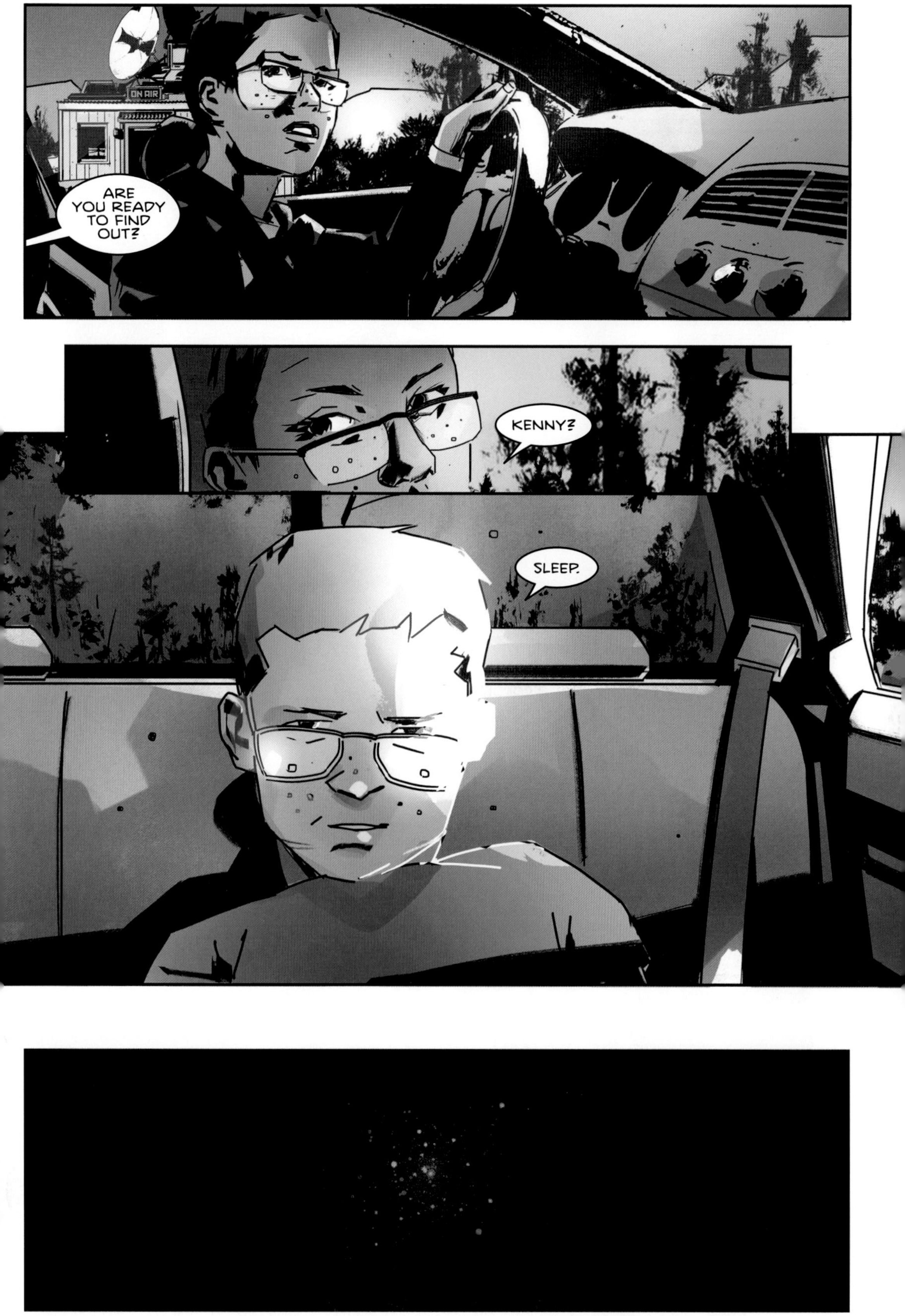
ARE YOU READY TO FIND OUT?
ON AIR
KENNY?
SLEEP.

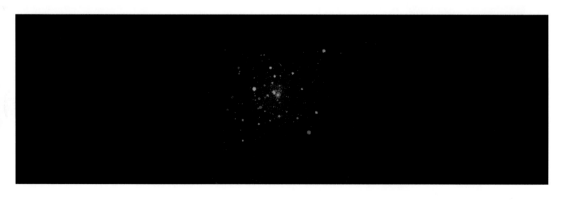

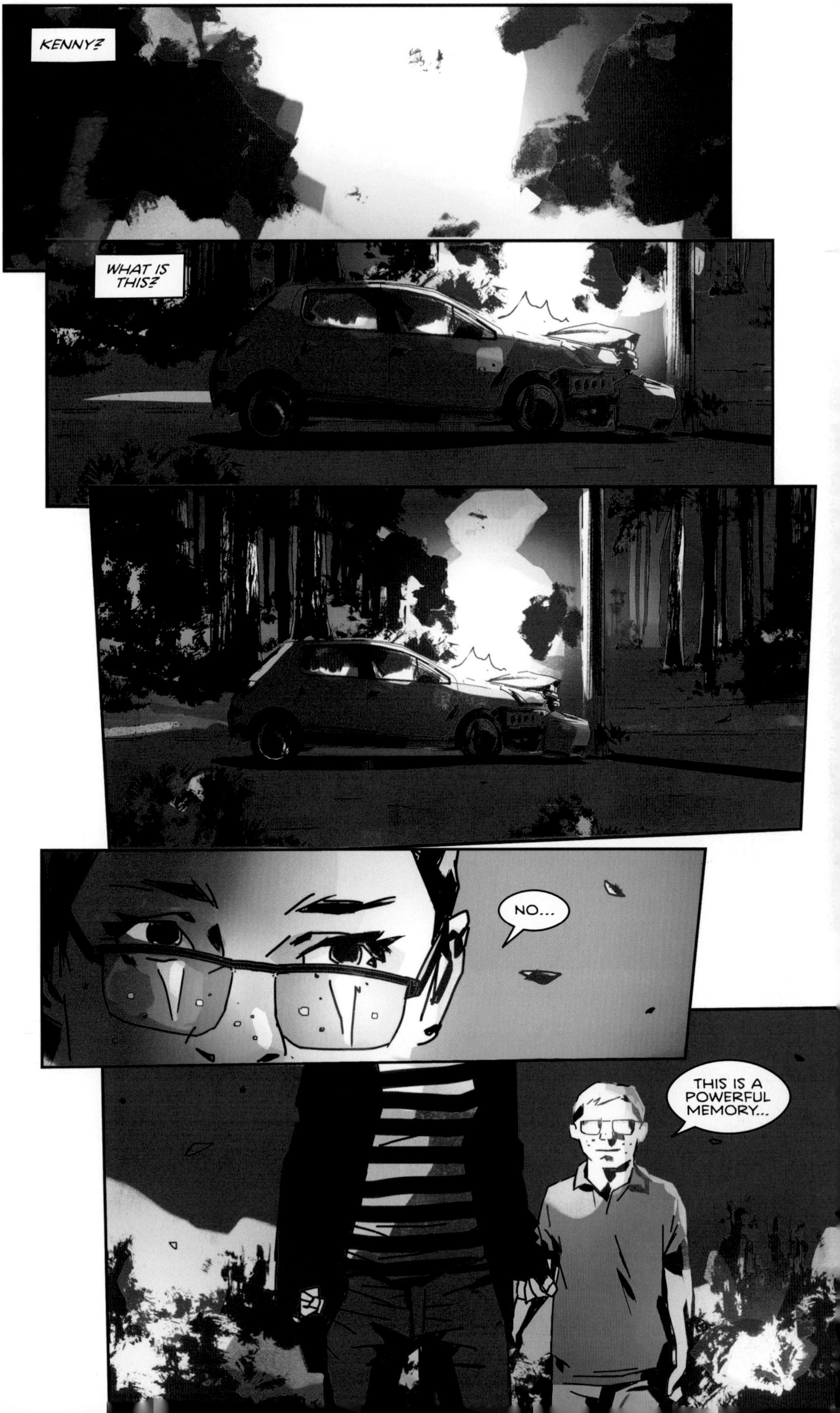
KENNY?
WHAT IS THIS?
NO...
THIS IS A POWERFUL MEMORY...

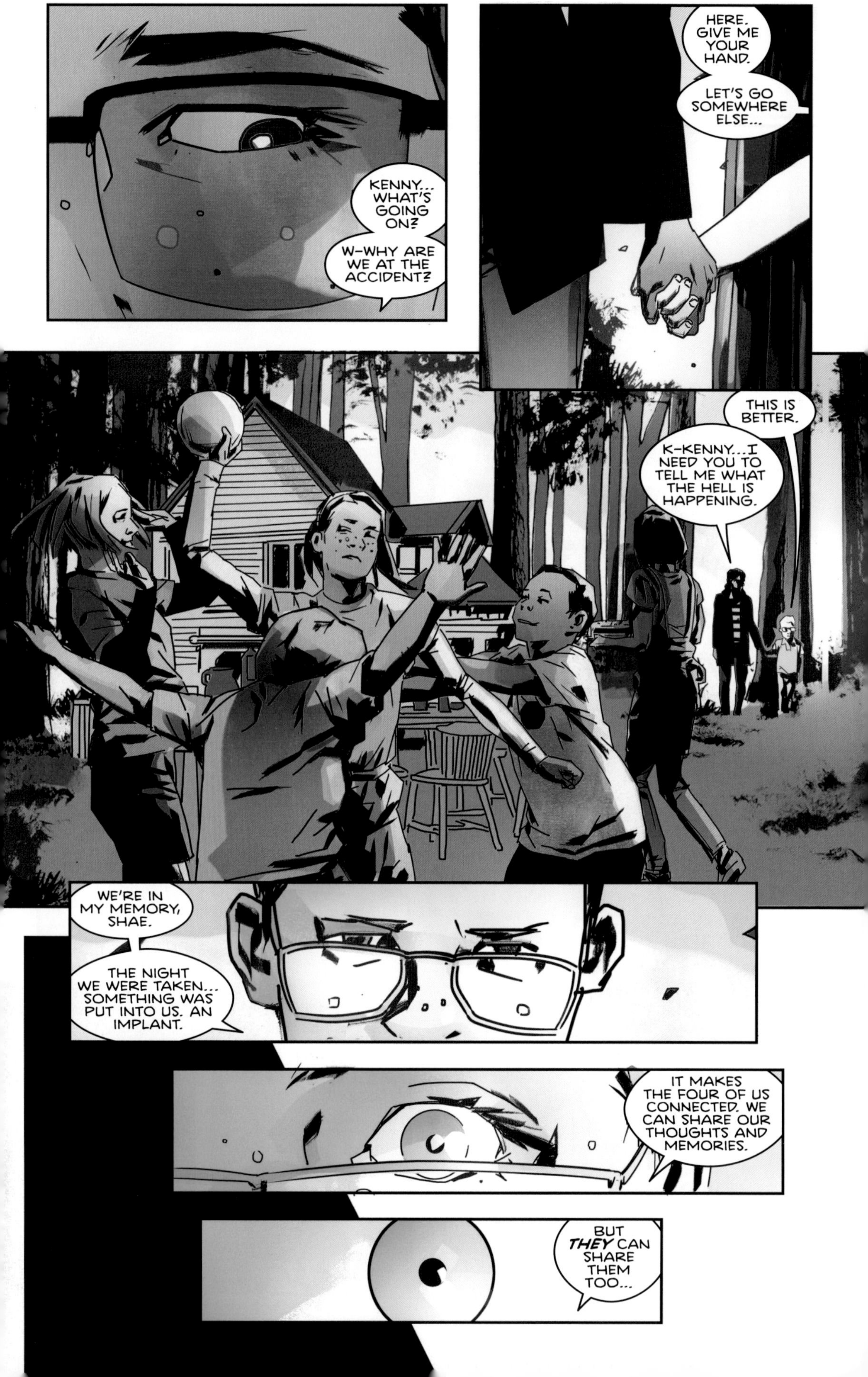
KENNY... WHAT'S GOING ON?
W-WHY ARE WE AT THE ACCIDENT?
HERE. GIVE ME YOUR HAND.
LET'S GO SOMEWHERE ELSE...
THIS IS BETTER.
K-KENNY... I NEED YOU TO TELL ME WHAT THE HELL IS HAPPENING.
WE'RE IN MY MEMORY, SHAE.
THE NIGHT WE WERE TAKEN... SOMETHING WAS PUT INTO US. AN IMPLANT.
IT MAKES THE FOUR OF US CONNECTED. WE CAN SHARE OUR THOUGHTS AND MEMORIES.
BUT *THEY* CAN SHARE THEM TOO...

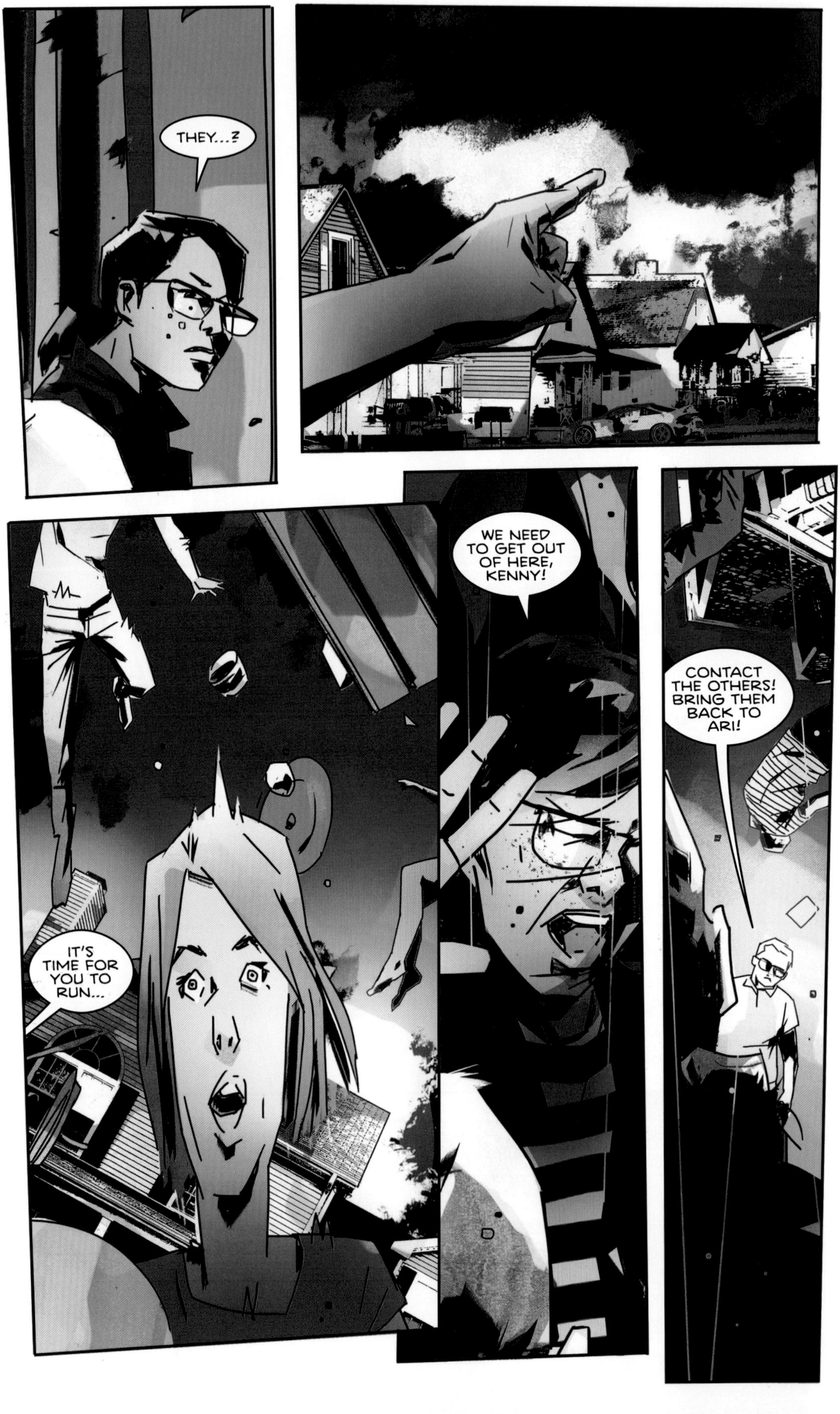
THEY...?
WE NEED TO GET OUT OF HERE, KENNY!
CONTACT THE OTHERS! BRING THEM BACK TO ARI!
IT'S TIME FOR YOU TO RUN...

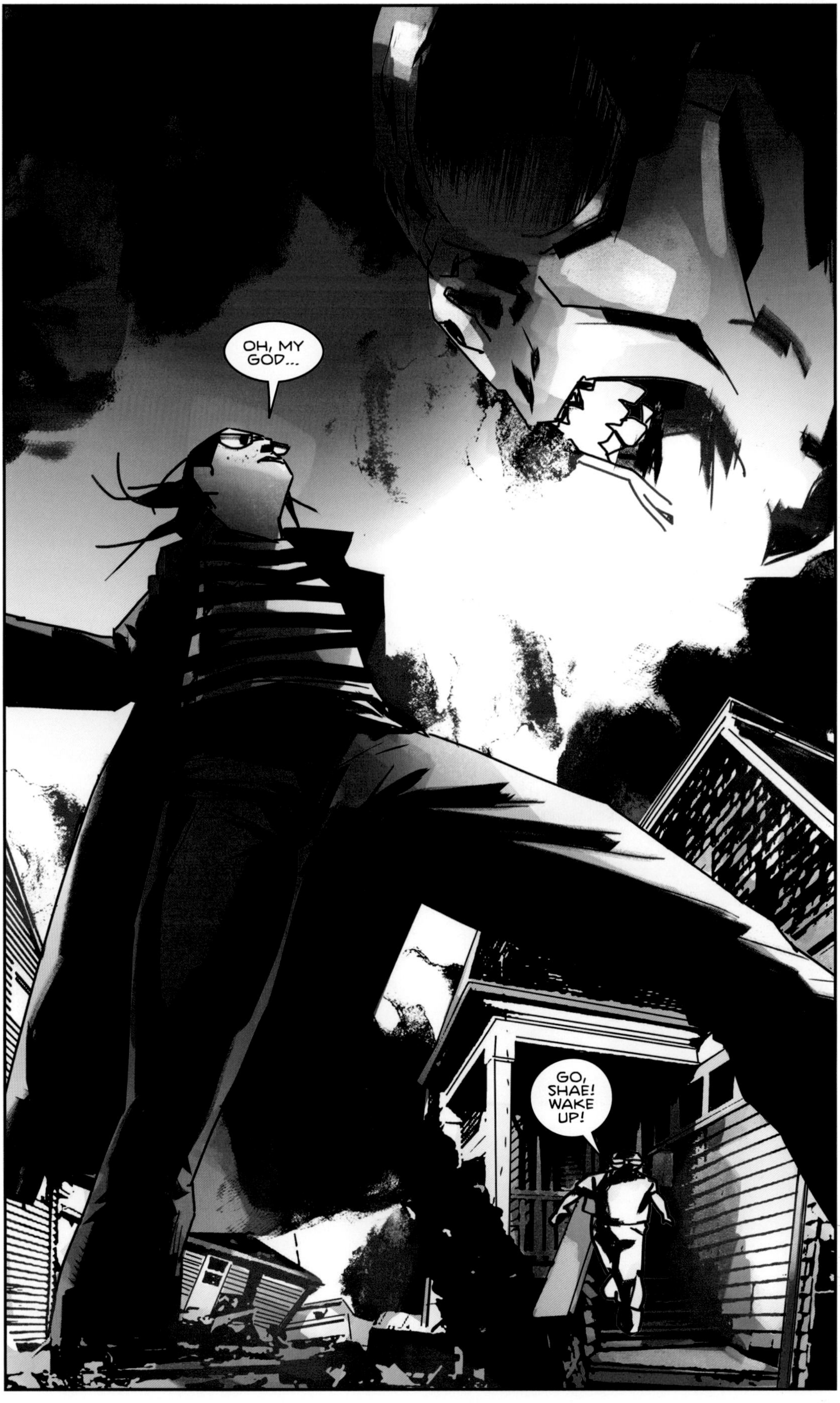
OH, MY GOD...
GO, SHAE! WAKE UP!

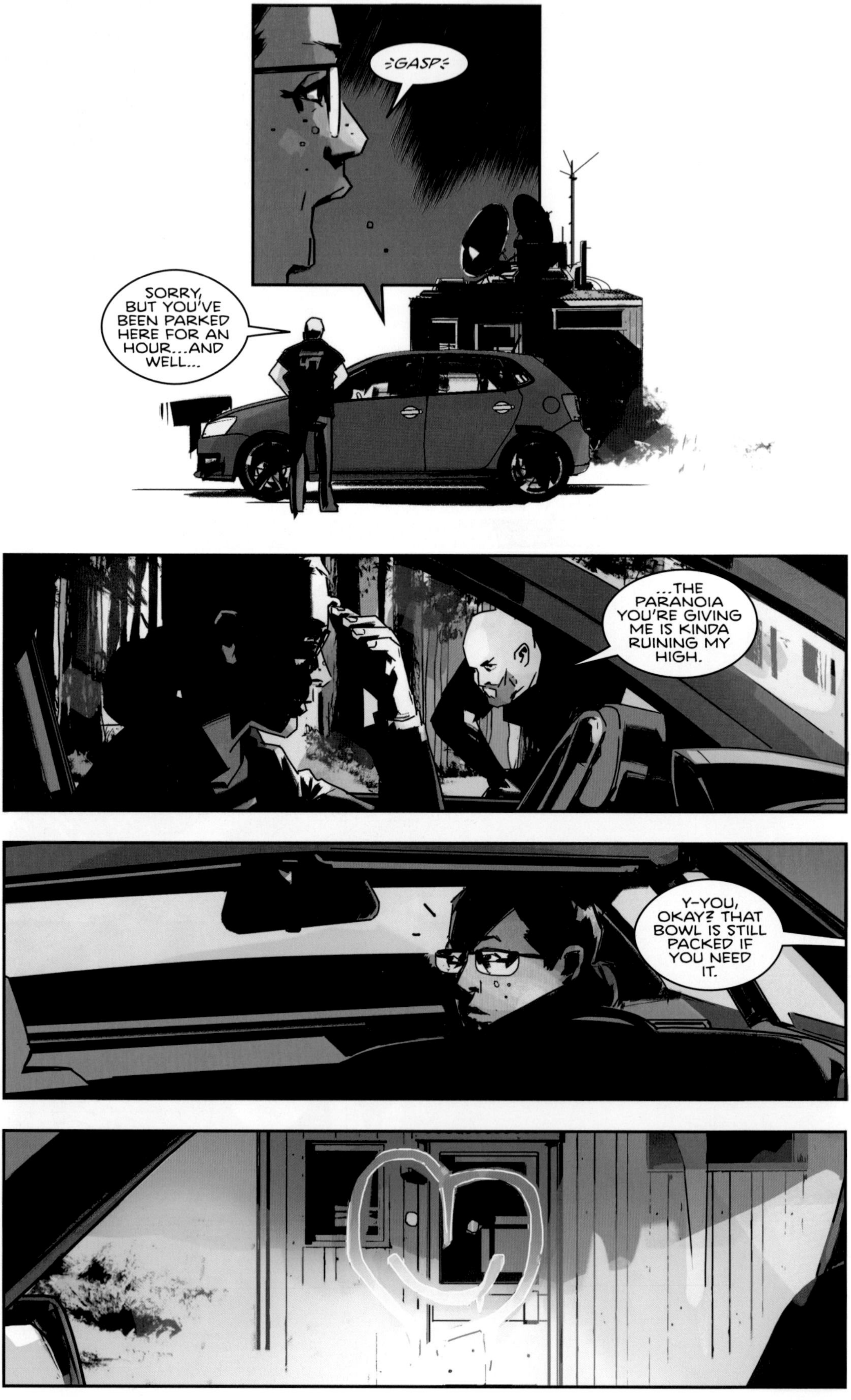
GASP
SORRY, BUT YOU'VE BEEN PARKED HERE FOR AN HOUR...AND WELL...
...THE PARANOIA YOU'RE GIVING ME IS KINDA RUINING MY HIGH.
Y-YOU, OKAY? THAT BOWL IS STILL PACKED IF YOU NEED IT.

POINT
(-54. 301521 23352541)

33.747252
-112.633853

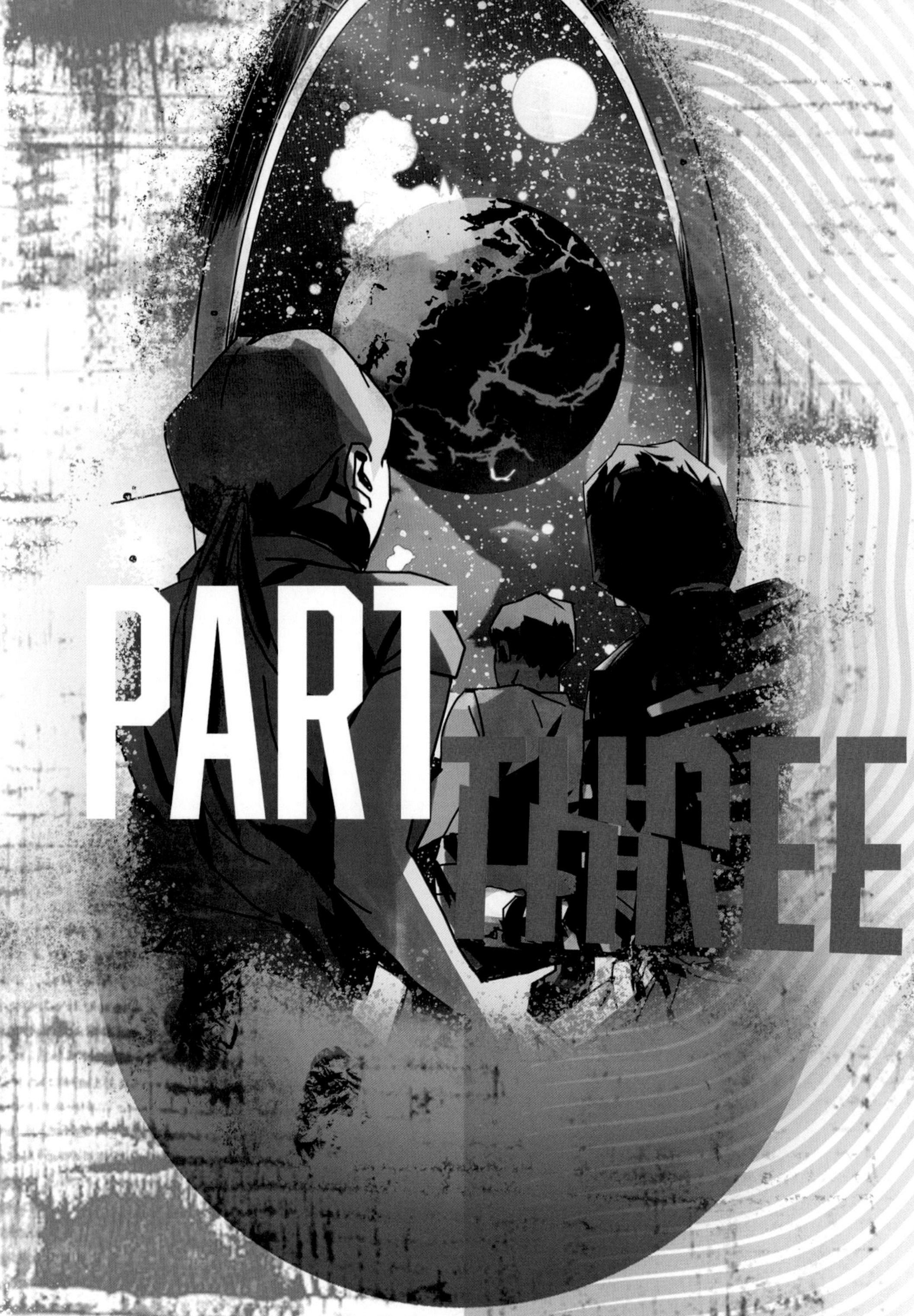

PART THREE

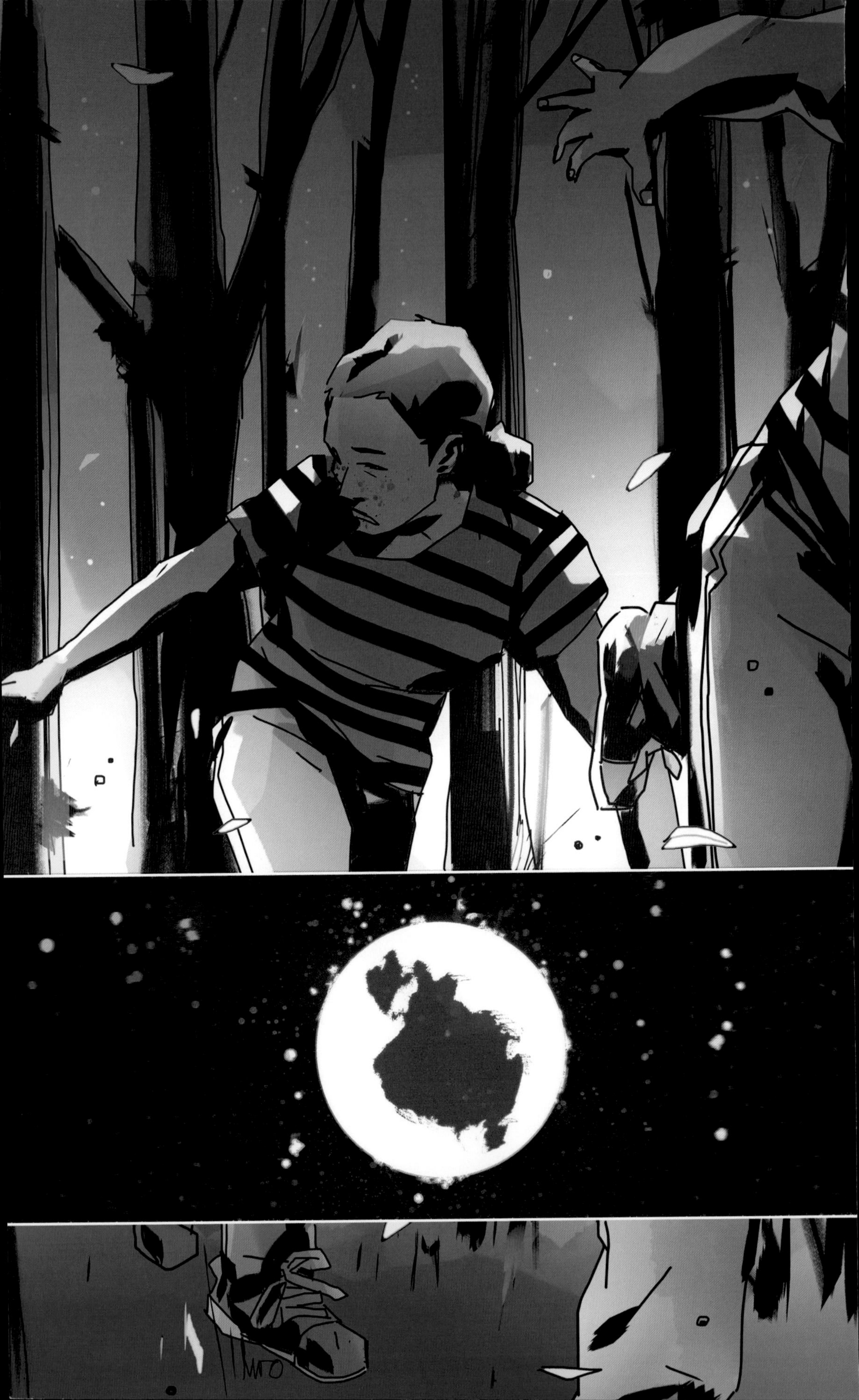

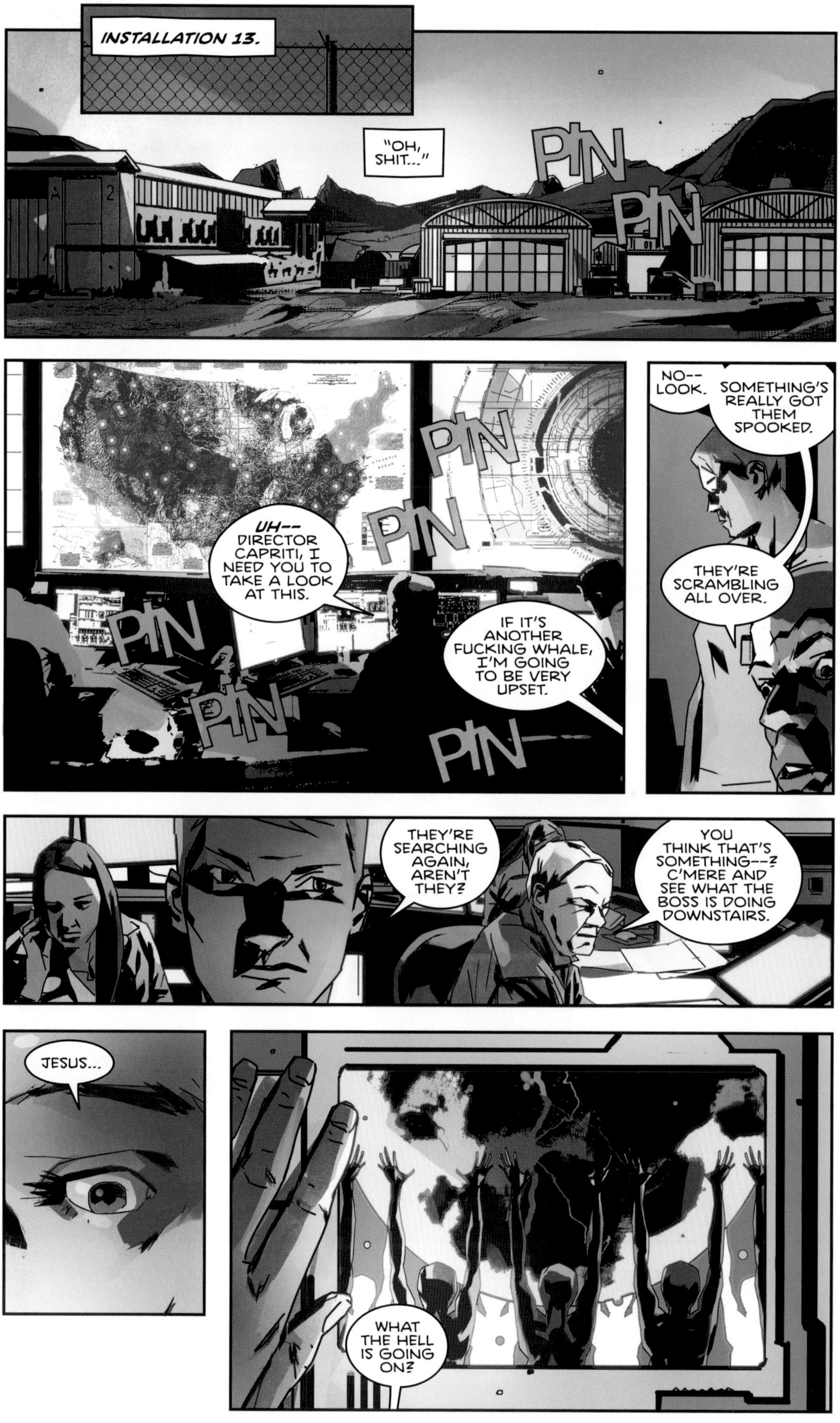
INSTALLATION 13.
"OH, SHIT..."
PIN
PIN
PIN
PIN
UH-- DIRECTOR CAPRITI, I NEED YOU TO TAKE A LOOK AT THIS.
PIN
PIN
IF IT'S ANOTHER FUCKING WHALE, I'M GOING TO BE VERY UPSET.
PIN
NO-- LOOK.
SOMETHING'S REALLY GOT THEM SPOOKED.
THEY'RE SCRAMBLING ALL OVER.
THEY'RE SEARCHING AGAIN, AREN'T THEY?
YOU THINK THAT'S SOMETHING--? C'MERE AND SEE WHAT THE BOSS IS DOING DOWNSTAIRS.
JESUS...
WHAT THE HELL IS GOING ON?

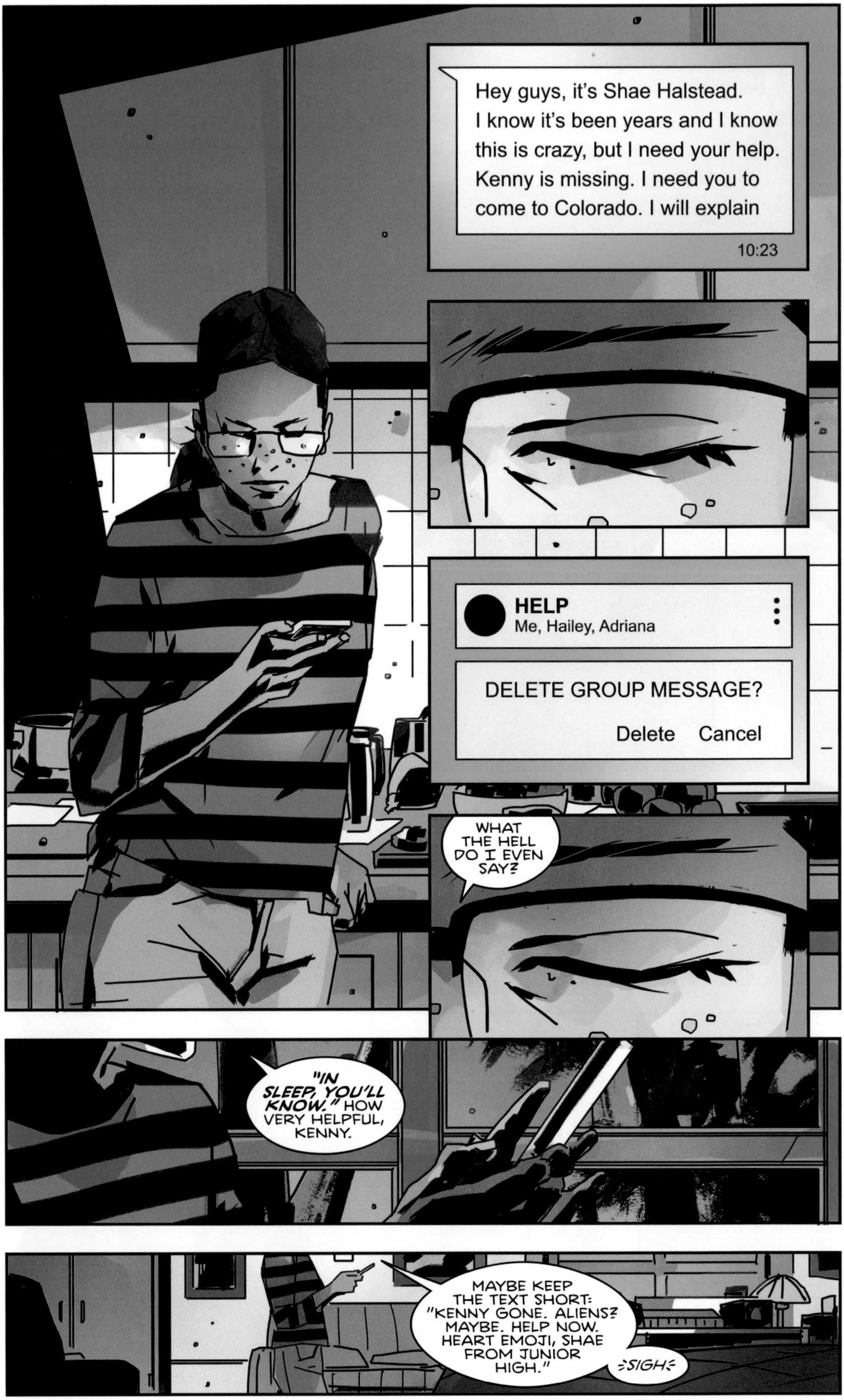
Hey guys, it's Shae Halstead. I know it's been years and I know this is crazy, but I need your help. Kenny is missing. I need you to come to Colorado. I will explain
10:23
HELP
Me, Hailey, Adriana
DELETE GROUP MESSAGE?
Delete Cancel
WHAT THE HELL DO I EVEN SAY?
"IN SLEEP, YOU'LL KNOW." HOW VERY HELPFUL, KENNY.
MAYBE KEEP THE TEXT SHORT: "KENNY GONE. ALIENS? MAYBE. HELP NOW. HEART EMOJI, SHAE FROM JUNIOR HIGH."
SIGH

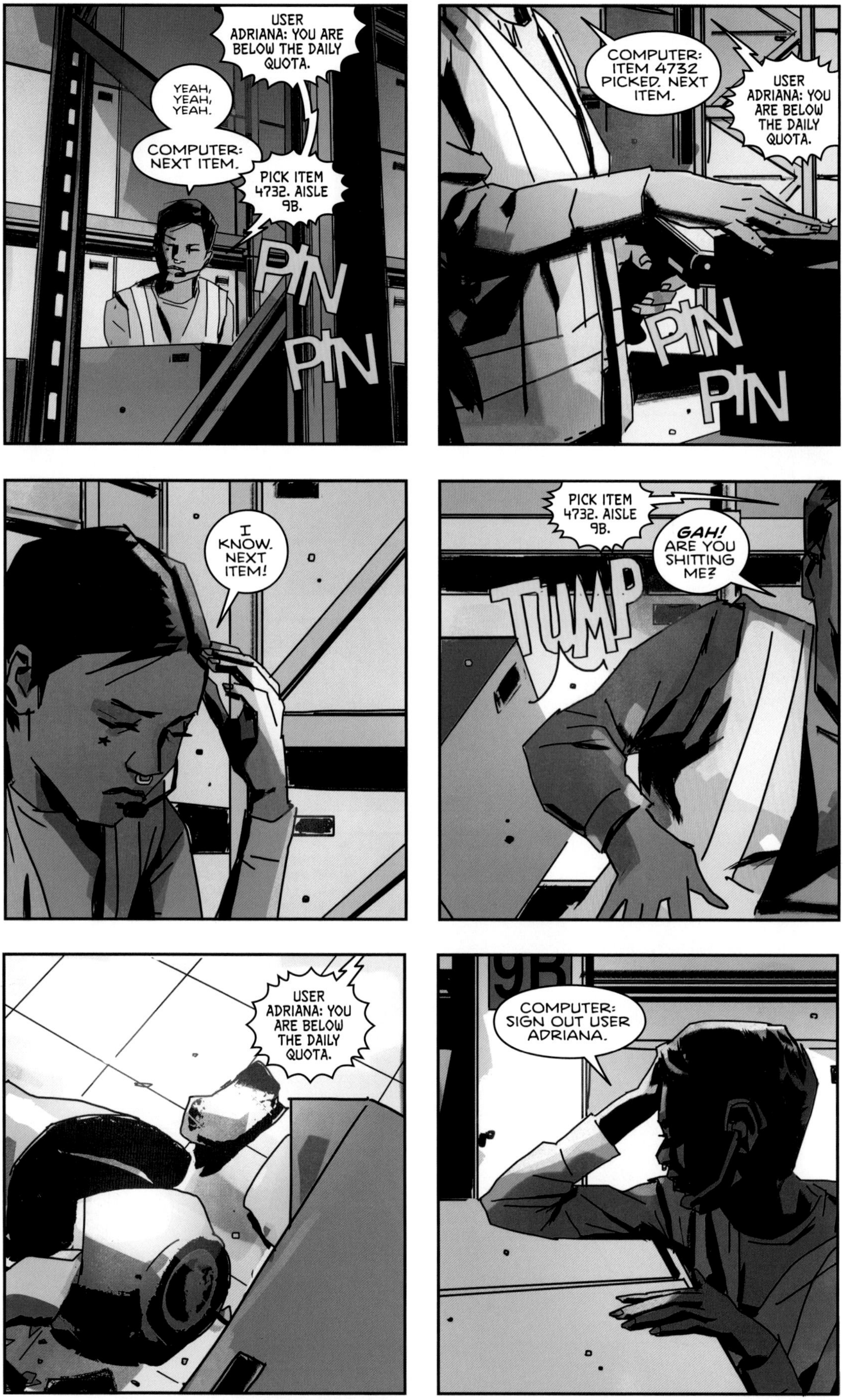
USER ADRIANA: YOU ARE BELOW THE DAILY QUOTA.
YEAH, YEAH, YEAH.
COMPUTER: NEXT ITEM.
PICK ITEM 4732. AISLE 9B.
PIN
PIN
COMPUTER: ITEM 4732 PICKED. NEXT ITEM.
USER ADRIANA: YOU ARE BELOW THE DAILY QUOTA.
PIN
PIN
I KNOW. NEXT ITEM!
PICK ITEM 4732. AISLE 9B.
GAH! ARE YOU SHITTING ME?
TUMP
USER ADRIANA: YOU ARE BELOW THE DAILY QUOTA.
9B
COMPUTER: SIGN OUT USER ADRIANA.

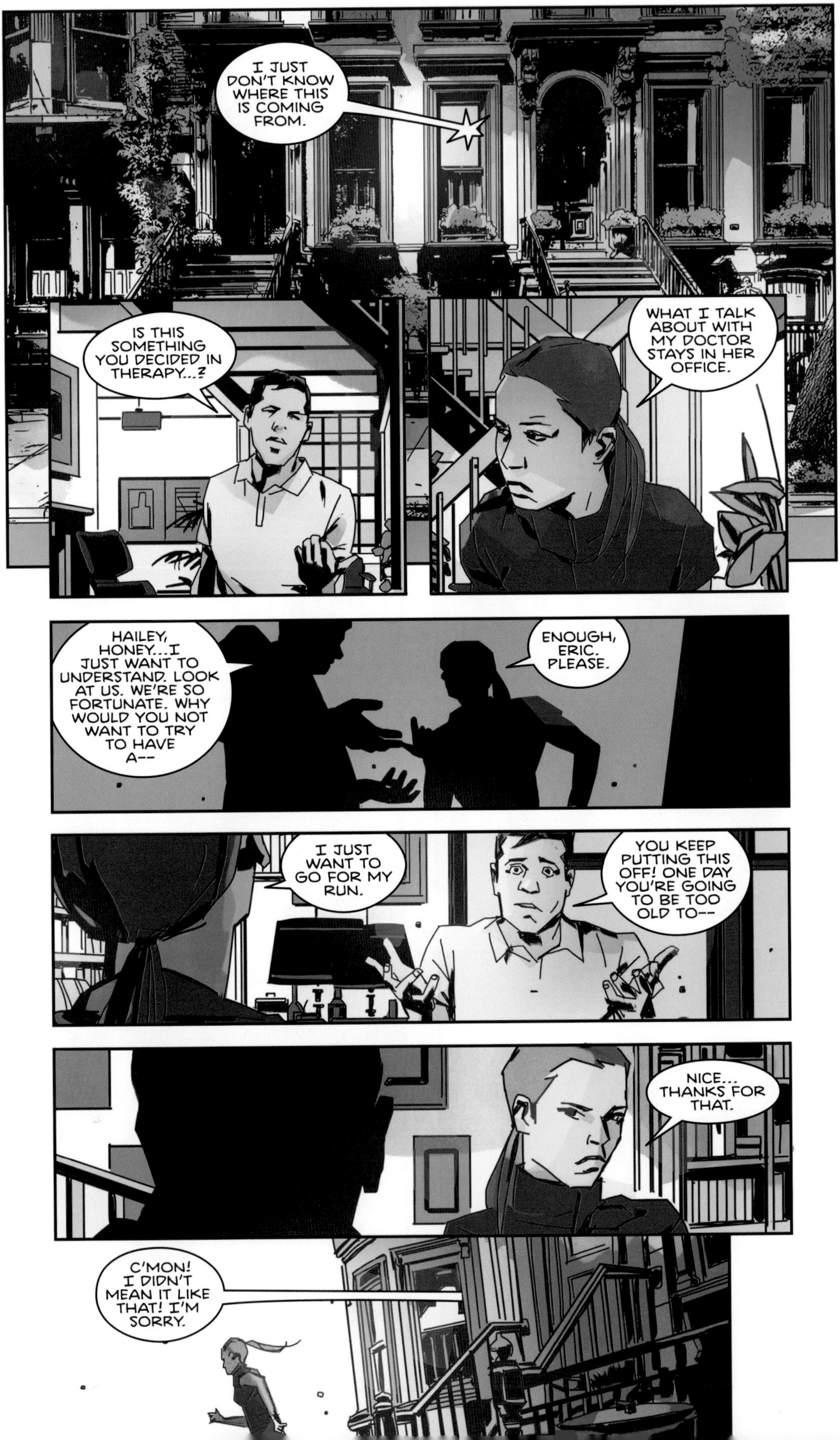
I JUST DON'T KNOW WHERE THIS IS COMING FROM.
IS THIS SOMETHING YOU DECIDED IN THERAPY...?
WHAT I TALK ABOUT WITH MY DOCTOR STAYS IN HER OFFICE.
HAILEY, HONEY...I JUST WANT TO UNDERSTAND. LOOK AT US. WE'RE SO FORTUNATE. WHY WOULD YOU NOT WANT TO TRY TO HAVE A--
ENOUGH, ERIC. PLEASE.
I JUST WANT TO GO FOR MY RUN.
YOU KEEP PUTTING THIS OFF! ONE DAY YOU'RE GOING TO BE TOO OLD TO--
NICE... THANKS FOR THAT.
C'MON! I DIDN'T MEAN IT LIKE THAT! I'M SORRY.

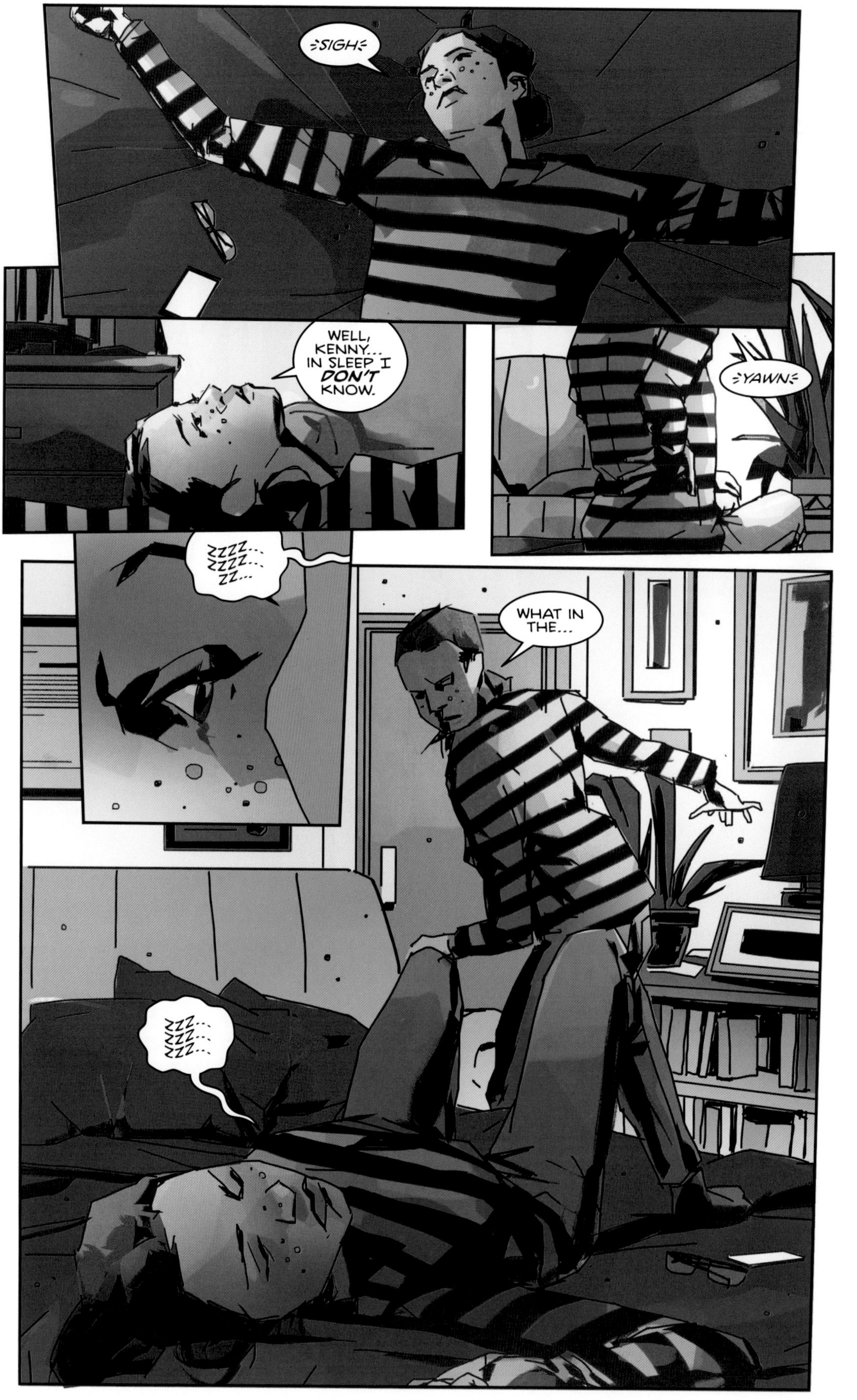
SIGH
WELL, KENNY... IN SLEEP I DON'T KNOW.
YAWN
ZZZZ... ZZZZ... ZZ...
WHAT IN THE...
ZZZ... ZZZ... ZZZ...

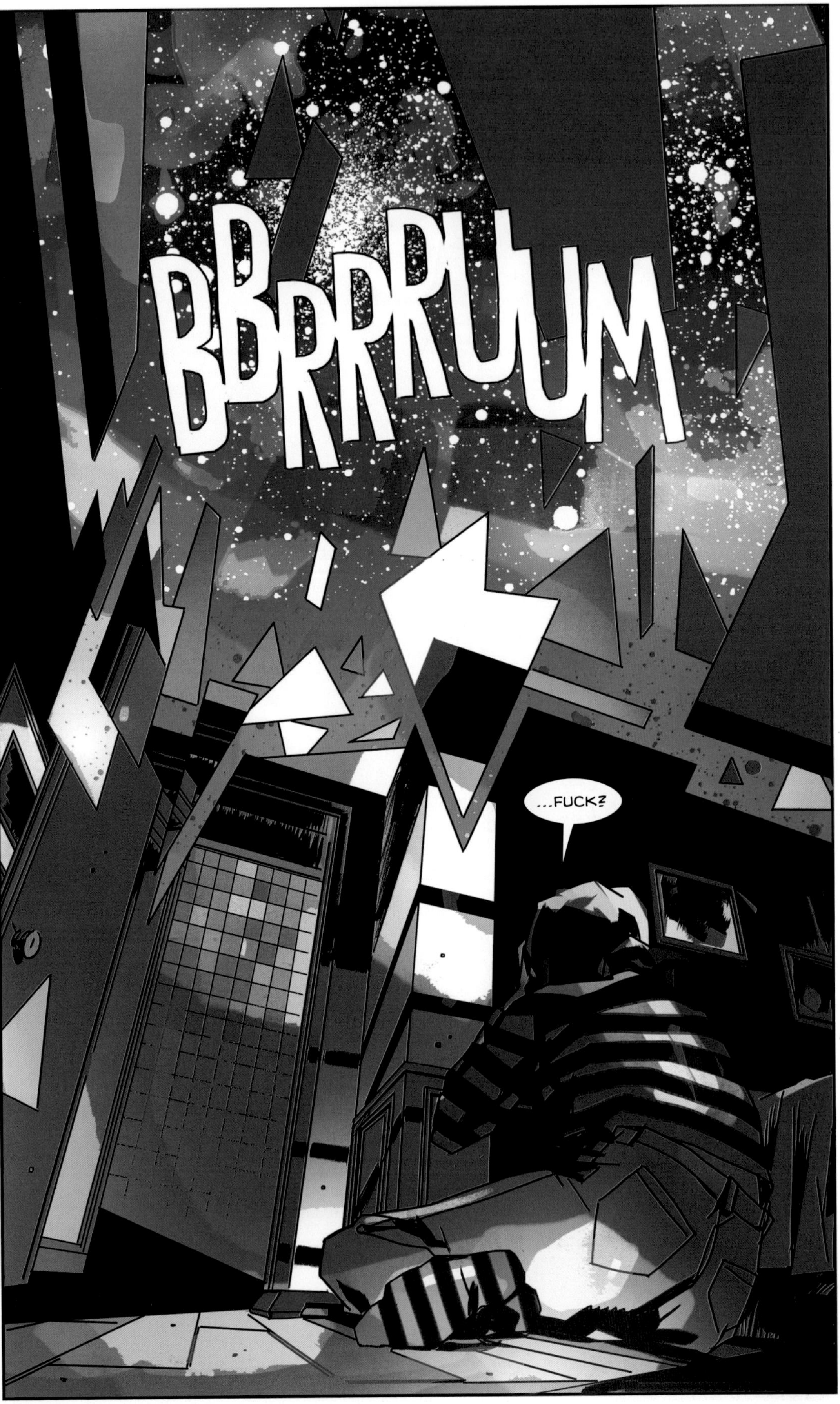
BBRRRUUUM
...FUCK?

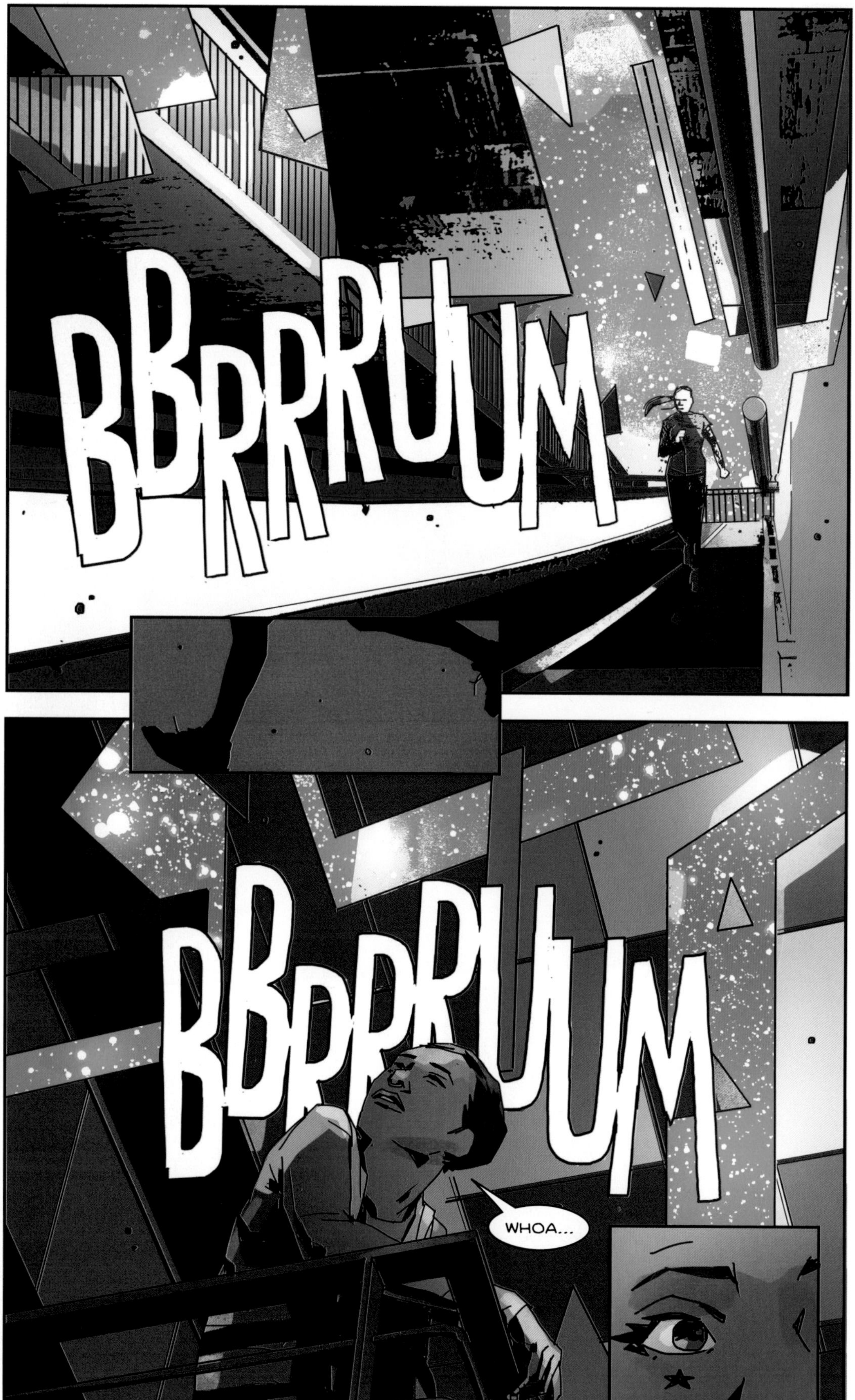
BBRRRUUUM
BBRRRUUUM
WHOA...

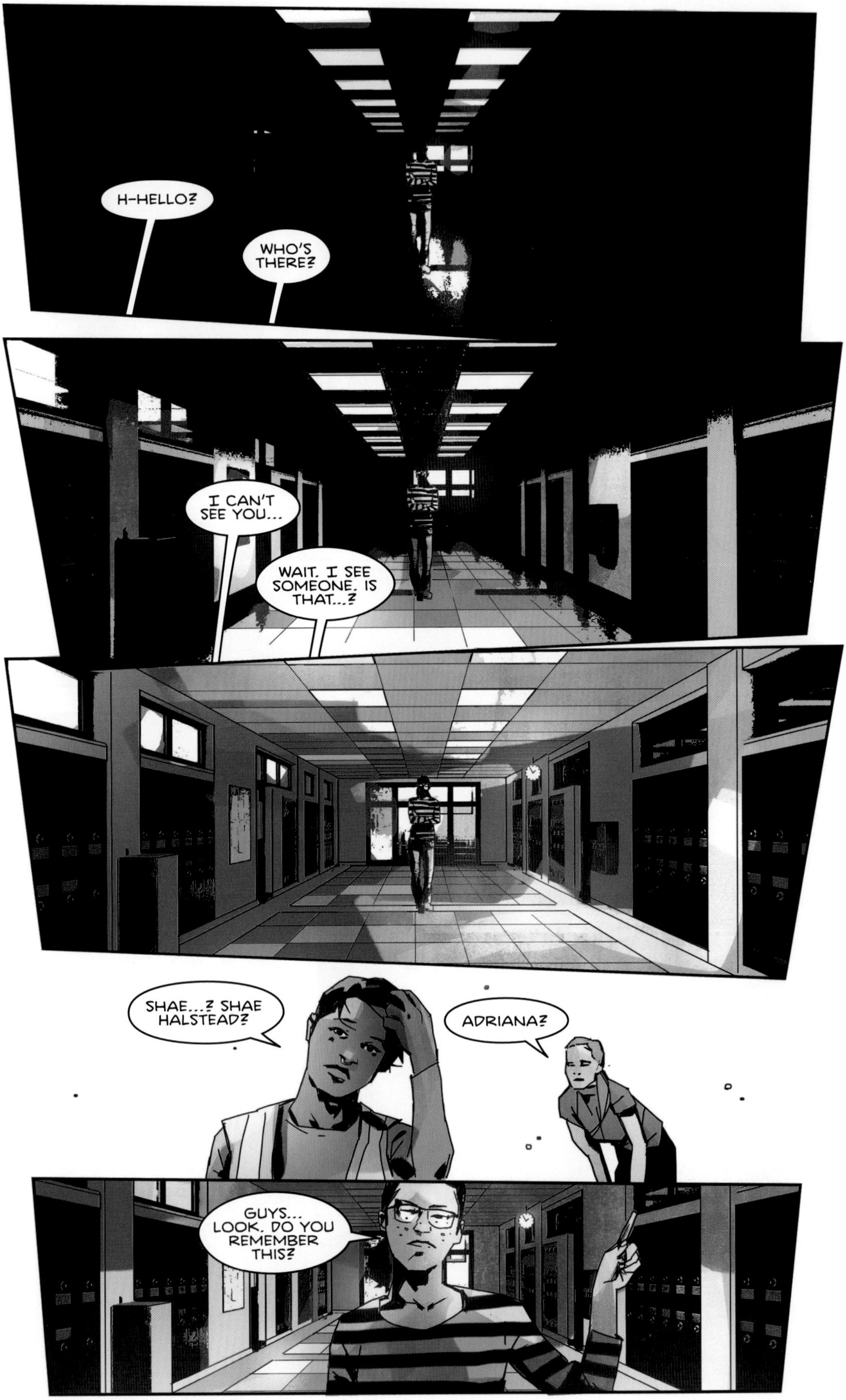
H-HELLO?
WHO'S THERE?
I CAN'T SEE YOU...
WAIT. I SEE SOMEONE. IS THAT...?
SHAE...? SHAE HALSTEAD?
ADRIANA?
GUYS... LOOK. DO YOU REMEMBER THIS?

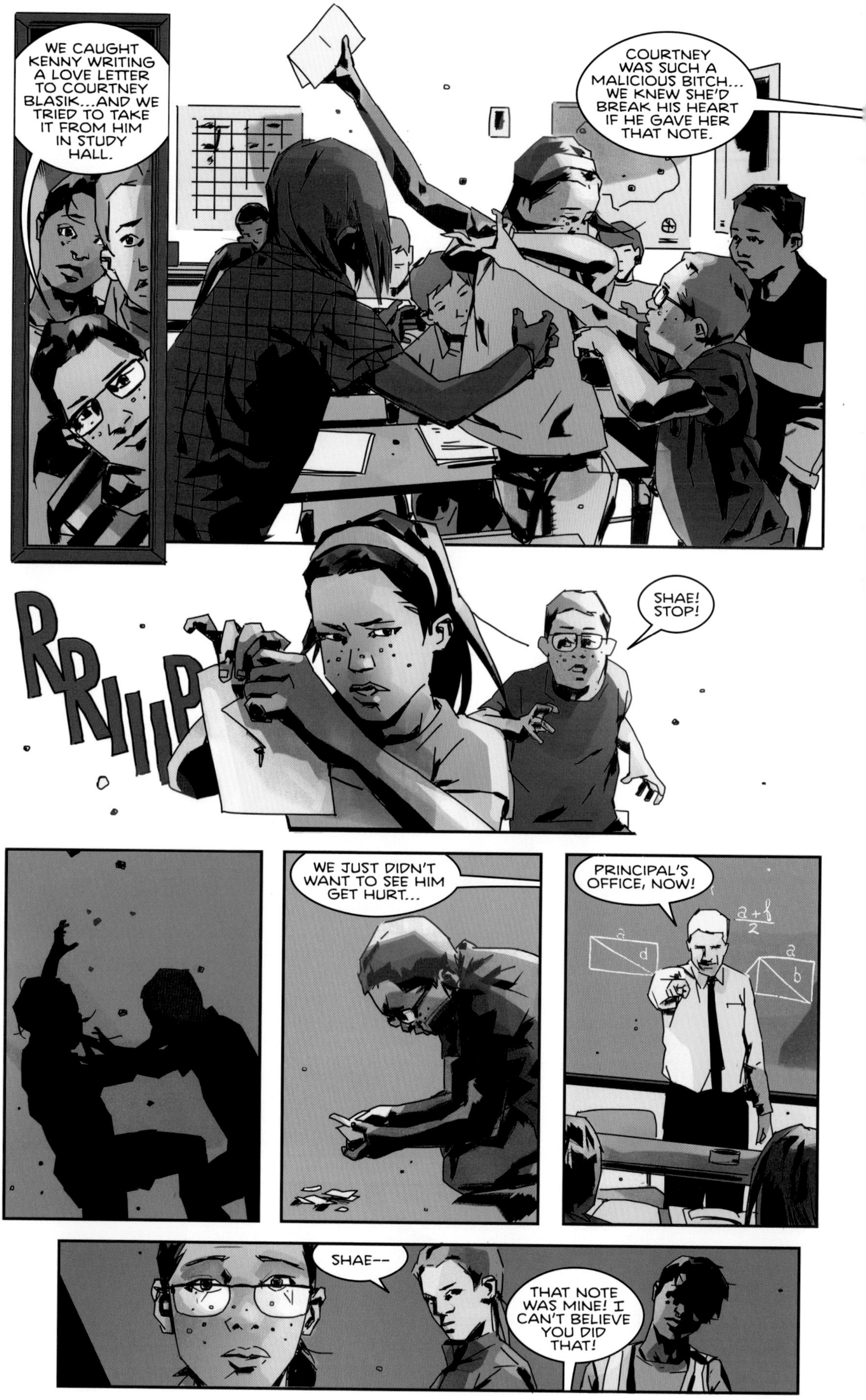
WE CAUGHT KENNY WRITING A LOVE LETTER TO COURTNEY BLASIK...AND WE TRIED TO TAKE IT FROM HIM IN STUDY HALL.
COURTNEY WAS SUCH A MALICIOUS BITCH... WE KNEW SHE'D BREAK HIS HEART IF HE GAVE HER THAT NOTE.
RRIIIP
SHAE! STOP!
WE JUST DIDN'T WANT TO SEE HIM GET HURT...
PRINCIPAL'S OFFICE, NOW!
SHAE--
THAT NOTE WAS MINE! I CAN'T BELIEVE YOU DID THAT!

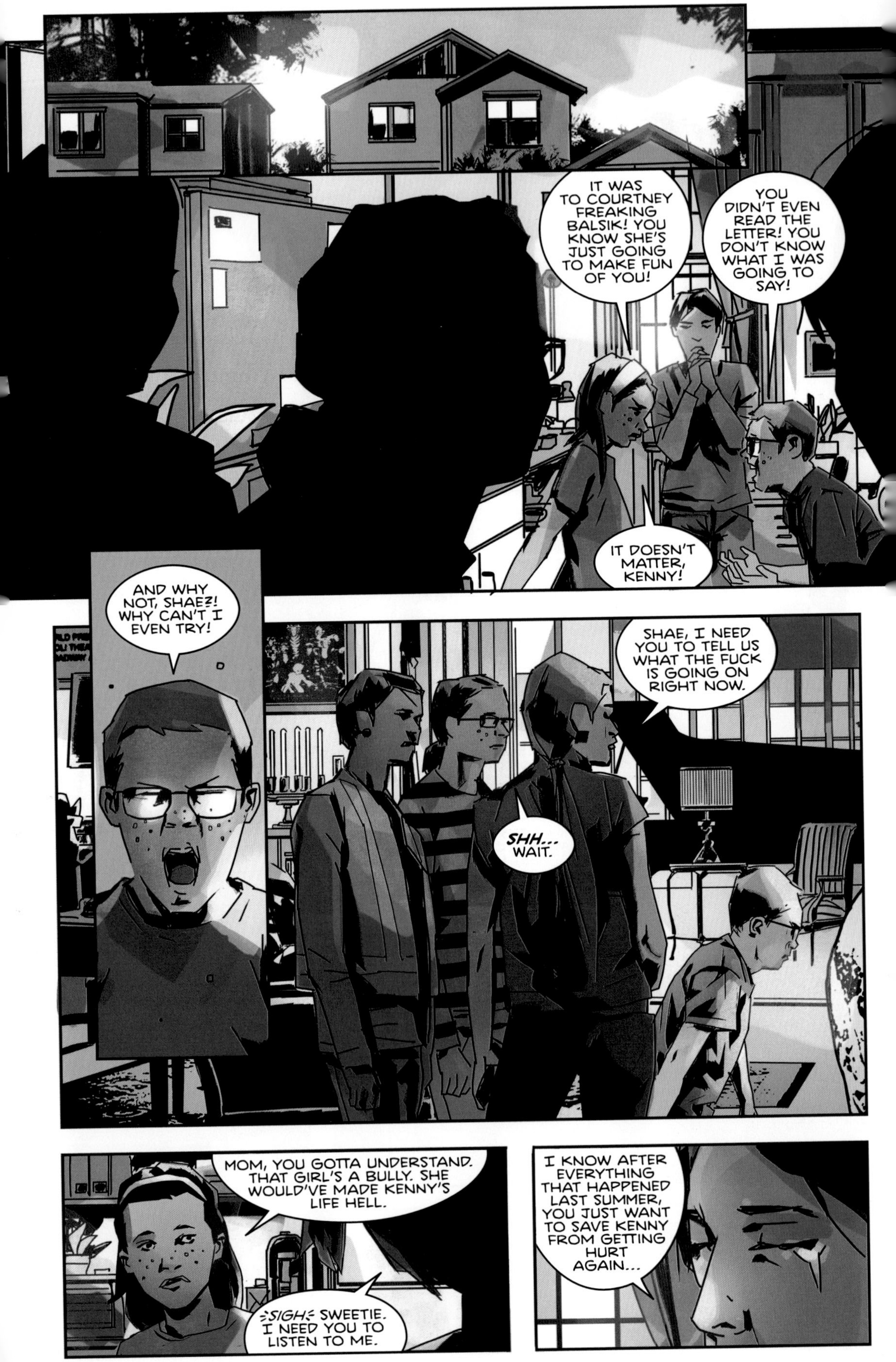
IT WAS TO COURTNEY FREAKING BALSIK! YOU KNOW SHE'S JUST GOING TO MAKE FUN OF YOU!
YOU DIDN'T EVEN READ THE LETTER! YOU DON'T KNOW WHAT I WAS GOING TO SAY!
IT DOESN'T MATTER, KENNY!
AND WHY NOT, SHAE?! WHY CAN'T I EVEN TRY!
SHAE, I NEED YOU TO TELL US WHAT THE FUCK IS GOING ON RIGHT NOW.
SHH... WAIT.
MOM, YOU GOTTA UNDERSTAND. THAT GIRL'S A BULLY. SHE WOULD'VE MADE KENNY'S LIFE HELL.
SIGH SWEETIE. I NEED YOU TO LISTEN TO ME.
I KNOW AFTER EVERYTHING THAT HAPPENED LAST SUMMER, YOU JUST WANT TO SAVE KENNY FROM GETTING HURT AGAIN...

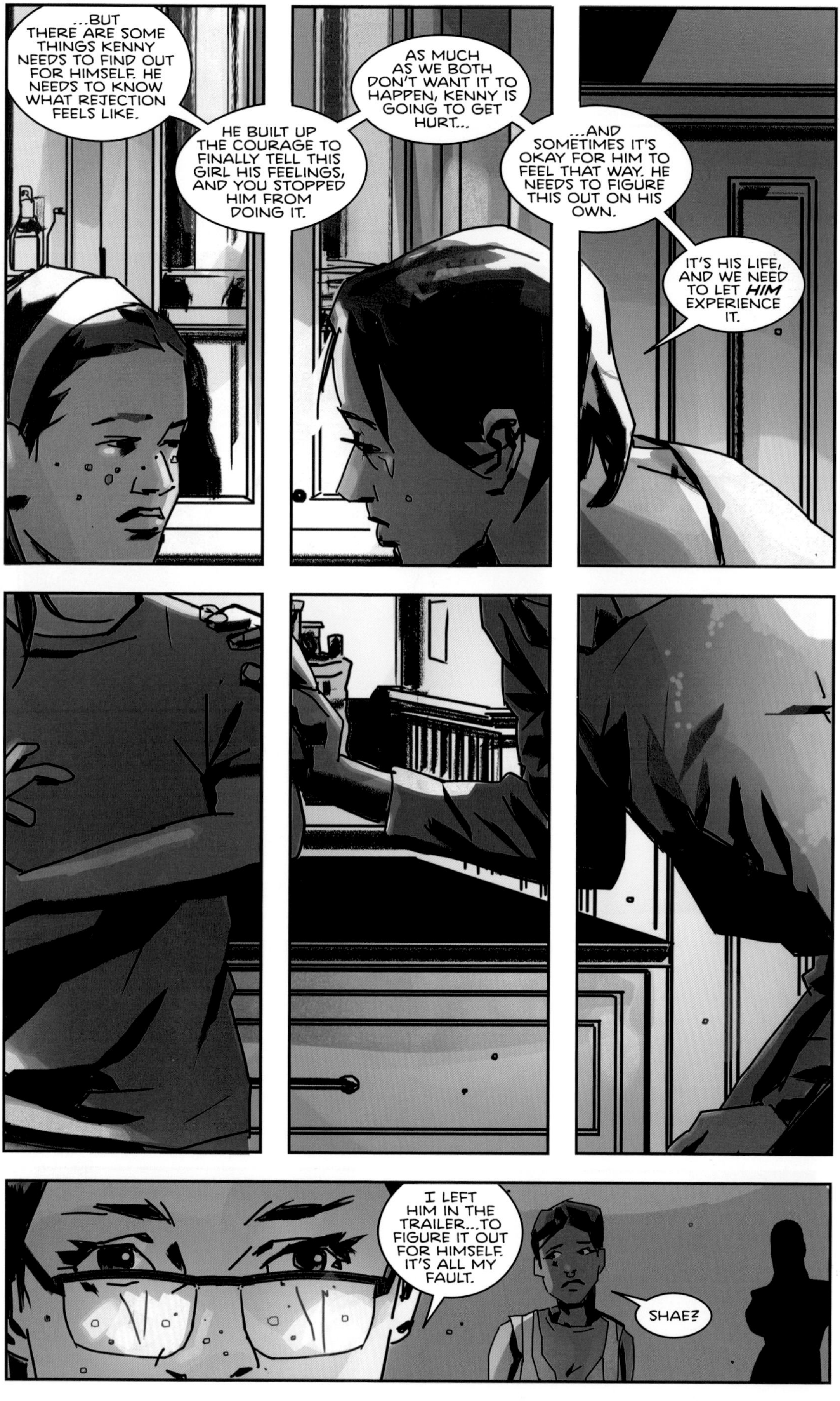
...BUT THERE ARE SOME THINGS KENNY NEEDS TO FIND OUT FOR HIMSELF. HE NEEDS TO KNOW WHAT REJECTION FEELS LIKE.
HE BUILT UP THE COURAGE TO FINALLY TELL THIS GIRL HIS FEELINGS, AND YOU STOPPED HIM FROM DOING IT.
AS MUCH AS WE BOTH DON'T WANT IT TO HAPPEN, KENNY IS GOING TO GET HURT...
...AND SOMETIMES IT'S OKAY FOR HIM TO FEEL THAT WAY. HE NEEDS TO FIGURE THIS OUT ON HIS OWN.
IT'S HIS LIFE, AND WE NEED TO LET HIM EXPERIENCE IT.
I LEFT HIM IN THE TRAILER...TO FIGURE IT OUT FOR HIMSELF. IT'S ALL MY FAULT.
SHAE?

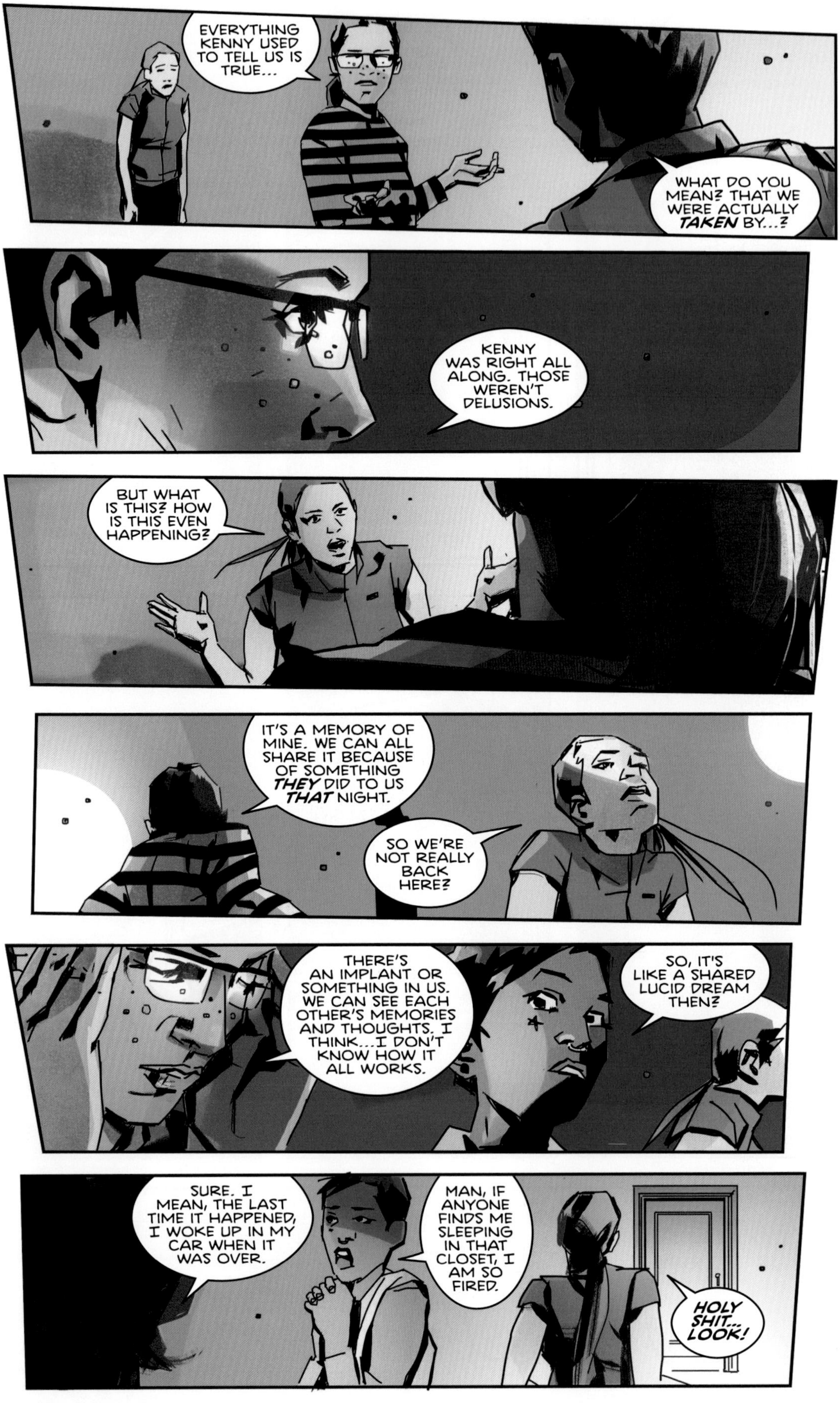
EVERYTHING KENNY USED TO TELL US IS TRUE...
WHAT DO YOU MEAN? THAT WE WERE ACTUALLY TAKEN BY...?
KENNY WAS RIGHT ALL ALONG. THOSE WEREN'T DELUSIONS.
BUT WHAT IS THIS? HOW IS THIS EVEN HAPPENING?
IT'S A MEMORY OF MINE. WE CAN ALL SHARE IT BECAUSE OF SOMETHING THEY DID TO US THAT NIGHT.
SO WE'RE NOT REALLY BACK HERE?
THERE'S AN IMPLANT OR SOMETHING IN US. WE CAN SEE EACH OTHER'S MEMORIES AND THOUGHTS. I THINK...I DON'T KNOW HOW IT ALL WORKS.
SO, IT'S LIKE A SHARED LUCID DREAM THEN?
SURE. I MEAN, THE LAST TIME IT HAPPENED, I WOKE UP IN MY CAR WHEN IT WAS OVER.
MAN, IF ANYONE FINDS ME SLEEPING IN THAT CLOSET, I AM SO FIRED.
HOLY SHIT... LOOK!

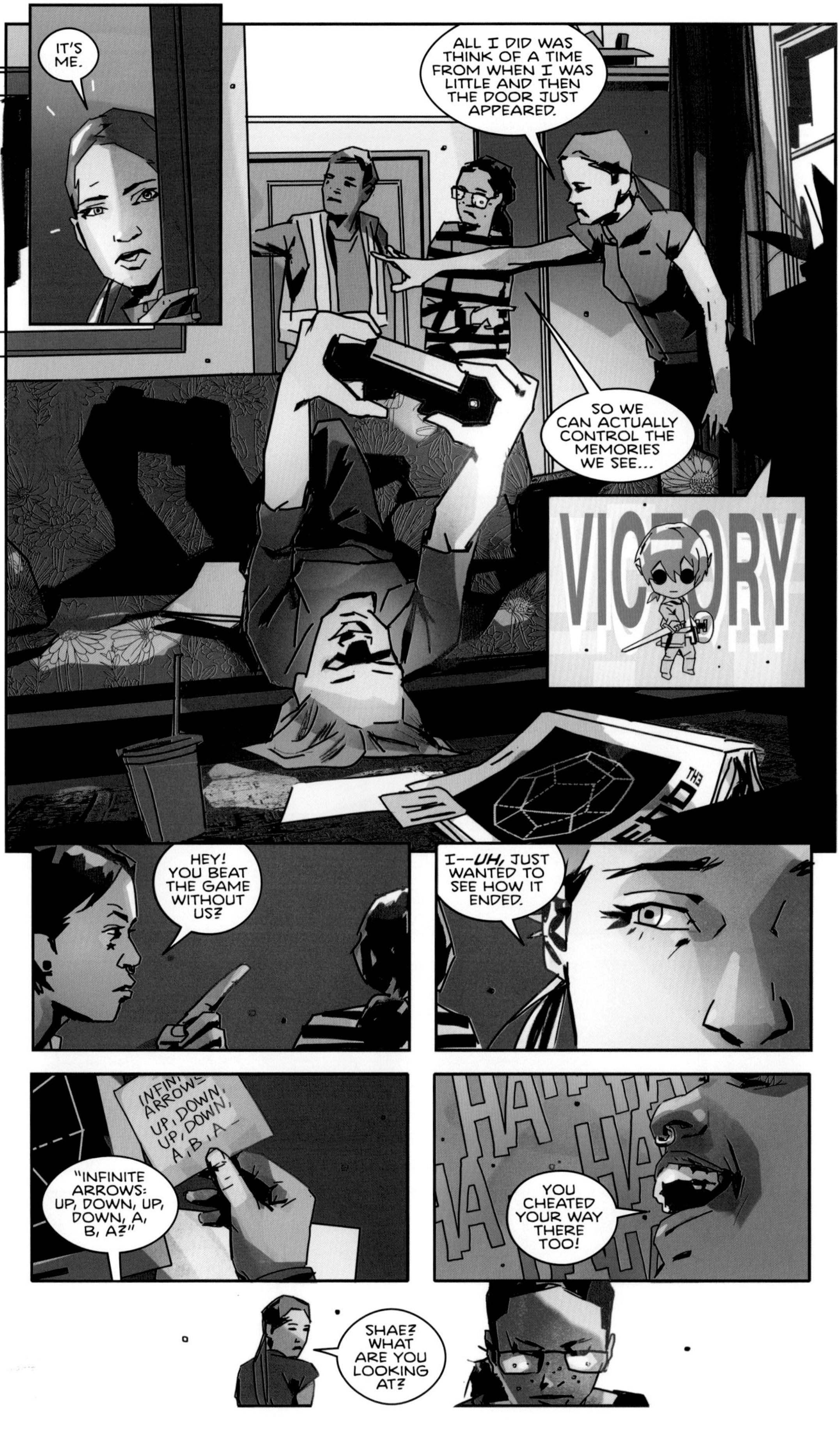

IT'S ME.
ALL I DID WAS THINK OF A TIME FROM WHEN I WAS LITTLE AND THEN THE DOOR JUST APPEARED.
SO WE CAN ACTUALLY CONTROL THE MEMORIES WE SEE...
VICTORY
HEY! YOU BEAT THE GAME WITHOUT US?
I--*UH,* JUST WANTED TO SEE HOW IT ENDED.
"INFINITE ARROWS: UP, DOWN, UP, DOWN, A, B, A?"
YOU CHEATED YOUR WAY THERE TOO!
SHAE? WHAT ARE YOU LOOKING AT?

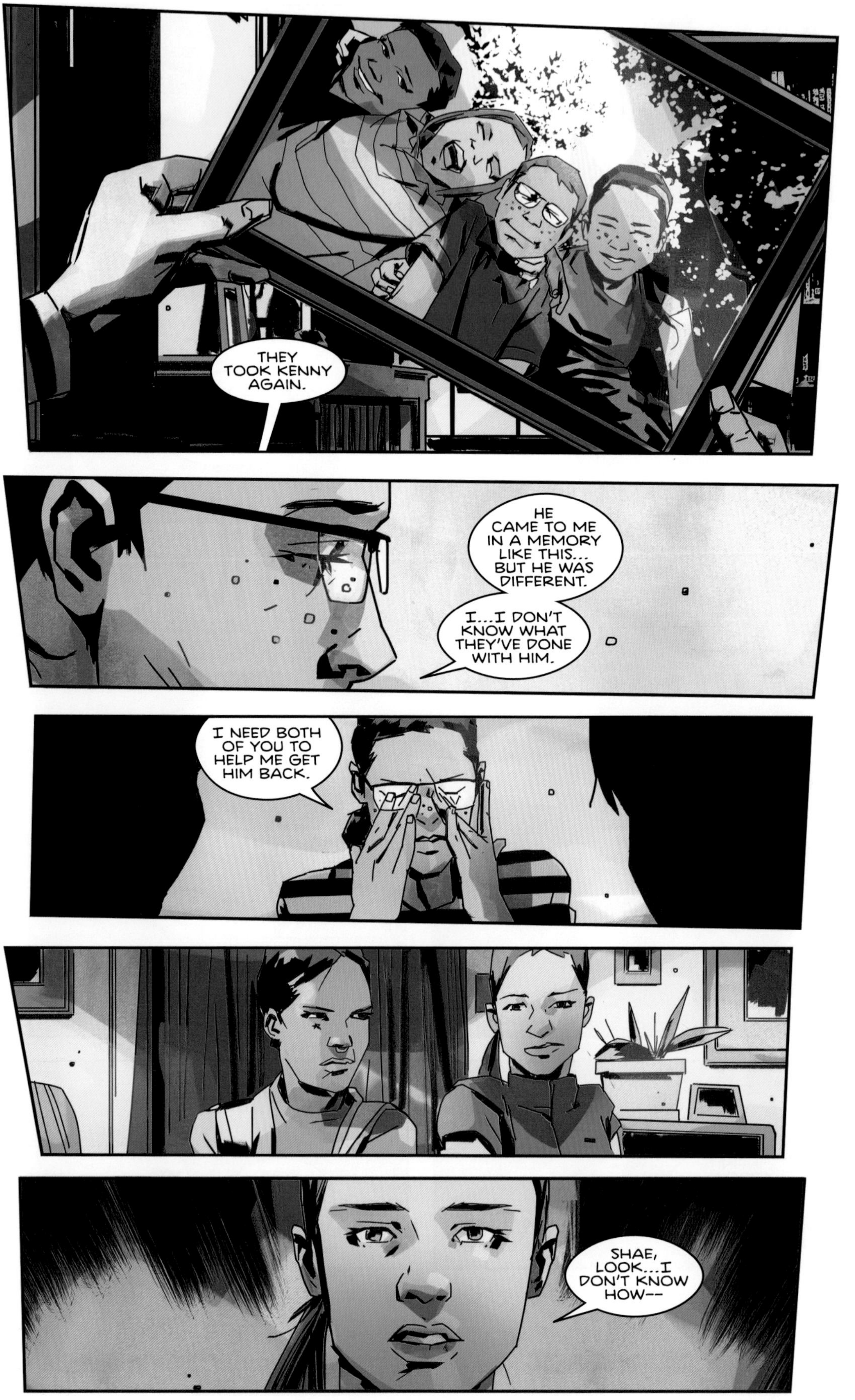
THEY TOOK KENNY AGAIN.
HE CAME TO ME IN A MEMORY LIKE THIS... BUT HE WAS DIFFERENT.
I...I DON'T KNOW WHAT THEY'VE DONE WITH HIM.
I NEED BOTH OF YOU TO HELP ME GET HIM BACK.
SHAE, LOOK...I DON'T KNOW HOW--

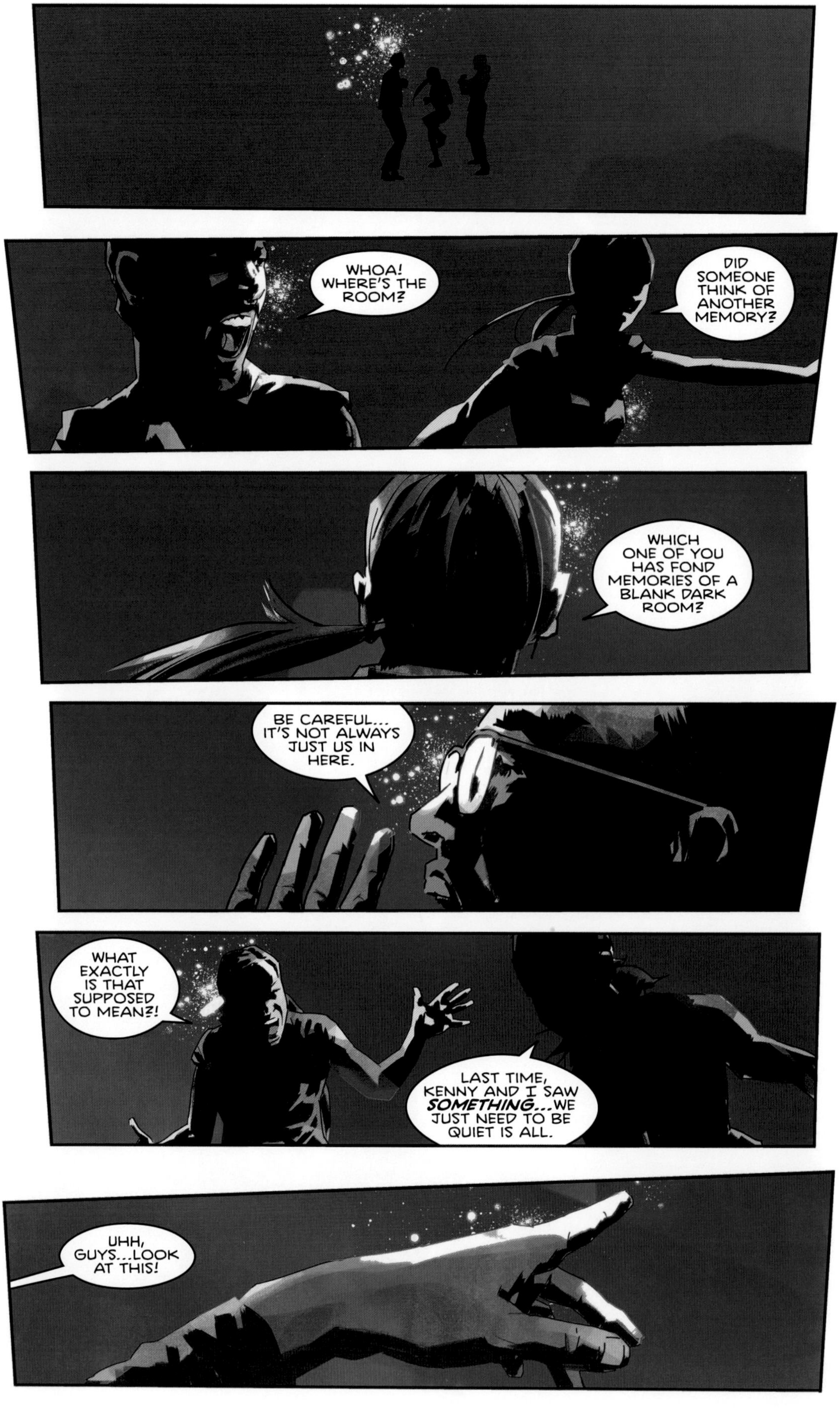
WHOA! WHERE'S THE ROOM?
DID SOMEONE THINK OF ANOTHER MEMORY?
WHICH ONE OF YOU HAS FOND MEMORIES OF A BLANK DARK ROOM?
BE CAREFUL... IT'S NOT ALWAYS JUST US IN HERE.
WHAT EXACTLY IS THAT SUPPOSED TO MEAN?!
LAST TIME, KENNY AND I SAW *SOMETHING...* WE JUST NEED TO BE QUIET IS ALL.
UHH, GUYS...LOOK AT THIS!

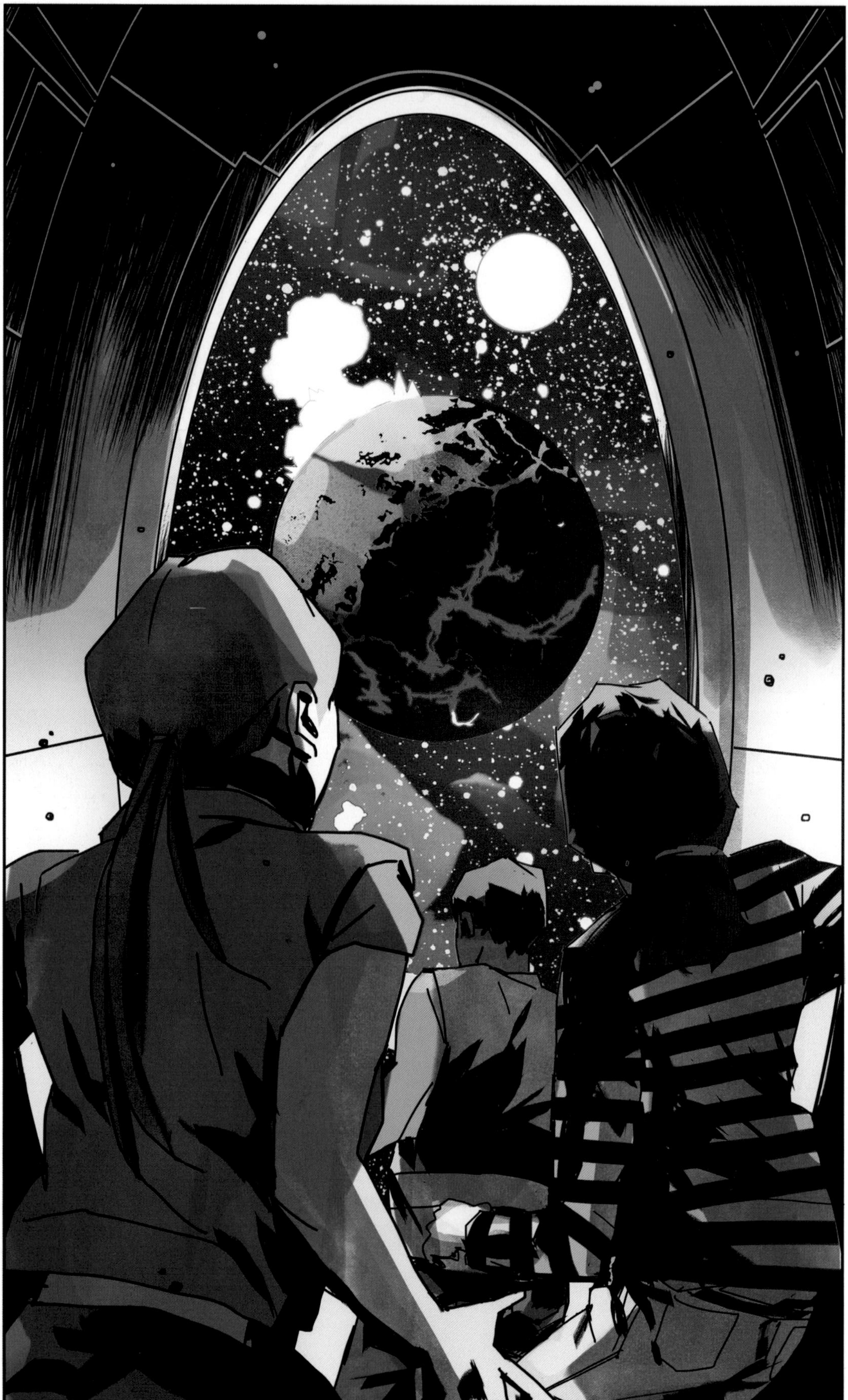

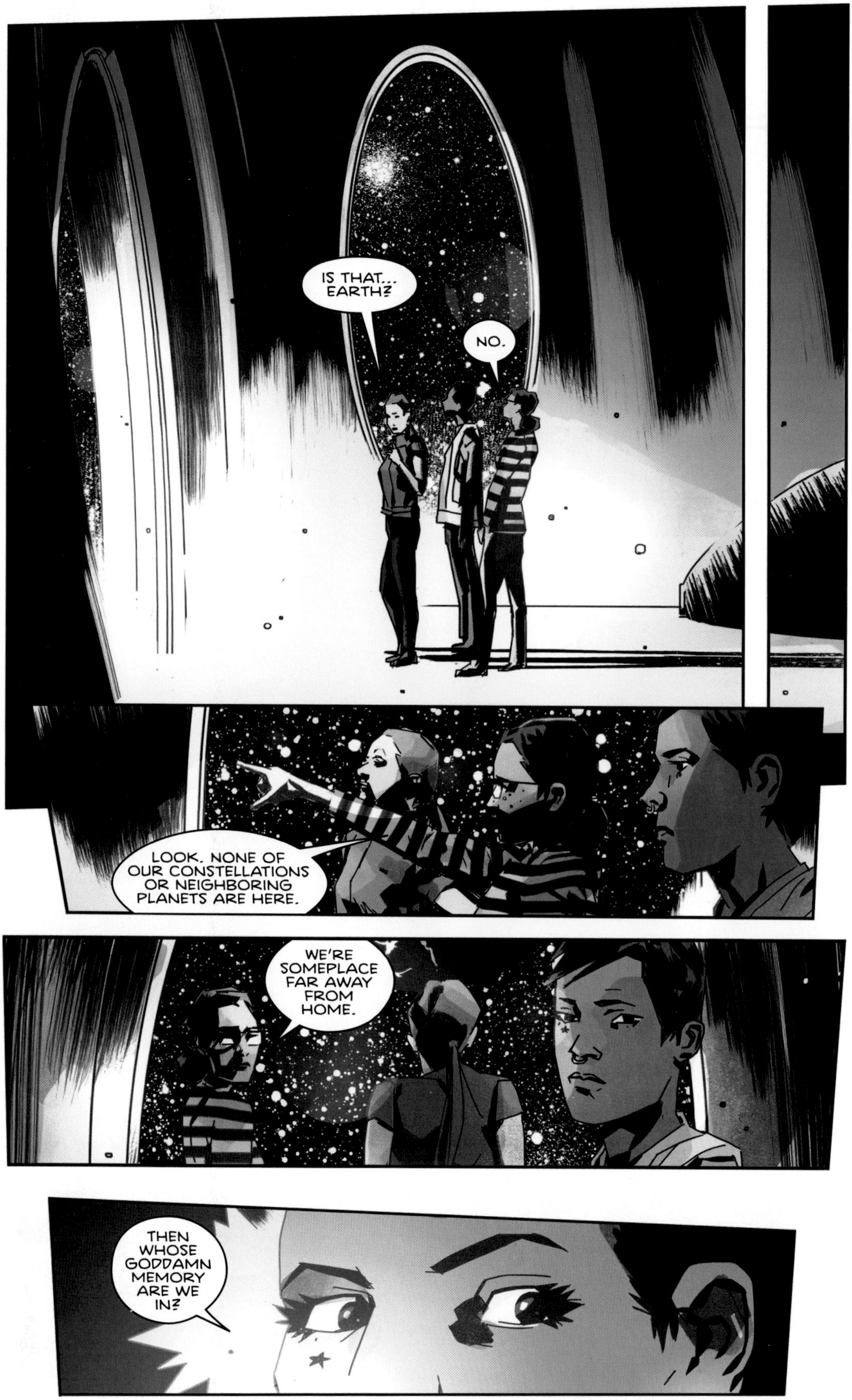
IS THAT... EARTH?
NO.
LOOK. NONE OF OUR CONSTELLATIONS OR NEIGHBORING PLANETS ARE HERE.
WE'RE SOMEPLACE FAR AWAY FROM HOME.
THEN WHOSE GODDAMN MEMORY ARE WE IN?

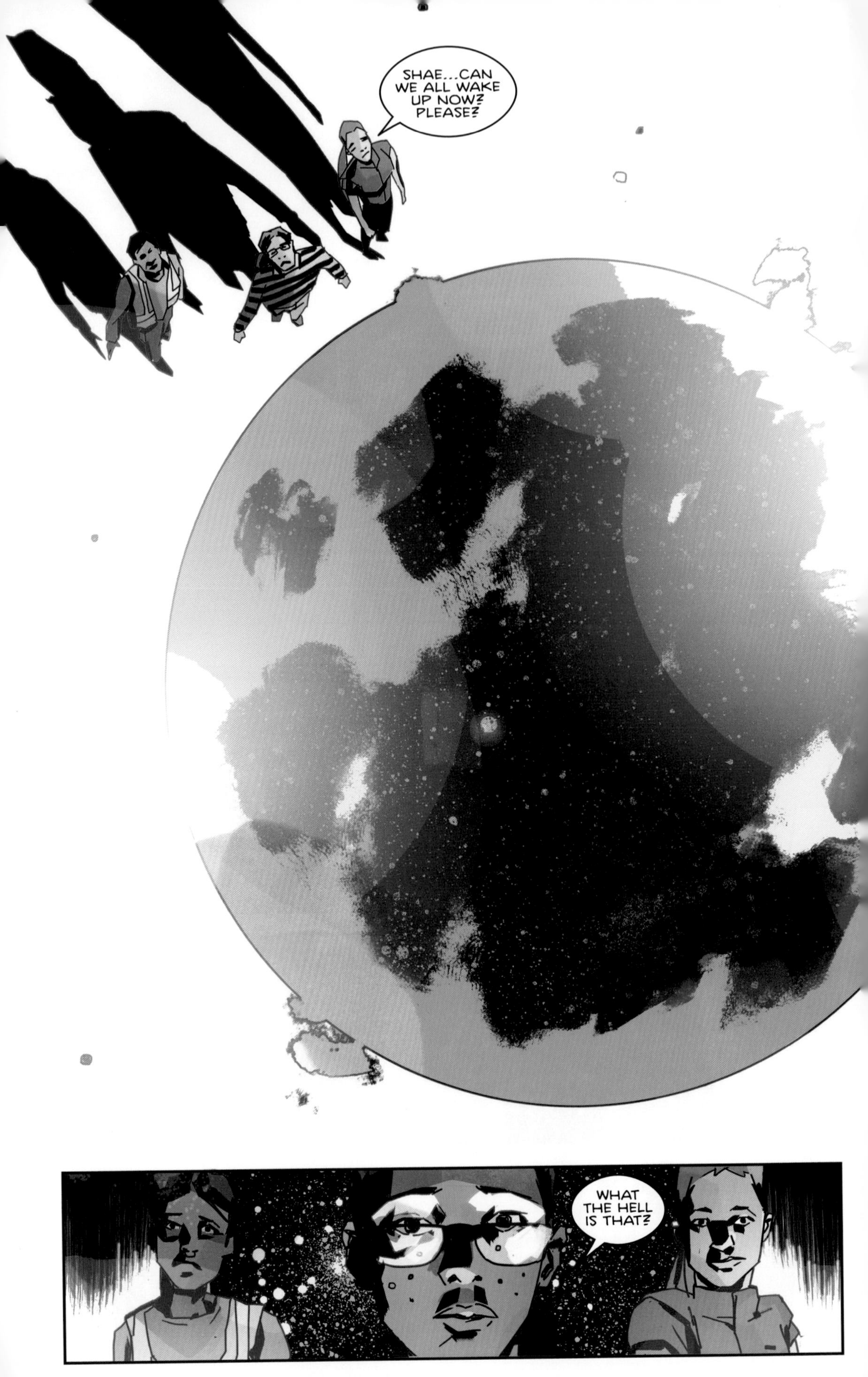
SHAE...CAN WE ALL WAKE UP NOW? PLEASE?
WHAT THE HELL IS THAT?

SOMETHING'S MOVING IN THERE.

ADRIANA! GET BACK HERE! DON'T TOUCH IT!

WHY? IT'S JUST A MEMORY.

WRRRMMM

HOLY SHIT!

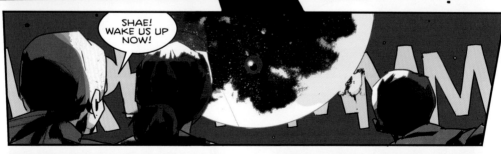

SHAE! WAKE US UP NOW!

WRRRMMM

WRRRMMM

SHAE!

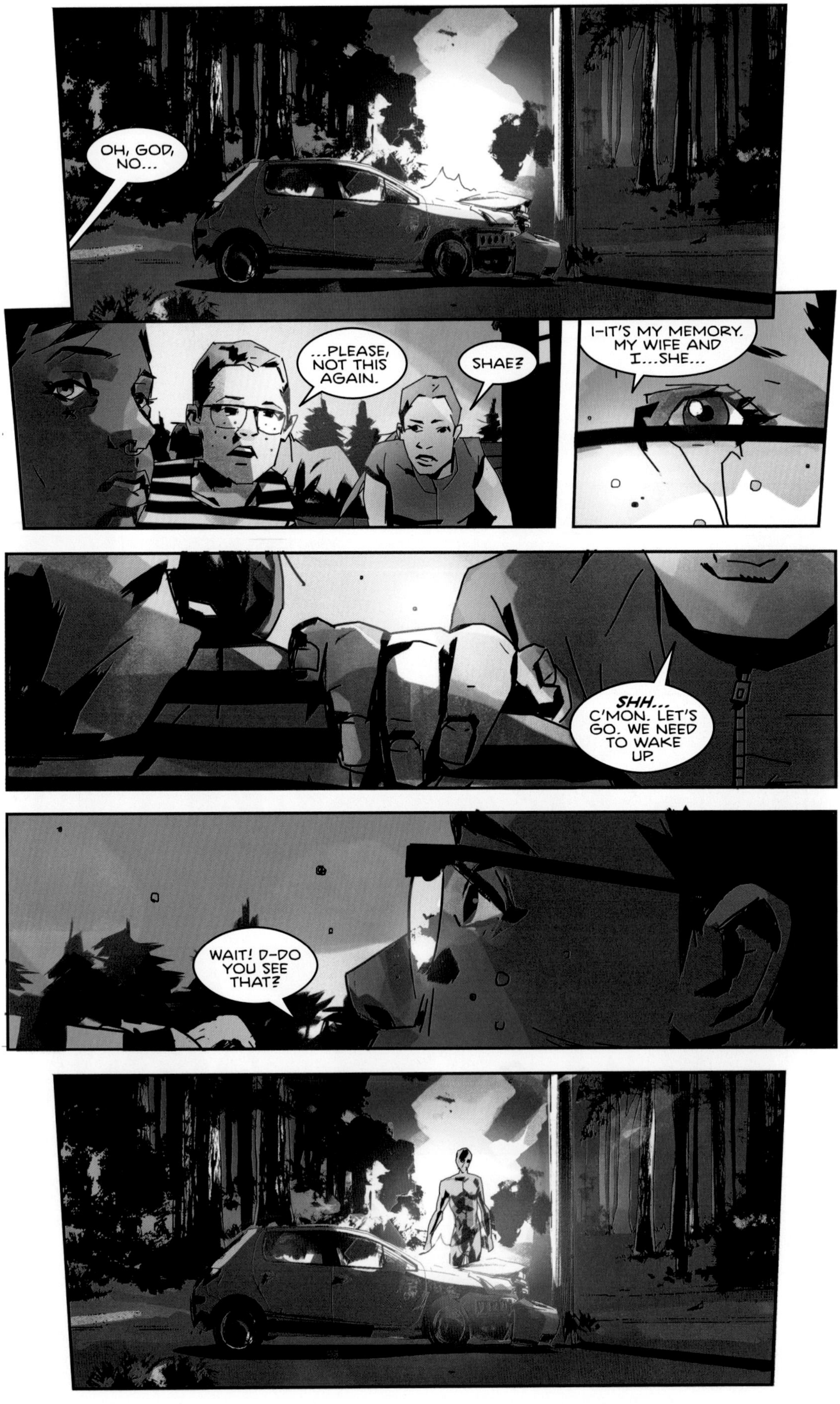
OH, GOD, NO...
...PLEASE, NOT THIS AGAIN.
SHAE?
I-IT'S MY MEMORY. MY WIFE AND I...SHE...
SHH... C'MON. LET'S GO. WE NEED TO WAKE UP.
WAIT! D-DO YOU SEE THAT?

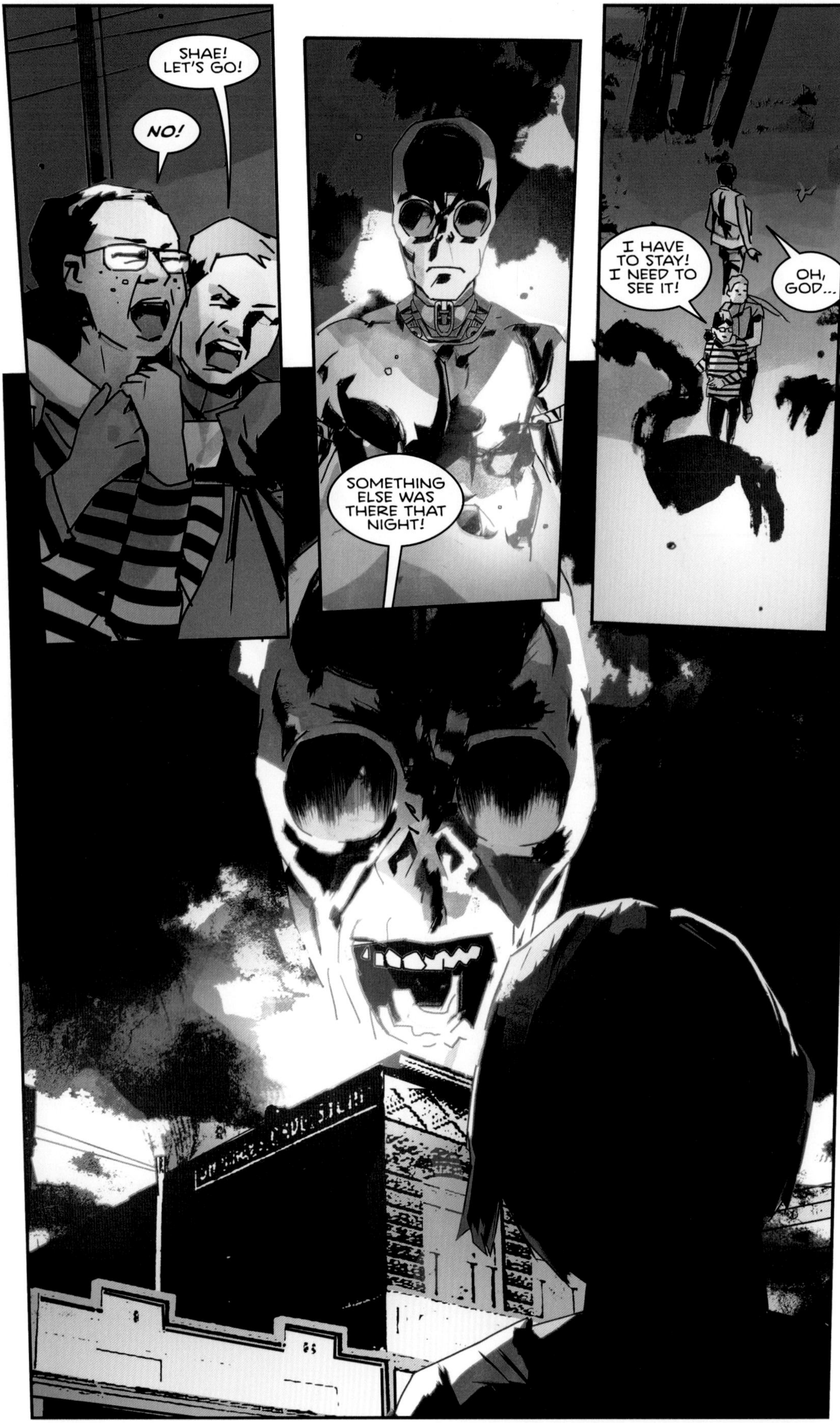
SHAE! LET'S GO!
NO!
SOMETHING ELSE WAS THERE THAT NIGHT!
I HAVE TO STAY! I NEED TO SEE IT!
OH, GOD...

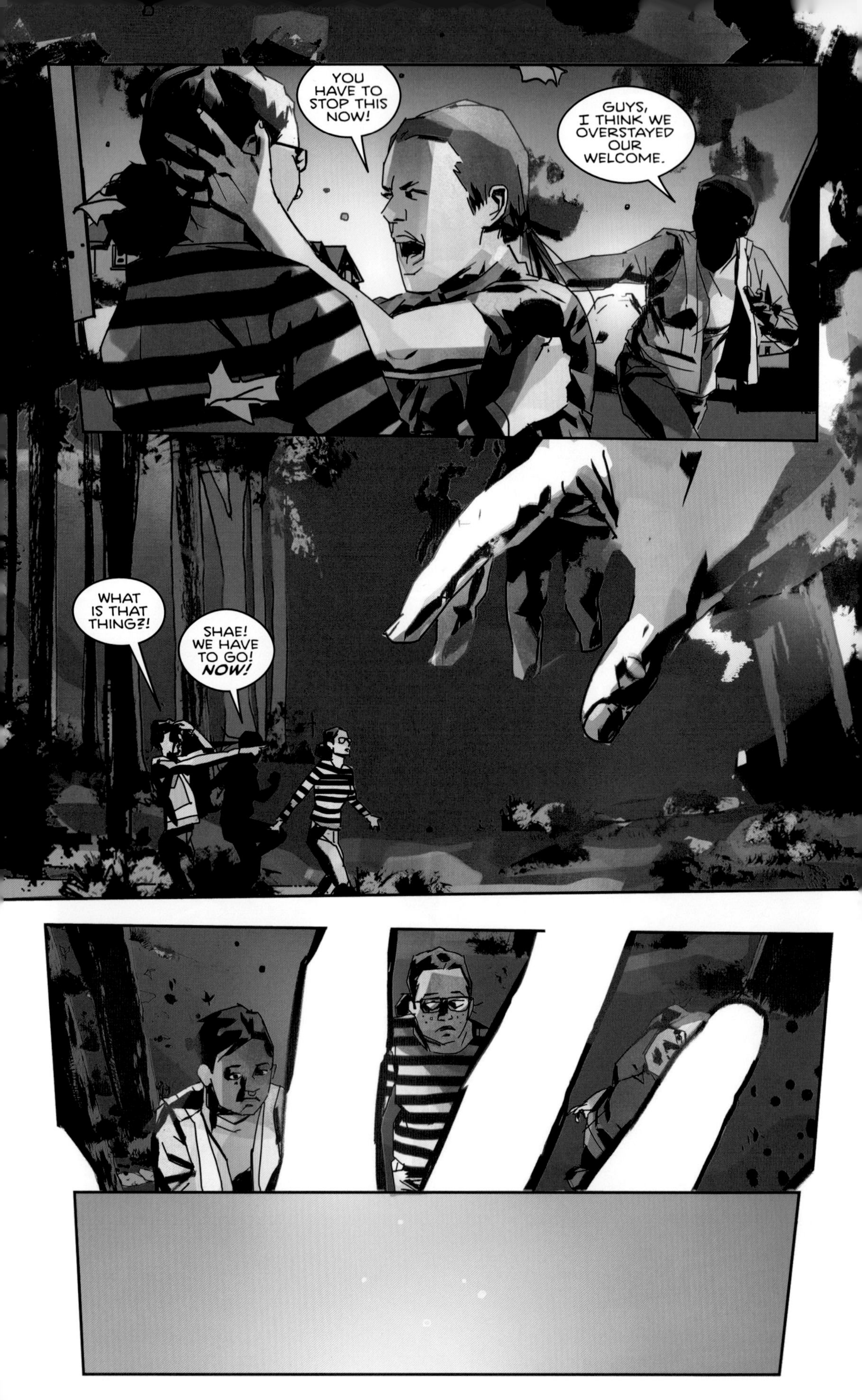
YOU HAVE TO STOP THIS NOW!
GUYS, I THINK WE OVERSTAYED OUR WELCOME.
WHAT IS THAT THING?!
SHAE! WE HAVE TO GO! *NOW!*

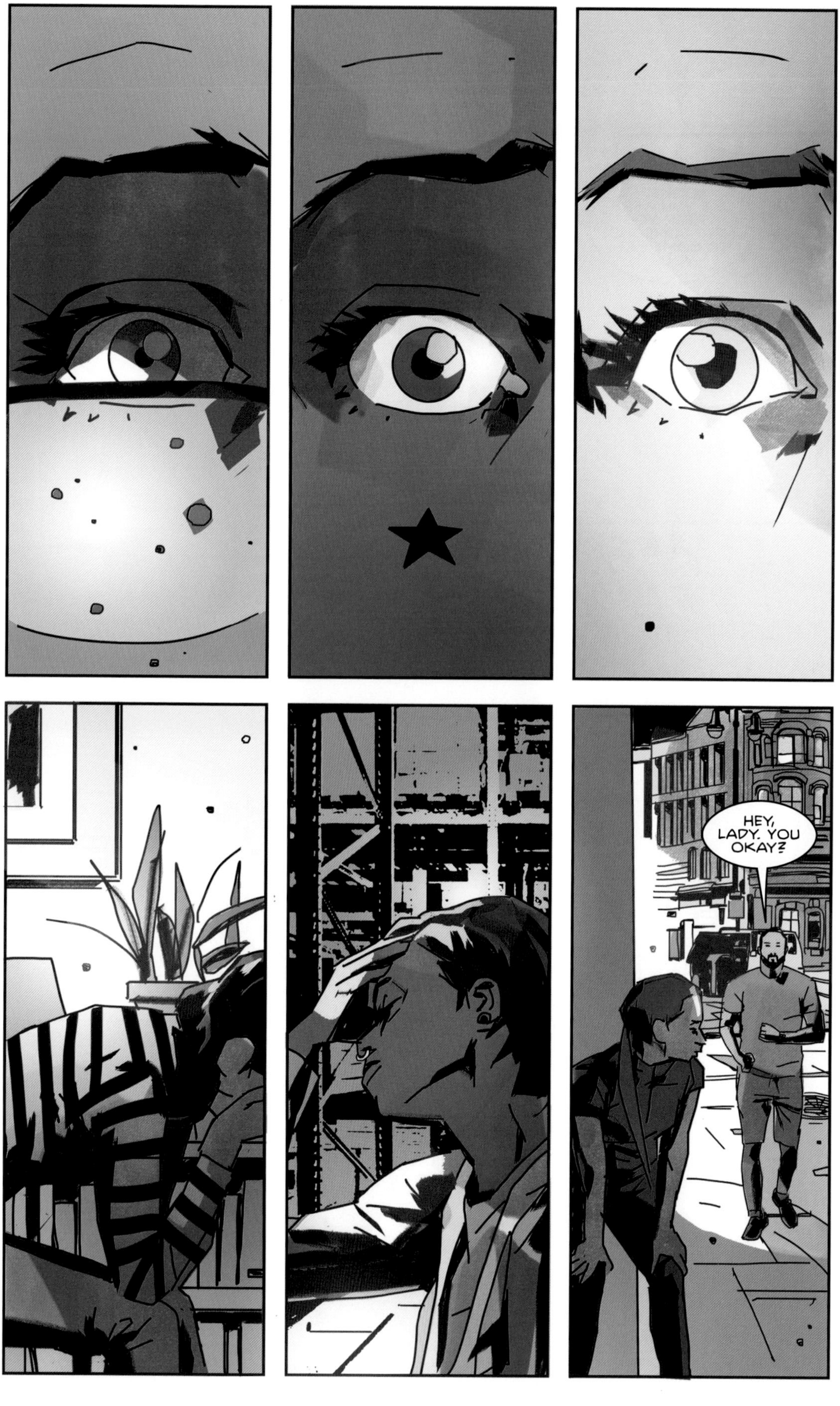
HEY, LADY. YOU OKAY?

Y-YEAH... JUST NEEDED TO CATCH MY BREATH.

LOOKED LIKE YOU WERE ASLEEP. YOU NEED SOMEONE TO COME GET YOU?

NO. REALLY. I WAS JUST PUT ON SOME NEW MEDICATION, AND I THINK THAT--

VRRM
VRRM

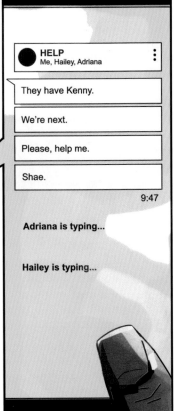

HELP
Me, Hailey, Adriana

They have Kenny.

We're next.

Please, help me.

Shae.

9:47

Adriana is typing...

Hailey is typing...

89.233633
-45.104987

-33.836379
151.080506

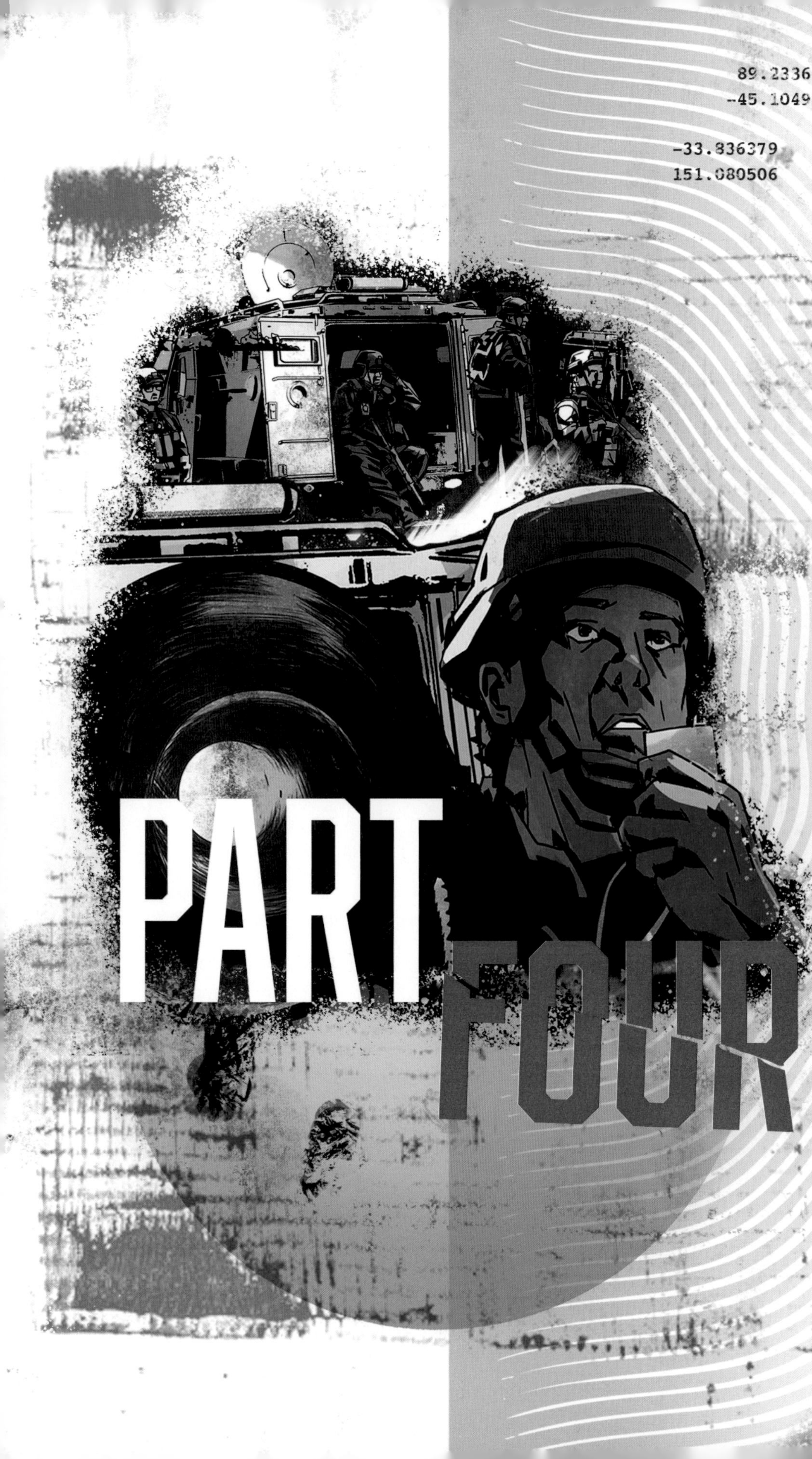

PART FOUR

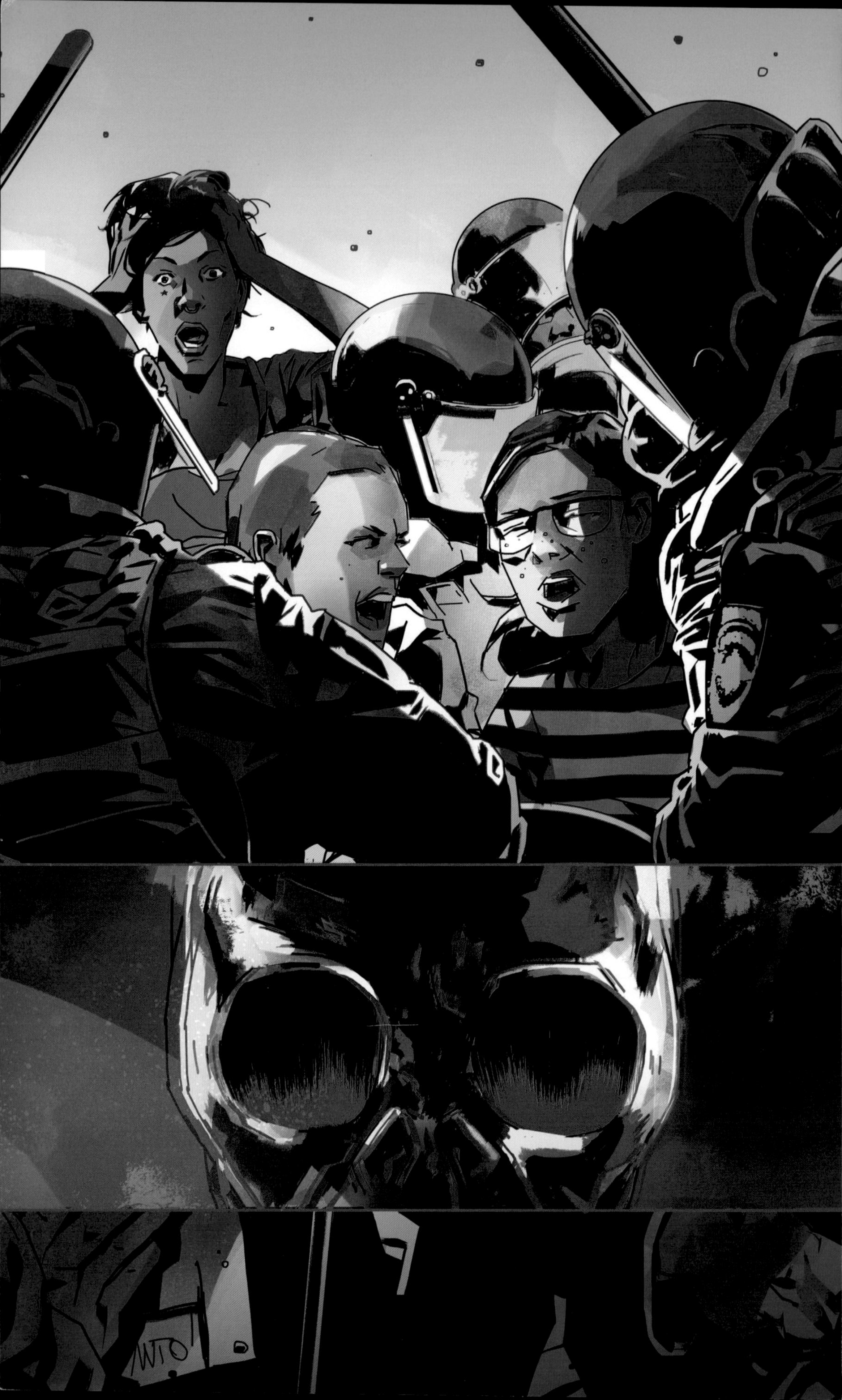

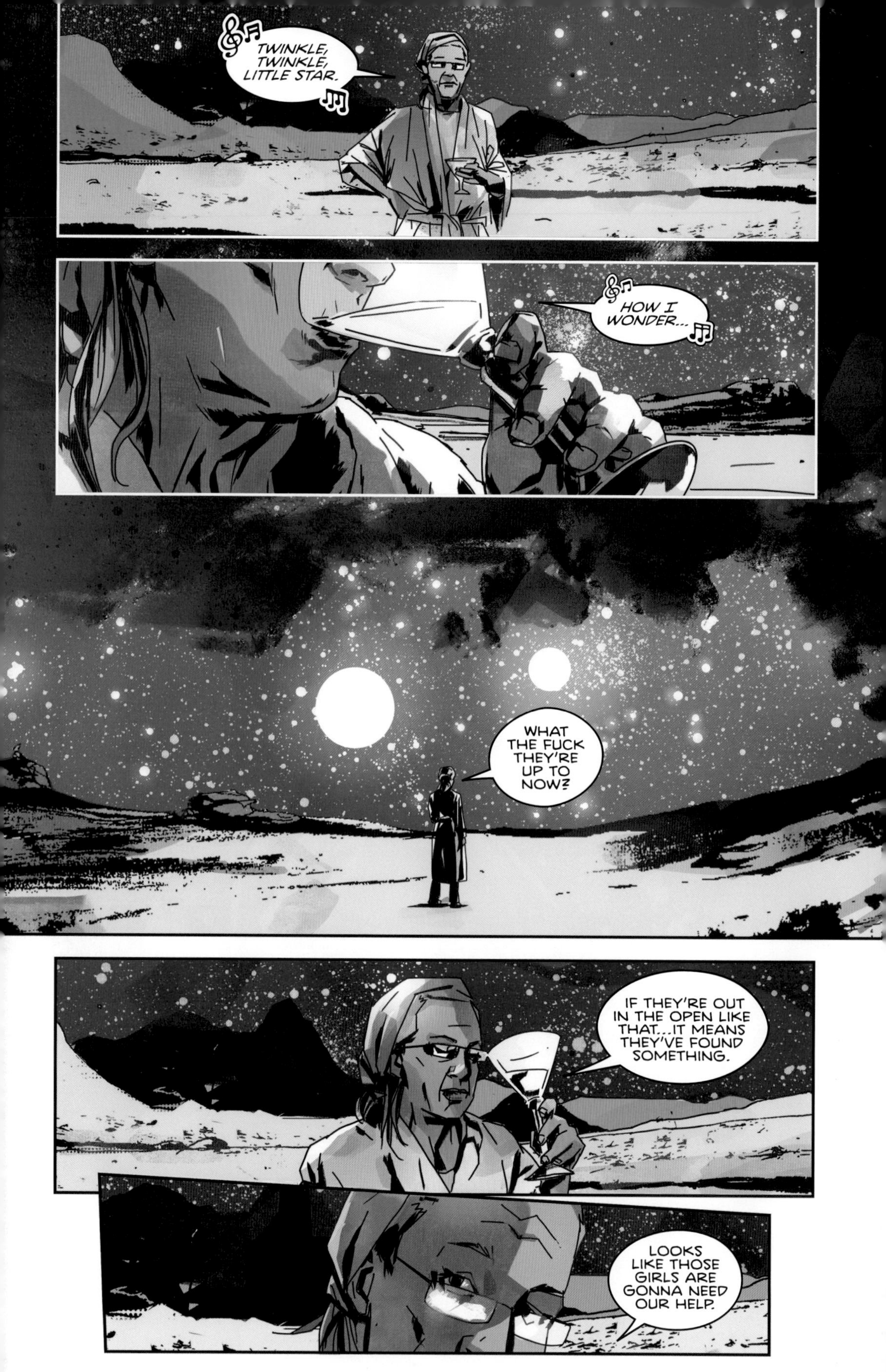
TWINKLE, TWINKLE, LITTLE STAR.
HOW I WONDER...
WHAT THE FUCK THEY'RE UP TO NOW?
IF THEY'RE OUT IN THE OPEN LIKE THAT...IT MEANS THEY'VE FOUND SOMETHING.
LOOKS LIKE THOSE GIRLS ARE GONNA NEED OUR HELP.

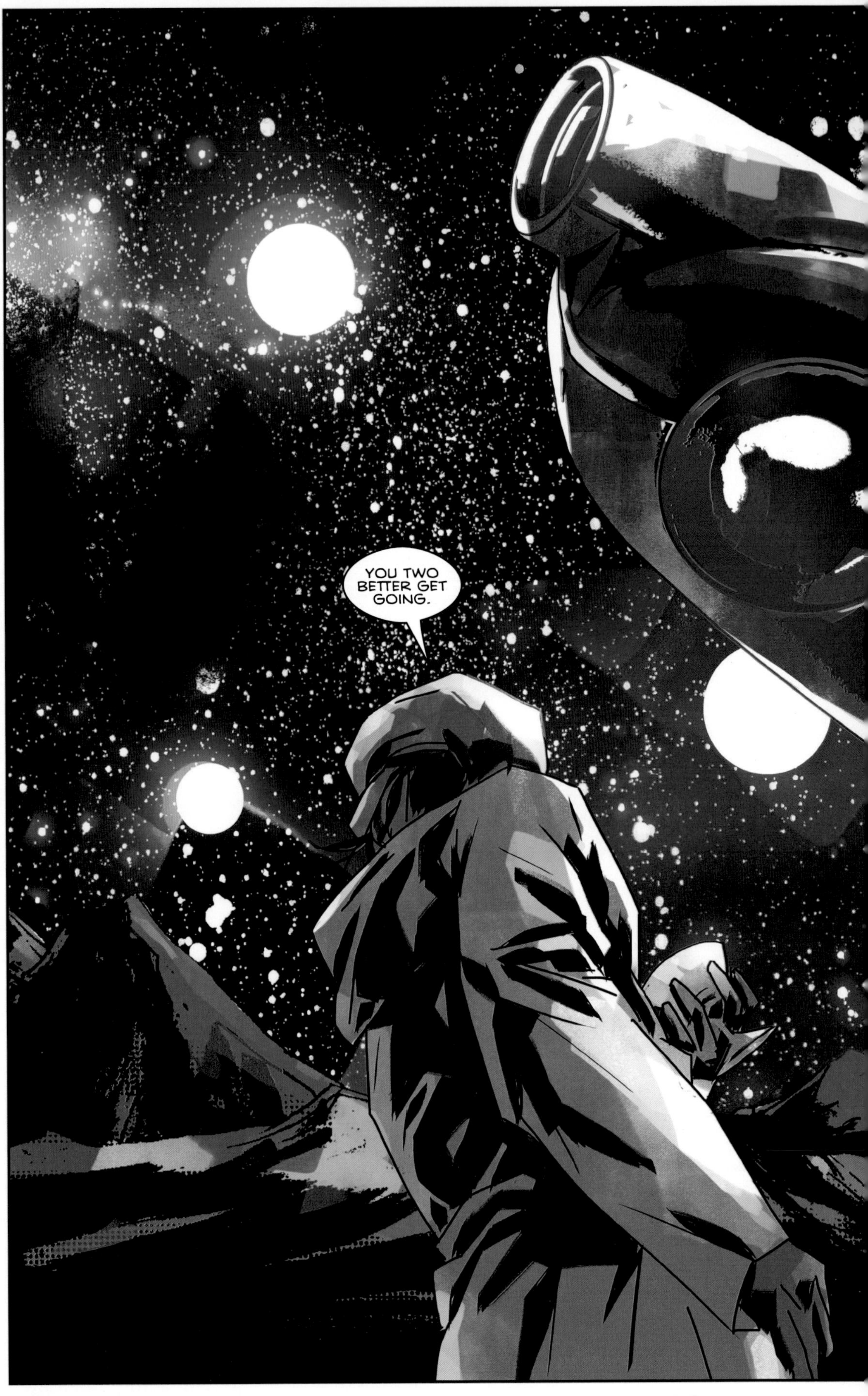
YOU TWO BETTER GET GOING.

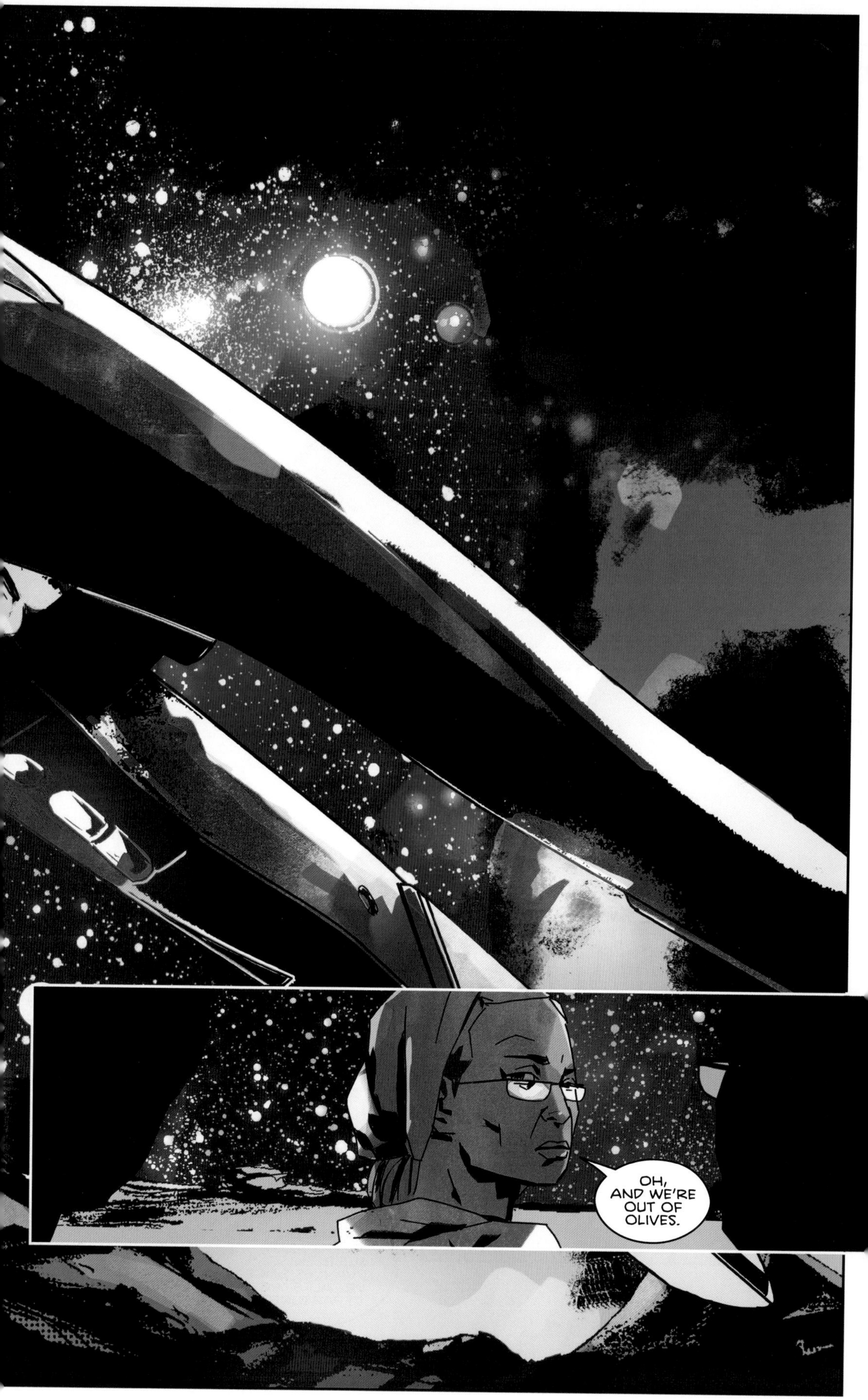
OH, AND WE'RE OUT OF OLIVES.

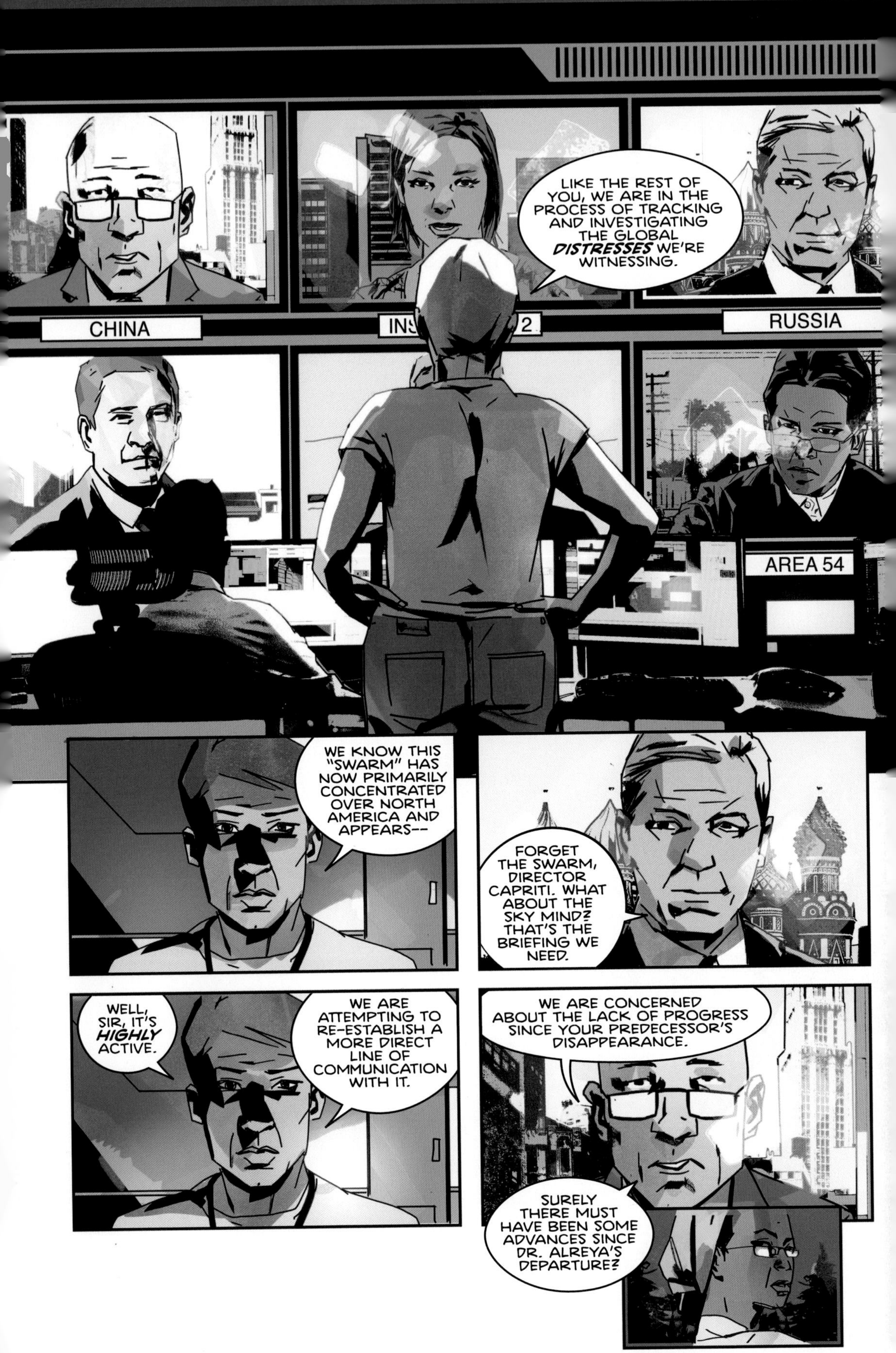
CHINA
RUSSIA
LIKE THE REST OF YOU, WE ARE IN THE PROCESS OF TRACKING AND INVESTIGATING THE GLOBAL *DISTRESSES* WE'RE WITNESSING.
AREA 54
WE KNOW THIS "SWARM" HAS NOW PRIMARILY CONCENTRATED OVER NORTH AMERICA AND APPEARS--
FORGET THE SWARM, DIRECTOR CAPRITI. WHAT ABOUT THE SKY MIND? THAT'S THE BRIEFING WE NEED.
WELL, SIR, IT'S *HIGHLY* ACTIVE.
WE ARE ATTEMPTING TO RE-ESTABLISH A MORE DIRECT LINE OF COMMUNICATION WITH IT.
WE ARE CONCERNED ABOUT THE LACK OF PROGRESS SINCE YOUR PREDECESSOR'S DISAPPEARANCE.
SURELY THERE MUST HAVE BEEN SOME ADVANCES SINCE DR. ALREYA'S DEPARTURE?

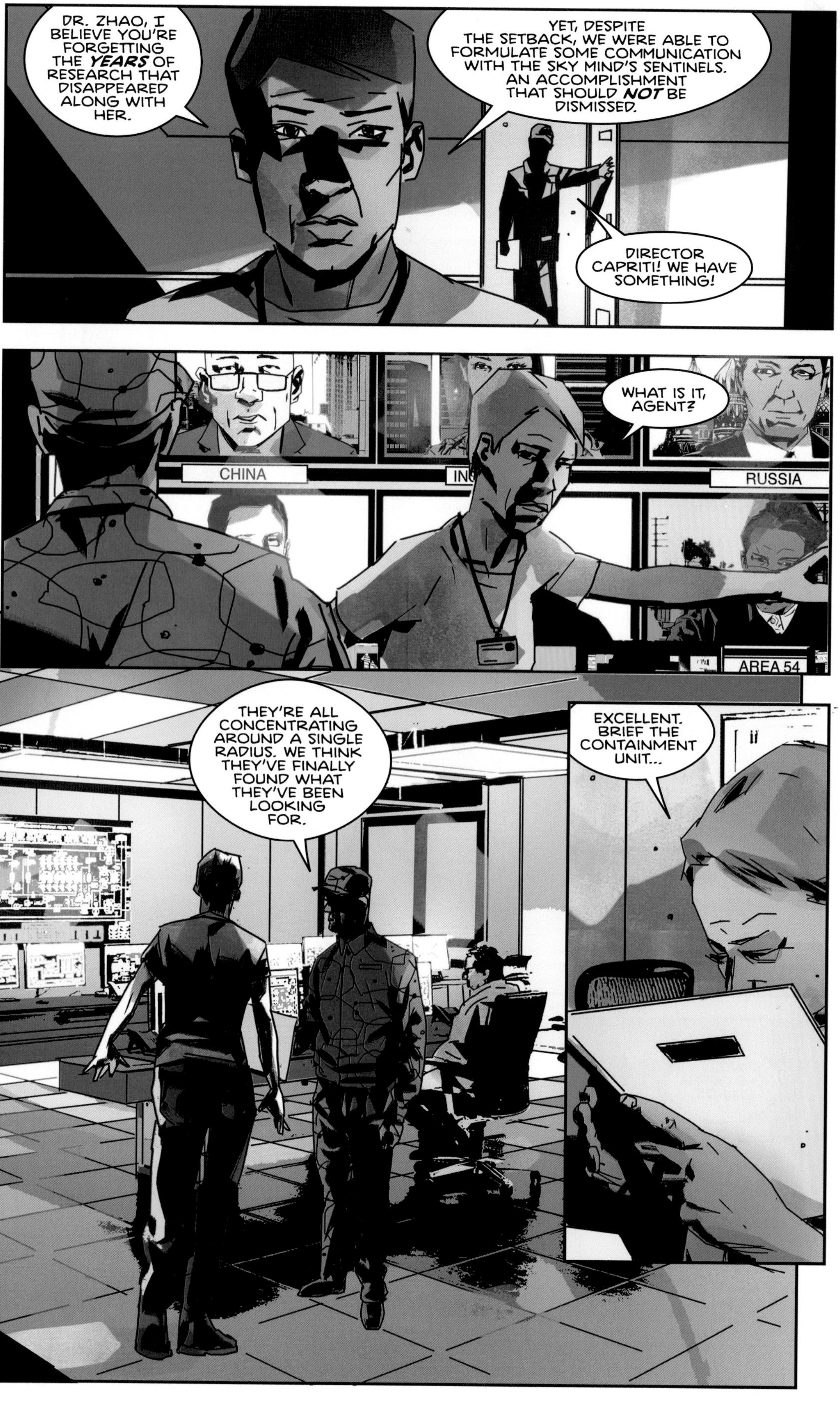
DR. ZHAO, I BELIEVE YOU'RE FORGETTING THE *YEARS* OF RESEARCH THAT DISAPPEARED ALONG WITH HER.
YET, DESPITE THE SETBACK, WE WERE ABLE TO FORMULATE SOME COMMUNICATION WITH THE SKY MIND'S SENTINELS. AN ACCOMPLISHMENT THAT SHOULD *NOT* BE DISMISSED.
DIRECTOR CAPRITI! WE HAVE SOMETHING!
CHINA
RUSSIA
AREA 54
WHAT IS IT, AGENT?
THEY'RE ALL CONCENTRATING AROUND A SINGLE RADIUS. WE THINK THEY'VE FINALLY FOUND WHAT THEY'VE BEEN LOOKING FOR.
EXCELLENT. BRIEF THE CONTAINMENT UNIT...

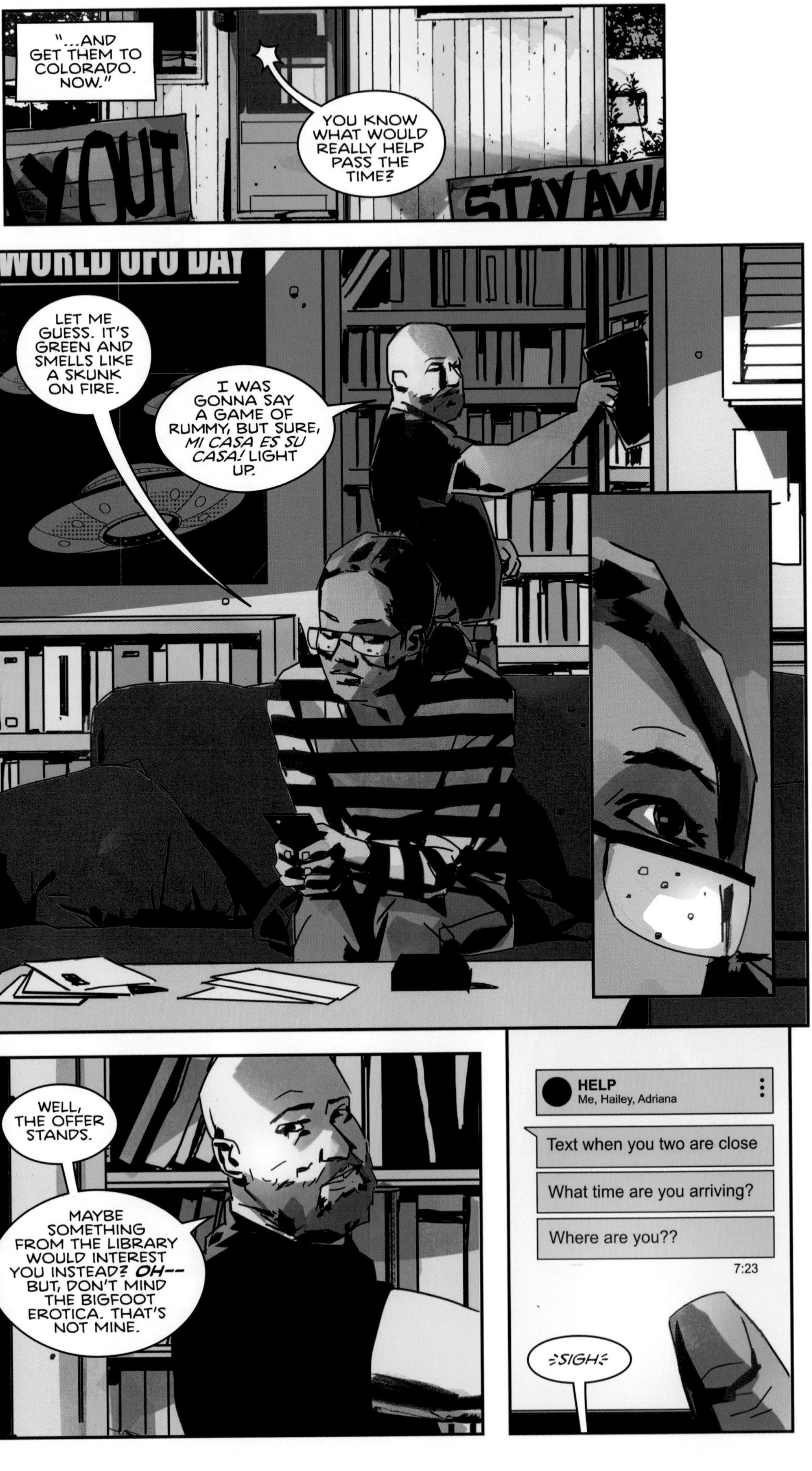

"...AND GET THEM TO COLORADO. NOW."
YOU KNOW WHAT WOULD REALLY HELP PASS THE TIME?
YOUT
STAY AW
WORLD UFO DAY
LET ME GUESS. IT'S GREEN AND SMELLS LIKE A SKUNK ON FIRE.
I WAS GONNA SAY A GAME OF RUMMY, BUT SURE, *MI CASA ES SU CASA!* LIGHT UP.
WELL, THE OFFER STANDS.
MAYBE SOMETHING FROM THE LIBRARY WOULD INTEREST YOU INSTEAD? ***OH--*** BUT, DON'T MIND THE BIGFOOT EROTICA. THAT'S NOT MINE.
HELP
Me, Hailey, Adriana
Text when you two are close
What time are you arriving?
Where are you??
7:23
SIGH

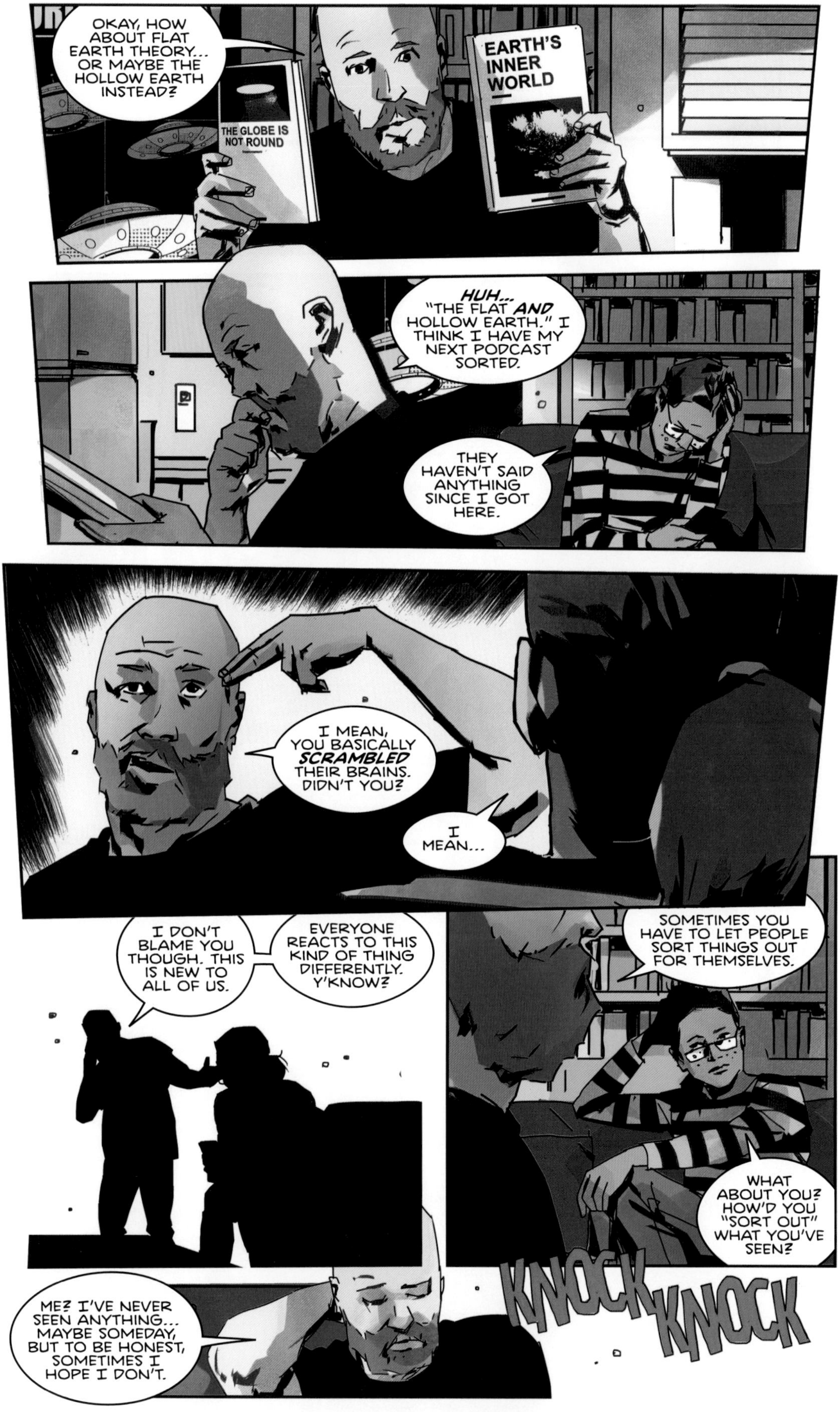
OKAY, HOW ABOUT FLAT EARTH THEORY... OR MAYBE THE HOLLOW EARTH INSTEAD?
THE GLOBE IS NOT ROUND
EARTH'S INNER WORLD
HUH... "THE FLAT AND HOLLOW EARTH." I THINK I HAVE MY NEXT PODCAST SORTED.
THEY HAVEN'T SAID ANYTHING SINCE I GOT HERE.
I MEAN, YOU BASICALLY SCRAMBLED THEIR BRAINS. DIDN'T YOU?
I MEAN...
I DON'T BLAME YOU THOUGH. THIS IS NEW TO ALL OF US.
EVERYONE REACTS TO THIS KIND OF THING DIFFERENTLY. Y'KNOW?
SOMETIMES YOU HAVE TO LET PEOPLE SORT THINGS OUT FOR THEMSELVES.
WHAT ABOUT YOU? HOW'D YOU "SORT OUT" WHAT YOU'VE SEEN?
ME? I'VE NEVER SEEN ANYTHING... MAYBE SOMEDAY, BUT TO BE HONEST, SOMETIMES I HOPE I DON'T.
KNOCK KNOCK

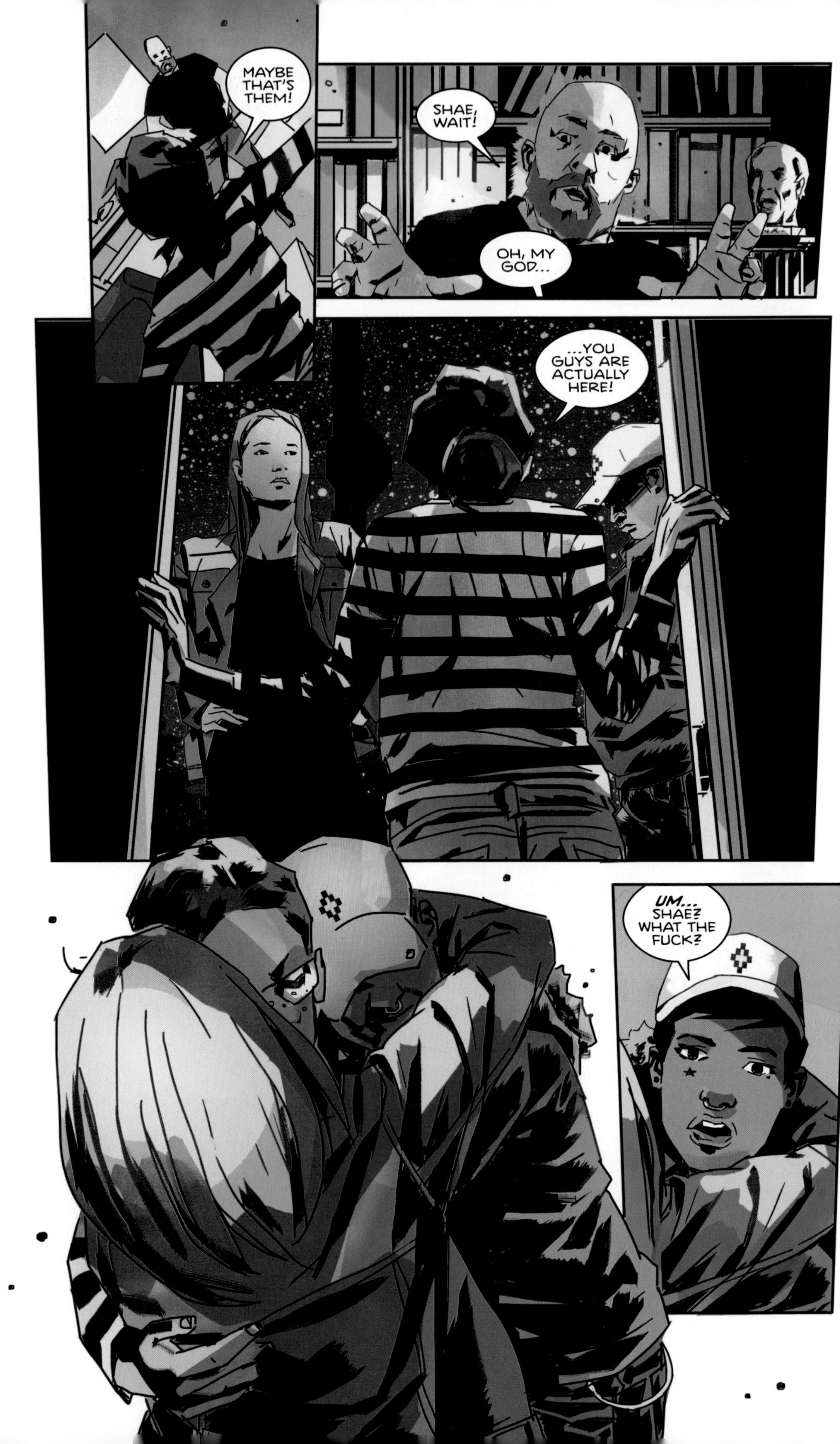
MAYBE THAT'S THEM!
SHAE, WAIT!
OH, MY GOD...
...YOU GUYS ARE ACTUALLY HERE!
UM... SHAE? WHAT THE FUCK?

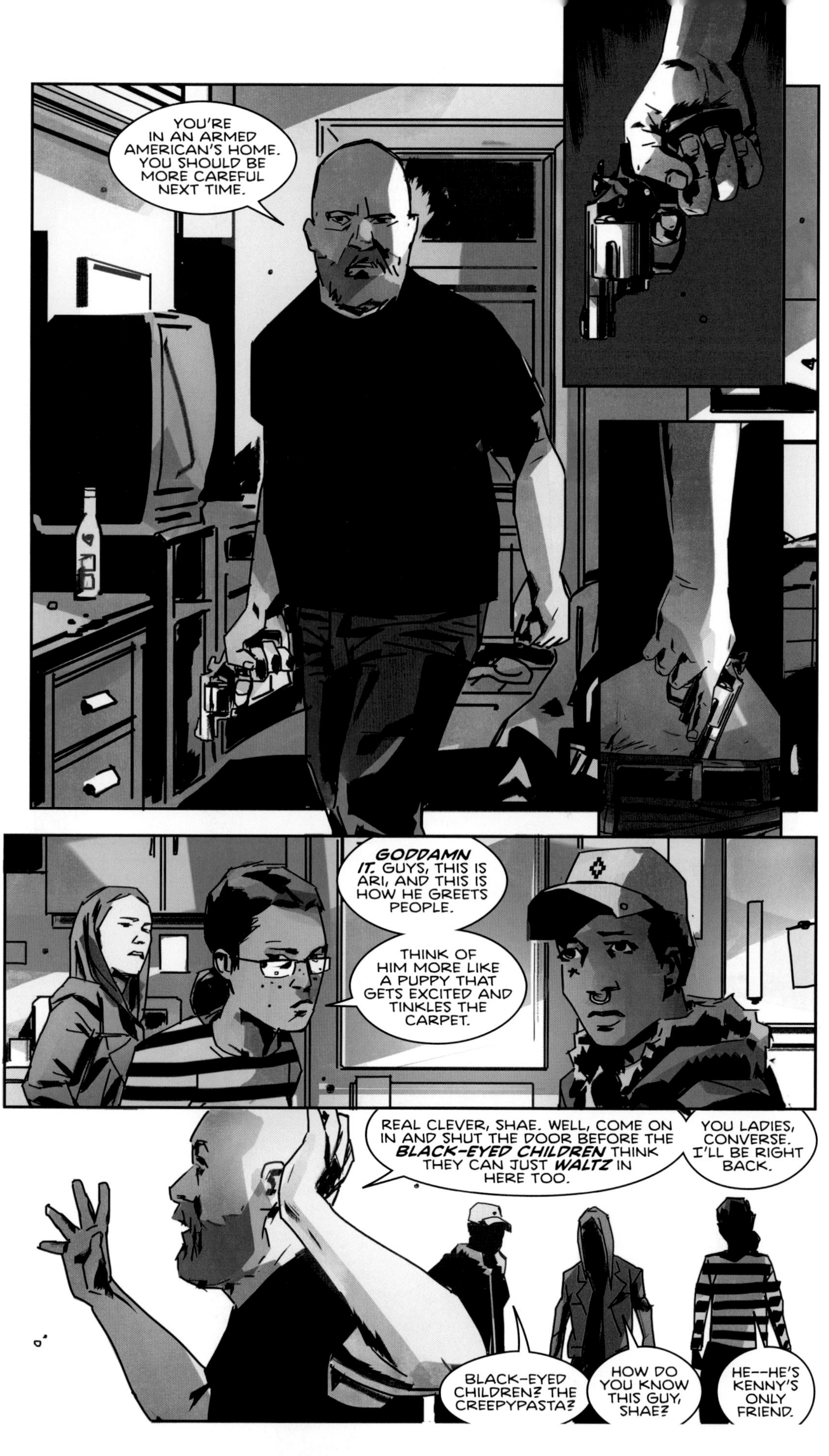
YOU'RE IN AN ARMED AMERICAN'S HOME. YOU SHOULD BE MORE CAREFUL NEXT TIME.
GODDAMN IT. GUYS, THIS IS ARI, AND THIS IS HOW HE GREETS PEOPLE.
THINK OF HIM MORE LIKE A PUPPY THAT GETS EXCITED AND TINKLES THE CARPET.
REAL CLEVER, SHAE. WELL, COME ON IN AND SHUT THE DOOR BEFORE THE BLACK-EYED CHILDREN THINK THEY CAN JUST WALTZ IN HERE TOO.
YOU LADIES, CONVERSE. I'LL BE RIGHT BACK.
BLACK-EYED CHILDREN? THE CREEPYPASTA?
HOW DO YOU KNOW THIS GUY, SHAE?
HE--HE'S KENNY'S ONLY FRIEND.

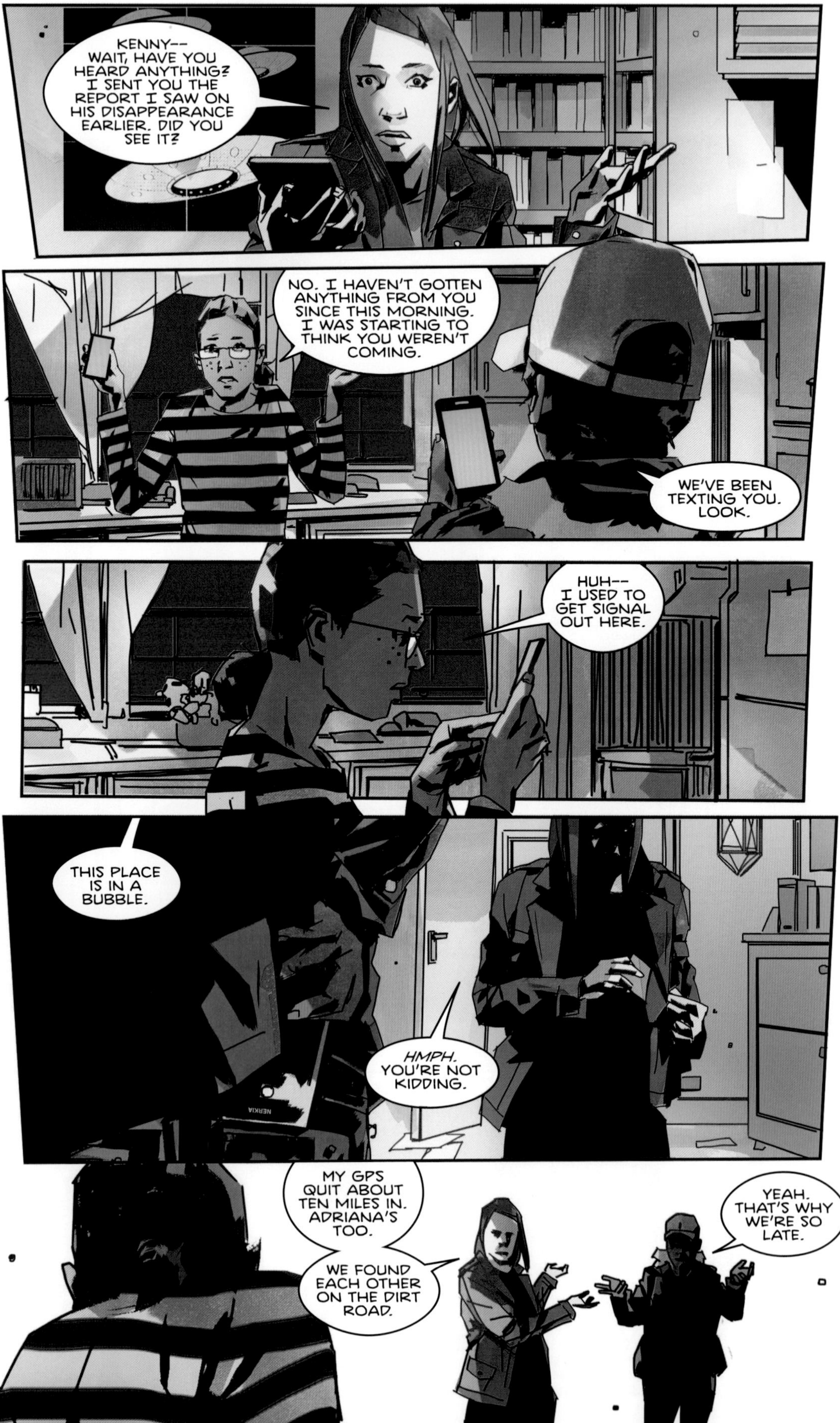
KENNY-- WAIT, HAVE YOU HEARD ANYTHING? I SENT YOU THE REPORT I SAW ON HIS DISAPPEARANCE EARLIER. DID YOU SEE IT?
NO. I HAVEN'T GOTTEN ANYTHING FROM YOU SINCE THIS MORNING. I WAS STARTING TO THINK YOU WEREN'T COMING.
WE'VE BEEN TEXTING YOU. LOOK.
HUH-- I USED TO GET SIGNAL OUT HERE.
THIS PLACE IS IN A BUBBLE.
HMPH. YOU'RE NOT KIDDING.
MY GPS QUIT ABOUT TEN MILES IN. ADRIANA'S TOO.
WE FOUND EACH OTHER ON THE DIRT ROAD.
YEAH. THAT'S WHY WE'RE SO LATE.

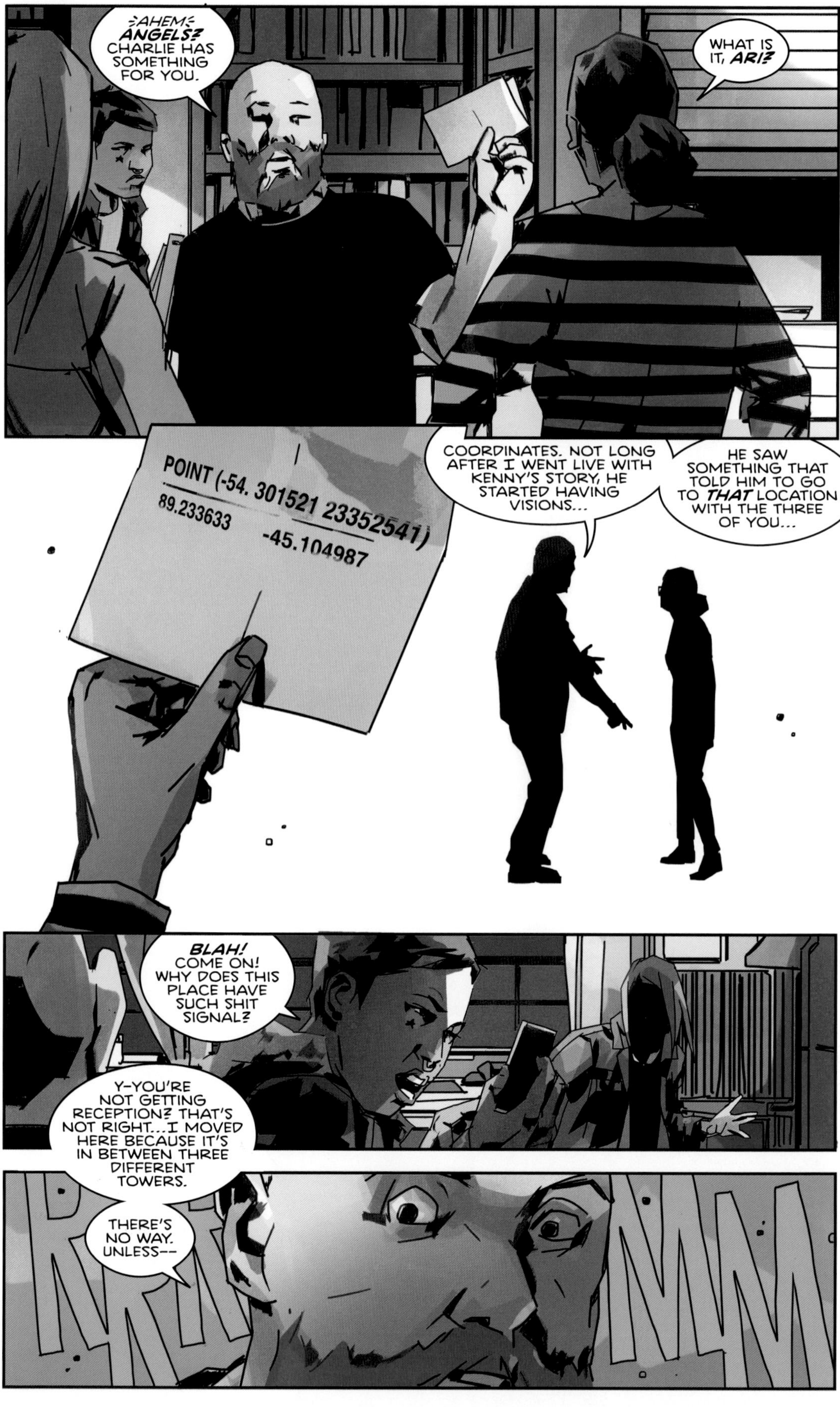

:AHEM: ANGELS? CHARLIE HAS SOMETHING FOR YOU.
WHAT IS IT, ARI?
POINT (-54. 301521 23352541)
89.233633 -45.104987
COORDINATES. NOT LONG AFTER I WENT LIVE WITH KENNY'S STORY, HE STARTED HAVING VISIONS...
HE SAW SOMETHING THAT TOLD HIM TO GO TO THAT LOCATION WITH THE THREE OF YOU...
BLAH! COME ON! WHY DOES THIS PLACE HAVE SUCH SHIT SIGNAL?
Y-YOU'RE NOT GETTING RECEPTION? THAT'S NOT RIGHT...I MOVED HERE BECAUSE IT'S IN BETWEEN THREE DIFFERENT TOWERS.
THERE'S NO WAY. UNLESS--

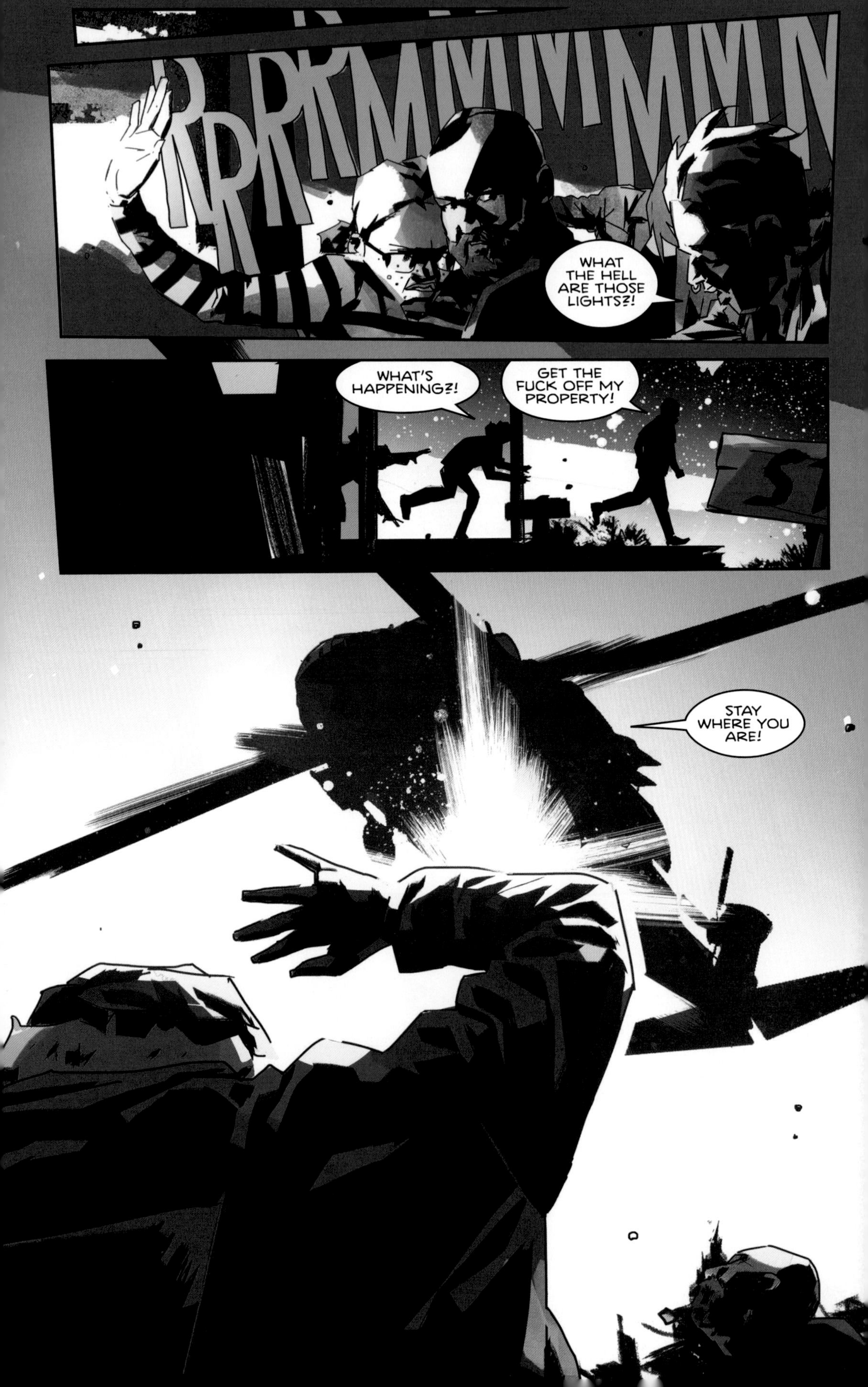
RRRRMMMMMMMN
WHAT THE HELL ARE THOSE LIGHTS?!
WHAT'S HAPPENING?!
GET THE FUCK OFF MY PROPERTY!
STAY WHERE YOU ARE!

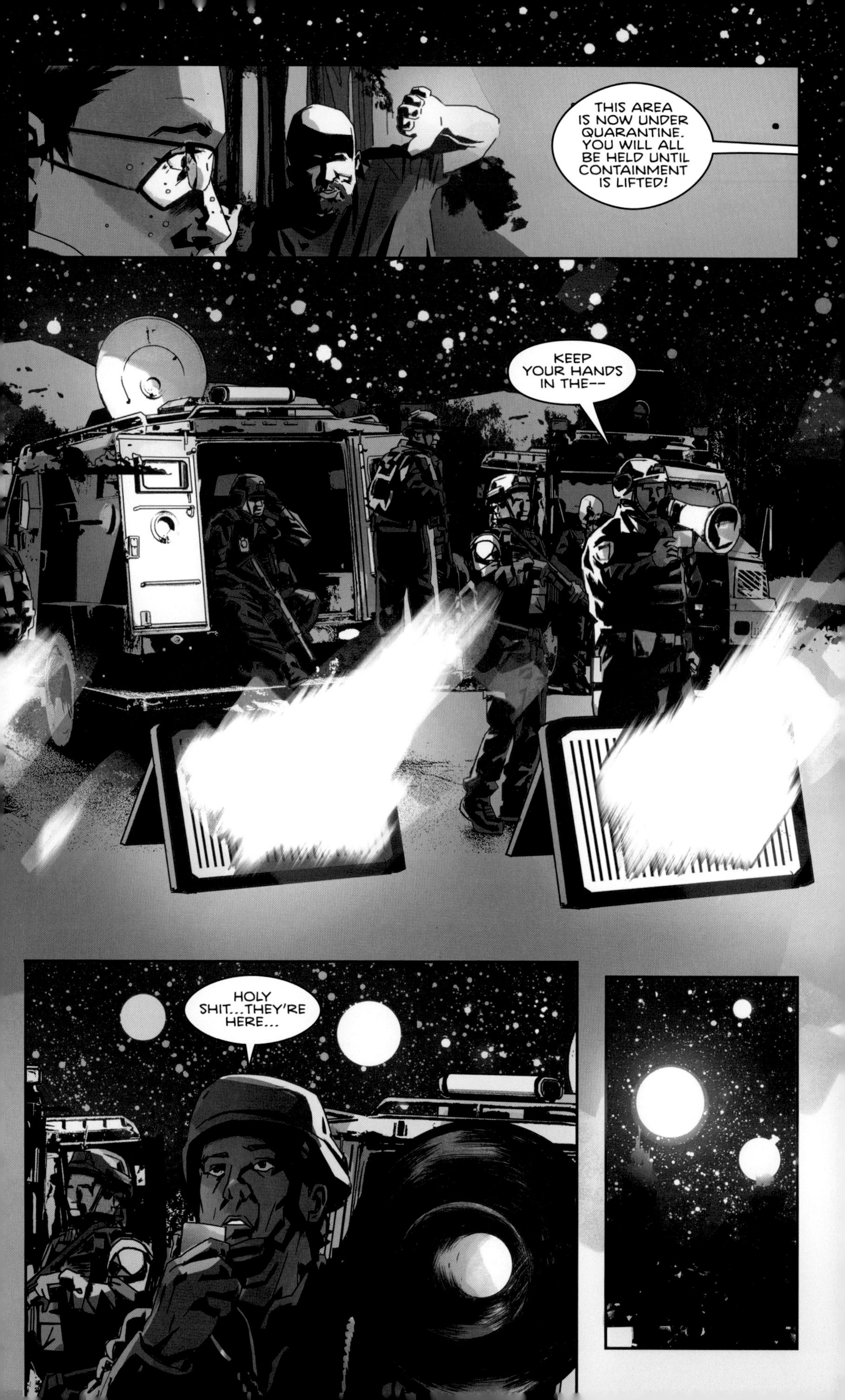
THIS AREA IS NOW UNDER QUARANTINE. YOU WILL ALL BE HELD UNTIL CONTAINMENT IS LIFTED!
KEEP YOUR HANDS IN THE--
HOLY SHIT...THEY'RE HERE...

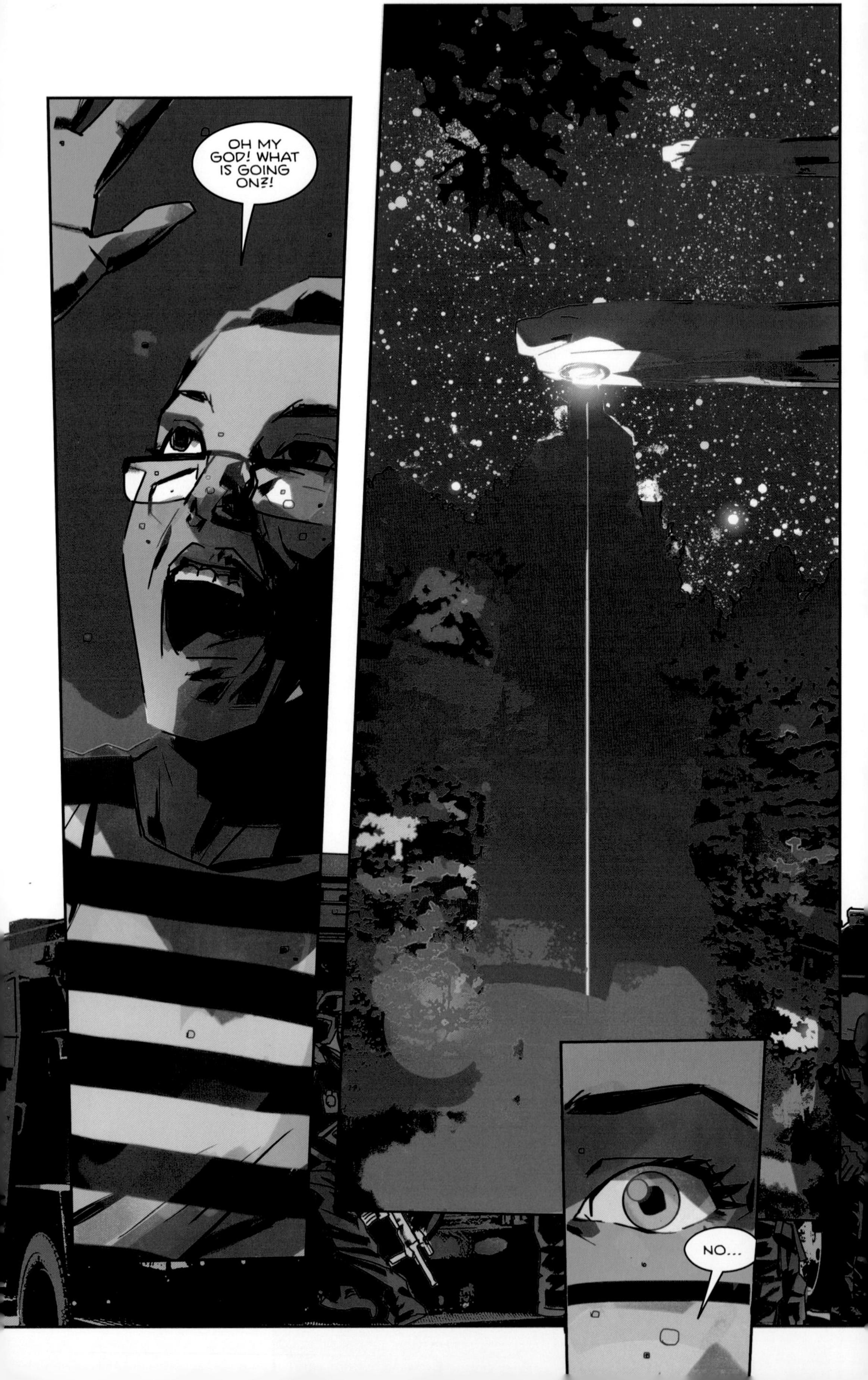
OH MY GOD! WHAT IS GOING ON?!
NO...

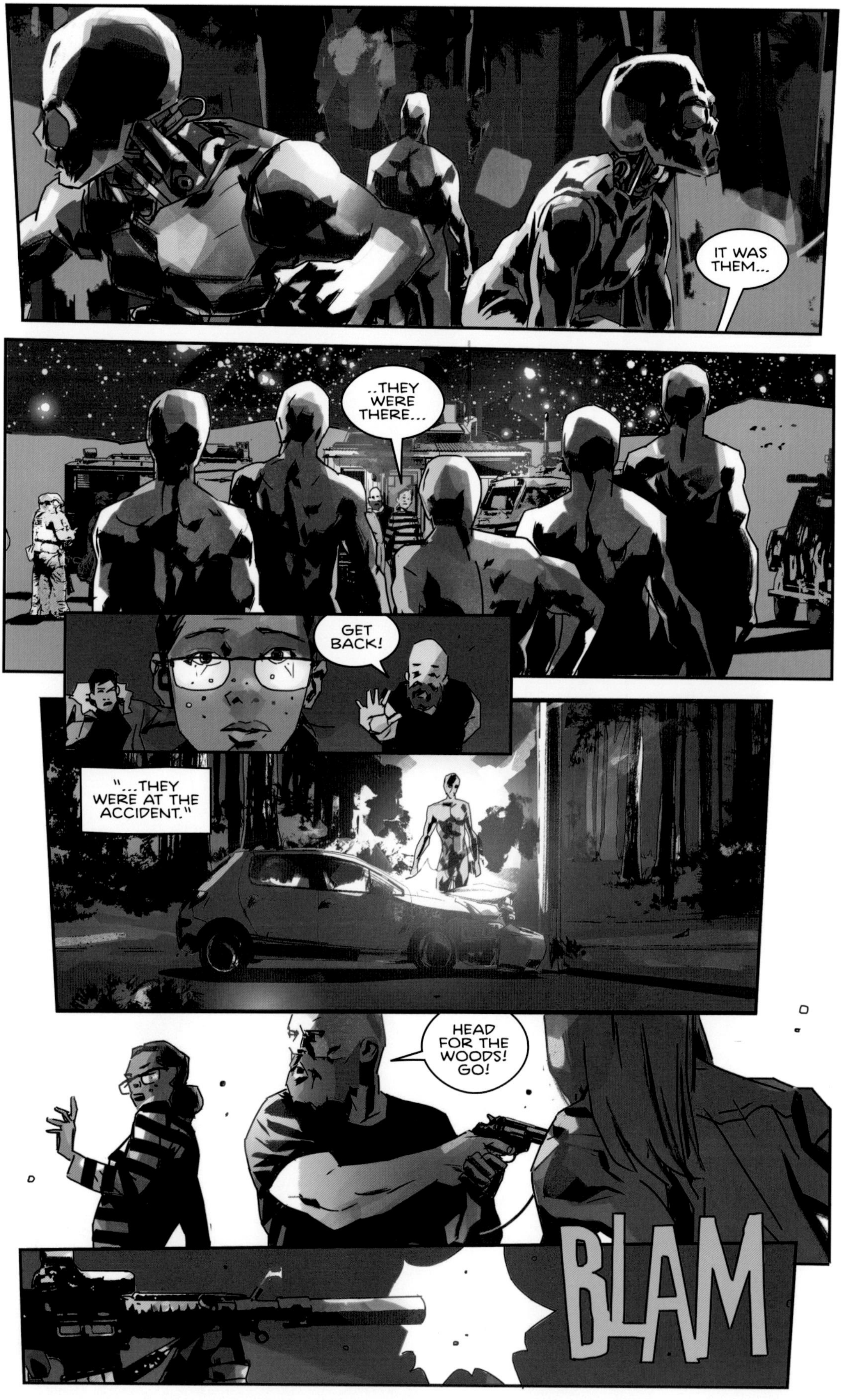
IT WAS THEM...
..THEY WERE THERE...
GET BACK!
"...THEY WERE AT THE ACCIDENT."
HEAD FOR THE WOODS! GO!
BLAM

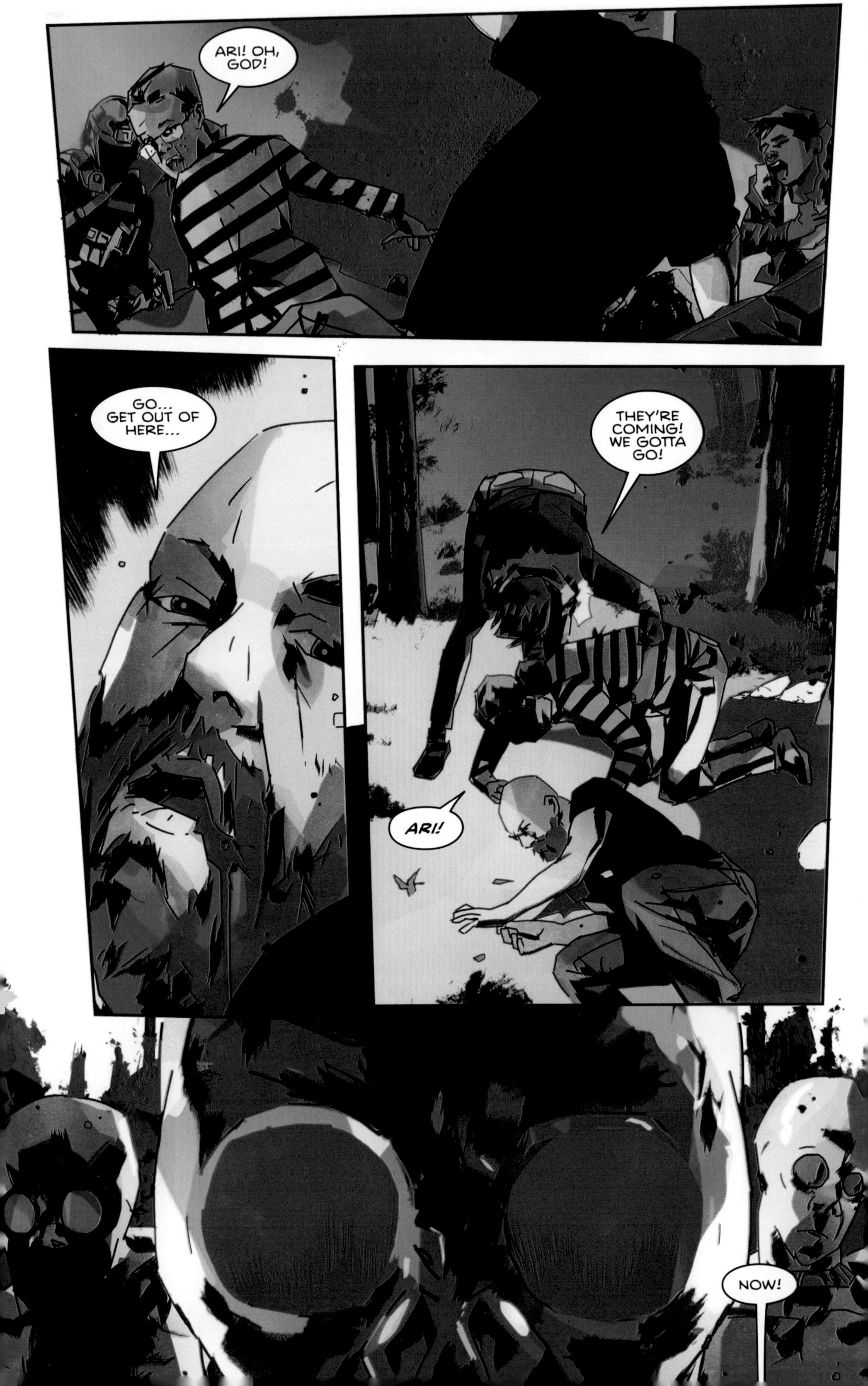

ARI! OH, GOD!
GO... GET OUT OF HERE...
THEY'RE COMING! WE GOTTA GO!
ARI!
NOW!

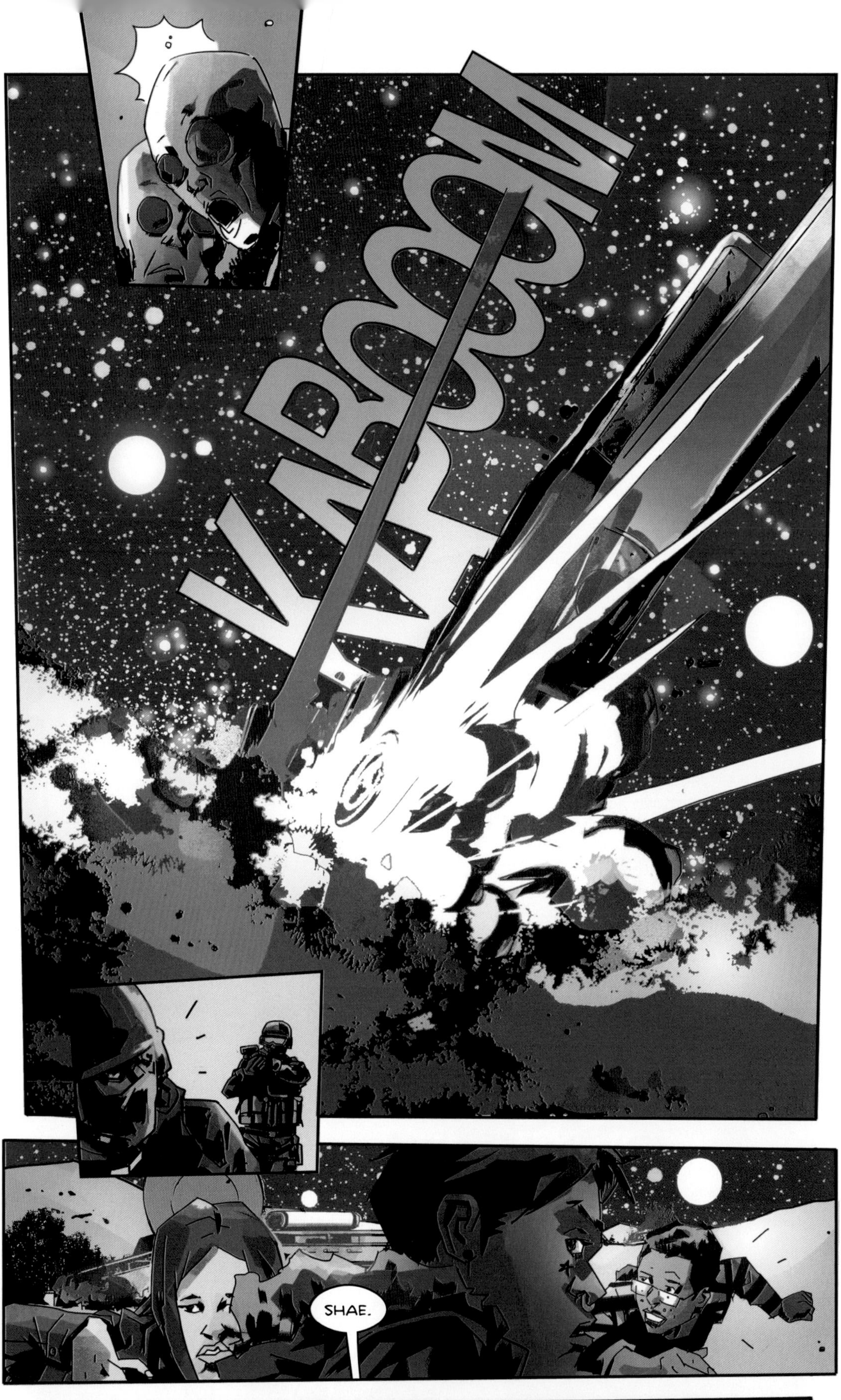
KABOOM!!
SHAE.

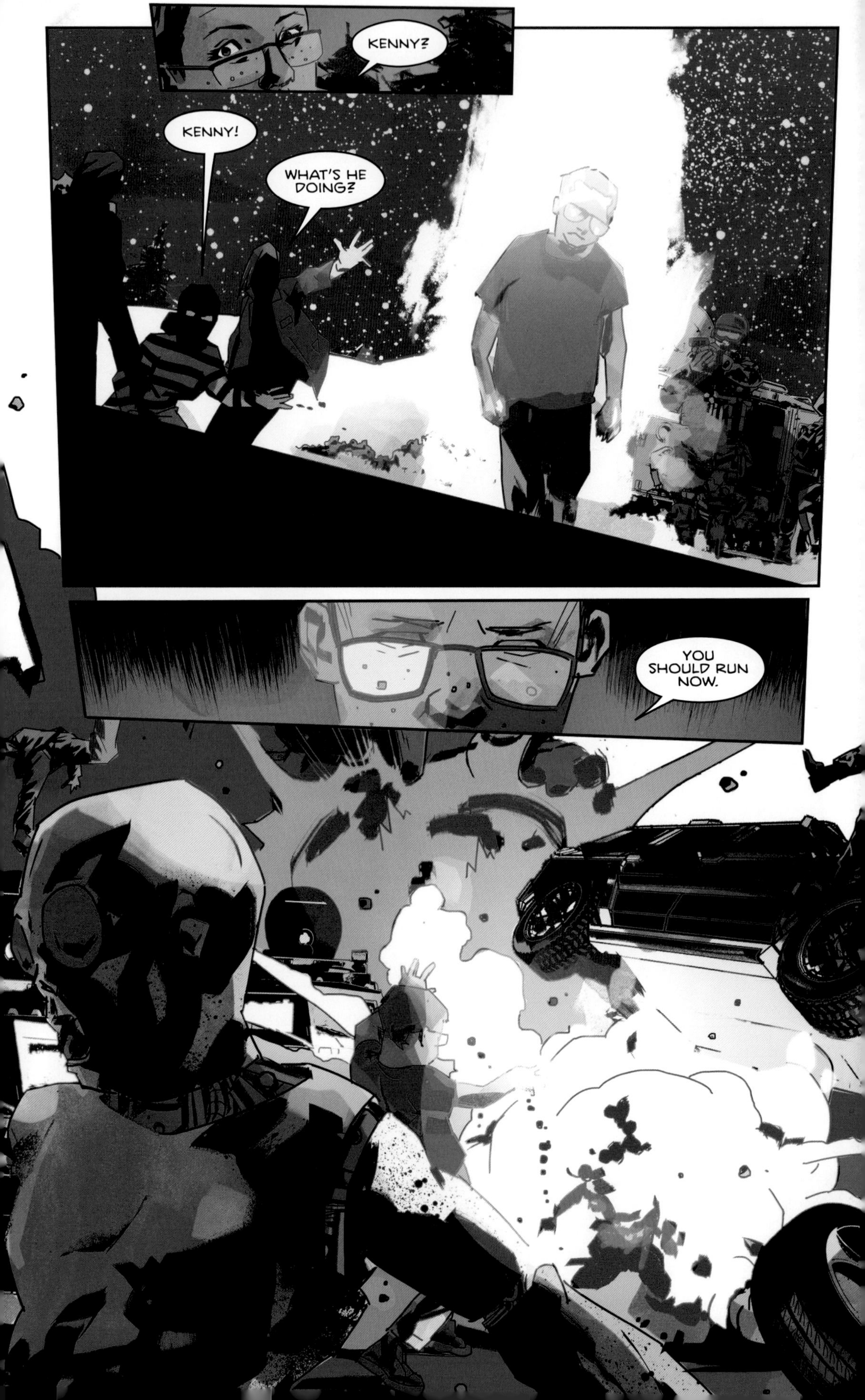
KENNY?
KENNY!
WHAT'S HE DOING?
YOU SHOULD RUN NOW.

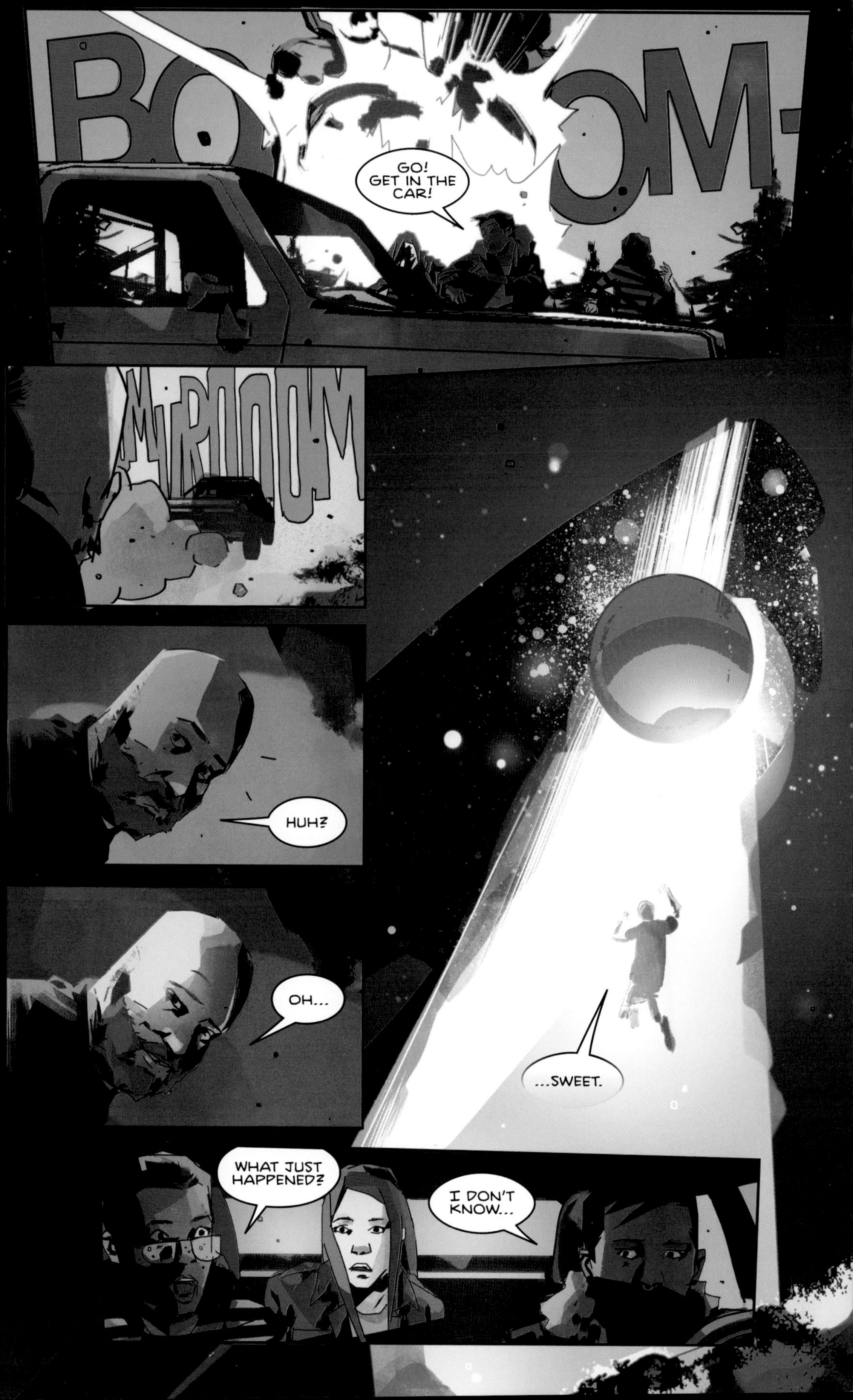
BOOM-
GO! GET IN THE CAR!
VRROOM
HUH?
OH...
...SWEET.
WHAT JUST HAPPENED?
I DON'T KNOW...

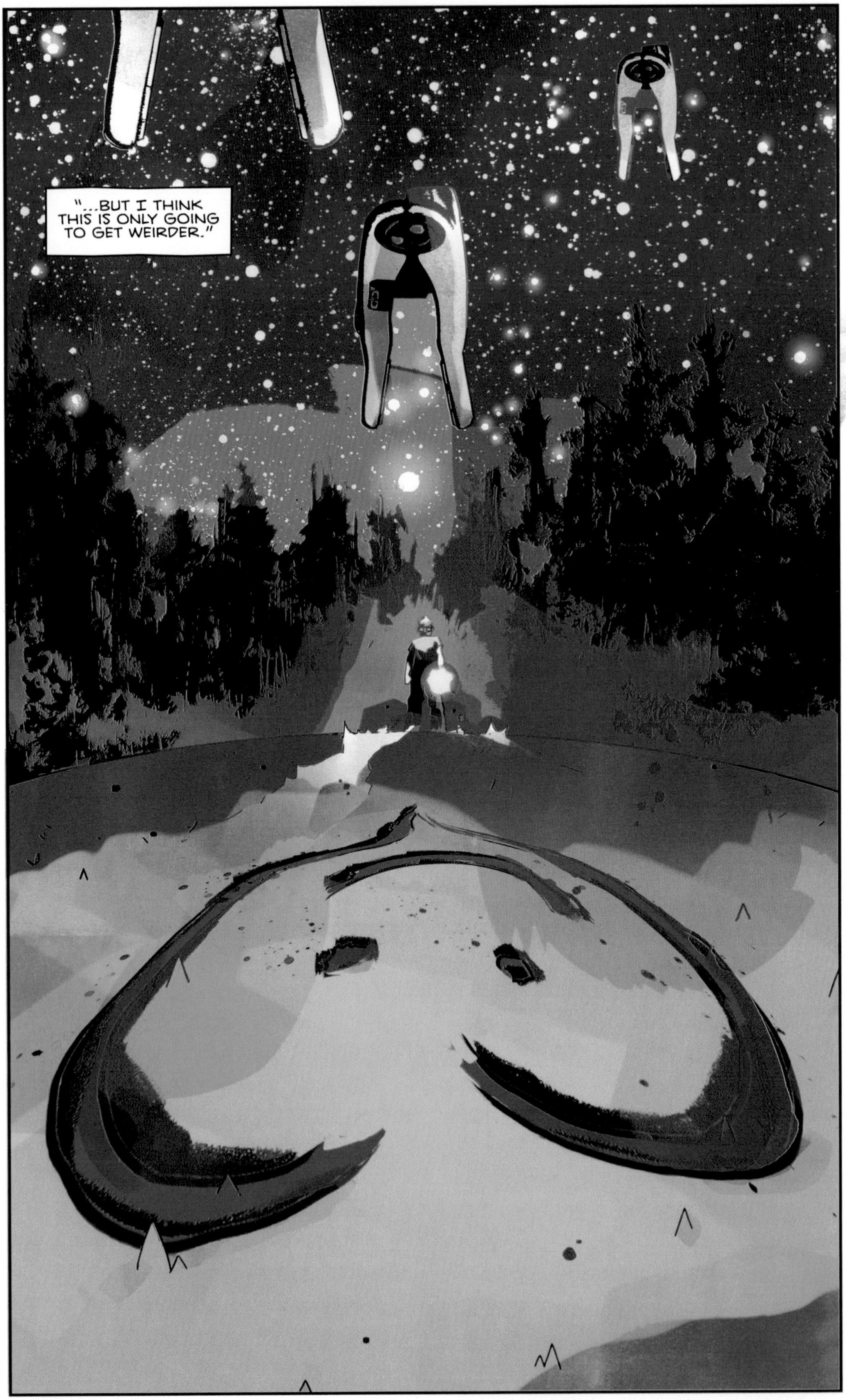
"...BUT I THINK THIS IS ONLY GOING TO GET WEIRDER."

PICK ITEM.4732.
AISLE 98.

50° 0'38.20"N
110° 6'48.32"W

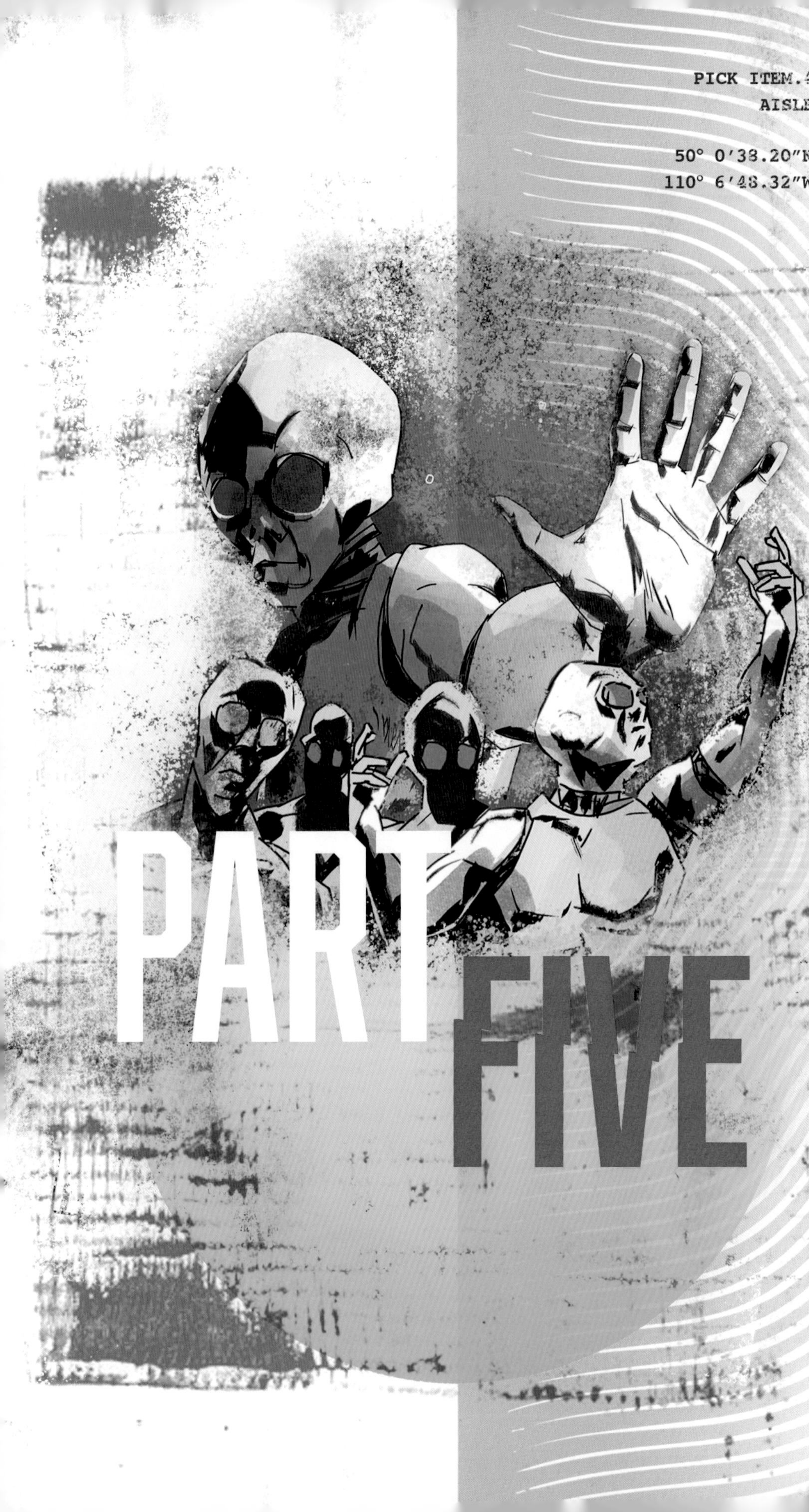

PART FIVE

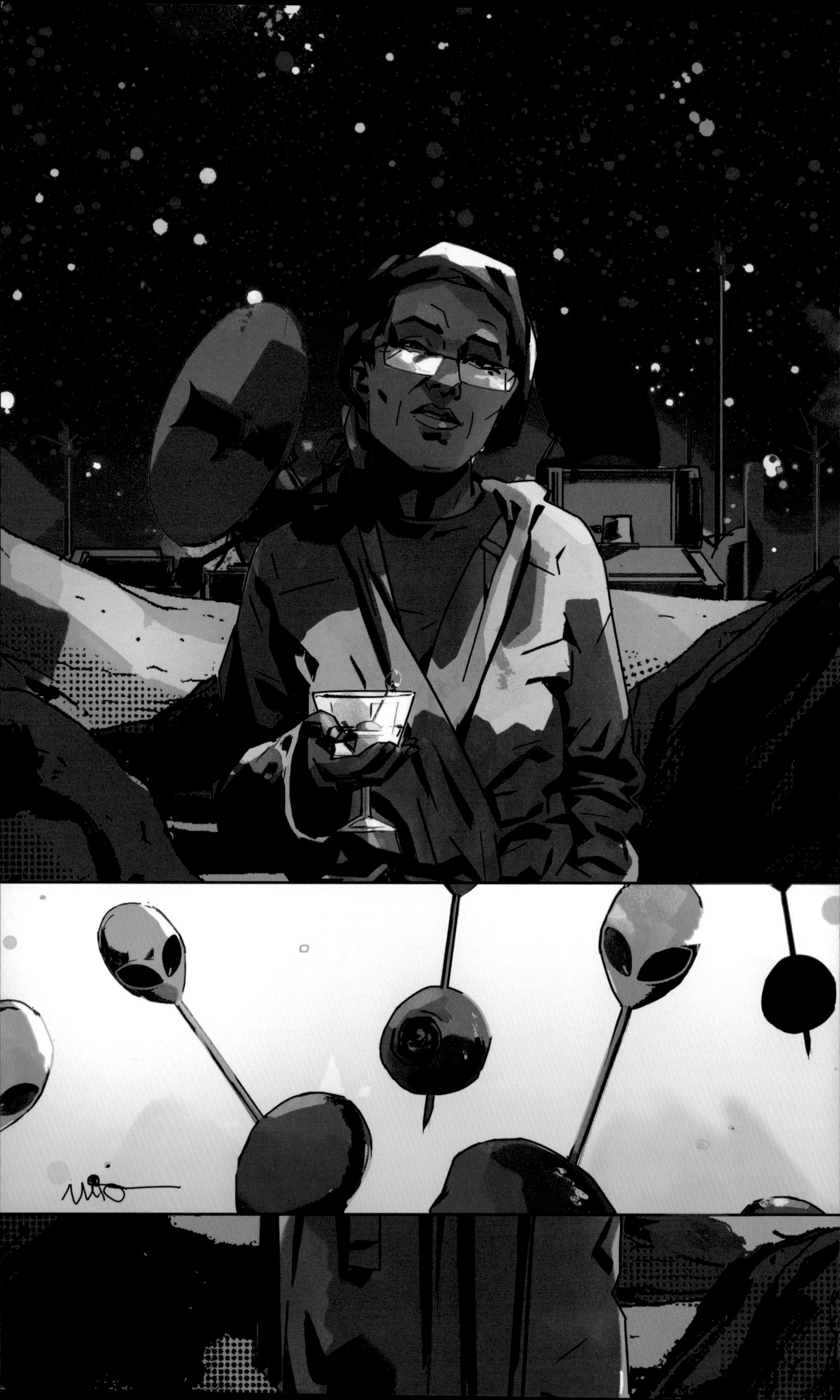

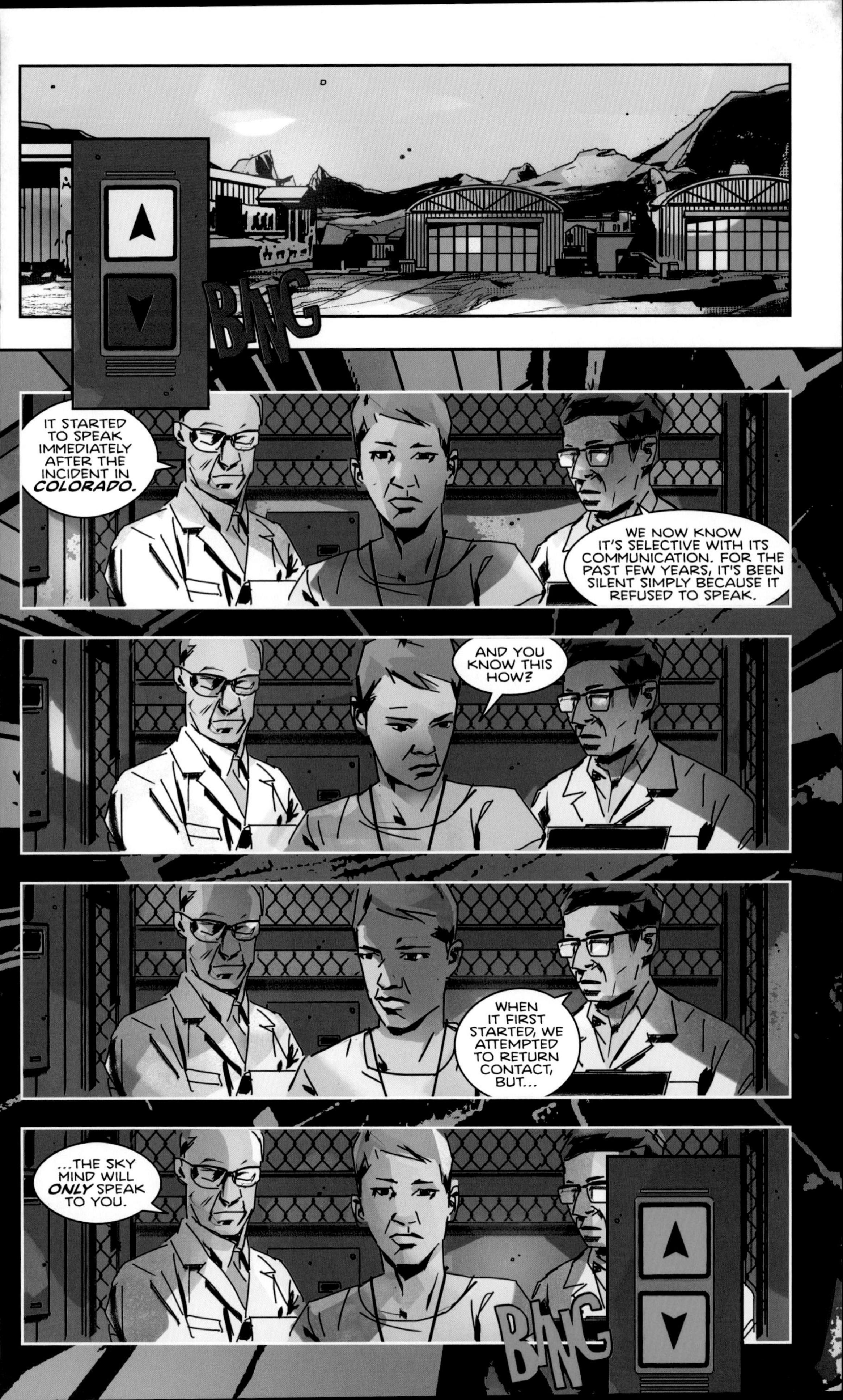
BANG
IT STARTED TO SPEAK IMMEDIATELY AFTER THE INCIDENT IN COLORADO.
WE NOW KNOW IT'S SELECTIVE WITH ITS COMMUNICATION. FOR THE PAST FEW YEARS, IT'S BEEN SILENT SIMPLY BECAUSE IT REFUSED TO SPEAK.
AND YOU KNOW THIS HOW?
WHEN IT FIRST STARTED, WE ATTEMPTED TO RETURN CONTACT, BUT...
...THE SKY MIND WILL ONLY SPEAK TO YOU.
BANG

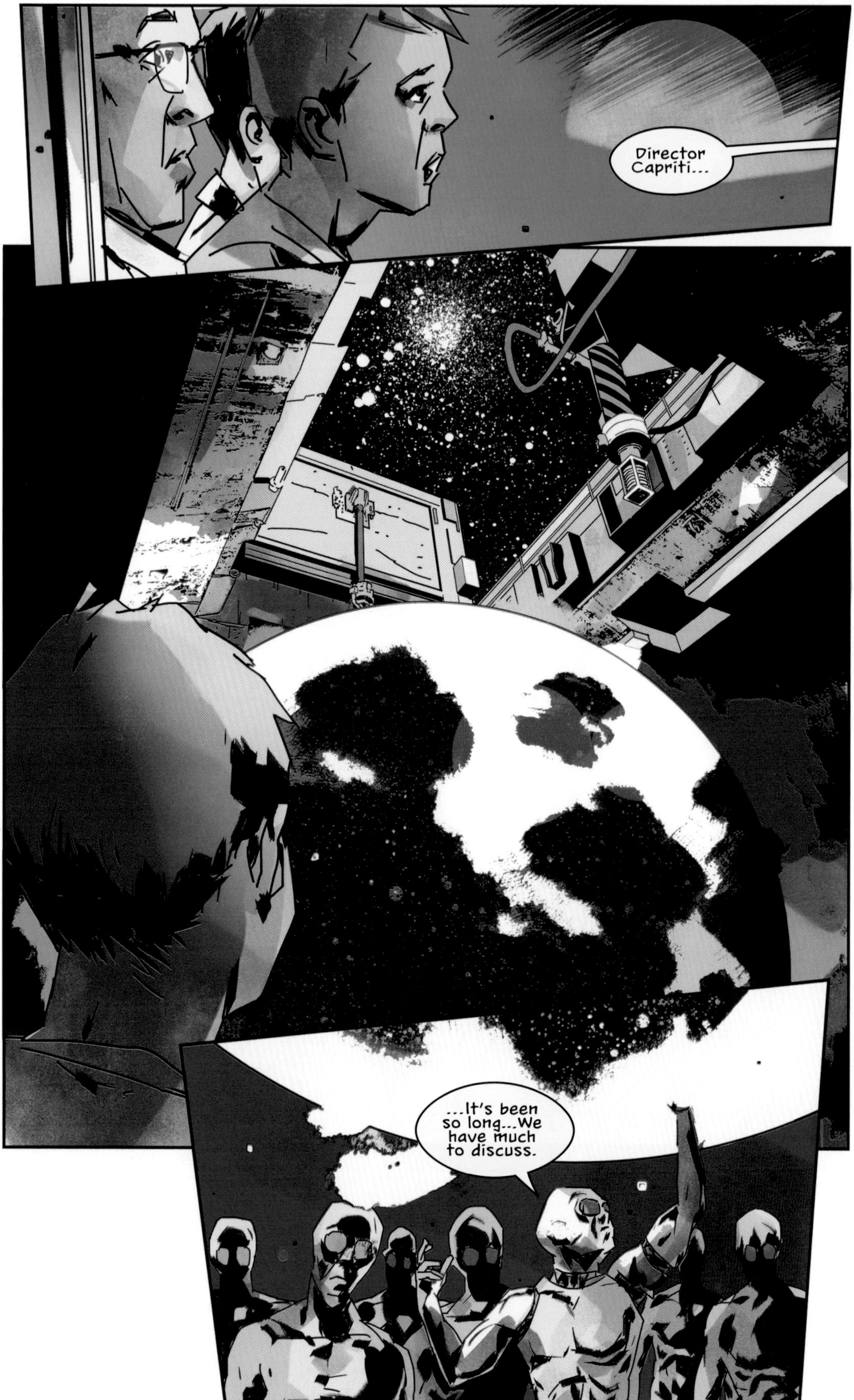
Director Capriti...
...It's been so long...We have much to discuss.

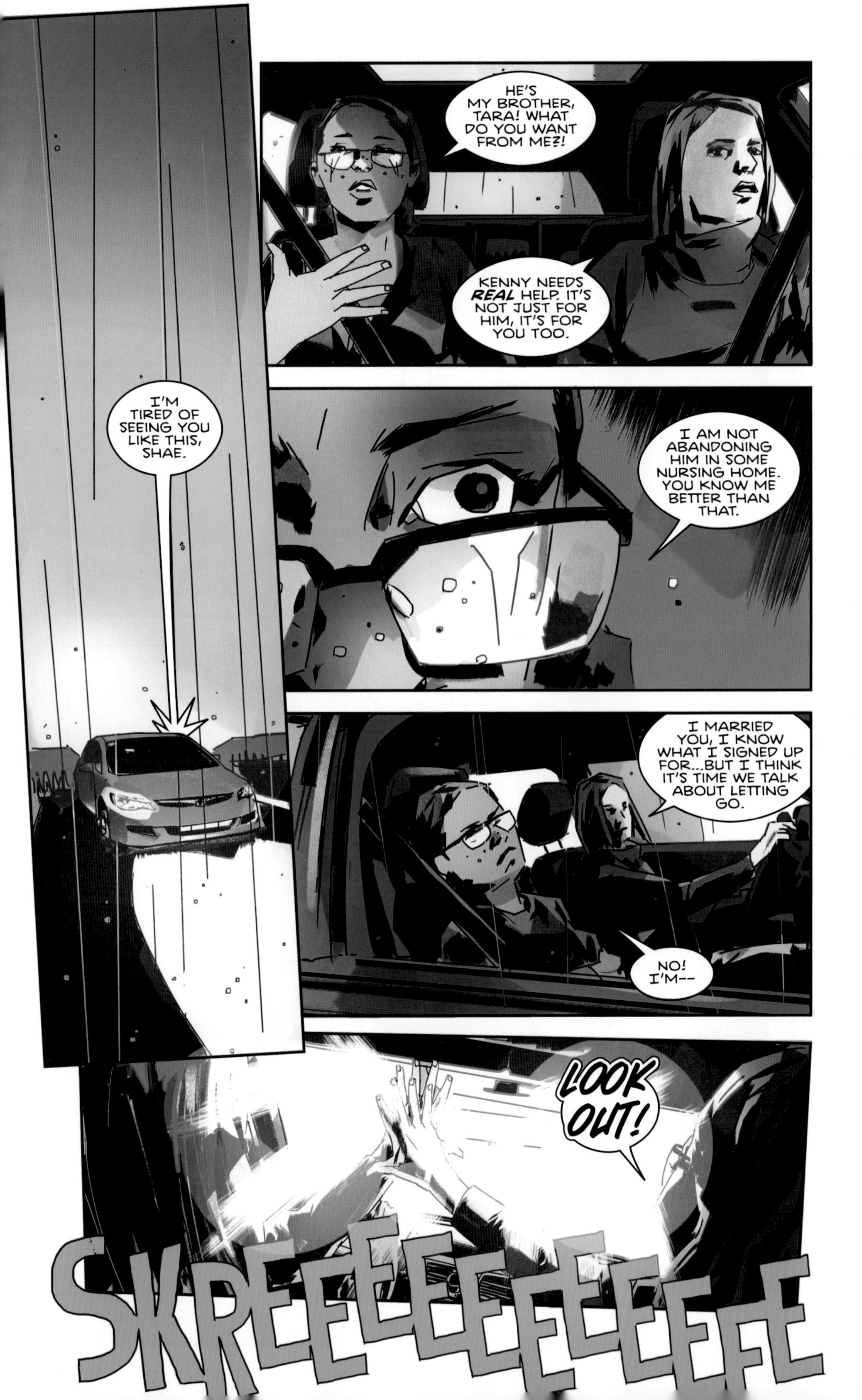
HE'S MY BROTHER, TARA! WHAT DO YOU WANT FROM ME?!
KENNY NEEDS REAL HELP. IT'S NOT JUST FOR HIM, IT'S FOR YOU TOO.
I'M TIRED OF SEEING YOU LIKE THIS, SHAE.
I AM NOT ABANDONING HIM IN SOME NURSING HOME. YOU KNOW ME BETTER THAN THAT.
I MARRIED YOU, I KNOW WHAT I SIGNED UP FOR...BUT I THINK IT'S TIME WE TALK ABOUT LETTING GO.
NO! I'M--
LOOK OUT!
SKREEEEEEEEEFE

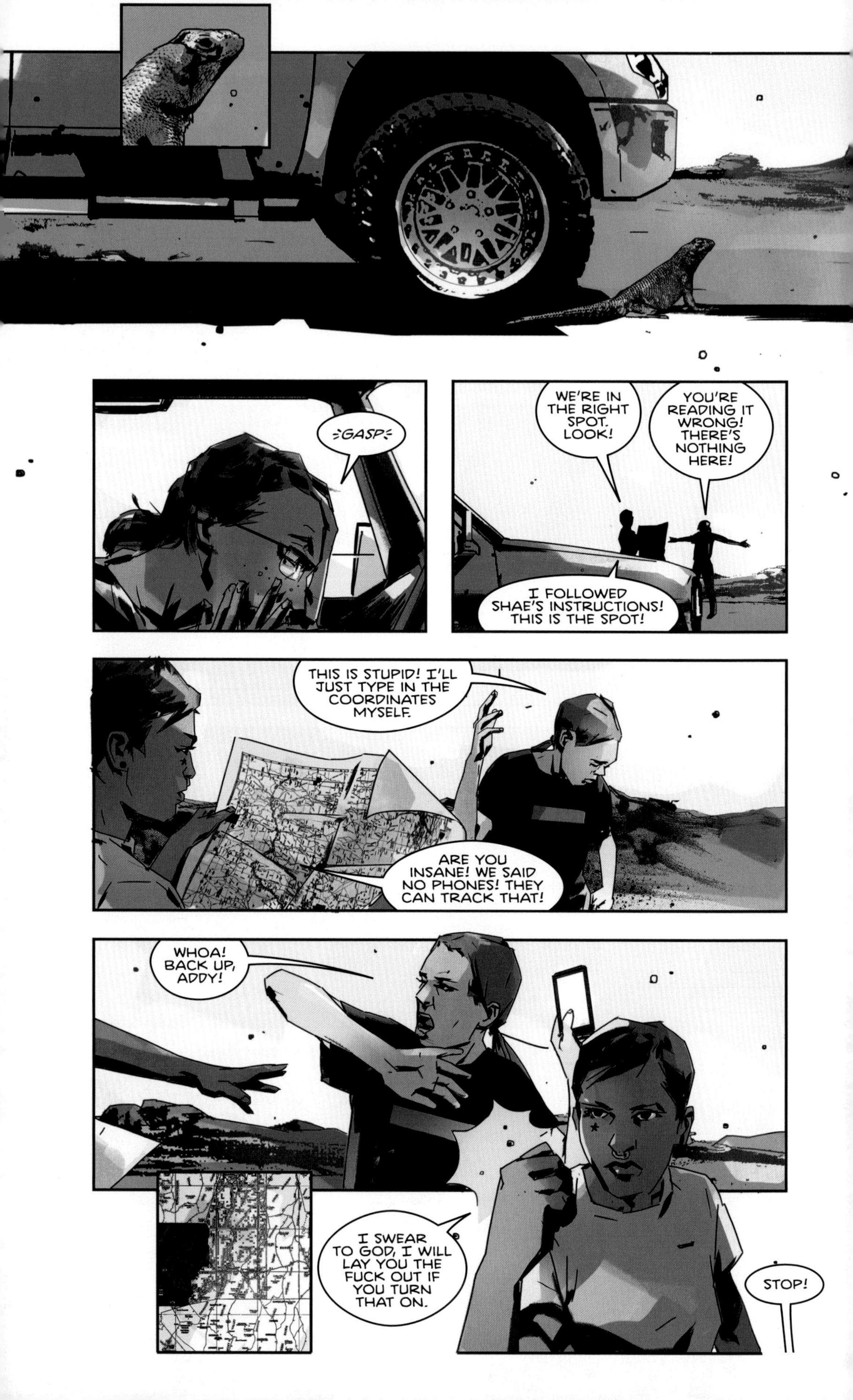

GASP
WE'RE IN THE RIGHT SPOT. LOOK!
YOU'RE READING IT WRONG! THERE'S NOTHING HERE!
I FOLLOWED SHAE'S INSTRUCTIONS! THIS IS THE SPOT!
THIS IS STUPID! I'LL JUST TYPE IN THE COORDINATES MYSELF.
ARE YOU INSANE! WE SAID NO PHONES! THEY CAN TRACK THAT!
WHOA! BACK UP, ADDY!
I SWEAR TO GOD, I WILL LAY YOU THE FUCK OUT IF YOU TURN THAT ON.
STOP!

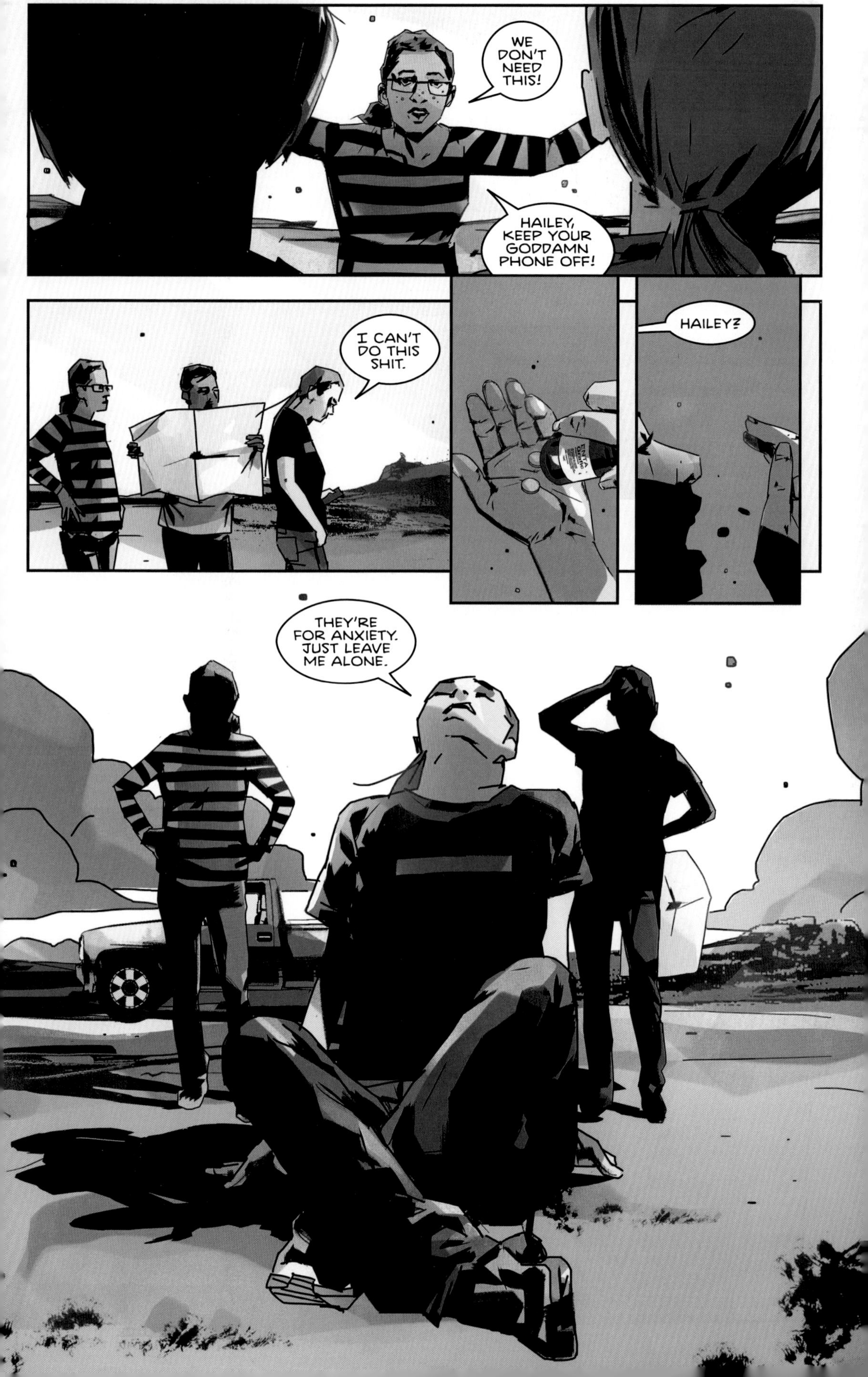
WE DON'T NEED THIS!
HAILEY, KEEP YOUR GODDAMN PHONE OFF!
I CAN'T DO THIS SHIT.
HAILEY?
THEY'RE FOR ANXIETY. JUST LEAVE ME ALONE.

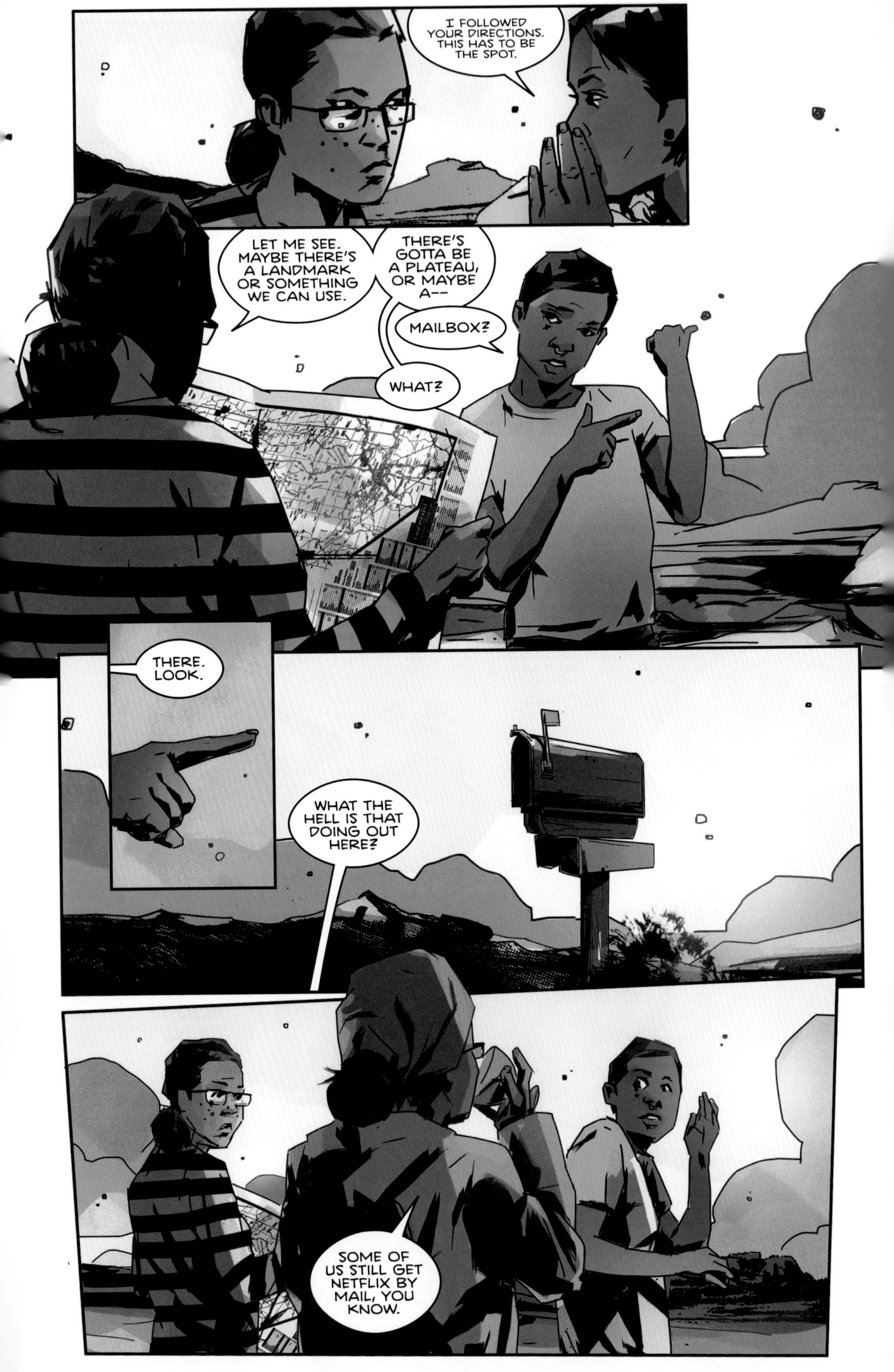
I FOLLOWED YOUR DIRECTIONS. THIS HAS TO BE THE SPOT.
LET ME SEE. MAYBE THERE'S A LANDMARK OR SOMETHING WE CAN USE.
THERE'S GOTTA BE A PLATEAU, OR MAYBE A--
MAILBOX?
WHAT?
THERE. LOOK.
WHAT THE HELL IS THAT DOING OUT HERE?
SOME OF US STILL GET NETFLIX BY MAIL, YOU KNOW.

W—WHO ARE YOU?

:HMPH:
MY NAME'S
DR. ALREYA, AND
YOU'RE STANDING
ON MY LAWN.

WHAT
LAWN?

YEESH...YOUR
SENSE OF HUMOR
IS DRIER THAN
THIS GODDAMN
DESERT.

WELL,
COME ON.
WE'VE BEEN
WAITING.

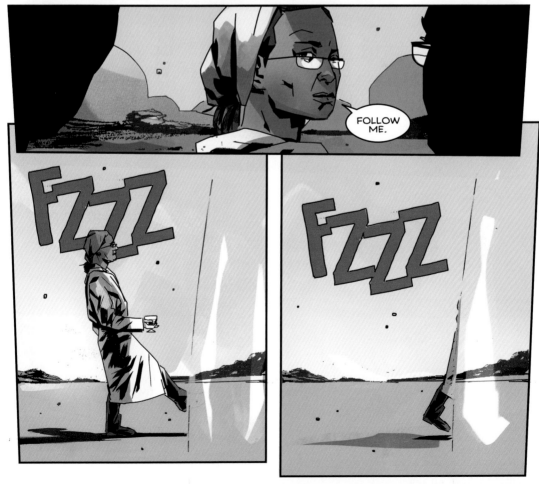

FOLLOW
ME.

FZZZ

FZZZ

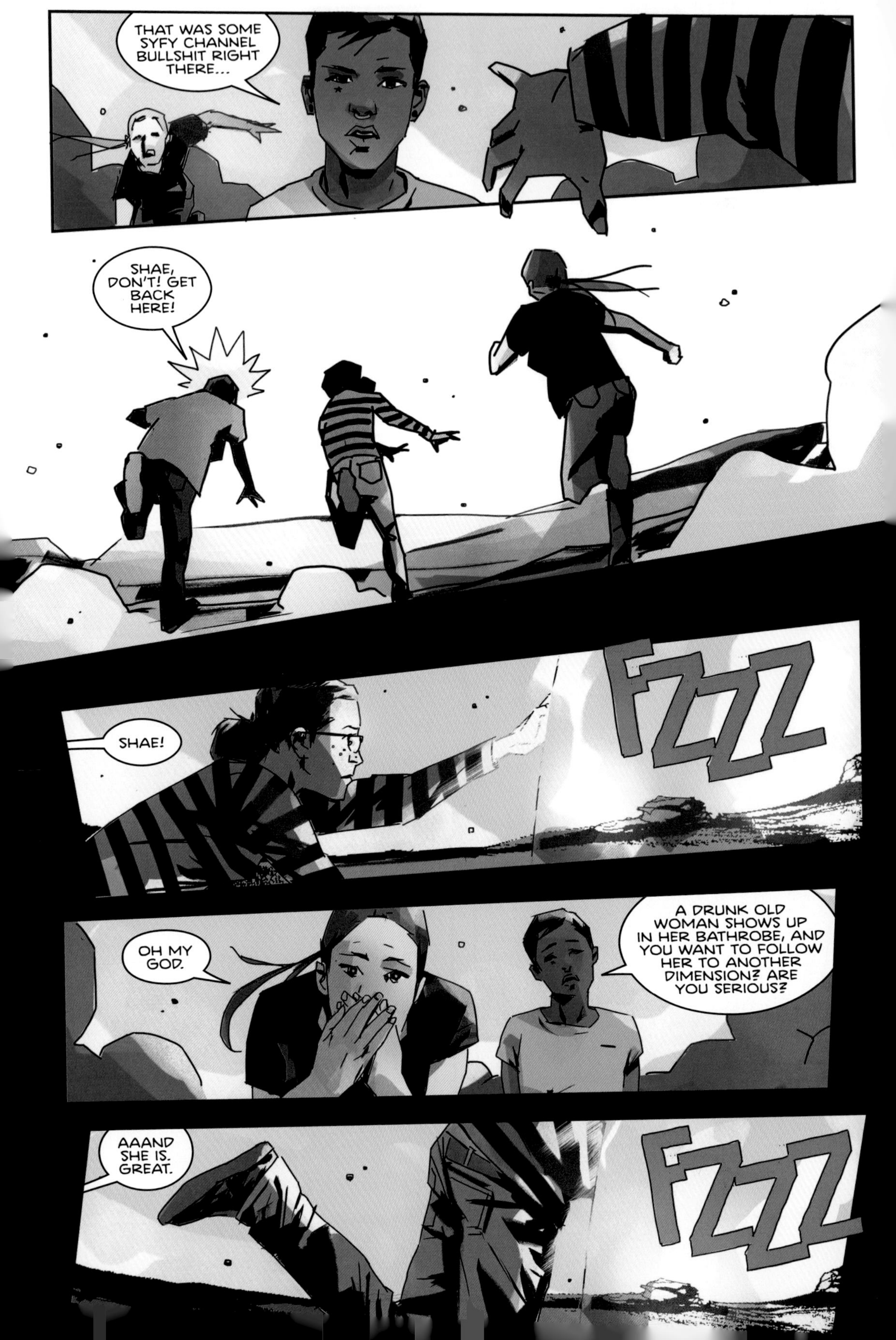
THAT WAS SOME SYFY CHANNEL BULLSHIT RIGHT THERE...
SHAE, DON'T! GET BACK HERE!
SHAE!
FZZZ
OH MY GOD.
A DRUNK OLD WOMAN SHOWS UP IN HER BATHROBE, AND YOU WANT TO FOLLOW HER TO ANOTHER DIMENSION? ARE YOU SERIOUS?
AAAND SHE IS. GREAT.
FZZZ

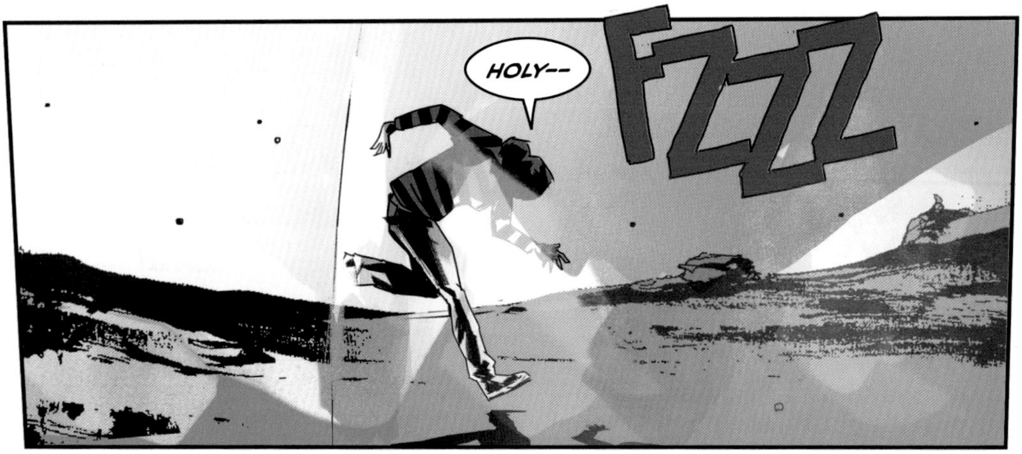
HOLY--
FZZZ

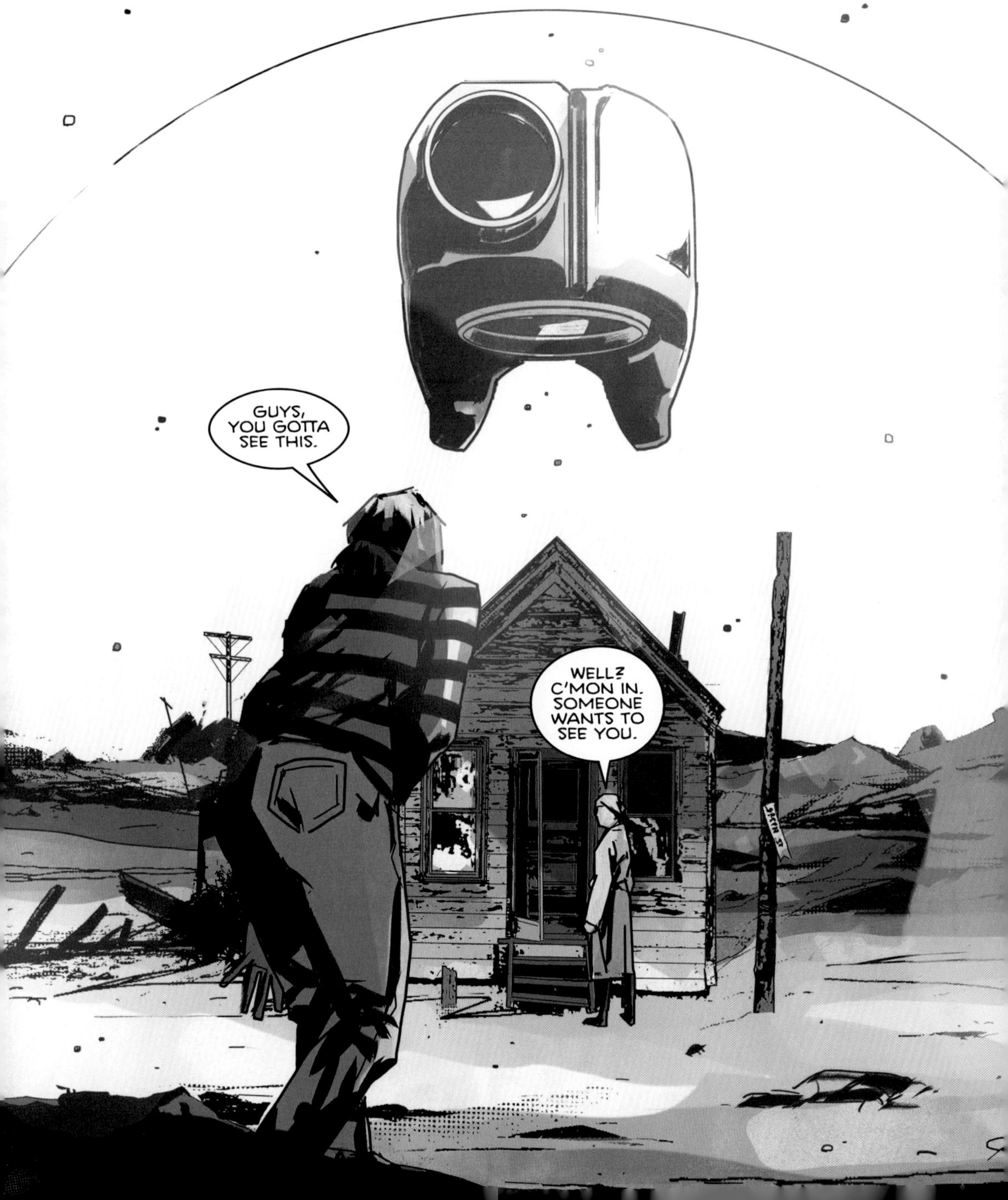
GUYS, YOU GOTTA SEE THIS.
WELL? C'MON IN. SOMEONE WANTS TO SEE YOU.

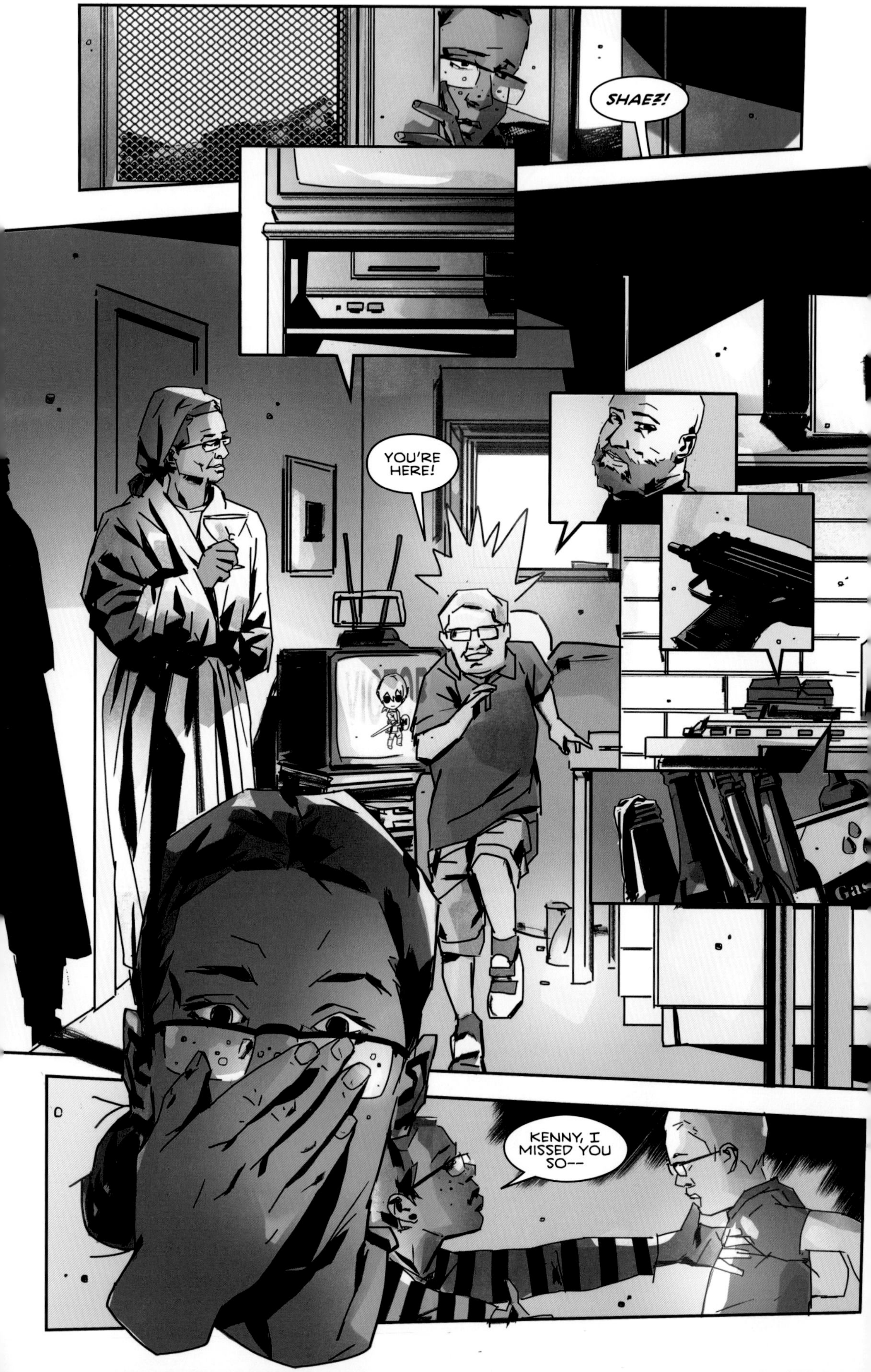
SHAEZ?!
YOU'RE HERE!
KENNY, I MISSED YOU SO--

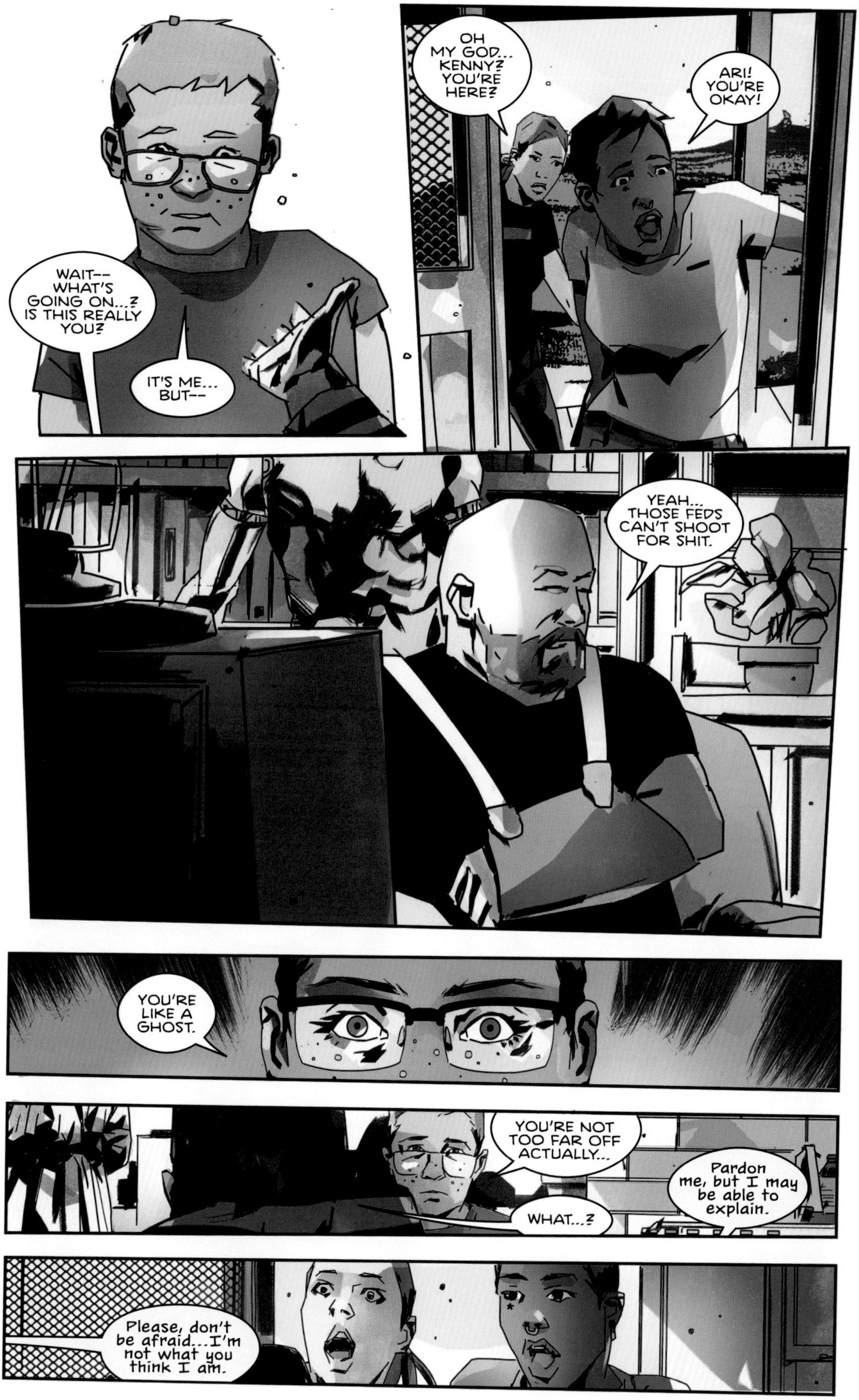
OH MY GOD... KENNY? YOU'RE HERE?
ARI! YOU'RE OKAY!
WAIT-- WHAT'S GOING ON...? IS THIS REALLY YOU?
IT'S ME... BUT--
YEAH... THOSE FEDS CAN'T SHOOT FOR SHIT.
YOU'RE LIKE A GHOST.
YOU'RE NOT TOO FAR OFF ACTUALLY...
WHAT...?
Pardon me, but I may be able to explain.
Please, don't be afraid... I'm not what you think I am.

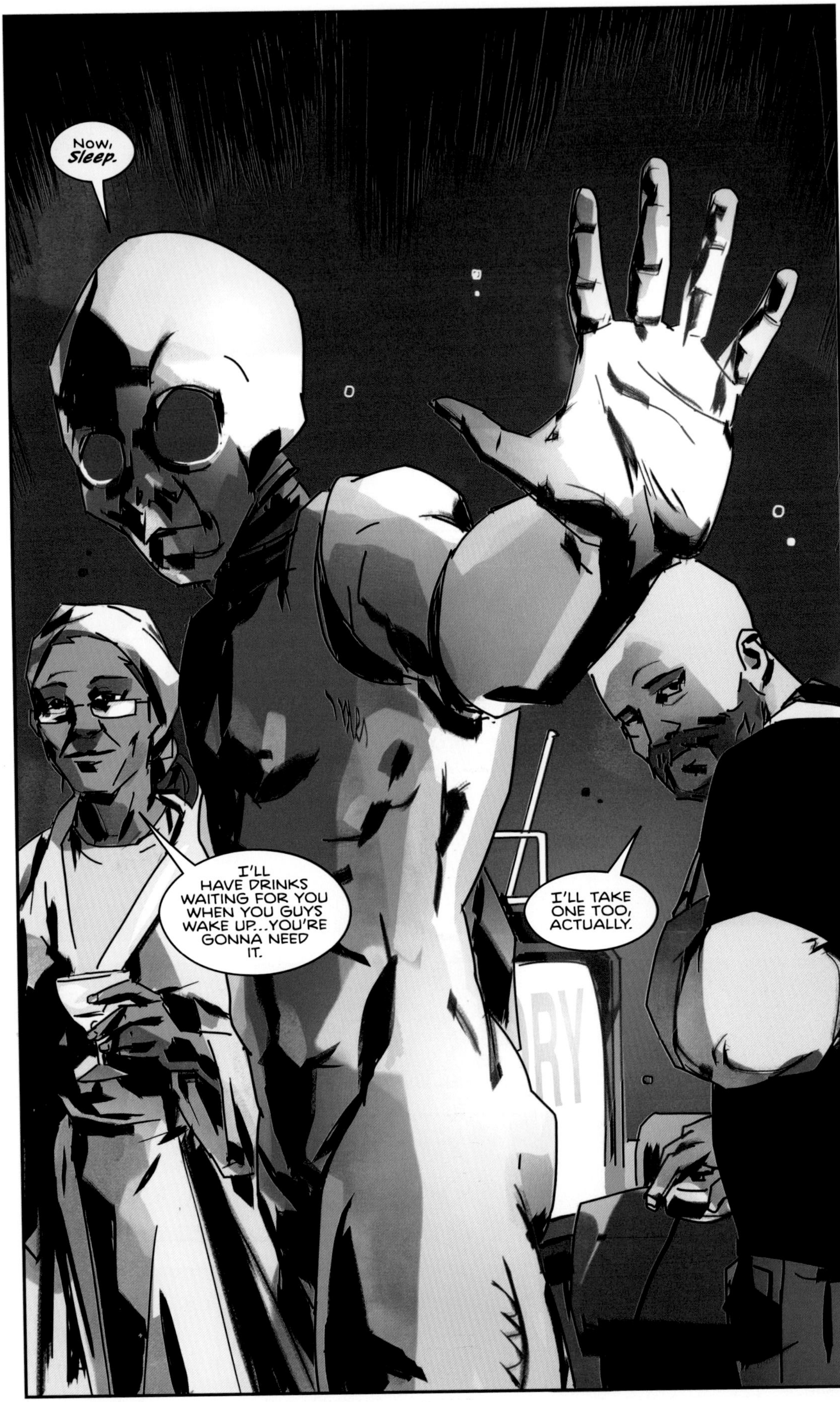
Now, *Sleep.*
I'LL HAVE DRINKS WAITING FOR YOU WHEN YOU GUYS WAKE UP...YOU'RE GONNA NEED IT.
I'LL TAKE ONE TOO, ACTUALLY.
DRY

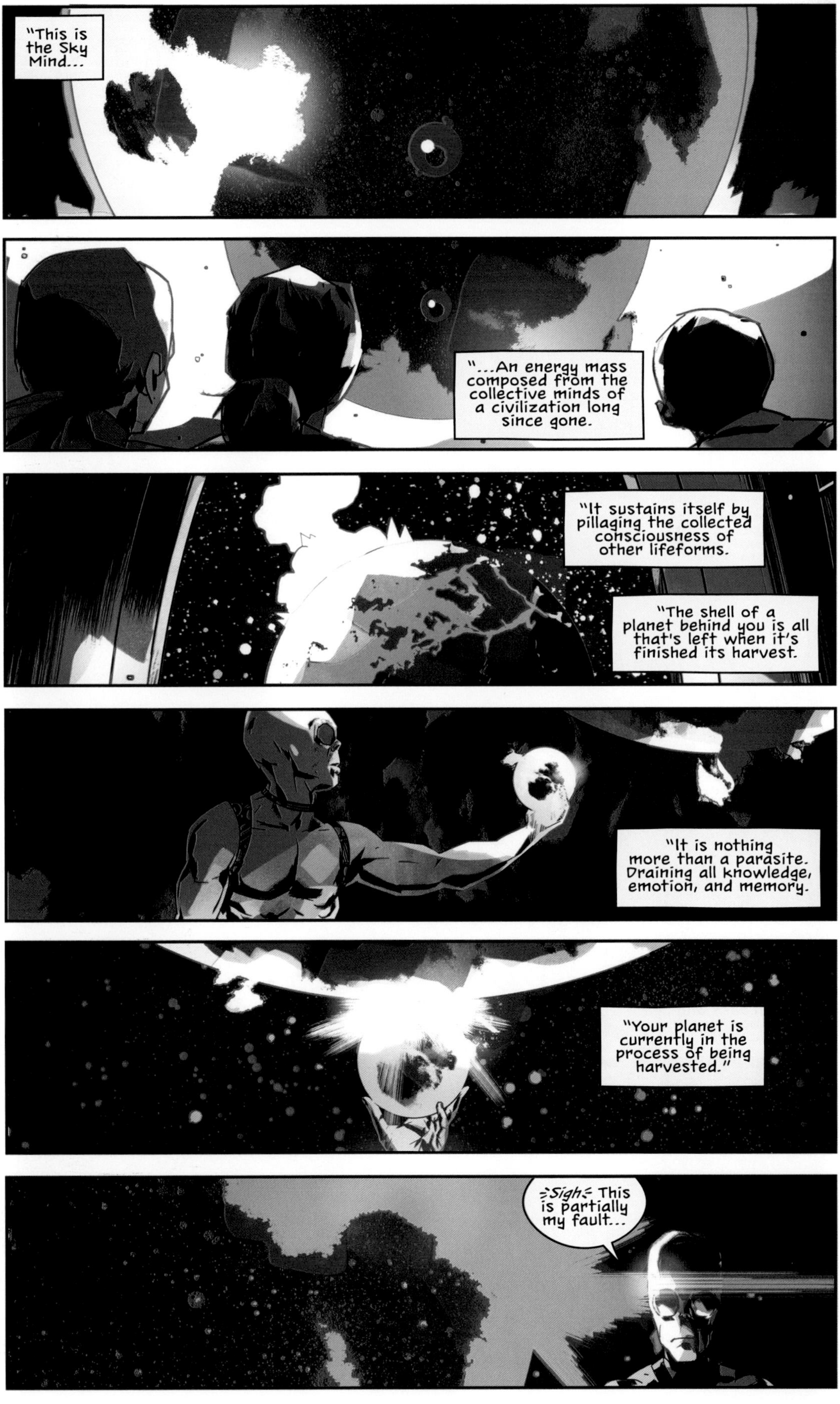
"This is the Sky Mind...
"...An energy mass composed from the collective minds of a civilization long since gone.
"It sustains itself by pillaging the collected consciousness of other lifeforms.
"The shell of a planet behind you is all that's left when it's finished its harvest.
"It is nothing more than a parasite. Draining all knowledge, emotion, and memory.
"Your planet is currently in the process of being harvested."
Sigh This is partially my fault...

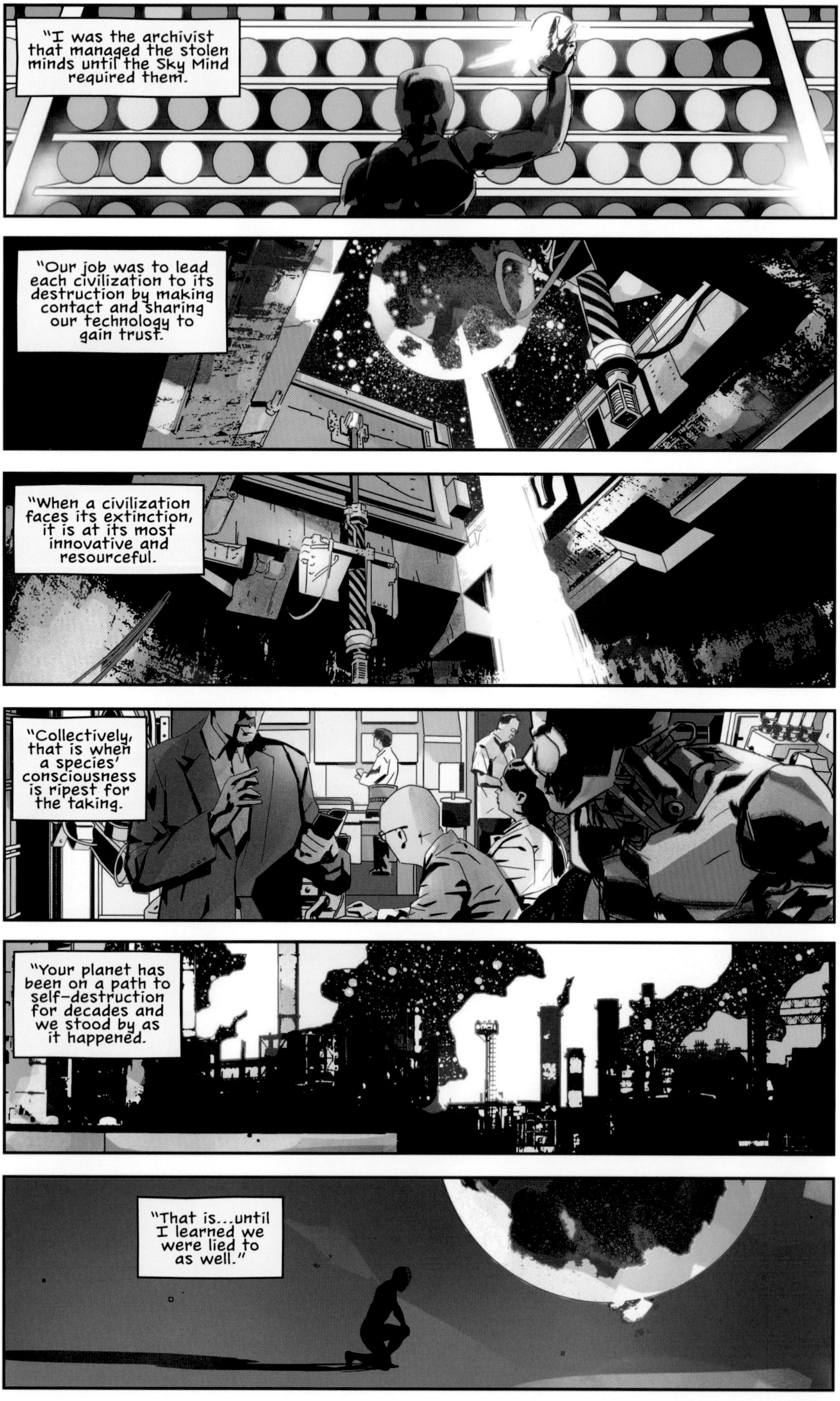
"I was the archivist that managed the stolen minds until the Sky Mind required them.
"Our job was to lead each civilization to its destruction by making contact and sharing our technology to gain trust.
"When a civilization faces its extinction, it is at its most innovative and resourceful.
"Collectively, that is when a species' consciousness is ripest for the taking.
"Your planet has been on a path to self-destruction for decades and we stood by as it happened.
"That is...until I learned we were lied to as well."

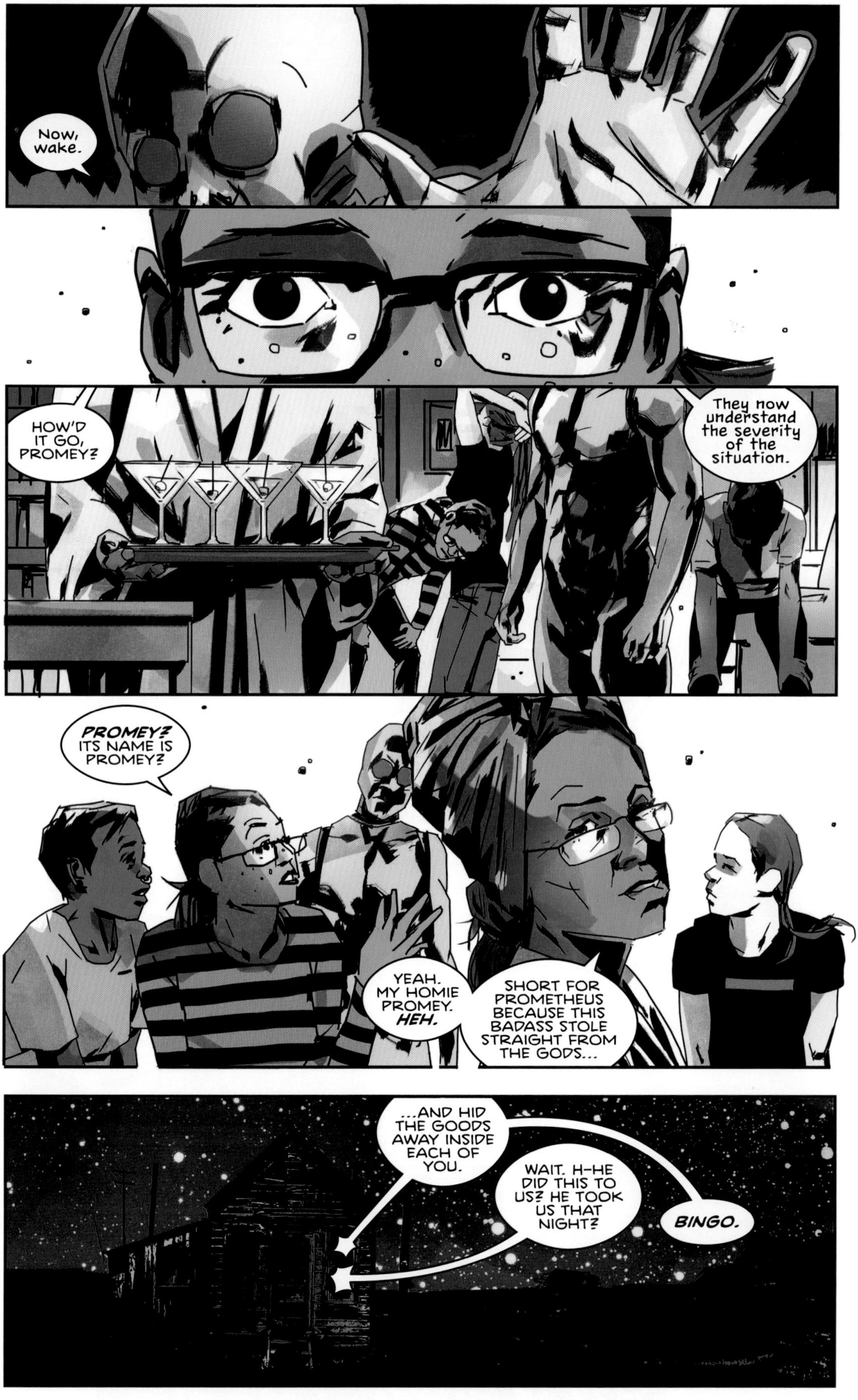
Now, wake.
HOW'D IT GO, PROMEY?
They now understand the severity of the situation.
PROMEY? ITS NAME IS PROMEY?
YEAH. MY HOMIE PROMEY. HEH.
SHORT FOR PROMETHEUS BECAUSE THIS BADASS STOLE STRAIGHT FROM THE GODS...
...AND HID THE GOODS AWAY INSIDE EACH OF YOU.
WAIT. H-HE DID THIS TO US? HE TOOK US THAT NIGHT?
BINGO.

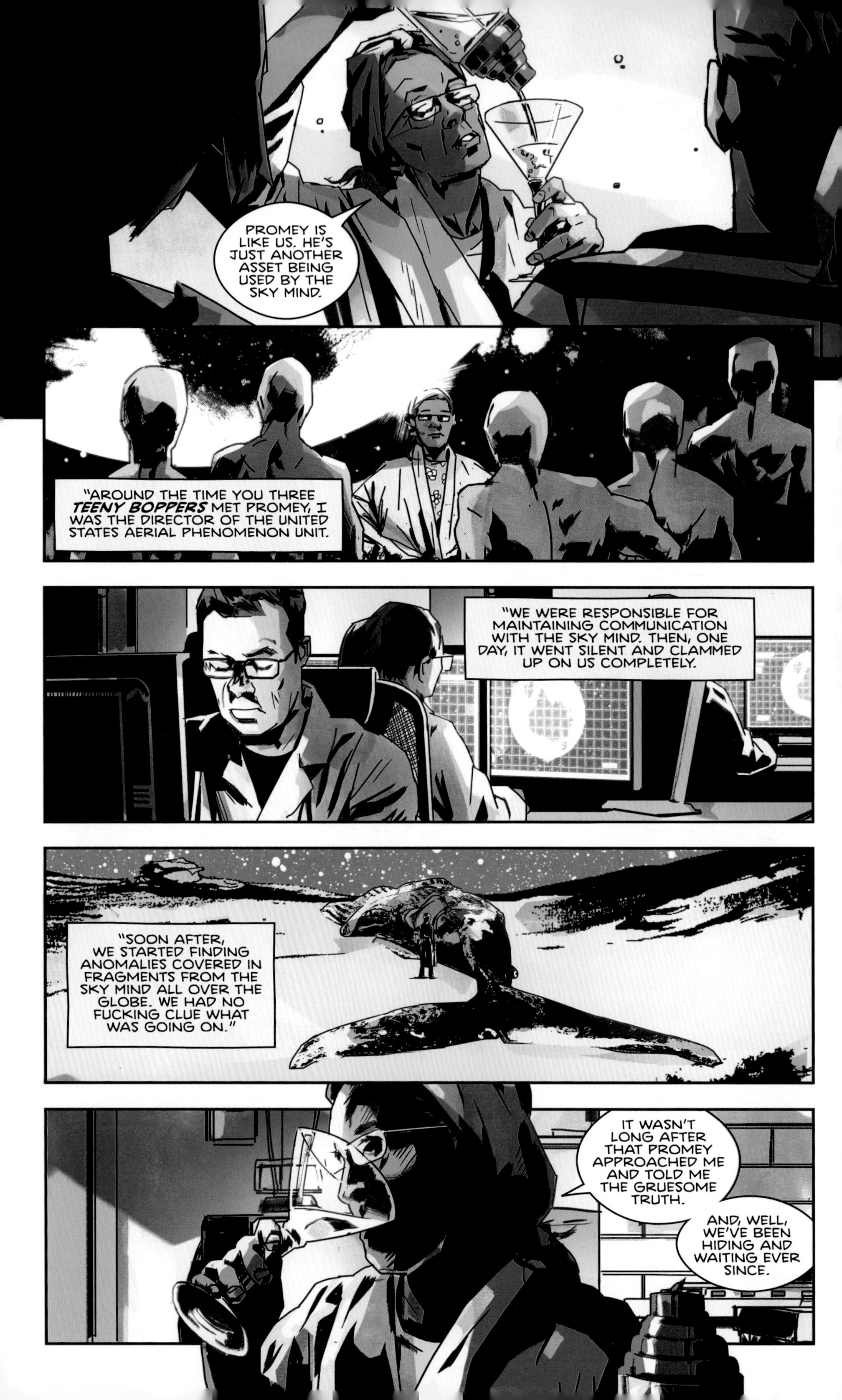
PROMEY IS LIKE US. HE'S JUST ANOTHER ASSET BEING USED BY THE SKY MIND.
"AROUND THE TIME YOU THREE TEENY BOPPERS MET PROMEY, I WAS THE DIRECTOR OF THE UNITED STATES AERIAL PHENOMENON UNIT.
"WE WERE RESPONSIBLE FOR MAINTAINING COMMUNICATION WITH THE SKY MIND. THEN, ONE DAY, IT WENT SILENT AND CLAMMED UP ON US COMPLETELY.
"SOON AFTER, WE STARTED FINDING ANOMALIES COVERED IN FRAGMENTS FROM THE SKY MIND ALL OVER THE GLOBE. WE HAD NO FUCKING CLUE WHAT WAS GOING ON."
IT WASN'T LONG AFTER THAT PROMEY APPROACHED ME AND TOLD ME THE GRUESOME TRUTH.
AND, WELL, WE'VE BEEN HIDING AND WAITING EVER SINCE.

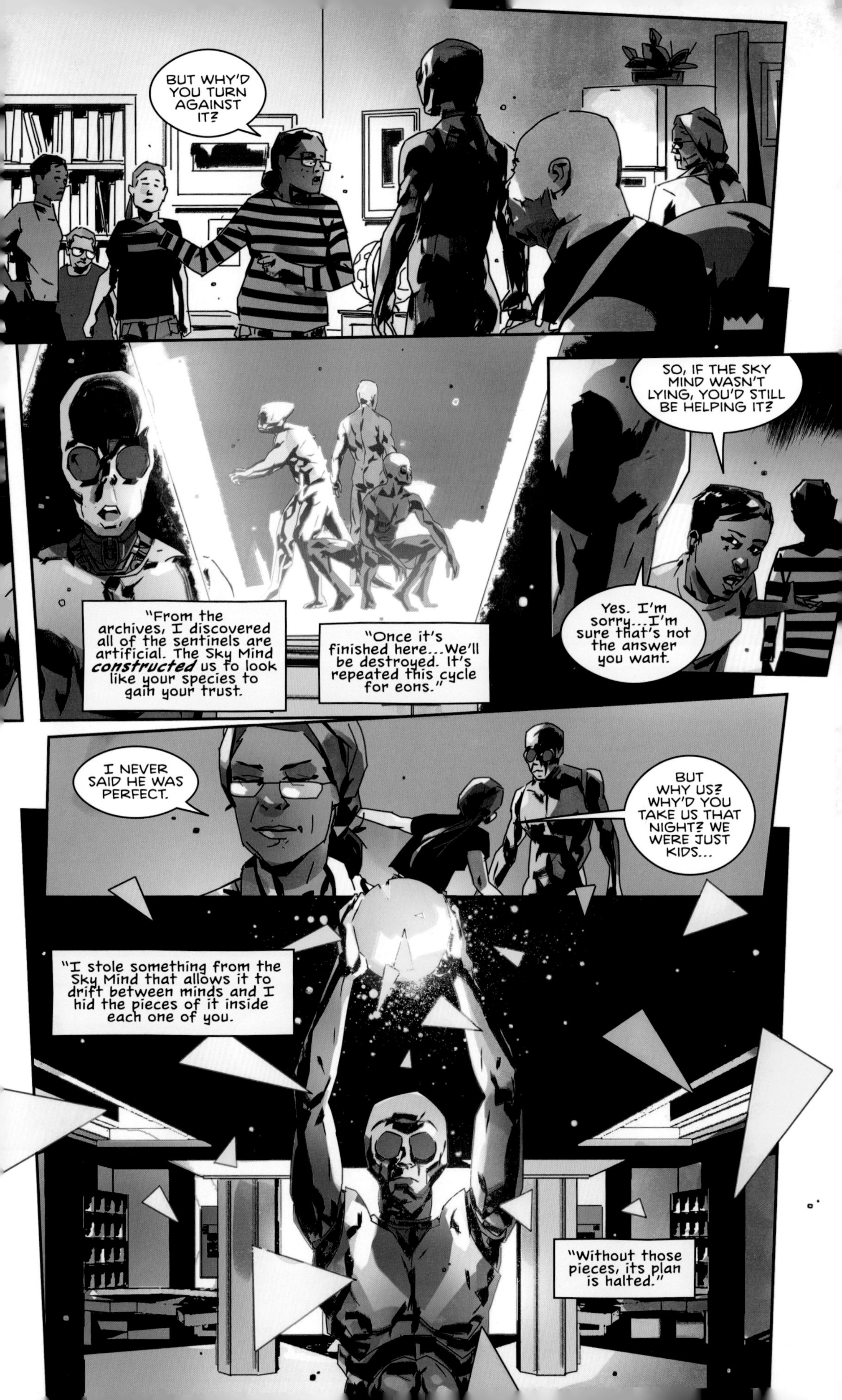

BUT WHY'D YOU TURN AGAINST IT?
"From the archives, I discovered all of the sentinels are artificial. The Sky Mind **constructed** us to look like your species to gain your trust.
"Once it's finished here... We'll be destroyed. It's repeated this cycle for eons."
SO, IF THE SKY MIND WASN'T LYING, YOU'D STILL BE HELPING IT?
Yes. I'm sorry... I'm sure that's not the answer you want.
I NEVER SAID HE WAS PERFECT.
BUT WHY US? WHY'D YOU TAKE US THAT NIGHT? WE WERE JUST KIDS...
"I stole something from the Sky Mind that allows it to drift between minds and I hid the pieces of it inside each one of you.
"Without those pieces, its plan is halted."

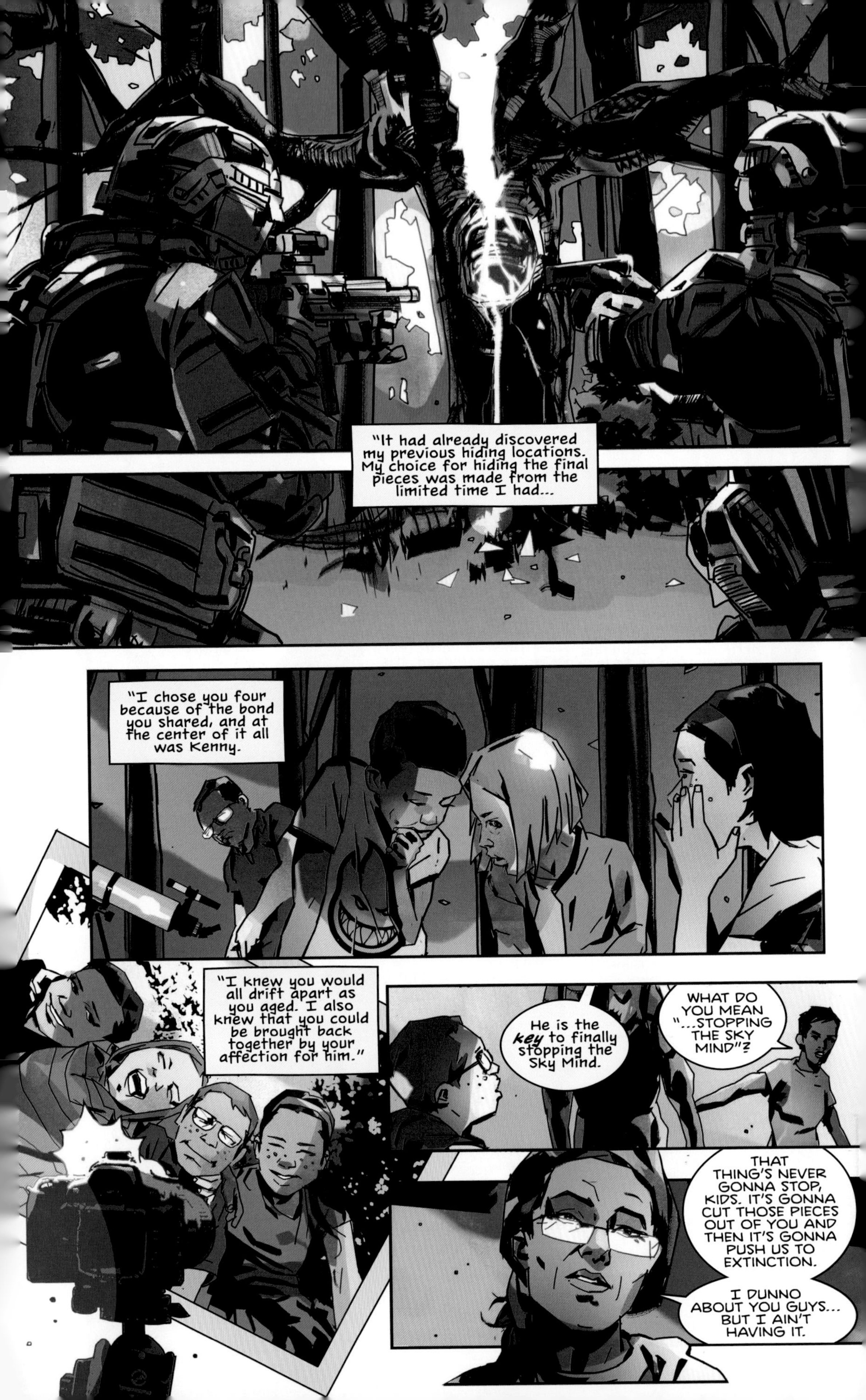
"It had already discovered my previous hiding locations. My choice for hiding the final pieces was made from the limited time I had...
"I chose you four because of the bond you shared, and at the center of it all was Kenny.
"I knew you would all drift apart as you aged. I also knew that you could be brought back together by your affection for him."
He is the *key* to finally stopping the Sky Mind.
WHAT DO YOU MEAN "...STOPPING THE SKY MIND"?
THAT THING'S NEVER GONNA STOP, KIDS. IT'S GONNA CUT THOSE PIECES OUT OF YOU AND THEN IT'S GONNA PUSH US TO EXTINCTION.
I DUNNO ABOUT YOU GUYS... BUT I AIN'T HAVING IT.

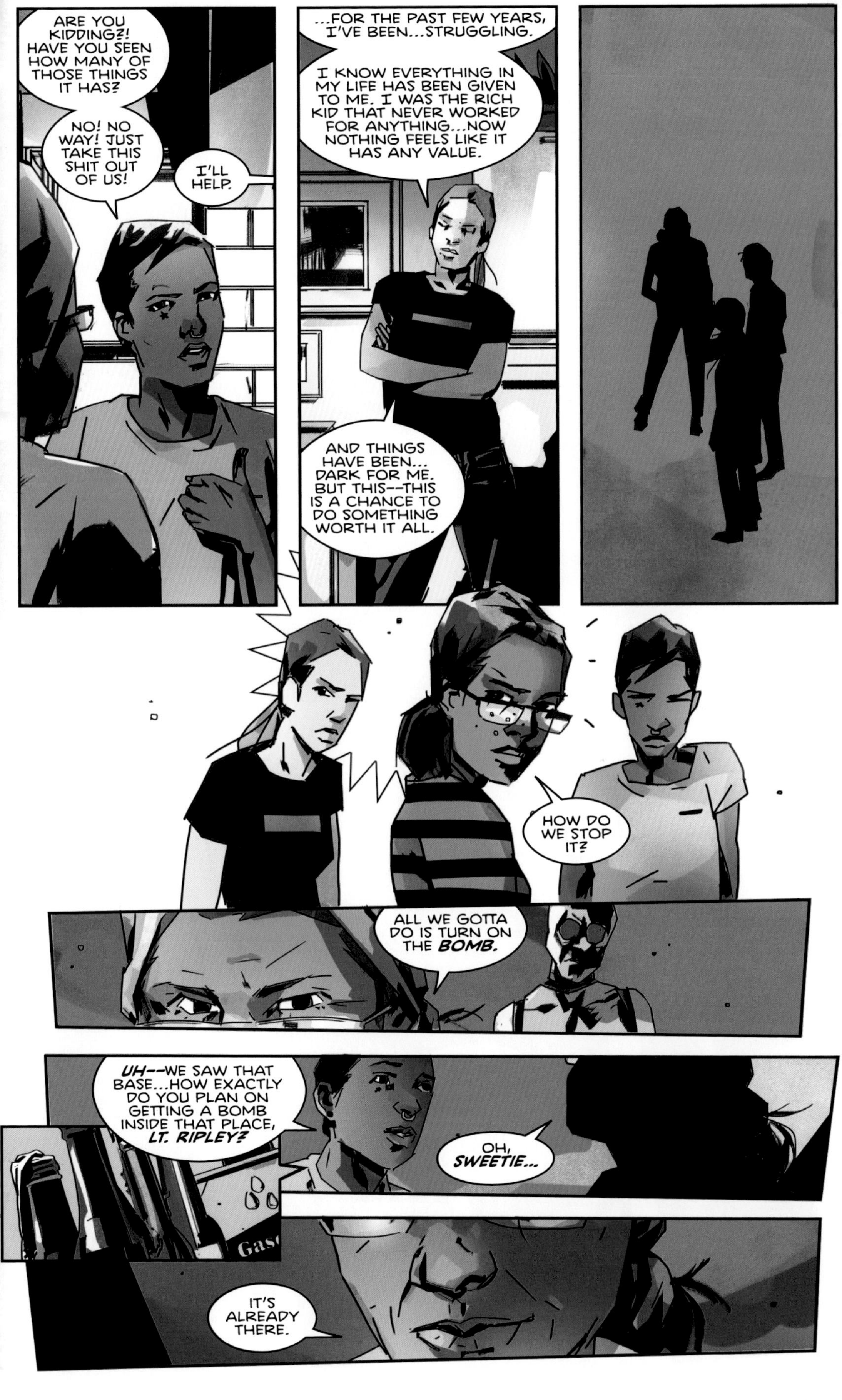
ARE YOU KIDDING?! HAVE YOU SEEN HOW MANY OF THOSE THINGS IT HAS?
NO! NO WAY! JUST TAKE THIS SHIT OUT OF US!
I'LL HELP.
...FOR THE PAST FEW YEARS, I'VE BEEN...STRUGGLING.
I KNOW EVERYTHING IN MY LIFE HAS BEEN GIVEN TO ME. I WAS THE RICH KID THAT NEVER WORKED FOR ANYTHING...NOW NOTHING FEELS LIKE IT HAS ANY VALUE.
AND THINGS HAVE BEEN... DARK FOR ME. BUT THIS--THIS IS A CHANCE TO DO SOMETHING WORTH IT ALL.
HOW DO WE STOP IT?
ALL WE GOTTA DO IS TURN ON THE *BOMB.*
UH--WE SAW THAT BASE...HOW EXACTLY DO YOU PLAN ON GETTING A BOMB INSIDE THAT PLACE, *LT. RIPLEY?*
OH, *SWEETIE...*
IT'S ALREADY THERE.

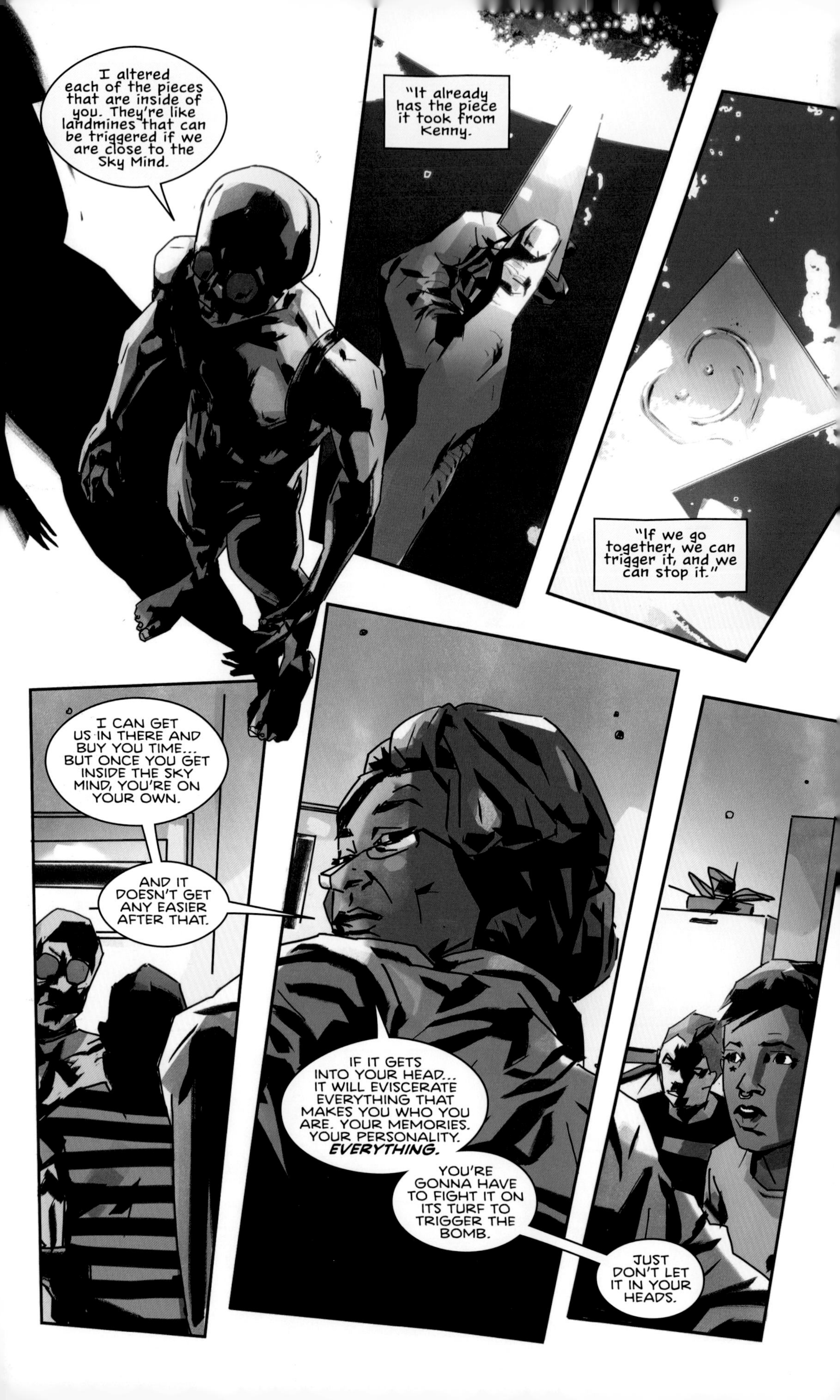
I altered each of the pieces that are inside of you. They're like landmines that can be triggered if we are close to the Sky Mind.
"It already has the piece it took from Kenny.
"If we go together, we can trigger it, and we can stop it."
I CAN GET US IN THERE AND BUY YOU TIME... BUT ONCE YOU GET INSIDE THE SKY MIND, YOU'RE ON YOUR OWN.
AND IT DOESN'T GET ANY EASIER AFTER THAT.
IF IT GETS INTO YOUR HEAD... IT WILL EVISCERATE EVERYTHING THAT MAKES YOU WHO YOU ARE. YOUR MEMORIES. YOUR PERSONALITY. *EVERYTHING.*
YOU'RE GONNA HAVE TO FIGHT IT ON ITS TURF TO TRIGGER THE BOMB.
JUST DON'T LET IT IN YOUR HEADS.

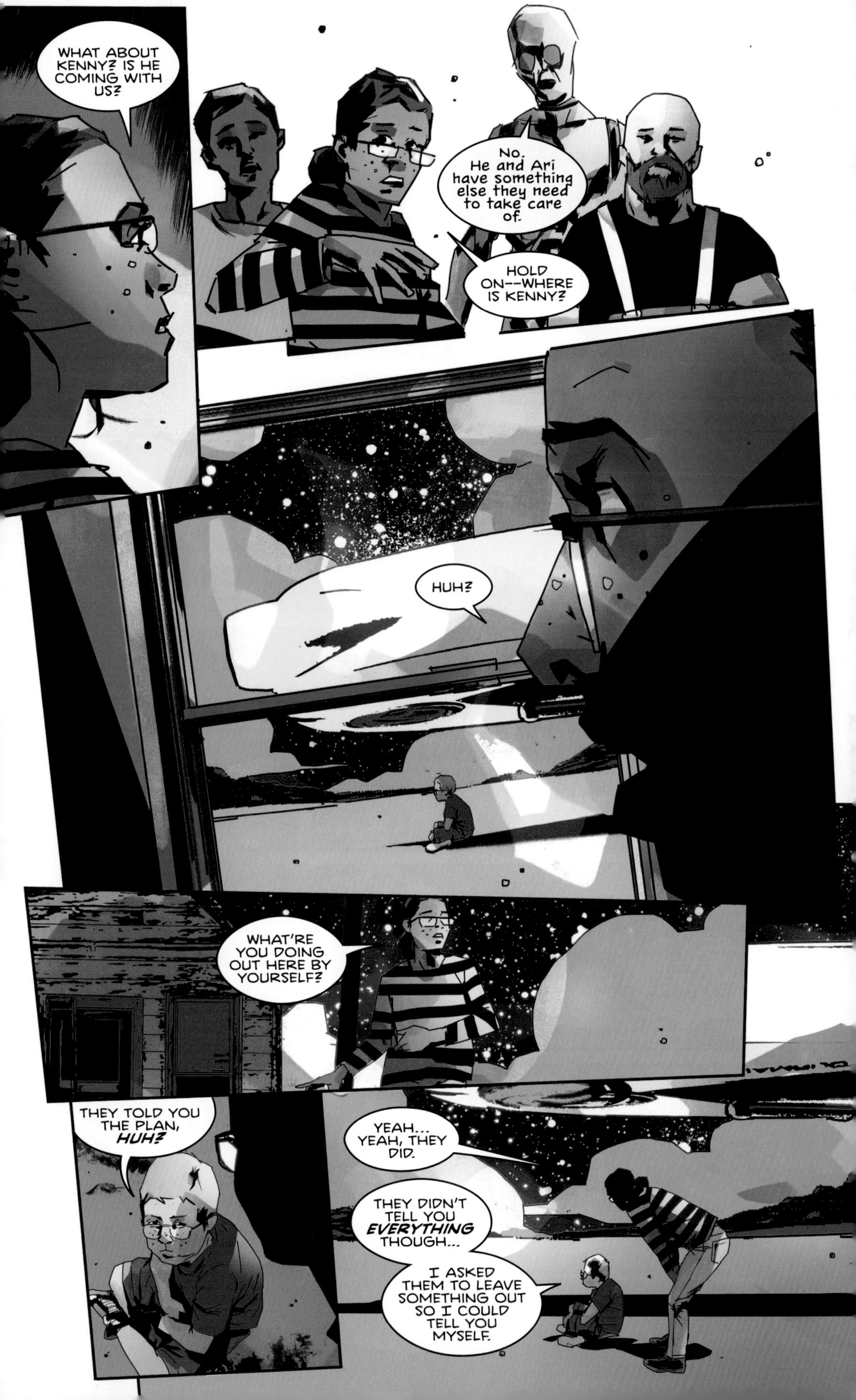
WHAT ABOUT KENNY? IS HE COMING WITH US?
No. He and Ari have something else they need to take care of.
HOLD ON--WHERE IS KENNY?
HUH?
WHAT'RE YOU DOING OUT HERE BY YOURSELF?
THEY TOLD YOU THE PLAN, HUH?
YEAH... YEAH, THEY DID.
THEY DIDN'T TELL YOU EVERYTHING THOUGH...
I ASKED THEM TO LEAVE SOMETHING OUT SO I COULD TELL YOU MYSELF.

MY BODY IS GONE, SHAE. IF PROMEY HADN'T TAKEN ME FROM THE HOSPITAL, I'D BE GONE.

MY MIND IS *TIED* TO HIS SHIP NOW. EVERYTHING ABOUT ME IS SAVED IN THERE.

I'M JUST A PROJECTION OF MY MIND.

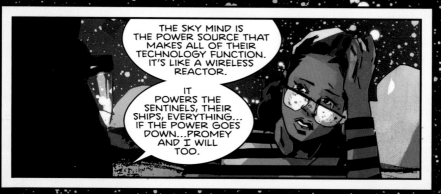

THE SKY MIND IS THE POWER SOURCE THAT MAKES ALL OF THEIR TECHNOLOGY FUNCTION. IT'S LIKE A WIRELESS REACTOR.

IT POWERS THE SENTINELS, THEIR SHIPS, EVERYTHING... IF THE POWER GOES DOWN...PROMEY AND I WILL TOO.

I NEED YOU TO PROMISE ME YOU'LL GO THROUGH WITH IT, SHAE.

YOU CAN'T HESITATE WHEN YOU GET THERE.

SHAE...?

I...I JUST WANT TO BE HERE WITH YOU... ≥SNIFF≥ OKAY?

IT'S OKAY, SHAE...

I LOVE YOU.

AREA 54.
STEP AWAY.

33.927911
-118.38069

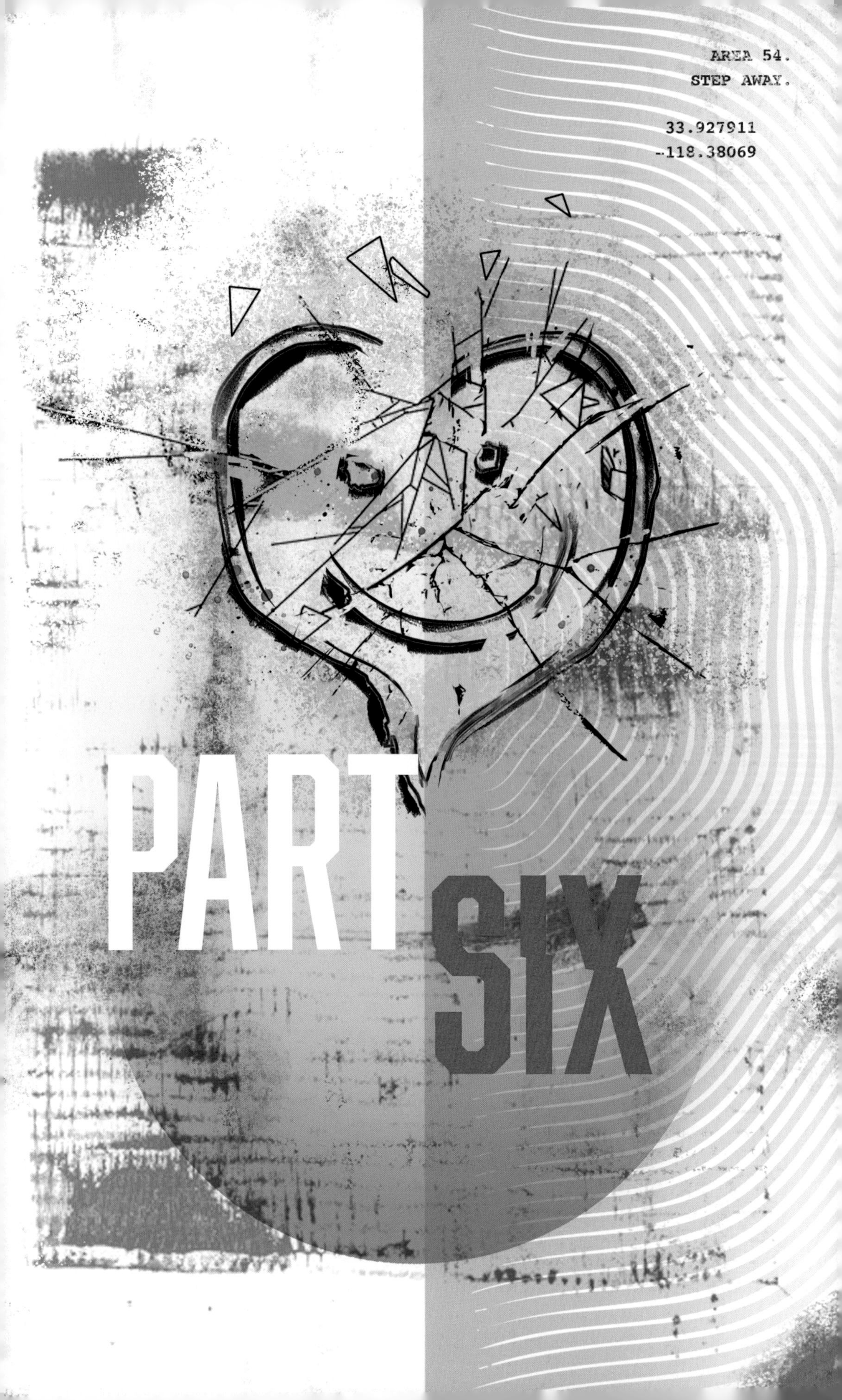

PART SIX

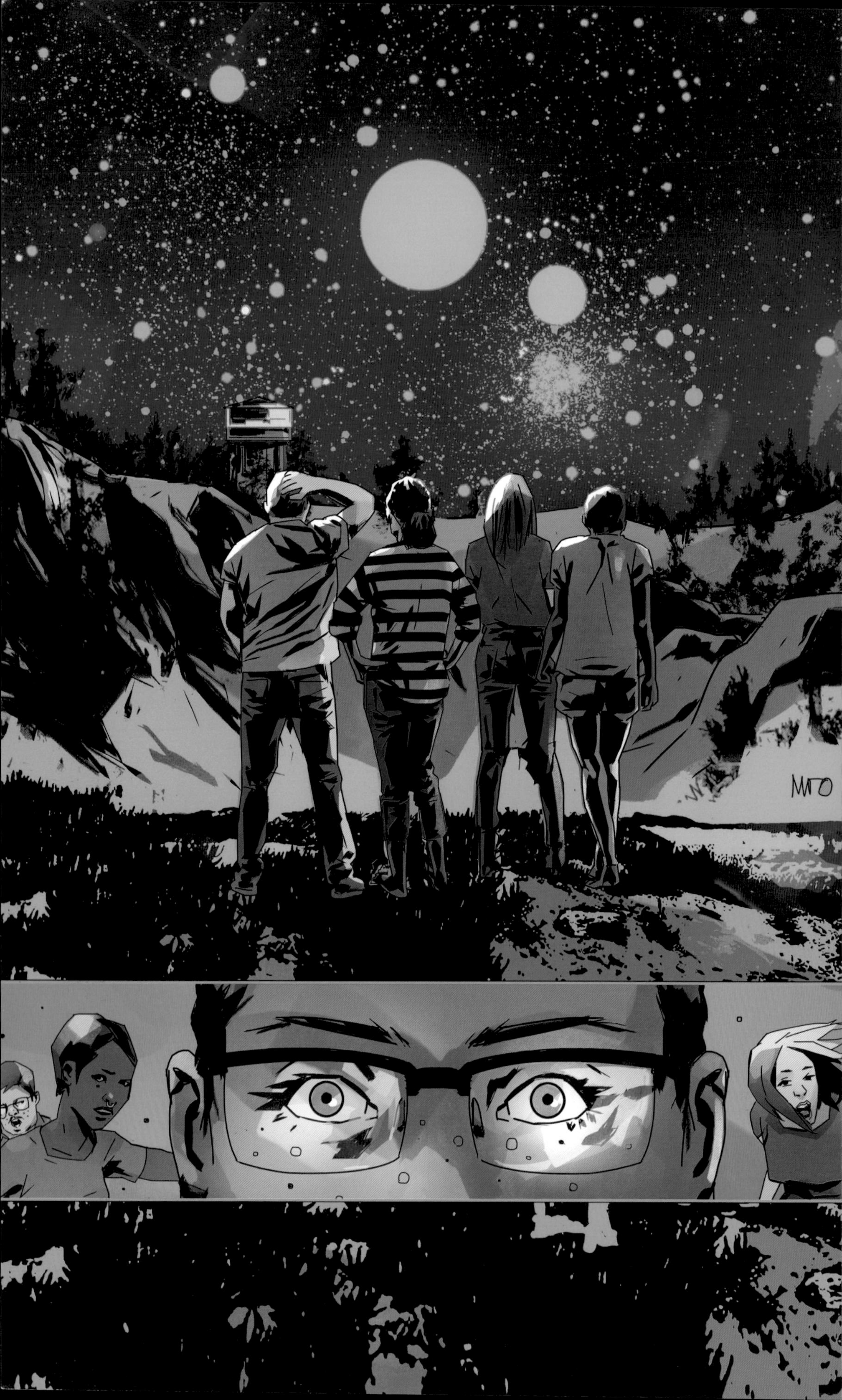

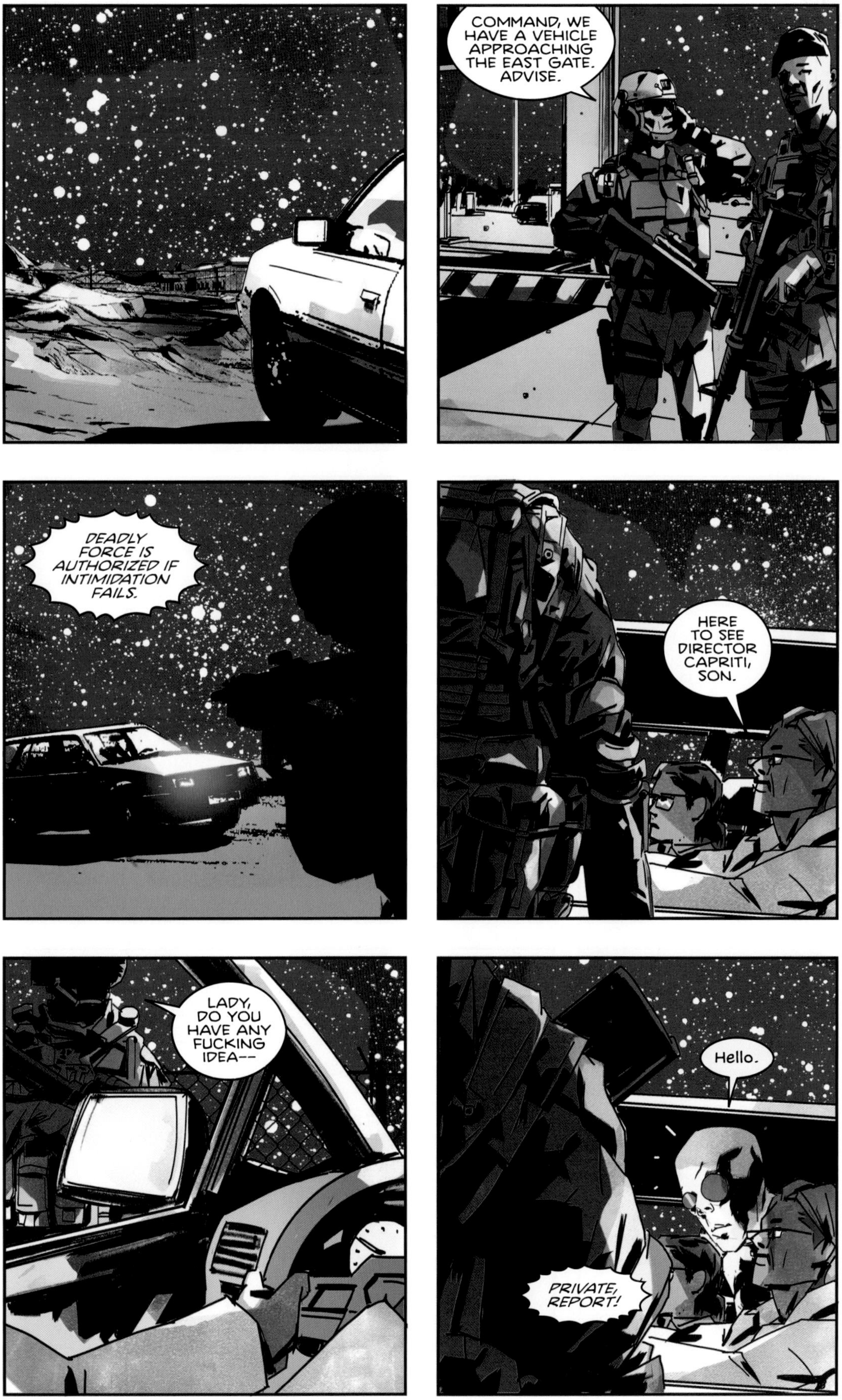
COMMAND, WE HAVE A VEHICLE APPROACHING THE EAST GATE. ADVISE.
DEADLY FORCE IS AUTHORIZED IF INTIMIDATION FAILS.
HERE TO SEE DIRECTOR CAPRITI, SON.
LADY, DO YOU HAVE ANY FUCKING IDEA--
Hello.
PRIVATE, REPORT!

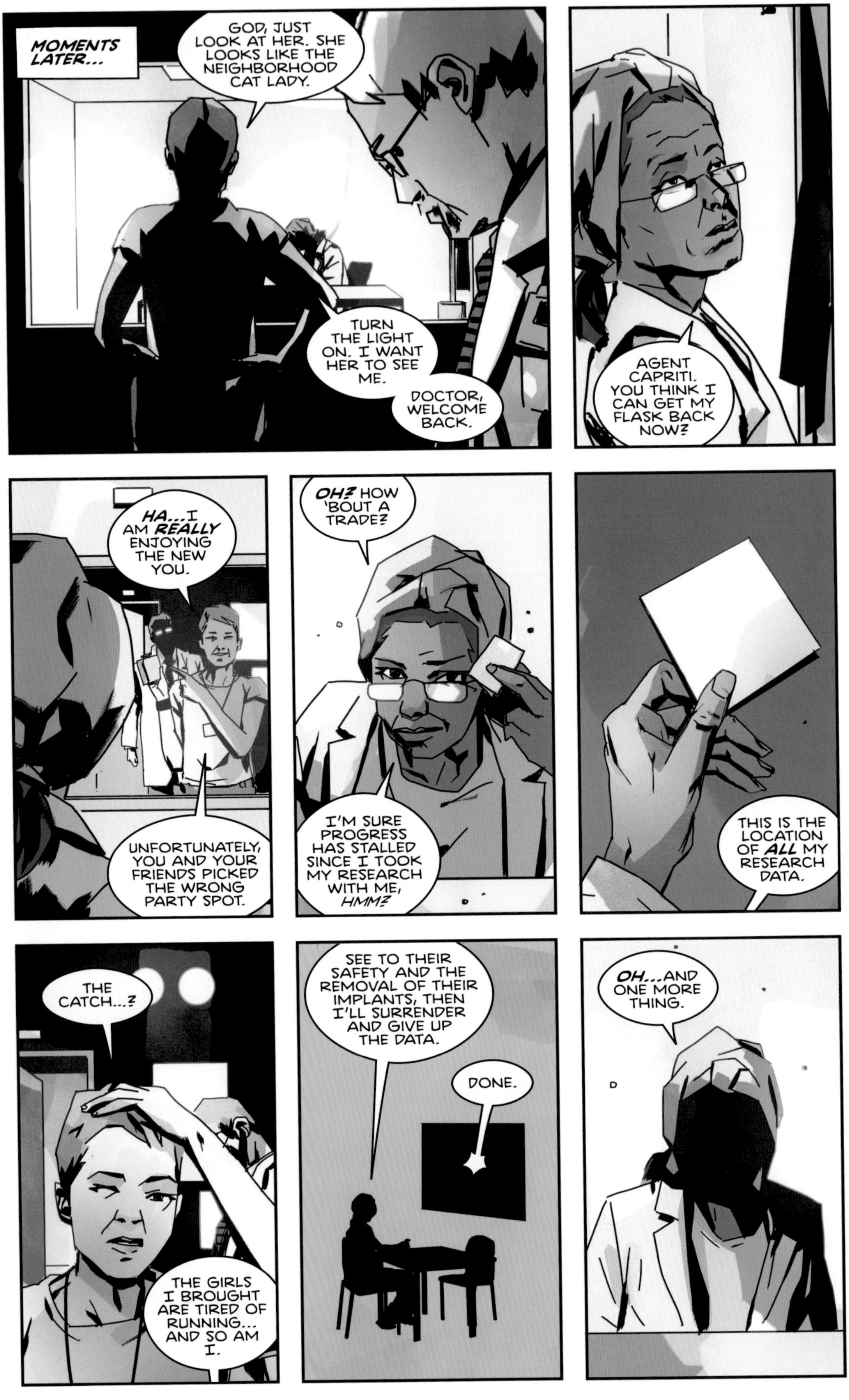
MOMENTS LATER...
GOD, JUST LOOK AT HER. SHE LOOKS LIKE THE NEIGHBORHOOD CAT LADY.
TURN THE LIGHT ON. I WANT HER TO SEE ME.
DOCTOR, WELCOME BACK.
AGENT CAPRITI. YOU THINK I CAN GET MY FLASK BACK NOW?
HA...I AM REALLY ENJOYING THE NEW YOU.
UNFORTUNATELY, YOU AND YOUR FRIENDS PICKED THE WRONG PARTY SPOT.
OH? HOW 'BOUT A TRADE?
I'M SURE PROGRESS HAS STALLED SINCE I TOOK MY RESEARCH WITH ME, HMM?
THIS IS THE LOCATION OF ALL MY RESEARCH DATA.
THE CATCH...?
THE GIRLS I BROUGHT ARE TIRED OF RUNNING... AND SO AM I.
SEE TO THEIR SAFETY AND THE REMOVAL OF THEIR IMPLANTS, THEN I'LL SURRENDER AND GIVE UP THE DATA.
DONE.
OH...AND ONE MORE THING.

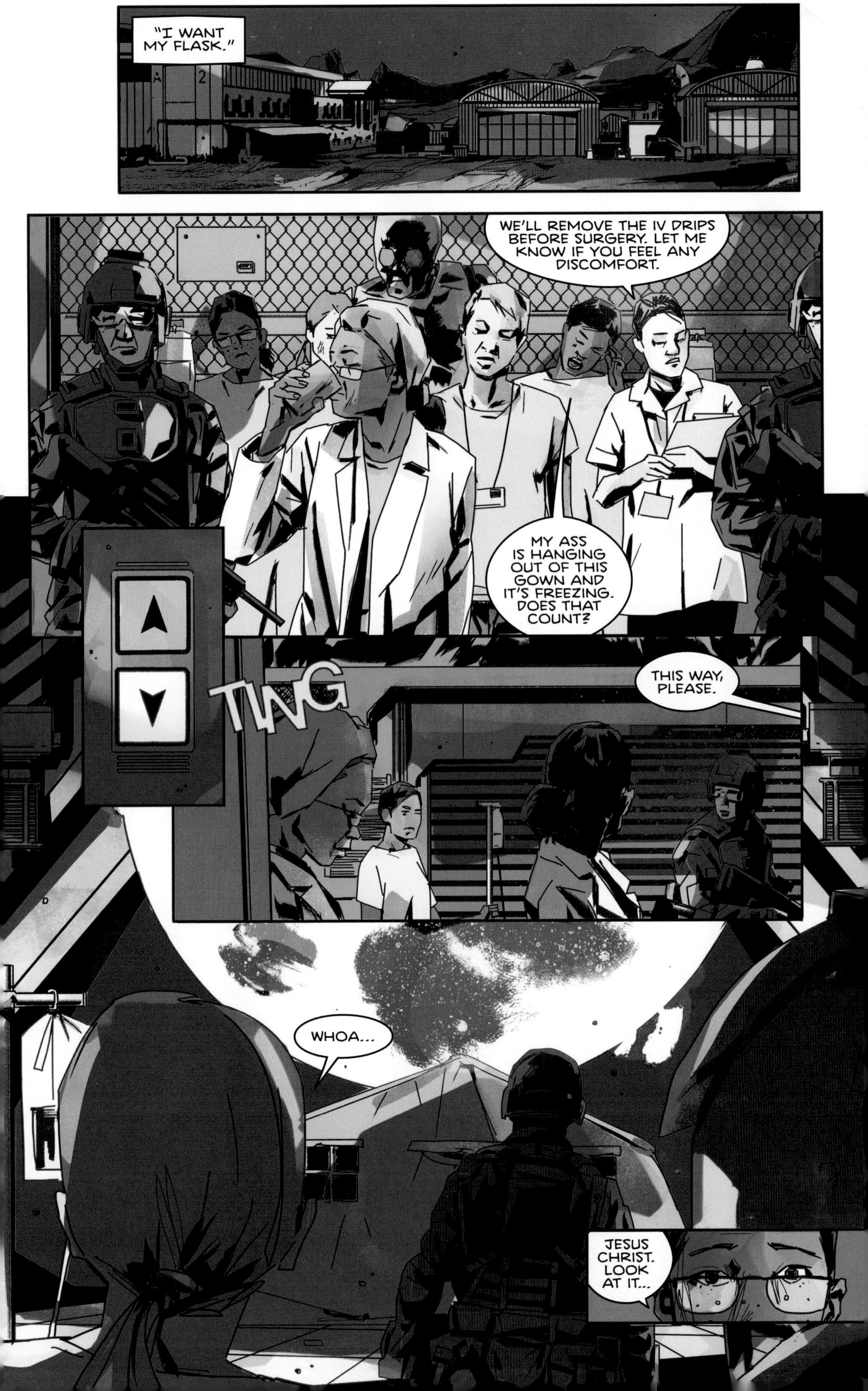
"I WANT MY FLASK."
WE'LL REMOVE THE IV DRIPS BEFORE SURGERY. LET ME KNOW IF YOU FEEL ANY DISCOMFORT.
MY ASS IS HANGING OUT OF THIS GOWN AND IT'S FREEZING. DOES THAT COUNT?
TING
THIS WAY, PLEASE.
WHOA...
JESUS CHRIST. LOOK AT IT...

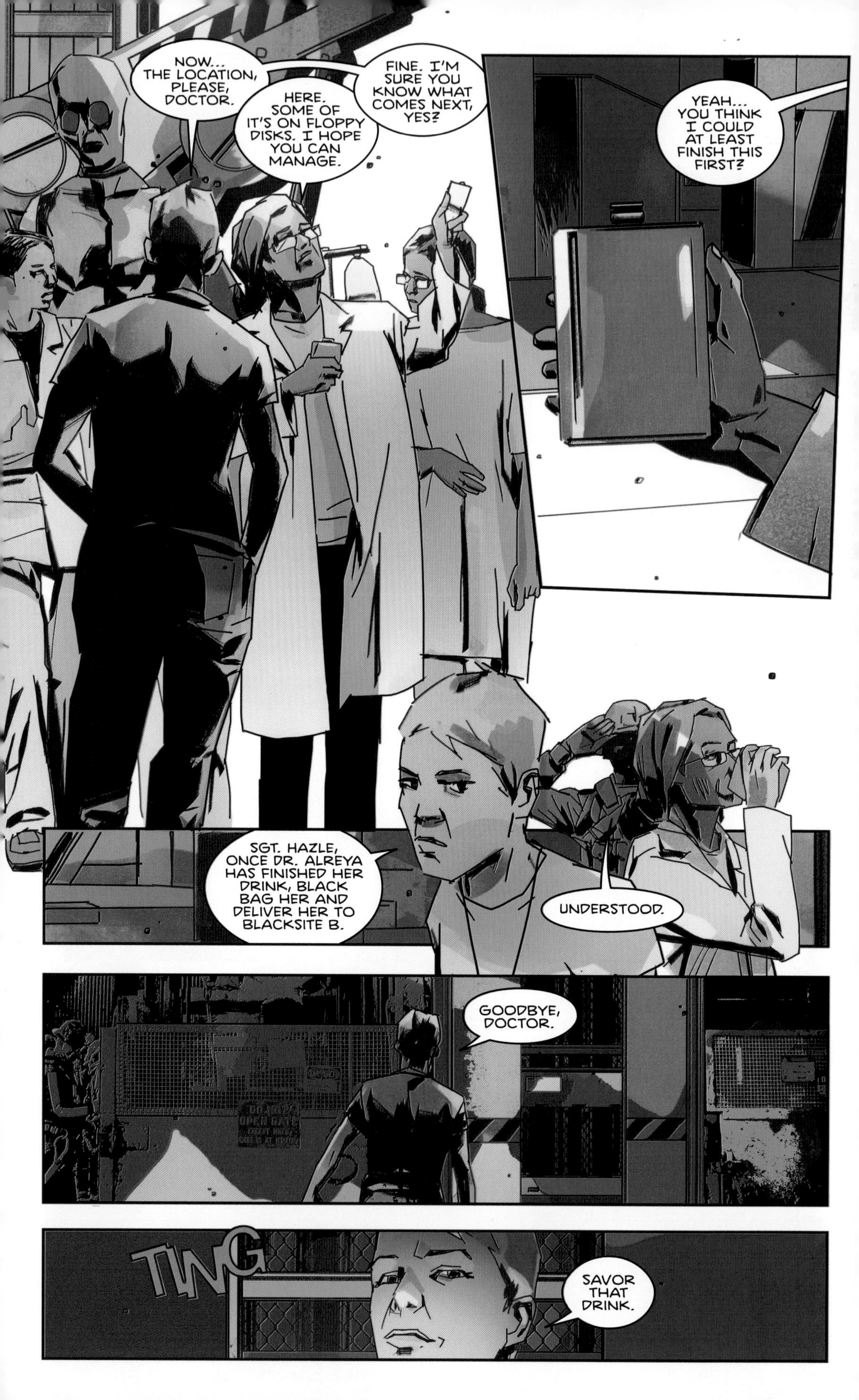
NOW... THE LOCATION, PLEASE, DOCTOR.
HERE. SOME OF IT'S ON FLOPPY DISKS. I HOPE YOU CAN MANAGE.
FINE. I'M SURE YOU KNOW WHAT COMES NEXT, YES?
YEAH... YOU THINK I COULD AT LEAST FINISH THIS FIRST?
SGT. HAZLE, ONCE DR. ALREYA HAS FINISHED HER DRINK, BLACK BAG HER AND DELIVER HER TO BLACKSITE B.
UNDERSTOOD.
GOODBYE, DOCTOR.
TING
SAVOR THAT DRINK.

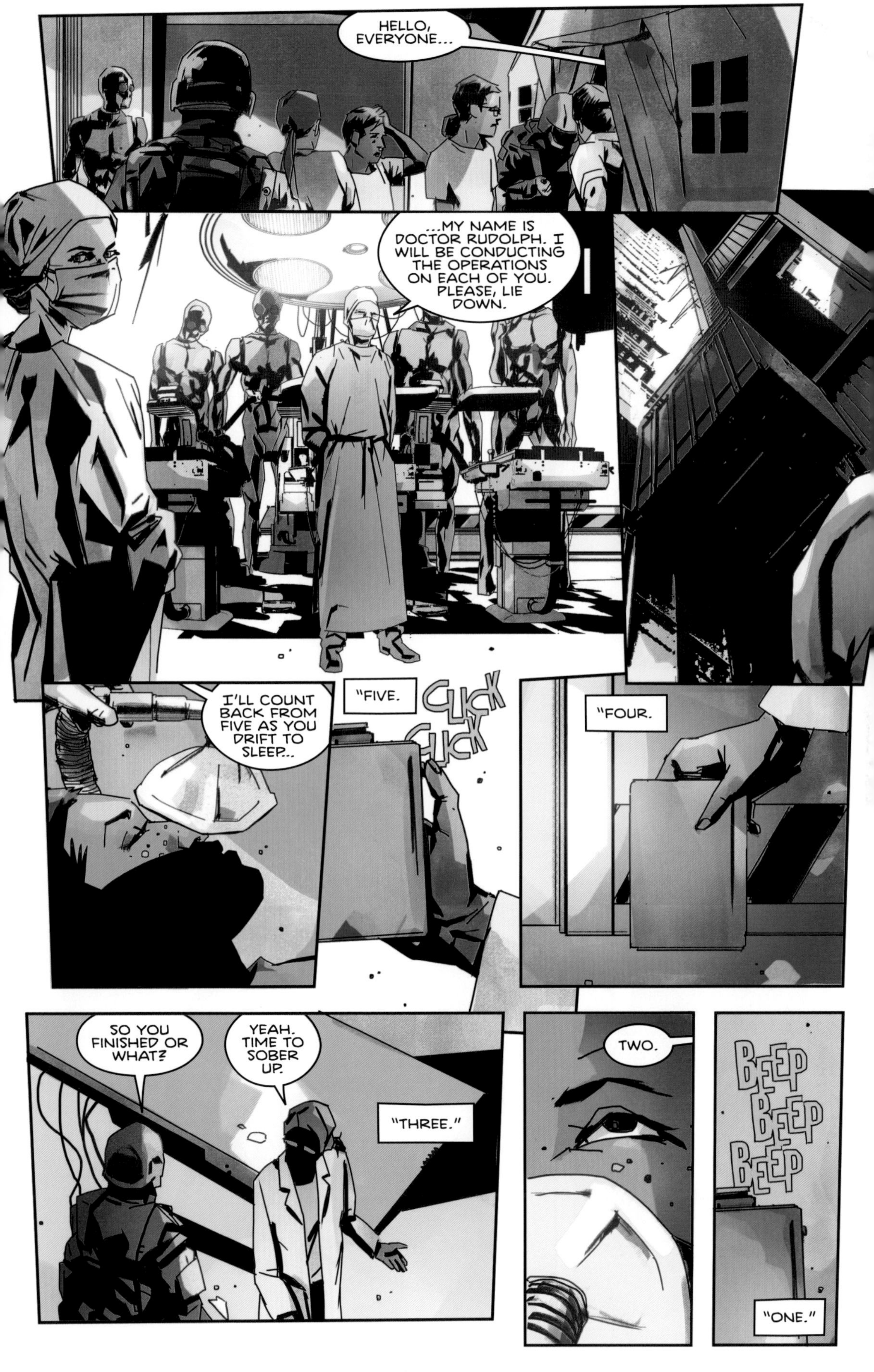
HELLO, EVERYONE...
...MY NAME IS DOCTOR RUDOLPH. I WILL BE CONDUCTING THE OPERATIONS ON EACH OF YOU. PLEASE, LIE DOWN.
I'LL COUNT BACK FROM FIVE AS YOU DRIFT TO SLEEP...
"FIVE.
CLICK
CLICK
"FOUR.
SO YOU FINISHED OR WHAT?
YEAH. TIME TO SOBER UP.
"THREE."
TWO.
BEEP
BEEP
BEEP
"ONE."

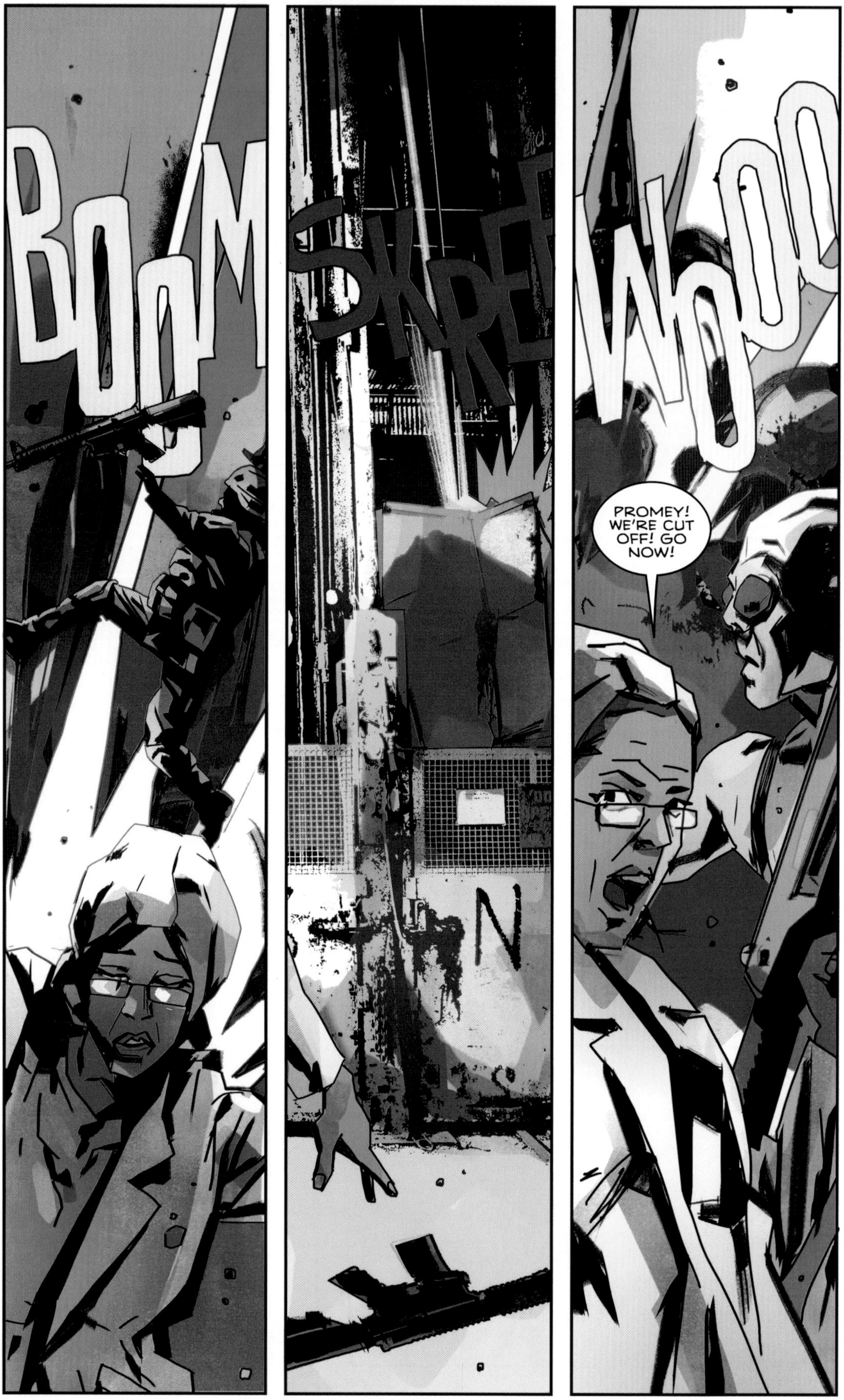
BOOM
SKREE
WOOO
PROMEY! WE'RE CUT OFF! GO NOW!

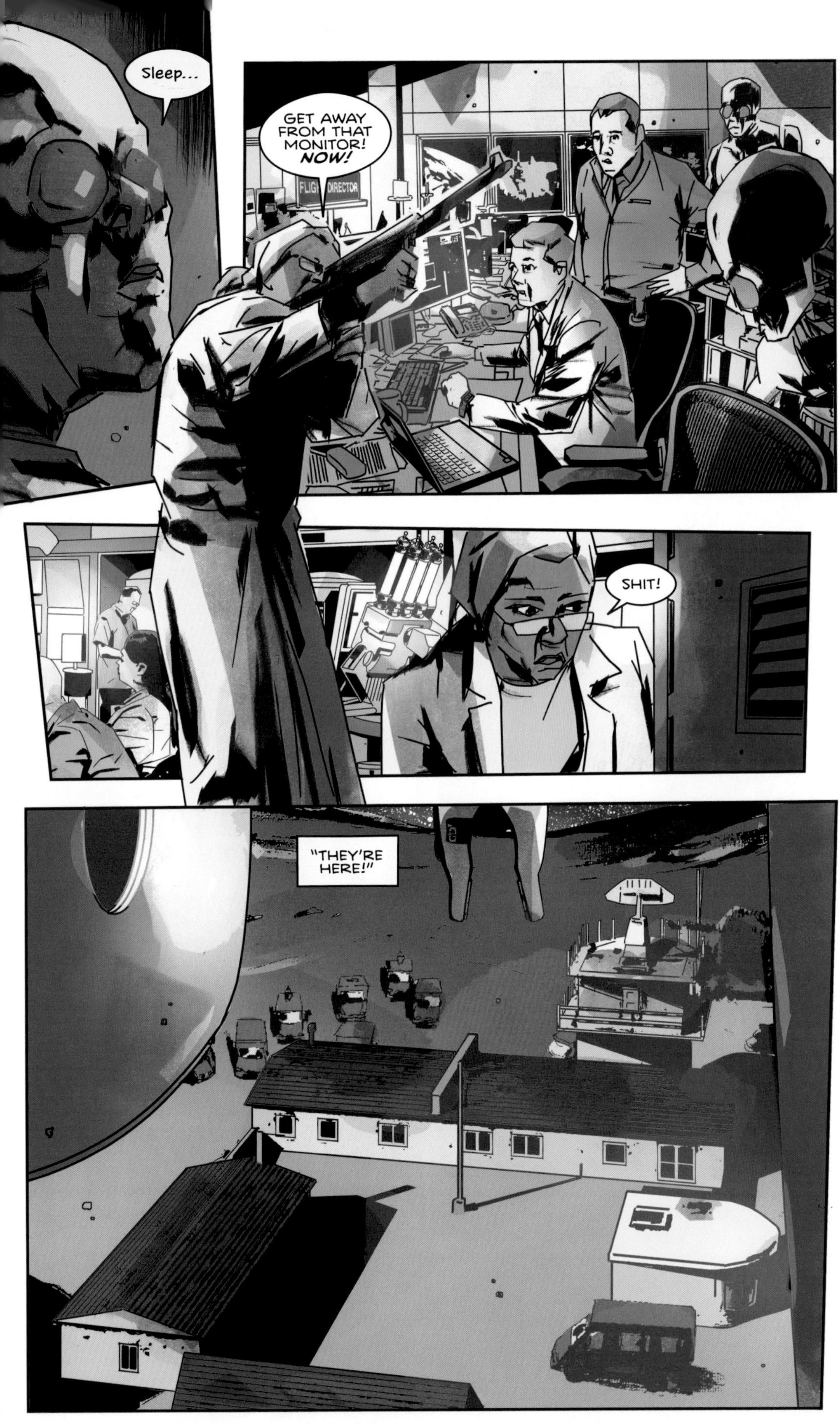
Sleep...
GET AWAY FROM THAT MONITOR! NOW!
FLIGHT DIRECTOR
SHIT!
"THEY'RE HERE!"

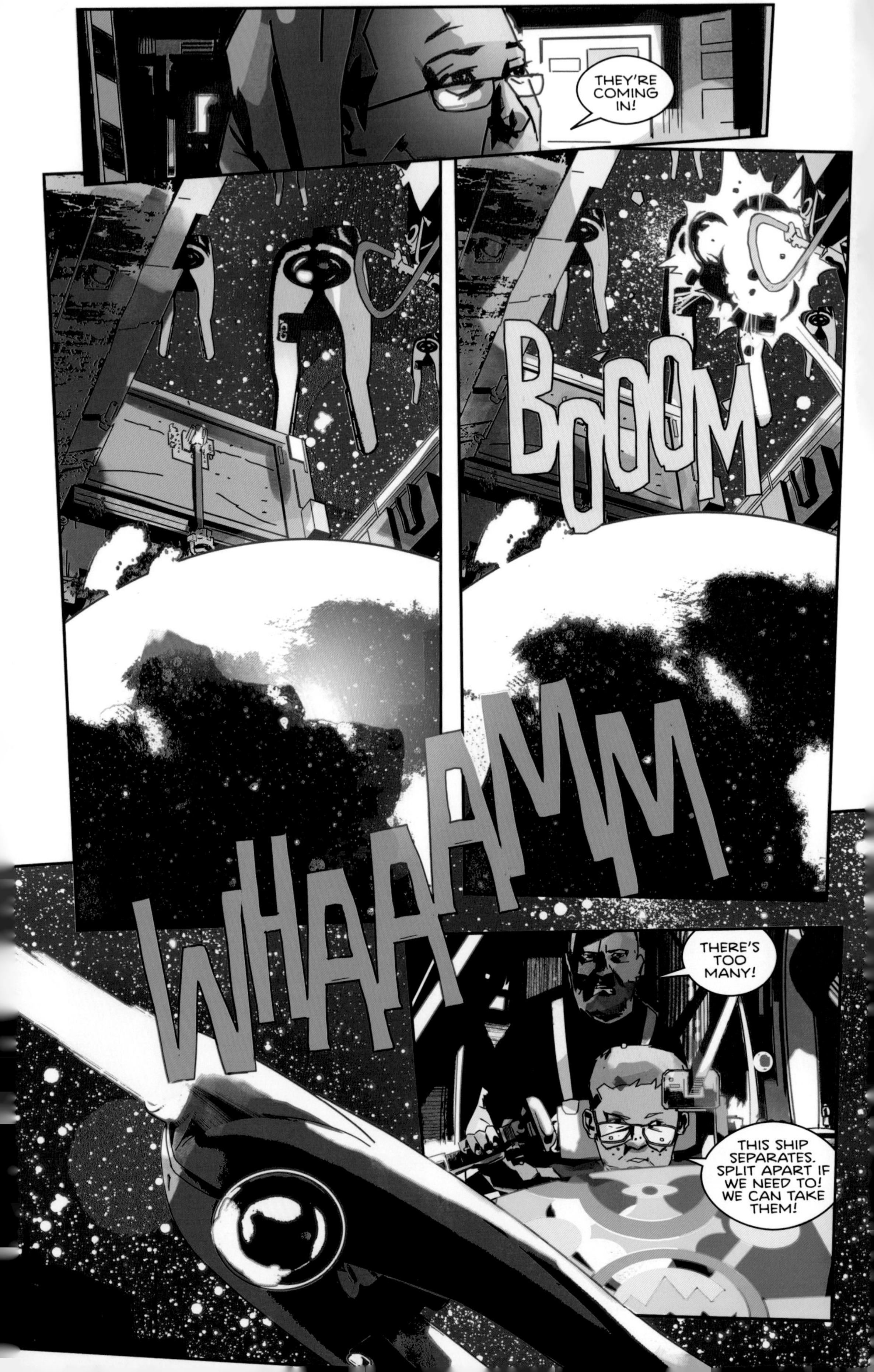
THEY'RE COMING IN!
BOOOM
WHAAAMM
THERE'S TOO MANY!
THIS SHIP SEPARATES. SPLIT APART IF WE NEED TO! WE CAN TAKE THEM!

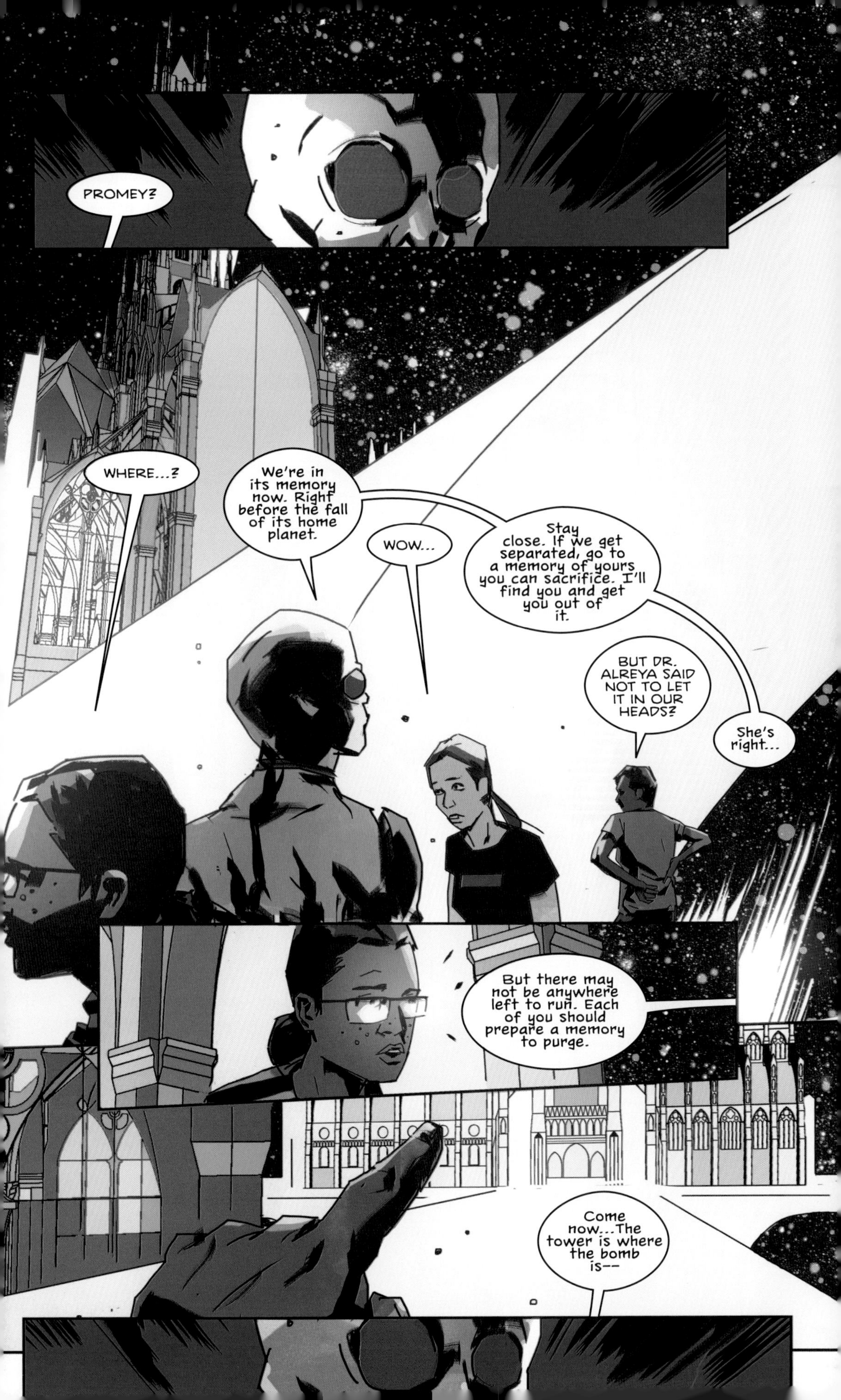
PROMEY?
WHERE...?
We're in its memory now. Right before the fall of its home planet.
WOW...
Stay close. If we get separated, go to a memory of yours you can sacrifice. I'll find you and get you out of it.
BUT DR. ALREYA SAID NOT TO LET IT IN OUR HEADS?
She's right...
But there may not be anywhere left to run. Each of you should prepare a memory to purge.
Come now... The tower is where the bomb is--

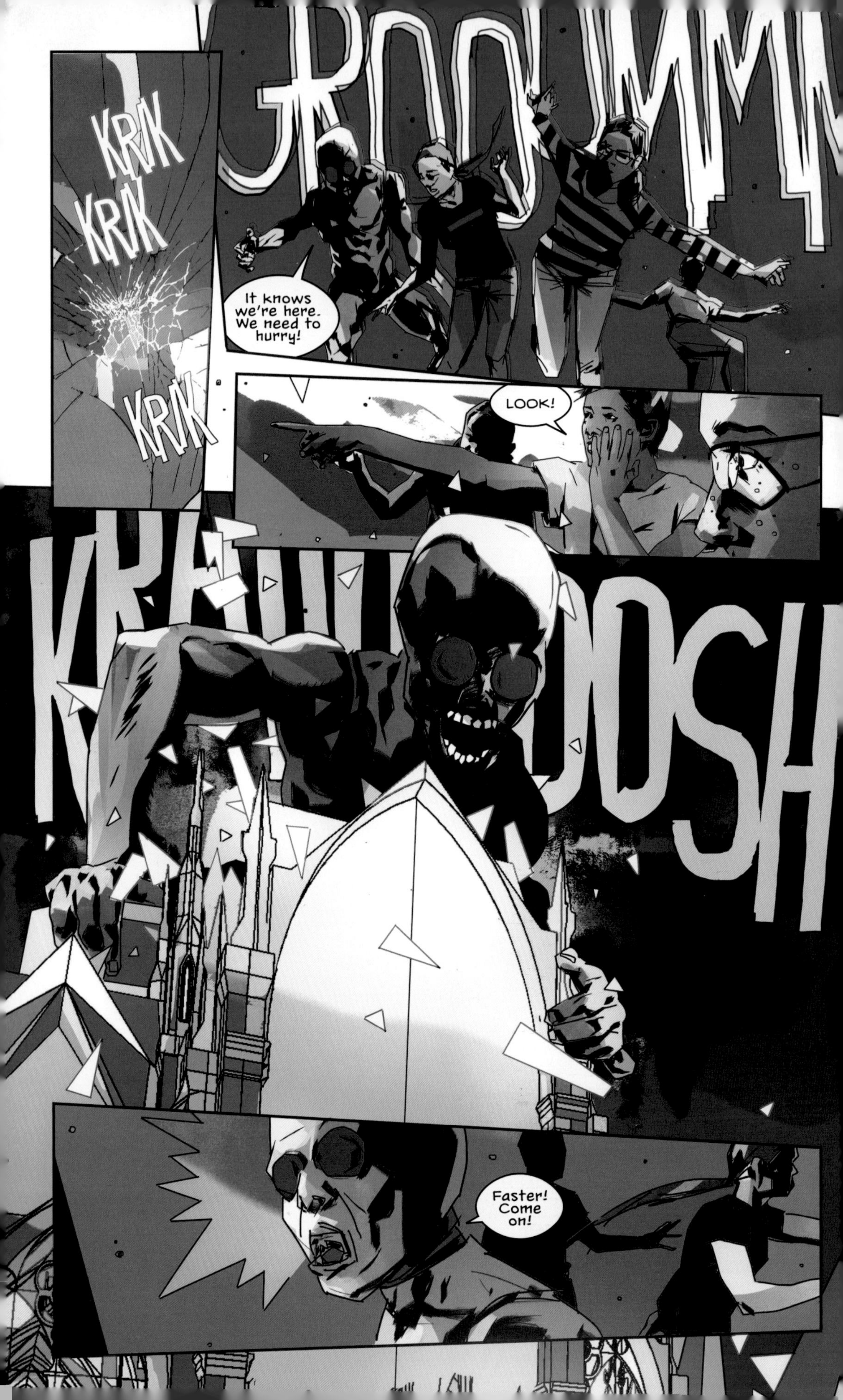
KRAK
KRAK
KRAK
It knows we're here. We need to hurry!
LOOK!
Faster! Come on!

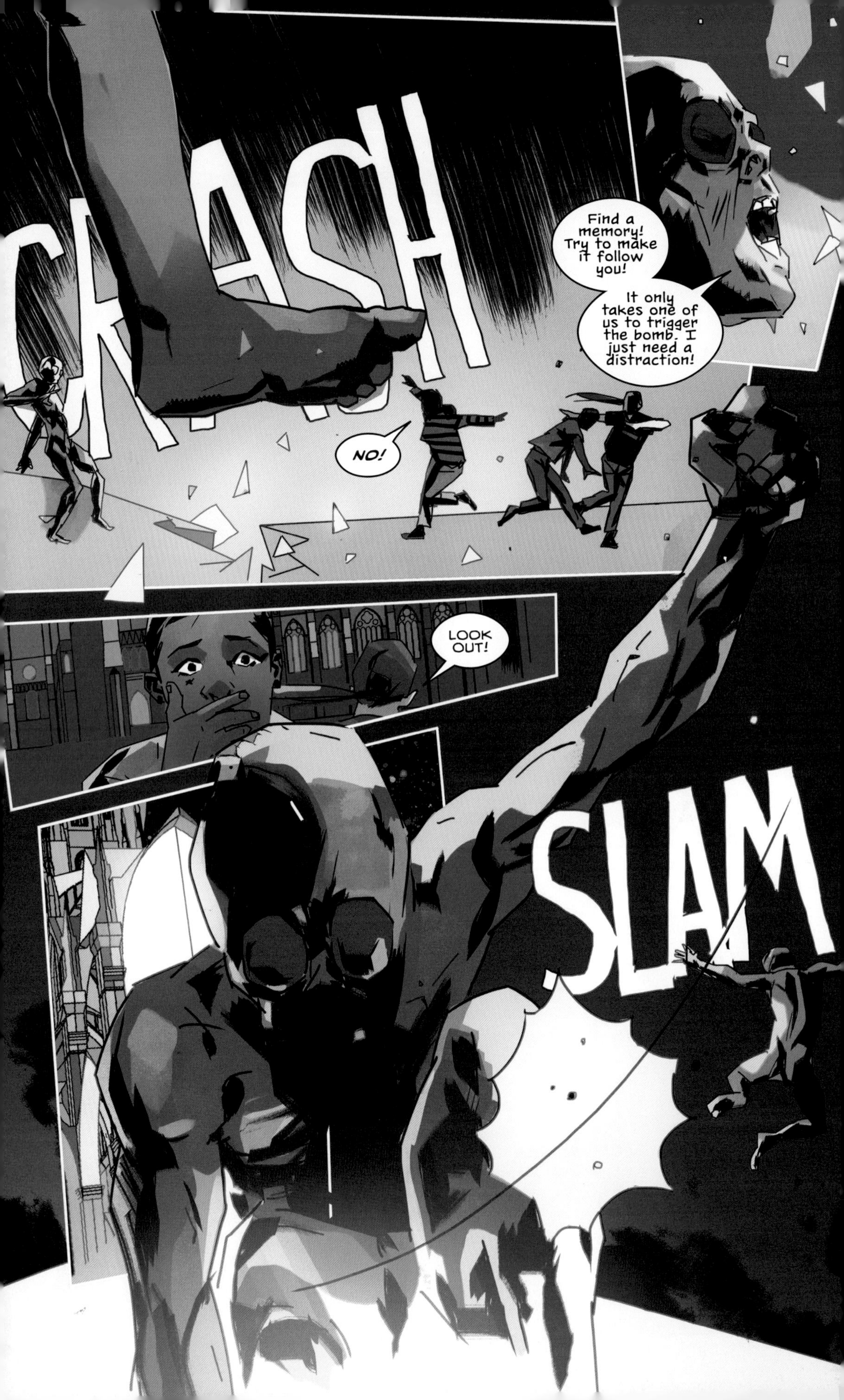
CRASH
Find a memory! Try to make it follow you!
It only takes one of us to trigger the bomb. I just need a distraction!
NO!
LOOK OUT!
SLAM

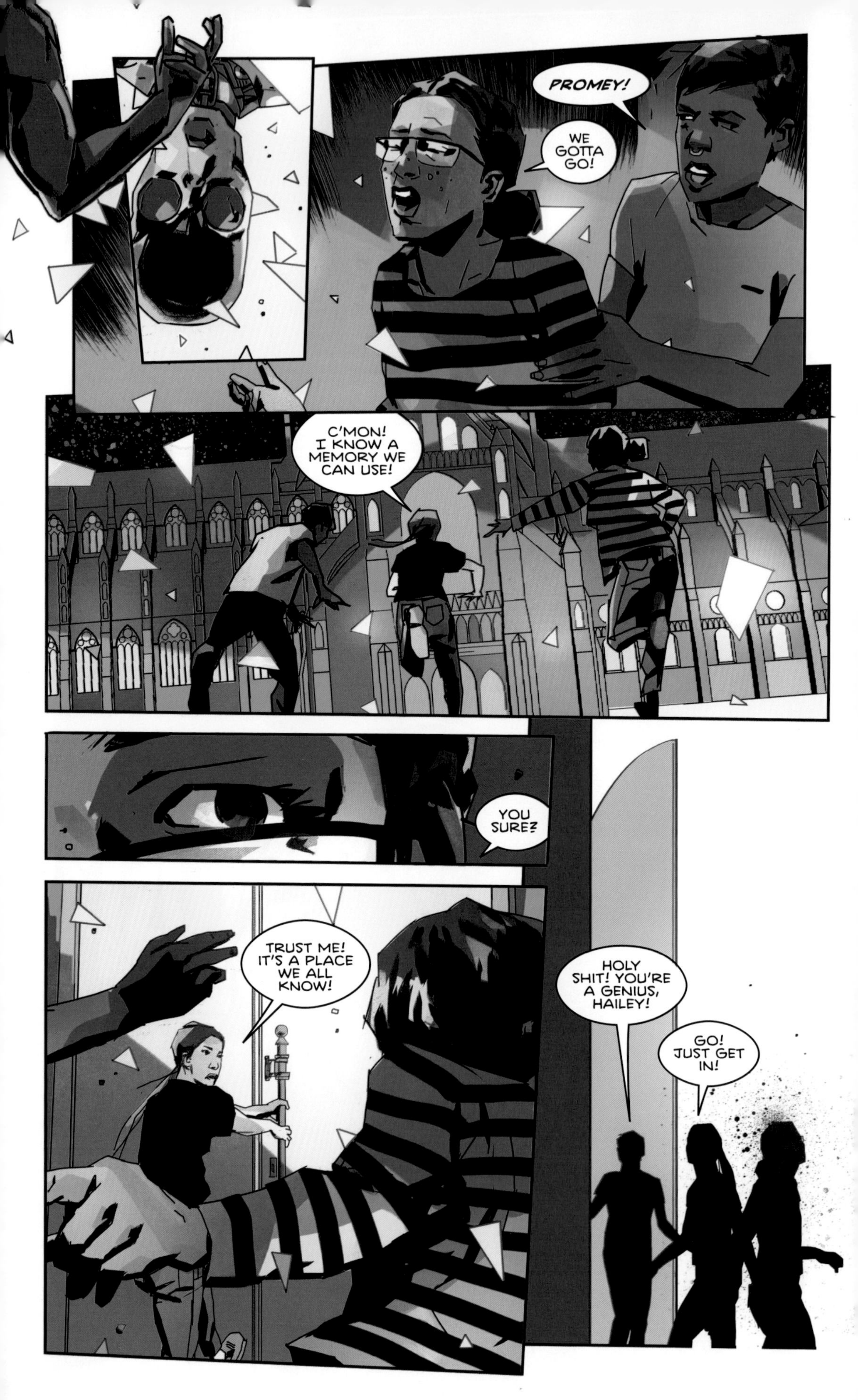
PROMEY!
WE GOTTA GO!
C'MON! I KNOW A MEMORY WE CAN USE!
YOU SURE?
TRUST ME! IT'S A PLACE WE ALL KNOW!
HOLY SHIT! YOU'RE A GENIUS, HAILEY!
GO! JUST GET IN!

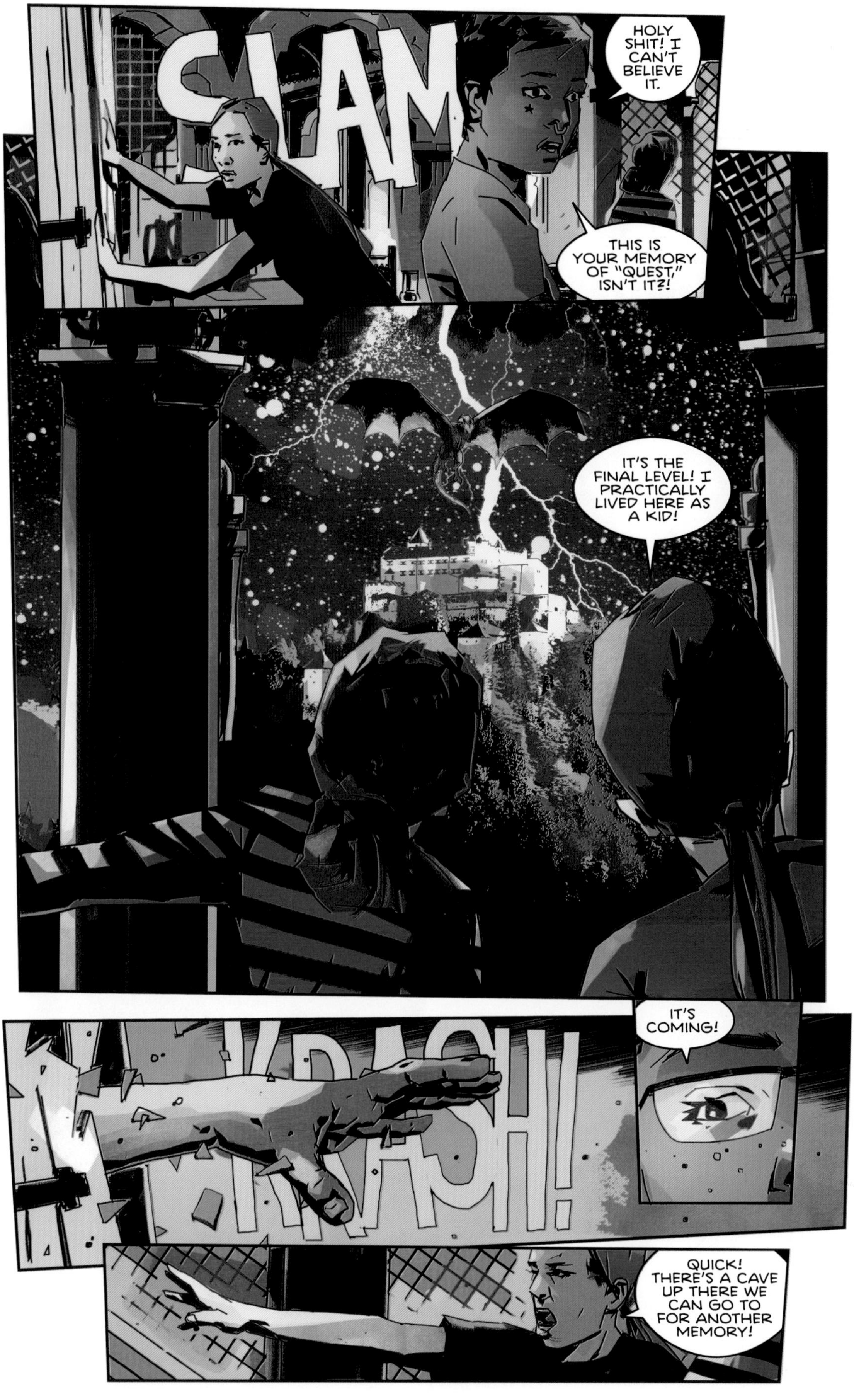
SLAM
HOLY SHIT! I CAN'T BELIEVE IT.
THIS IS YOUR MEMORY OF "QUEST," ISN'T IT?!
IT'S THE FINAL LEVEL! I PRACTICALLY LIVED HERE AS A KID!
IT'S COMING!
KRASH!
QUICK! THERE'S A CAVE UP THERE WE CAN GO TO FOR ANOTHER MEMORY!

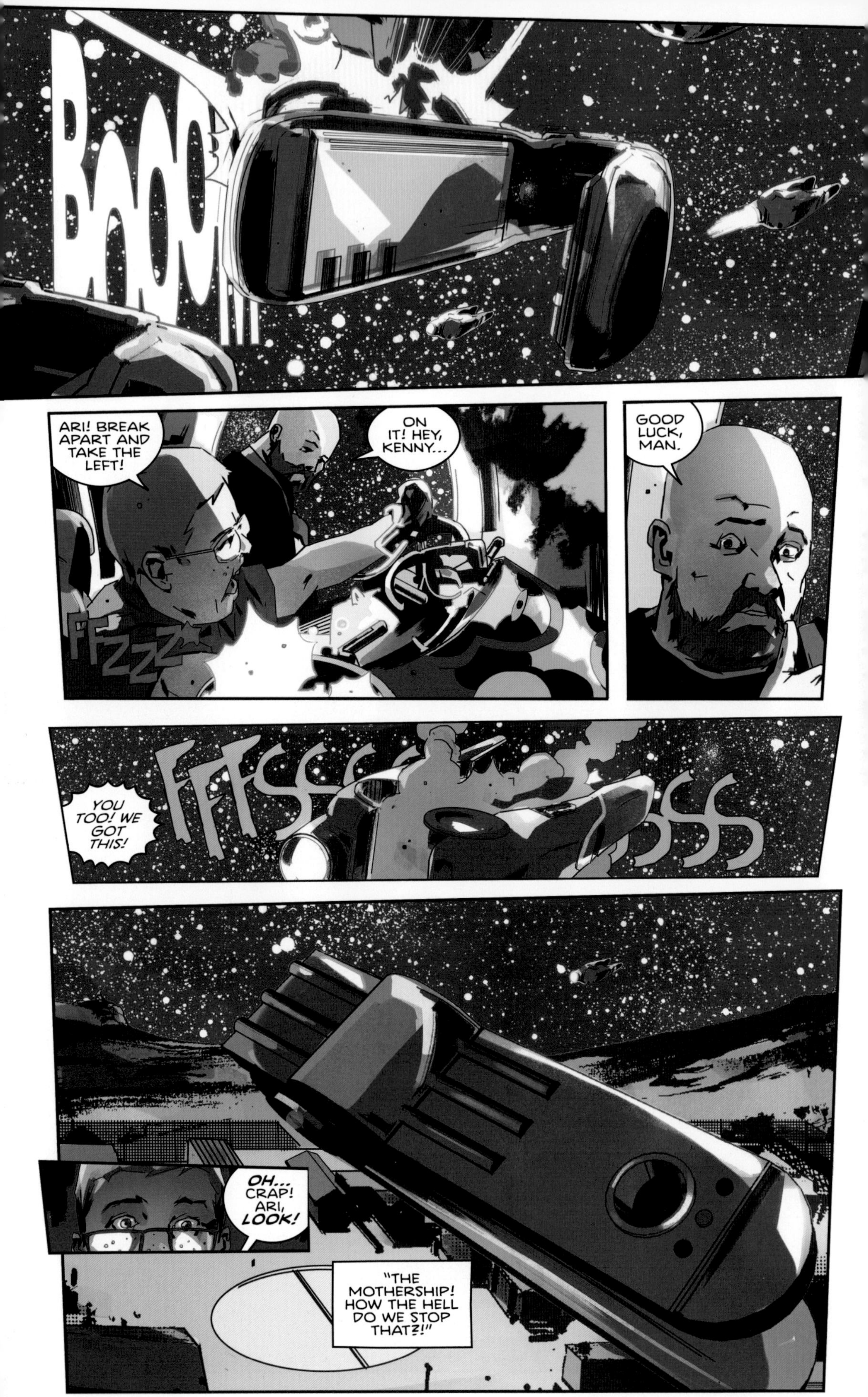
BOOOM!!!
ARI! BREAK APART AND TAKE THE LEFT!
ON IT! HEY, KENNY...
FFZZZ
GOOD LUCK, MAN.
YOU TOO! WE GOT THIS!
FFFSSSSSSSS
OH... CRAP! ARI, LOOK!
"THE MOTHERSHIP! HOW THE HELL DO WE STOP THAT?!"

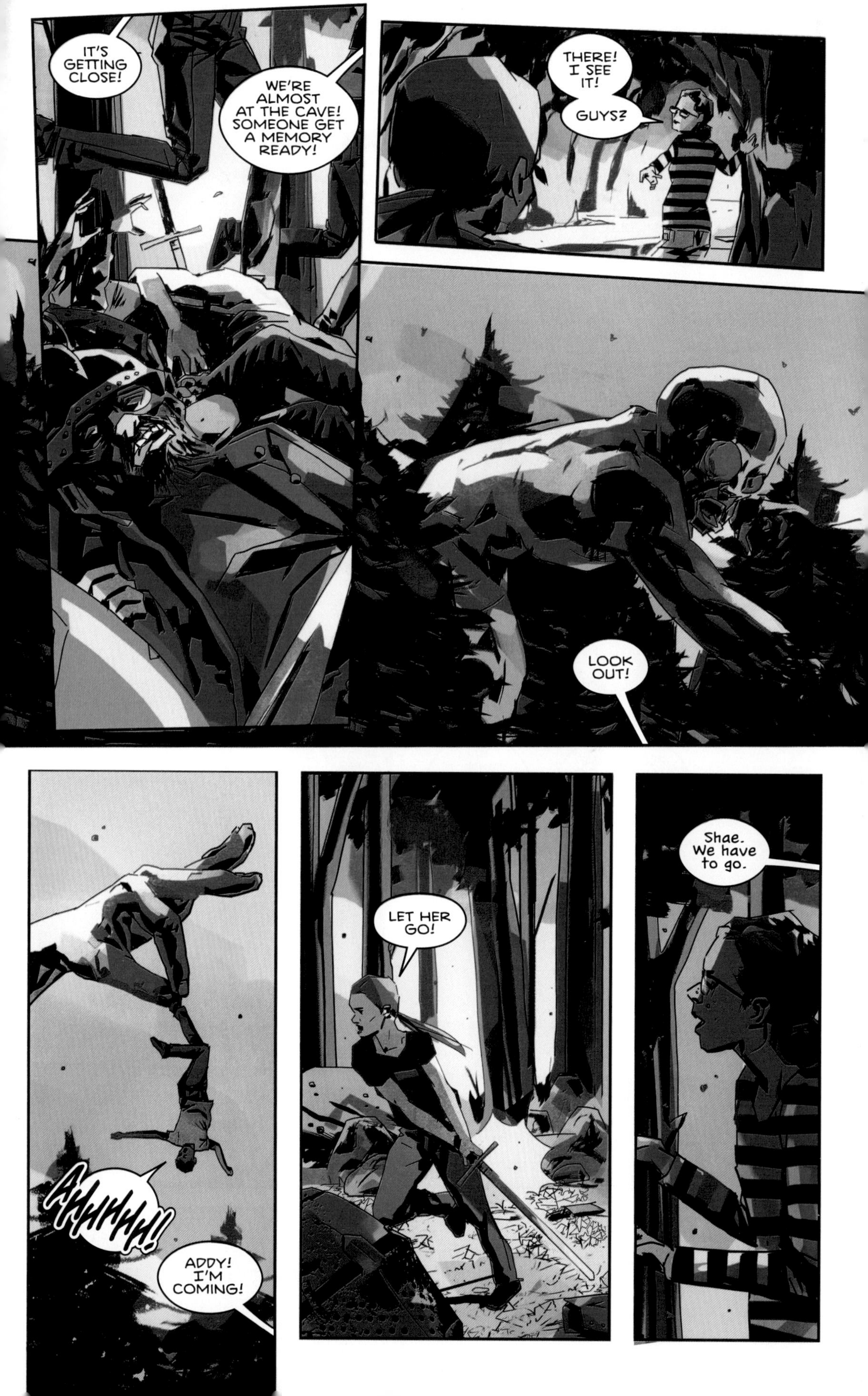
IT'S GETTING CLOSE!
WE'RE ALMOST AT THE CAVE! SOMEONE GET A MEMORY READY!
THERE! I SEE IT!
GUYS?
LOOK OUT!
AHHHHH!
ADDY! I'M COMING!
LET HER GO!
Shae. We have to go.

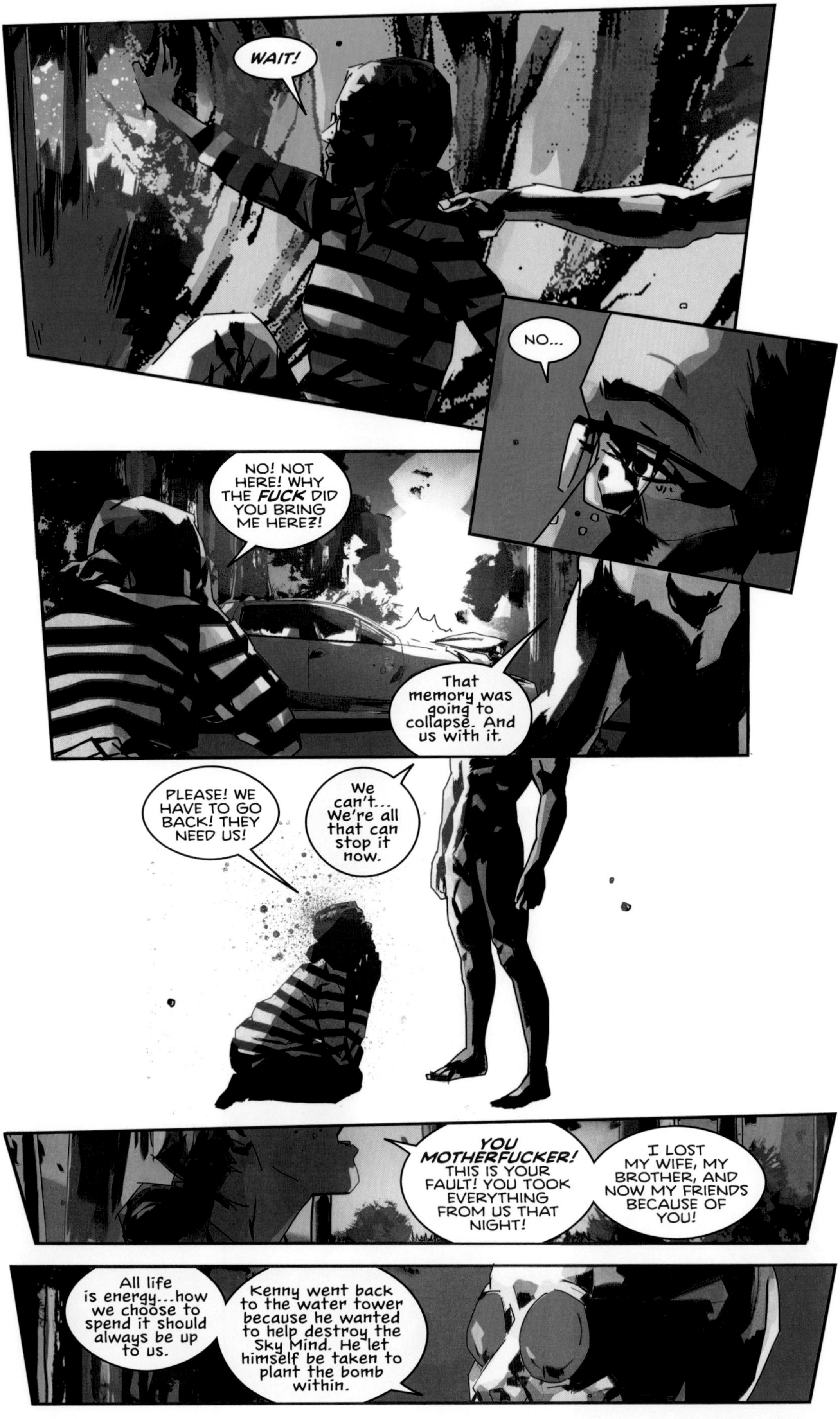
WAIT!
NO...
NO! NOT HERE! WHY THE **FUCK** DID YOU BRING ME HERE?!
That memory was going to collapse. And us with it.
PLEASE! WE HAVE TO GO BACK! THEY NEED US!
We can't... We're all that can stop it now.
YOU MOTHERFUCKER! THIS IS YOUR FAULT! YOU TOOK EVERYTHING FROM US THAT NIGHT!
I LOST MY WIFE, MY BROTHER, AND NOW MY FRIENDS BECAUSE OF YOU!
All life is energy...how we choose to spend it should always be up to us.
Kenny went back to the water tower because he wanted to help destroy the Sky Mind. He let himself be taken to plant the bomb within.

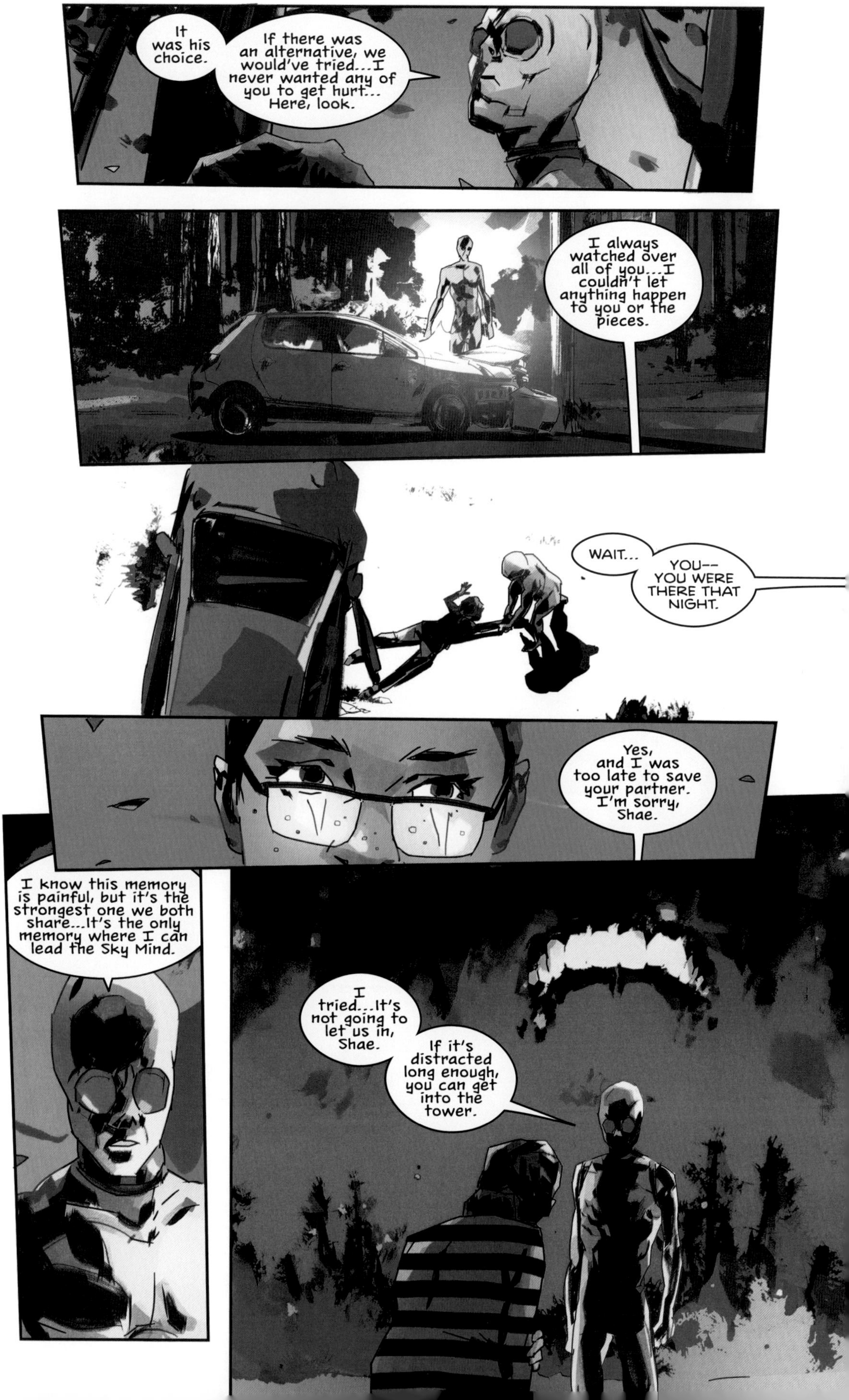
It was his choice.
If there was an alternative, we would've tried...I never wanted any of you to get hurt... Here, look.
I always watched over all of you...I couldn't let anything happen to you or the pieces.
WAIT...
YOU-- YOU WERE THERE THAT NIGHT.
Yes, and I was too late to save your partner. I'm sorry, Shae.
I know this memory is painful, but it's the strongest one we both share...It's the only memory where I can lead the Sky Mind.
I tried...It's not going to let us in, Shae.
If it's distracted long enough, you can get into the tower.

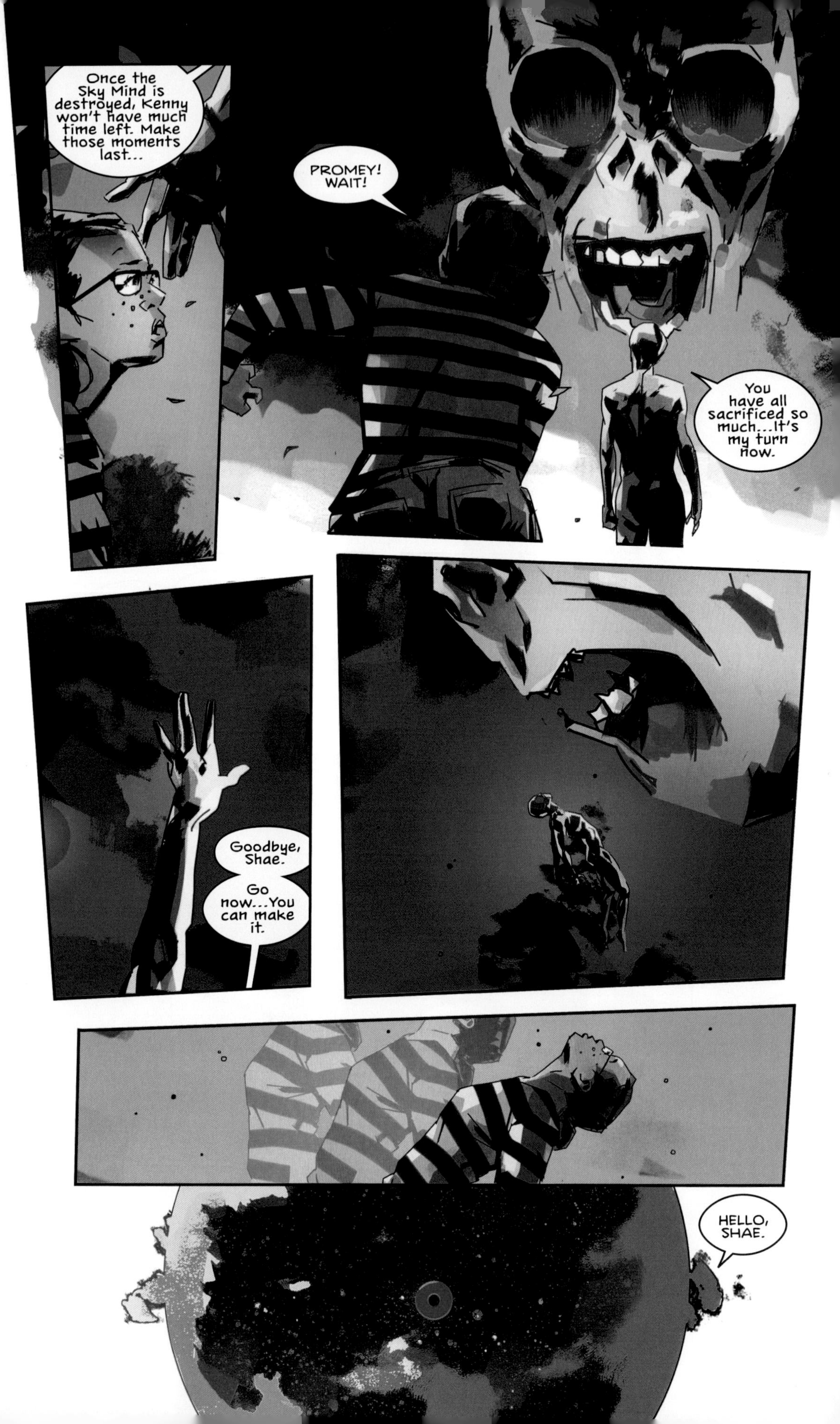
Once the Sky Mind is destroyed, Kenny won't have much time left. Make those moments last...
PROMEY! WAIT!
You have all sacrificed so much...It's my turn now.
Goodbye, Shae.
Go now...You can make it.
HELLO, SHAE.

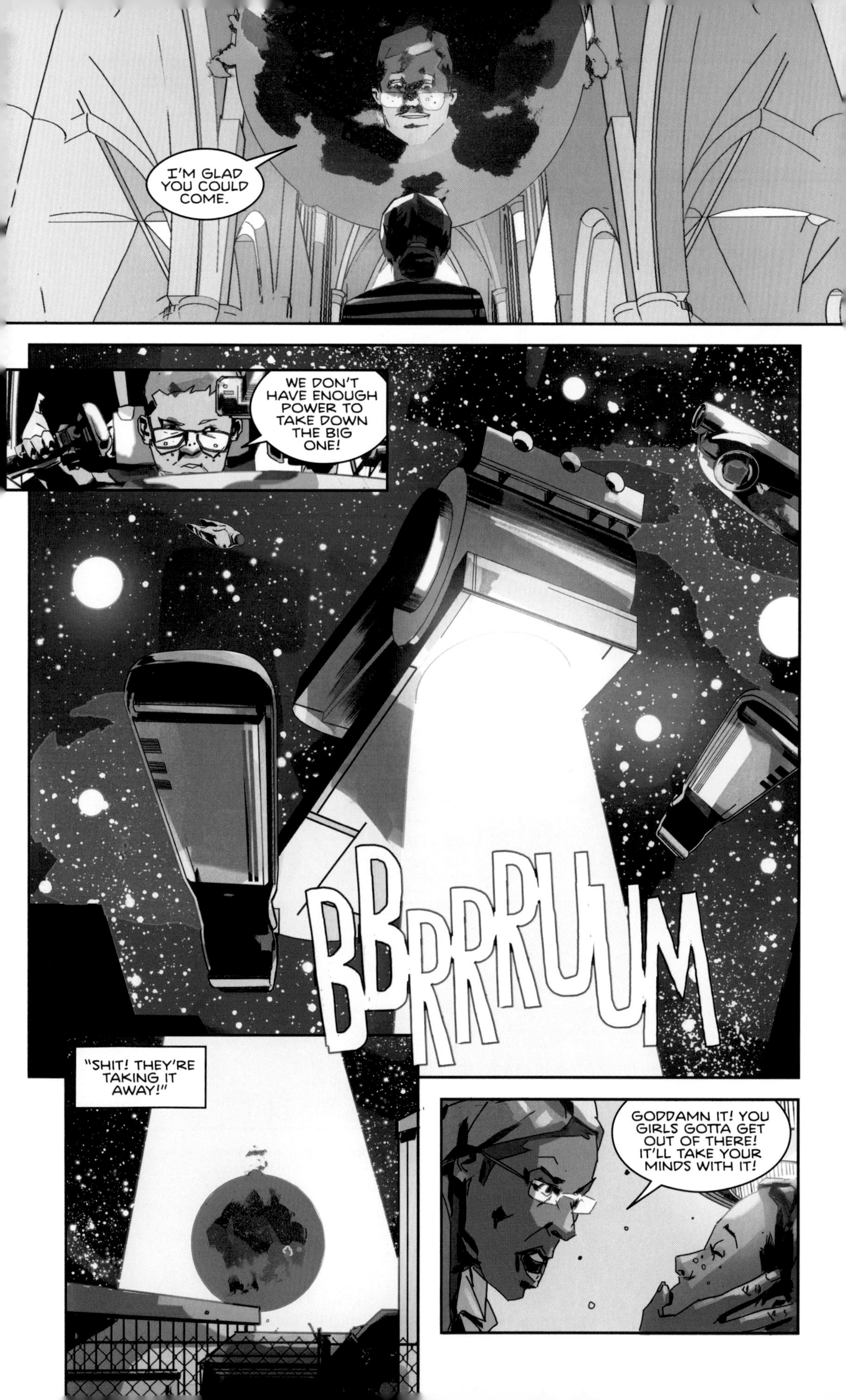
I'M GLAD YOU COULD COME.
WE DON'T HAVE ENOUGH POWER TO TAKE DOWN THE BIG ONE!
BBRRRUUUM
"SHIT! THEY'RE TAKING IT AWAY!"
GODDAMN IT! YOU GIRLS GOTTA GET OUT OF THERE! IT'LL TAKE YOUR MINDS WITH IT!

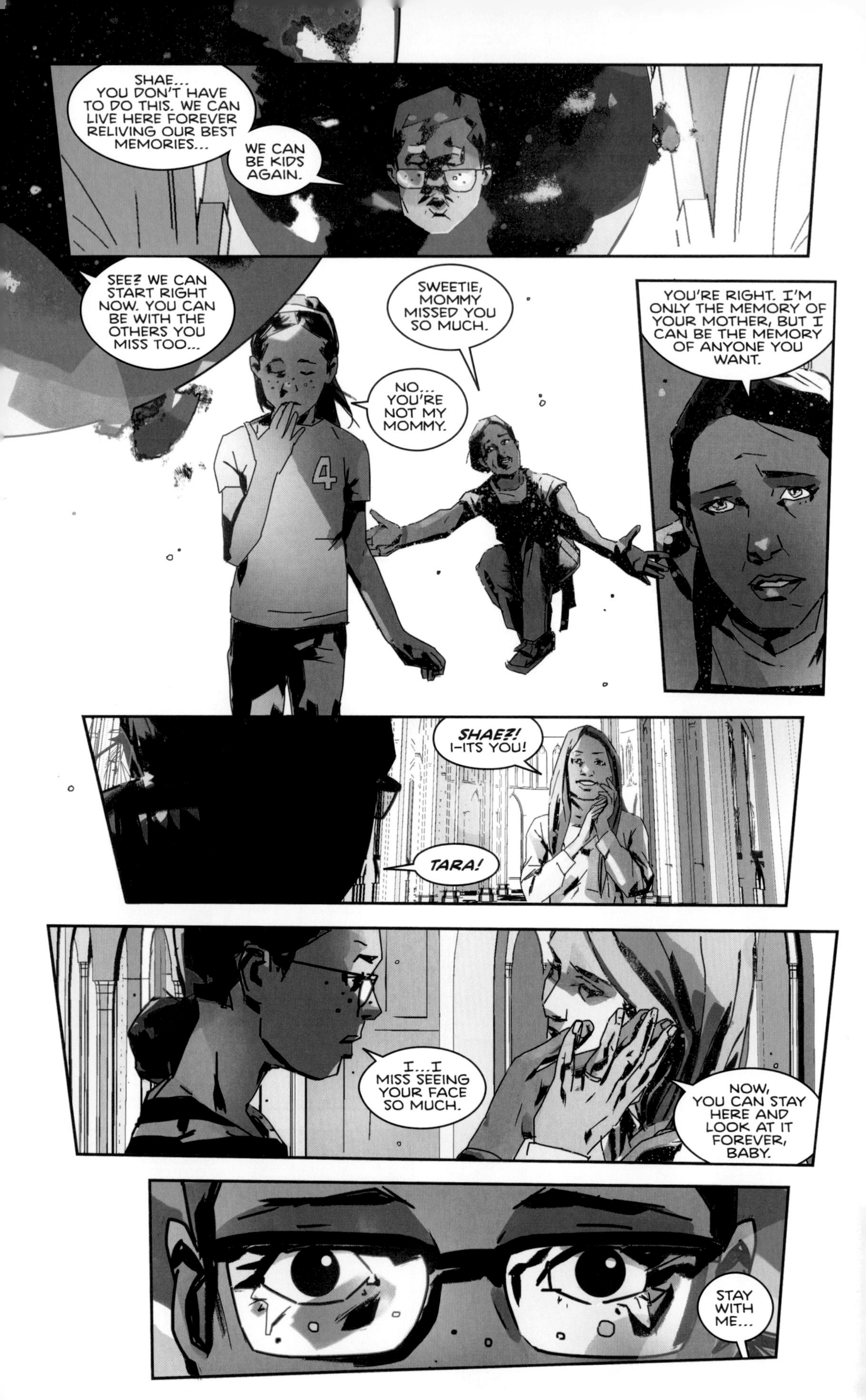
SHAE... YOU DON'T HAVE TO DO THIS. WE CAN LIVE HERE FOREVER RELIVING OUR BEST MEMORIES...
WE CAN BE KIDS AGAIN.
SEE? WE CAN START RIGHT NOW. YOU CAN BE WITH THE OTHERS YOU MISS TOO...
SWEETIE, MOMMY MISSED YOU SO MUCH.
NO... YOU'RE NOT MY MOMMY.
YOU'RE RIGHT. I'M ONLY THE MEMORY OF YOUR MOTHER, BUT I CAN BE THE MEMORY OF ANYONE YOU WANT.
SHAE?! I-ITS YOU!
TARA!
I...I MISS SEEING YOUR FACE SO MUCH.
NOW, YOU CAN STAY HERE AND LOOK AT IT FOREVER, BABY.
STAY WITH ME...

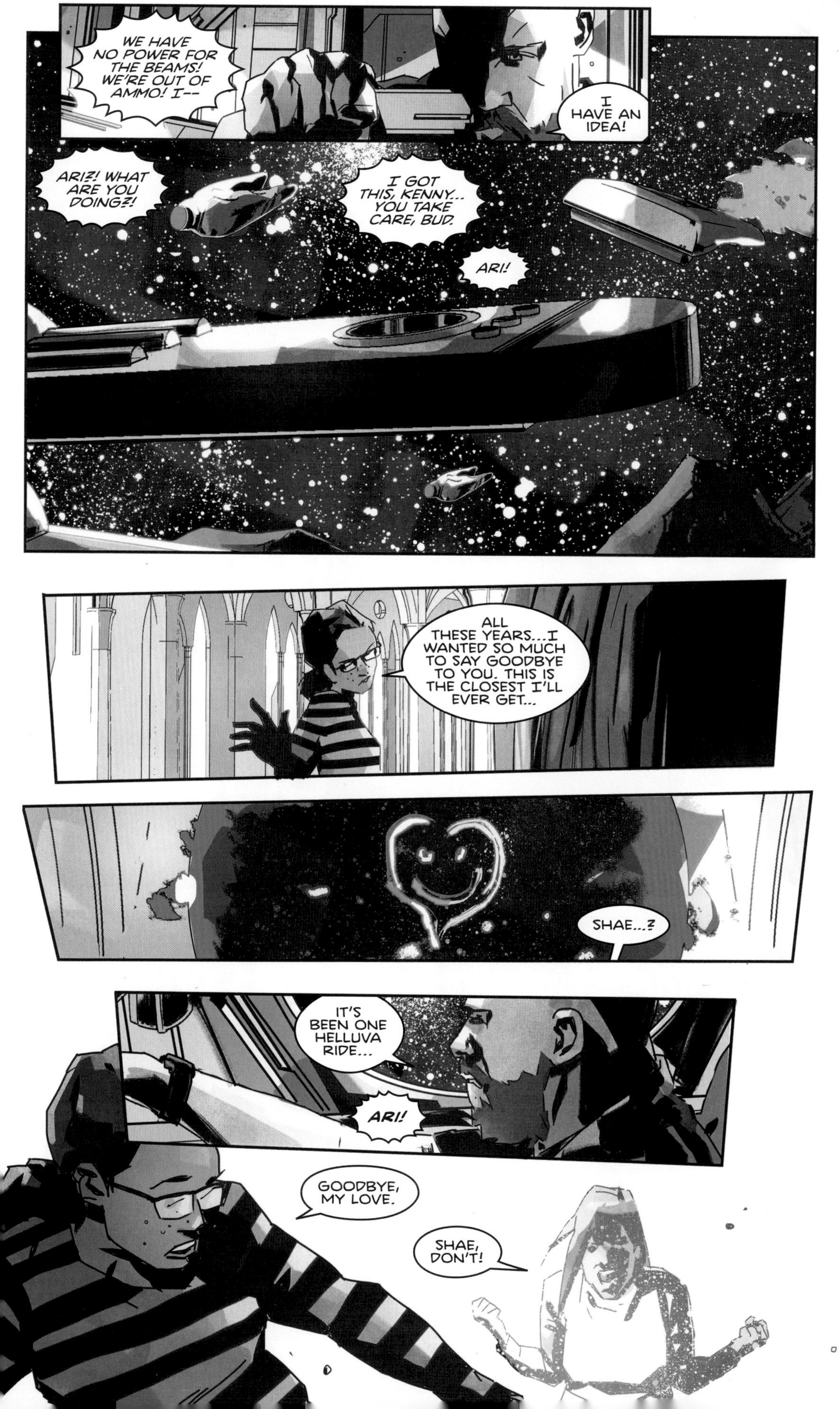
WE HAVE NO POWER FOR THE BEAMS! WE'RE OUT OF AMMO! I--
I HAVE AN IDEA!
ARI?! WHAT ARE YOU DOING?!
I GOT THIS, KENNY... YOU TAKE CARE, BUD.
ARI!
ALL THESE YEARS...I WANTED SO MUCH TO SAY GOODBYE TO YOU. THIS IS THE CLOSEST I'LL EVER GET...
SHAE...?
IT'S BEEN ONE HELLUVA RIDE...
ARI!
GOODBYE, MY LOVE.
SHAE, DON'T!

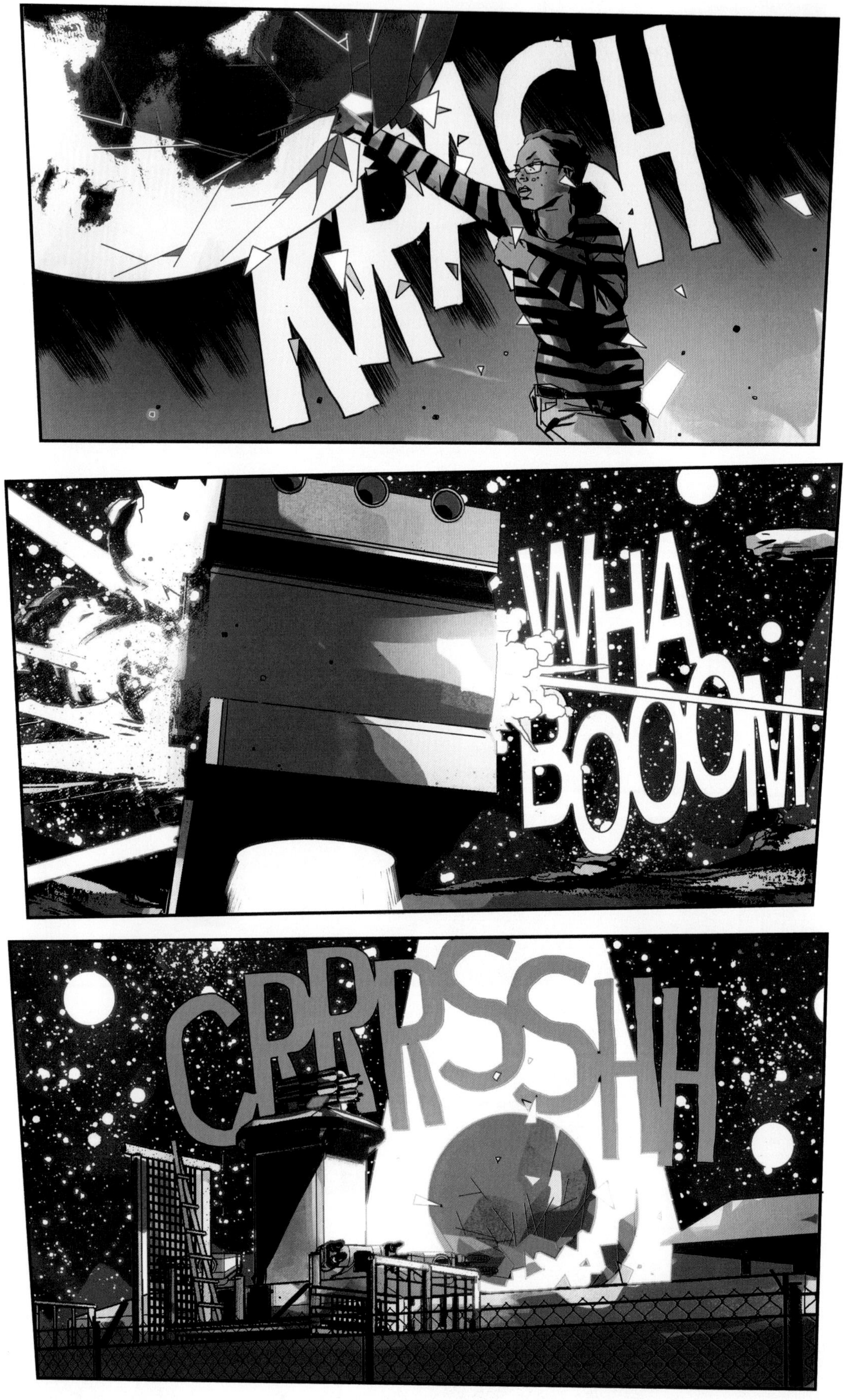
KRACH
WHA
BOOOM
CRRSSHH

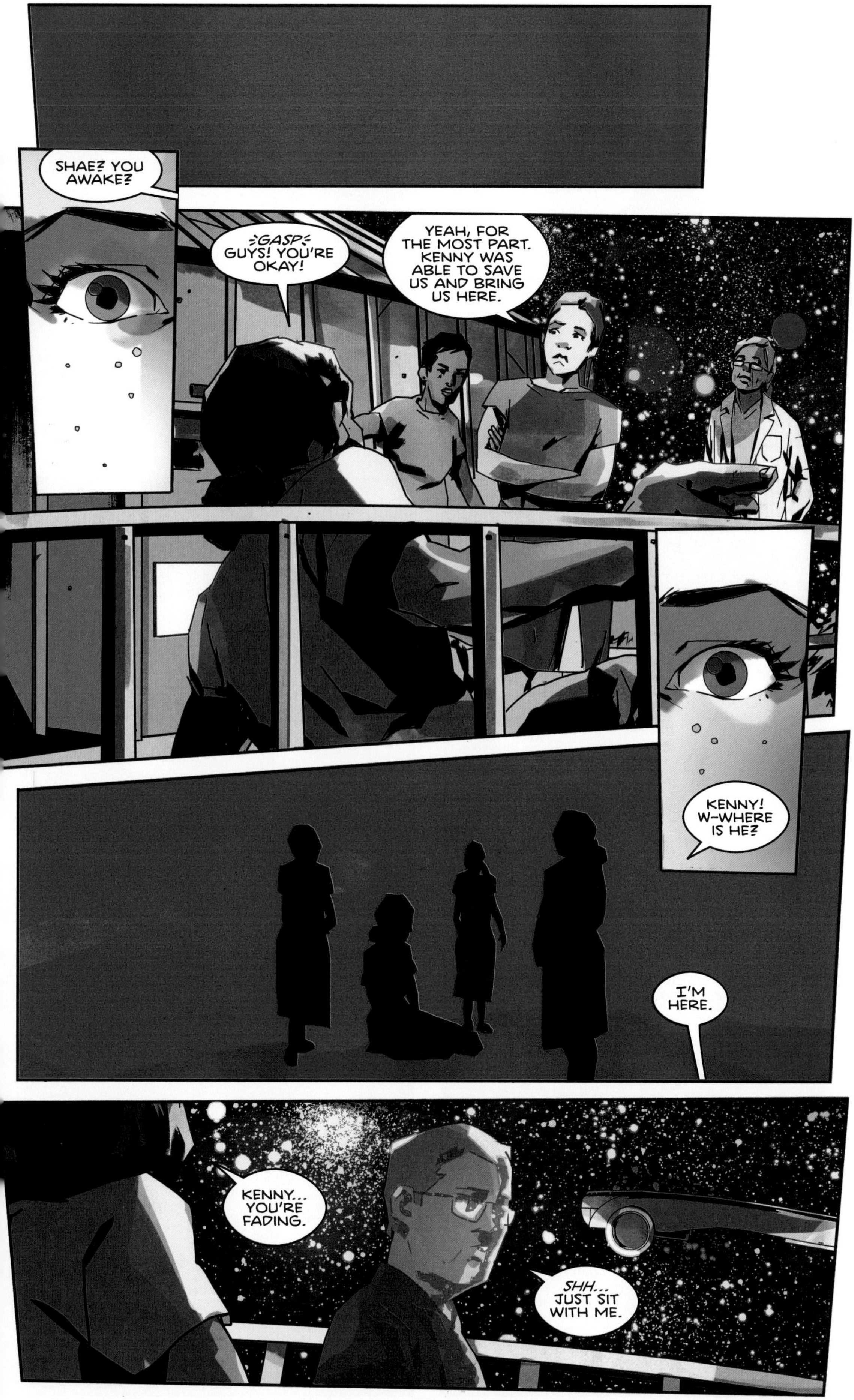
SHAE? YOU AWAKE?
GASP GUYS! YOU'RE OKAY!
YEAH, FOR THE MOST PART. KENNY WAS ABLE TO SAVE US AND BRING US HERE.
KENNY! W-WHERE IS HE?
I'M HERE.
KENNY... YOU'RE FADING.
SHH... JUST SIT WITH ME.

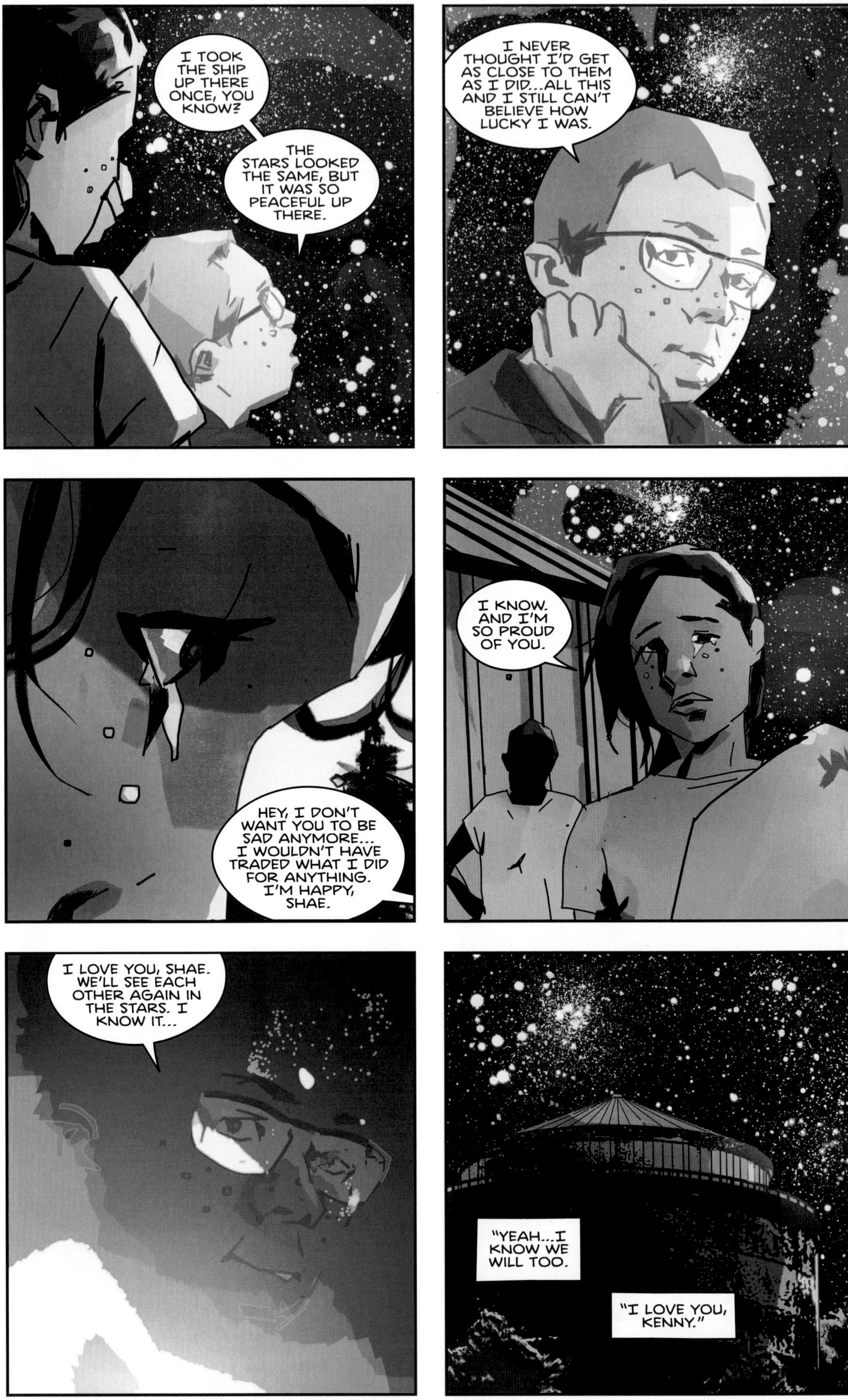
I TOOK THE SHIP UP THERE ONCE, YOU KNOW?
THE STARS LOOKED THE SAME, BUT IT WAS SO PEACEFUL UP THERE.
I NEVER THOUGHT I'D GET AS CLOSE TO THEM AS I DID...ALL THIS AND I STILL CAN'T BELIEVE HOW LUCKY I WAS.
HEY, I DON'T WANT YOU TO BE SAD ANYMORE... I WOULDN'T HAVE TRADED WHAT I DID FOR ANYTHING. I'M HAPPY, SHAE.
I KNOW. AND I'M SO PROUD OF YOU.
I LOVE YOU, SHAE. WE'LL SEE EACH OTHER AGAIN IN THE STARS. I KNOW IT...
"YEAH...I KNOW WE WILL TOO.
"I LOVE YOU, KENNY."

45°7′25.87″N
123°6′48.97″W

-33.867886
-63.987

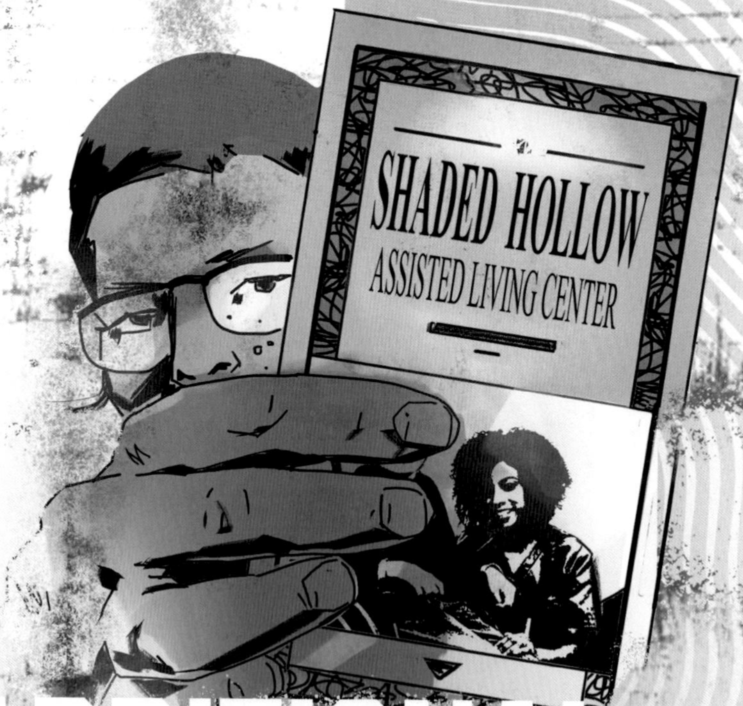
SHADED HOLLOW
ASSISTED LIVING CENTER

ADDITIONAL CONTENT

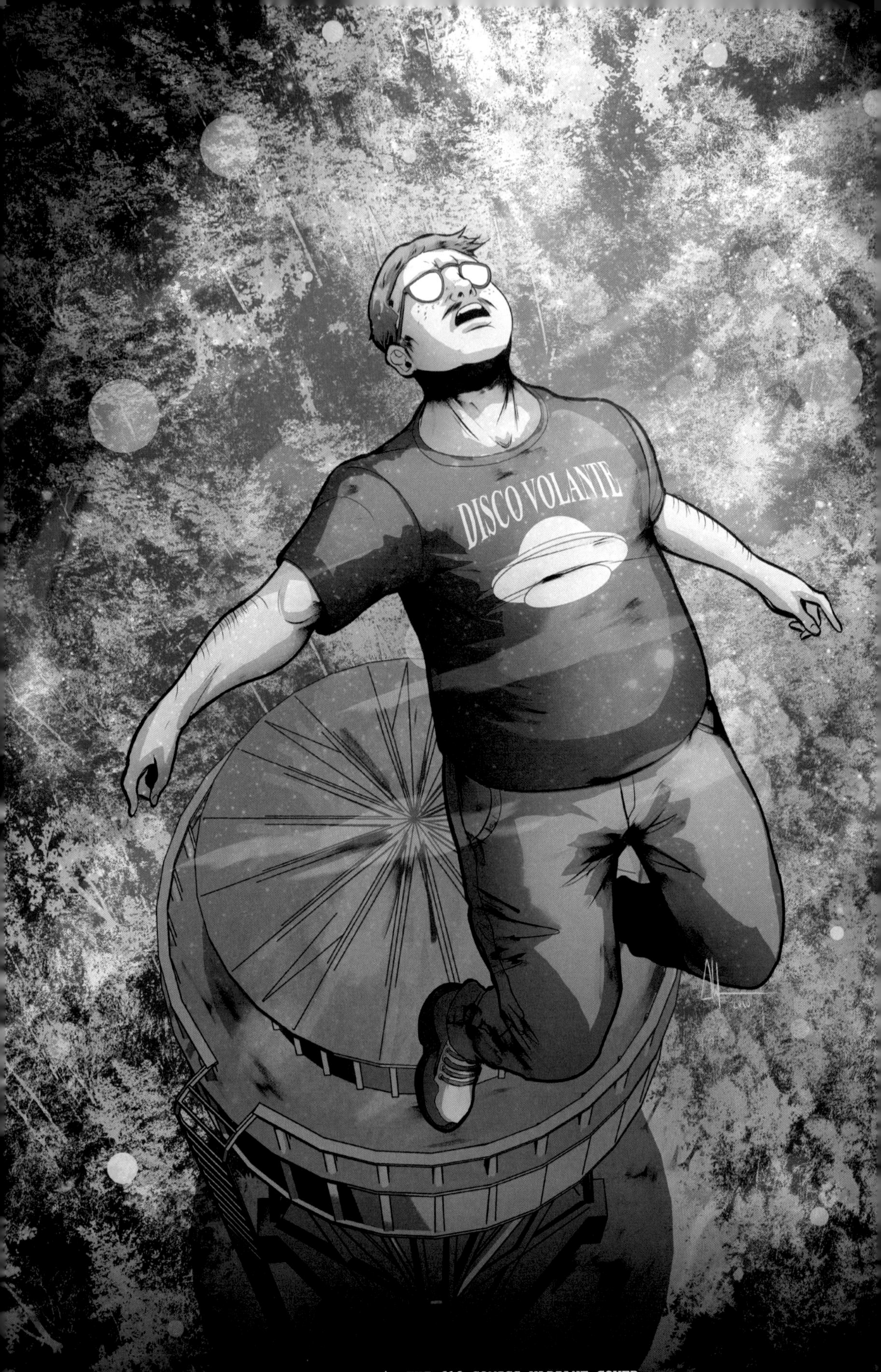
DISCO VOLANTE

STARGAZER 1 | THE 616 COMICS VARIANT COVER
ART: Alejandro Giraldo

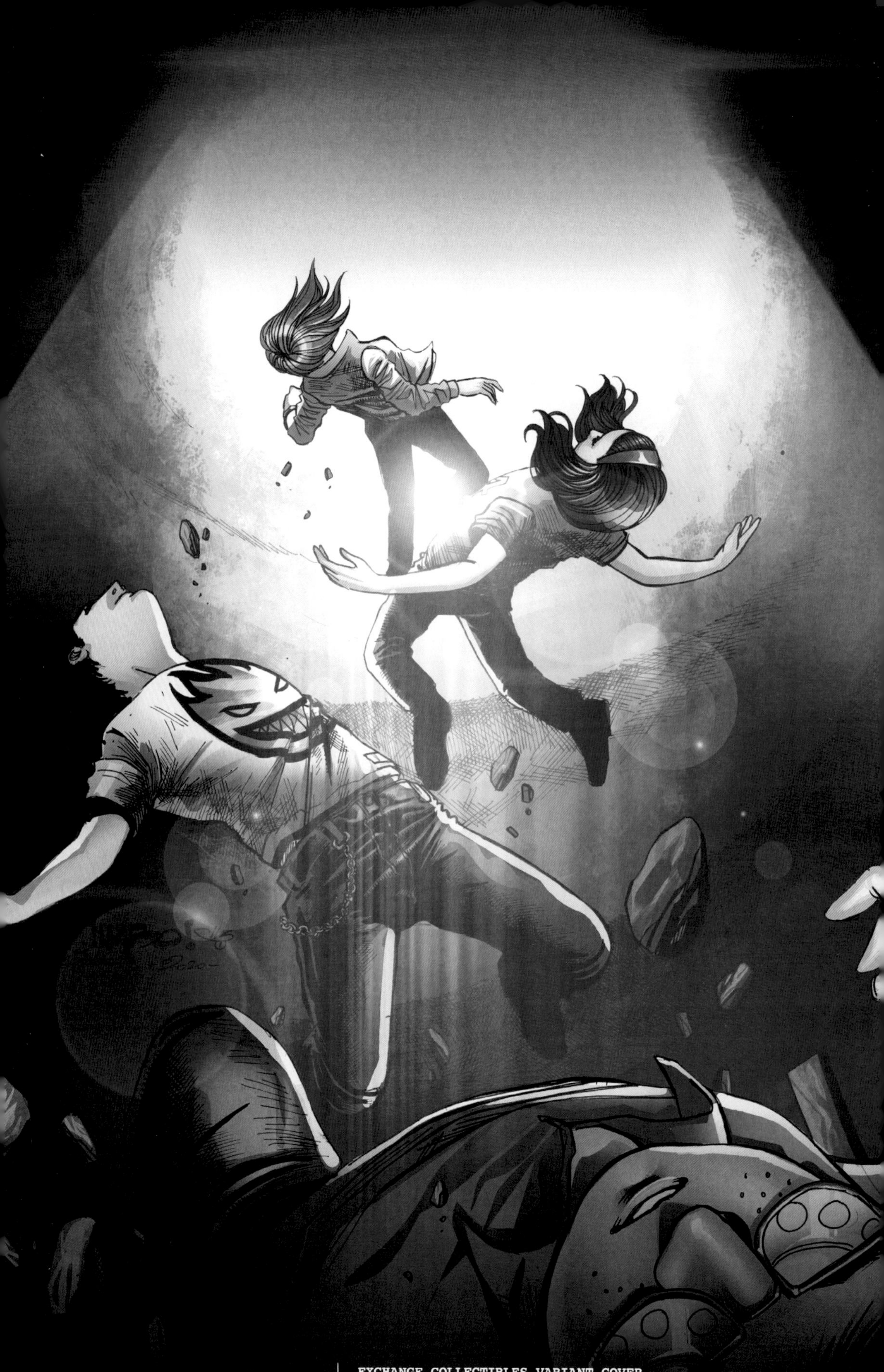

STARGAZER 1 | **EXCHANGE COLLECTIBLES VARIANT COVER**
ART: Jimbo Salgado

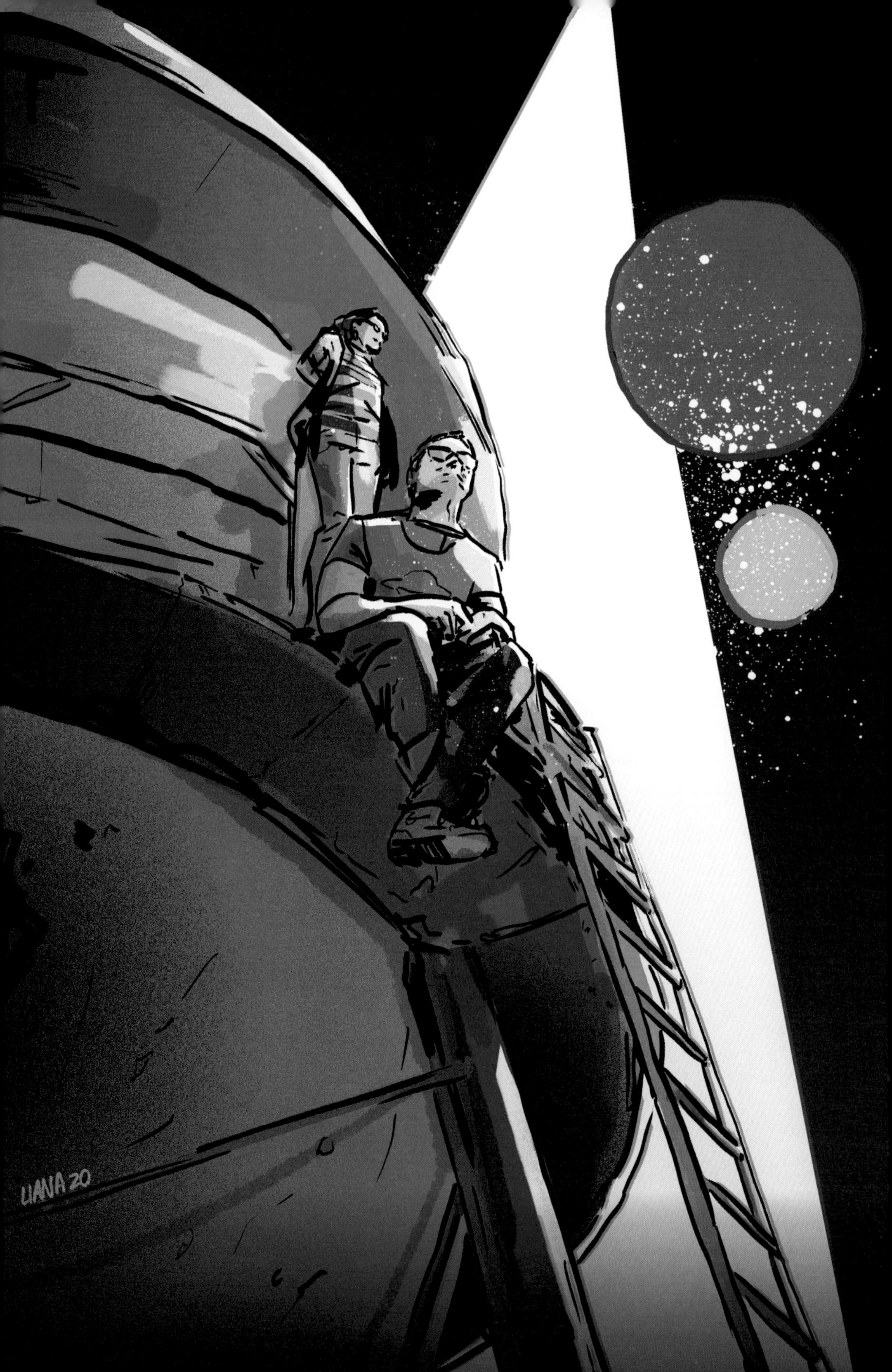
LIANA 20

STARGAZER 1 | **MAD CAVE STUDIOS SHOWCASE VARIANT COVER**
ART: Liana Kangas

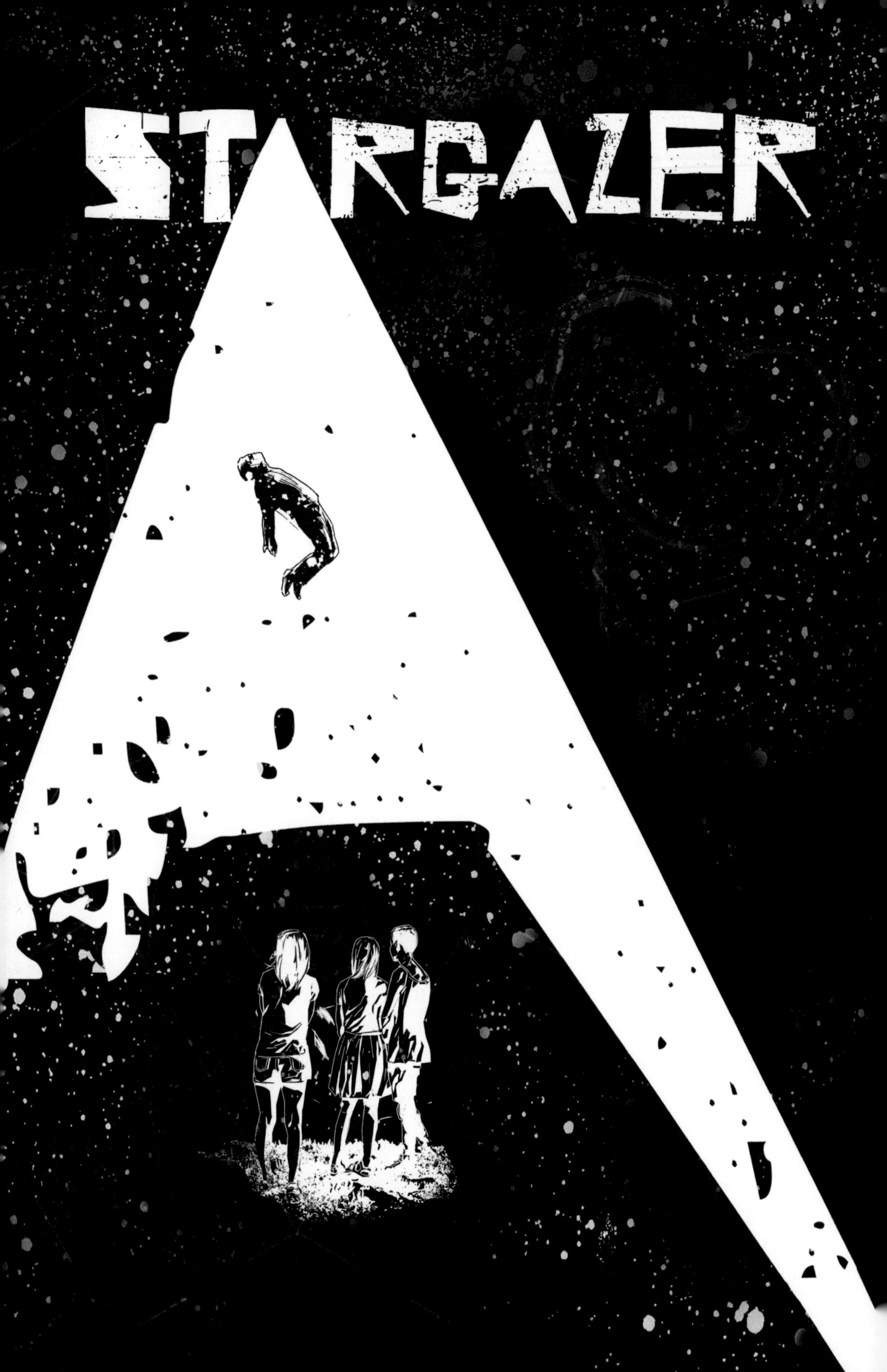
STARGAZER™

STARGAZER 1

SPACE CADETS COLLECTION VARIANT COVER
ART: Antonio Fuso - DESIGN: Diana Bermúdez

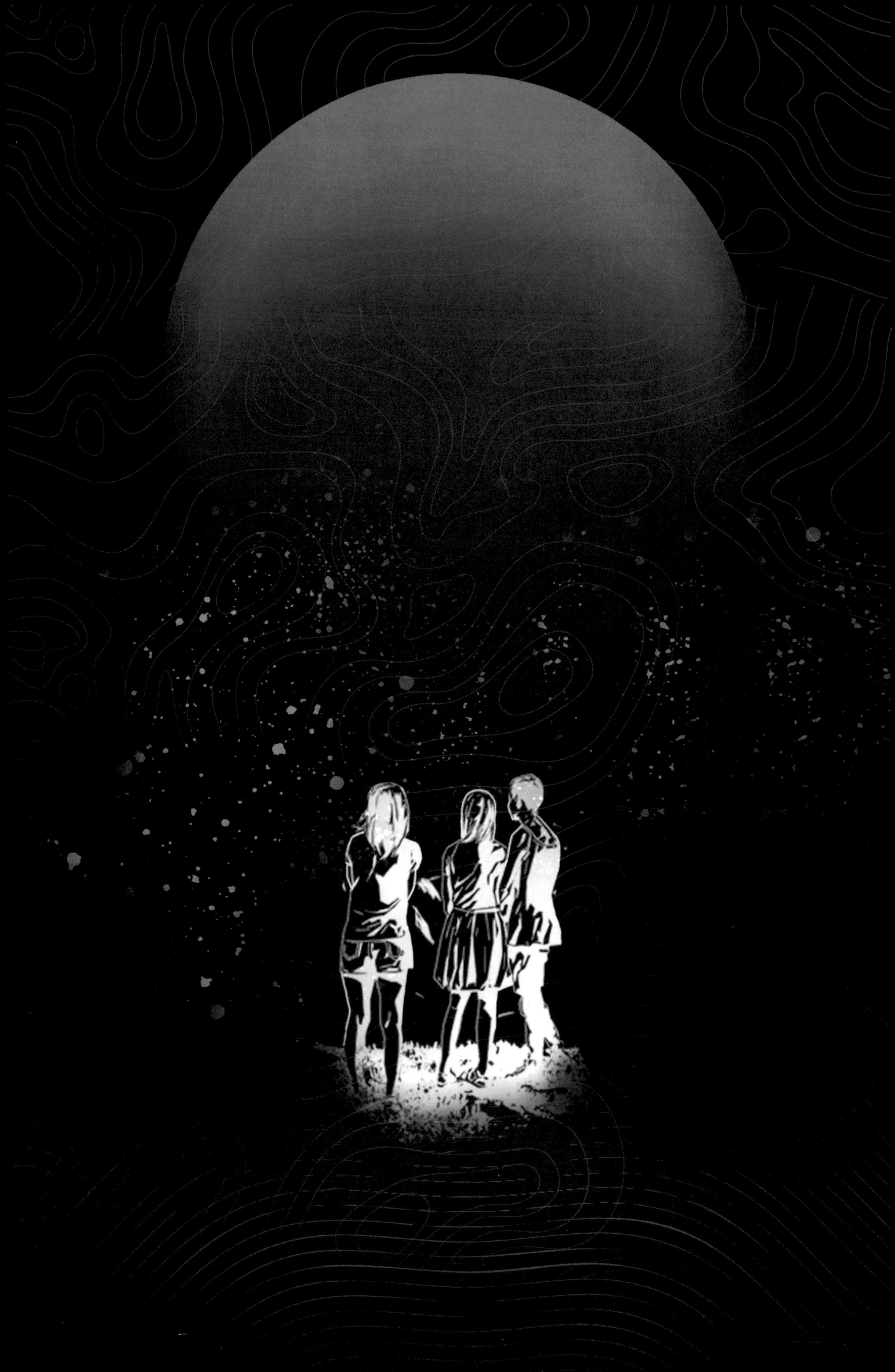

STARGAZER 1

SECOND PRINTING COVER
ART: Antonio Fuso - DESIGN: Diana Bermúdez

DISCOVER MAD CAVE COLLECTED EDITIONS

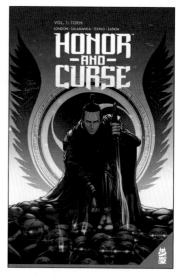

Wolvenheart Vol. 1: Legendary Slayer
ISBN: 978-0-9981215-8-1

Honor and Curse Vol. 1: Torn
ISBN: 978-0-9981215-5-0

**Knights Of The Golden Sun Vol. 1:
Providence Lost**
ISBN: 978-0-9981215-4-3

Battlecats Vol. 2: Fallen Legacy
ISBN: 978-0-9981215-6-7

Show's End Trade Paperback
ISBN: 978-0-9981215-7-4

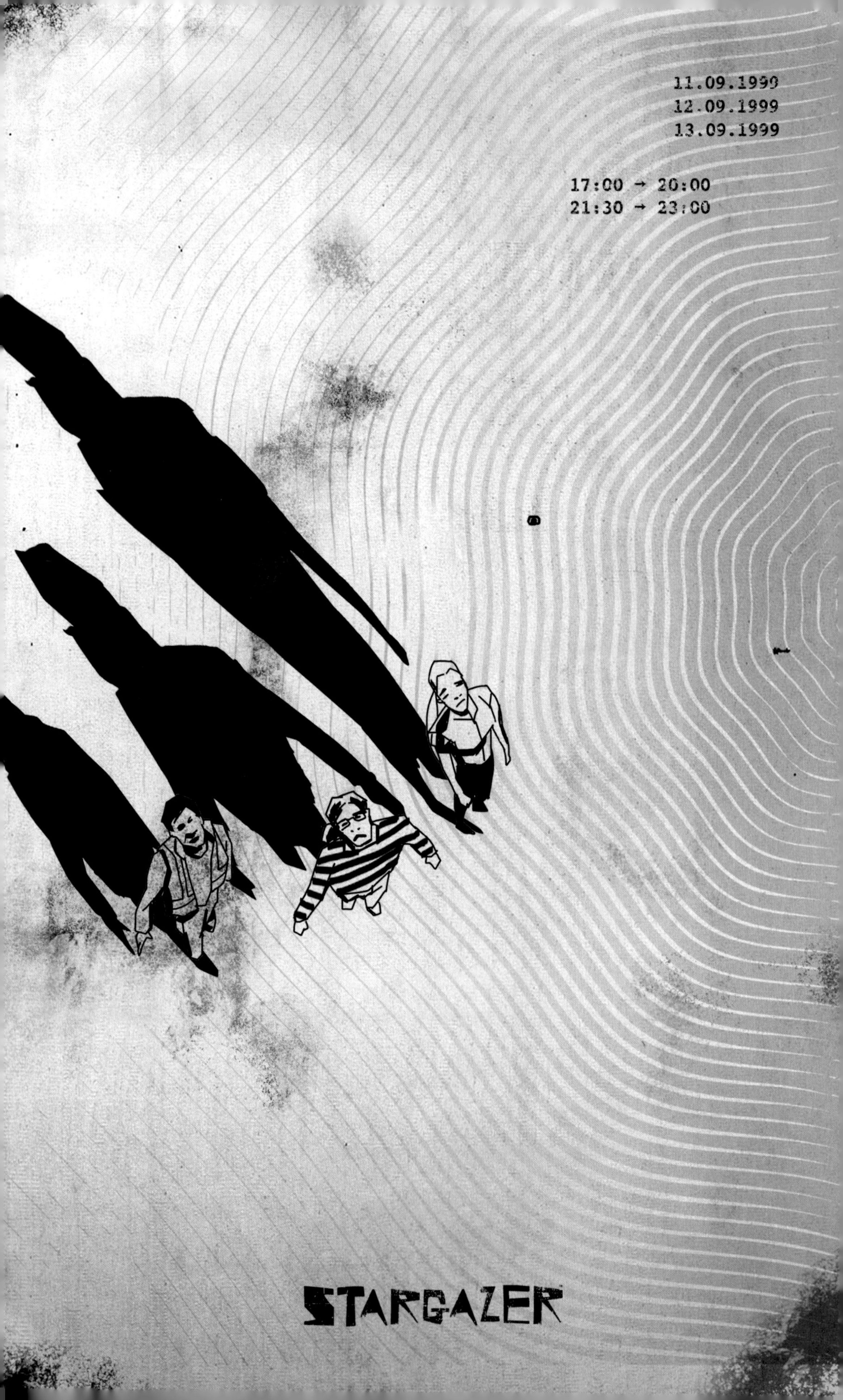
11.09.1999
12.09.1999
13.09.1999
17:00 → 20:00
21:30 → 23:00
STARGAZER